LEGAL WRITING CITATION

IN A NUTSHELL

By

LARRY L. TEPLY
Professor of Law
Creighton University

THOMSON
™
WEST

Mat #40498426

© 2008 Thomson/West
    610 Opperman Drive
    St. Paul, MN 55123
    1–800–313–9378

Printed in the United States of America

ISBN: 978–0–314–16938–9

TEXT IS PRINTED ON 10% POST
CONSUMER RECYCLED PAPER

*To My Family—Frannie, Robert, Benjamin,
Alison, Anna, and Nicholas Teply*

*

PREFACE

———————

"The devil is in the details." That proverb high-lights the basic problem that lawyers, law students, legal assistants, and others face in conforming legal citations to a particular citation system. To make matters worse, individual legal writers ordinarily do not control the choice of citation form. Instead, it is set by a court to which a document will be submitted, a law firm that has its own style manual for all law firm documents, a journal that has adopted a partic-ular citation system in which an article or student work will be published, a professor who requires students to follow a particular citation manual in a writing assignment, a governmental agency or department that has an internal style manual for agency writing, etc. Even in absence of an imposed choice of citation form, the customs and norms of the practice of law place limits on citation form. Thus, like it or not, it is imperative to learn how to cite legal sources in "proper" form.

Those learning legal citation, however, too often focus on all the details and not enough on **the pro-cess of legal citation and knowing what the "issues" are: how to go about citation, recognizing what needs to be looked up, and**

knowing where differences in citation systems are likely to occur. That is one of the primary functions of this book.

As it turns out, formatting a citation into proper form is actually only a minor part of using citations in legal writing. Although the following is discussed in detail in Chapter 1(F), it is important to understand from the outset that the process of legal citation involves several basic steps:

Step 1. Identify the basic information needed to construct the citation. If a citation is generated as part of taking research notes and may or may not be used later, sufficient information should be recorded so that a citation can be constructed at a later time *regardless of the system of citation ultimately used*. All citation systems generally require the same basic elements in the citation, even if they are presented differently. For example, as discussed in Chapter 1(B), a case citation in any system will ordinarily utilize the name of the case, the volume number of the reporter, the (abbreviated) name of the reporter, the page number on which the opinion begins, the page number identifying specific material of importance within the opinion, the (abbreviated) name of the court, including its geographic jurisdiction, and, finally, the year (or date) of the decision.

Step 2. Apply the detailed requirements of a system of citation or otherwise refining the

citation to comply a requirement of the recipient (*e.g.*, a court rule, a law firm policy, a law school requirement, a law review style guide, etc.), **reader expectations, or local practice.** In this regard, Chapter 1 discusses the citation conventions developed through customary "accretion" that underlie all modern citation systems. In fact, these conventions represent, as one commentator has aptly stated, the "standard language that allows one writer to refer to legal authorities with sufficient precision and generality that others can follow the references." With this fundamental understanding of citation conventions, it becomes easy to navigate any citation system, style guide, or citation manual. Likewise, it also becomes easy to understand why readers will regard some citations as evidencing careful and proper citation as opposed to sloppy citation.

Step 3. Incorporate the citations into the document, using appropriate signals, citation sentences or phrases, appropriate citation order, explanatory parentheticals, short forms, and typeface. As one of the citation manuals explicitly states, it is expected that citations be placed "immediately after each sentence, or part of a sentence, that contains a statement of legal principle, a reference to or description of a legal authority, or an idea, a thought, or an expression borrowed from another source." Thus, it is critically important to remember that citations do not appear in a vacuum. They are, in fact, an integral part of persuading the reader and establishing credibility of what is stated in a document.

Step 4. Make sure that the authorities are up to date, proofread the document, and check all citations. Citing authorities that have been over-ruled, amended, or superseded undermines an entire legal argument and causes serious damage to one's reputation (as well as one's grade in a legal research and writing class). Subsequent history must be appropriately indicated in the document.

Step 5. Proofread the document carefully and make sure that the citation form is correct and internally consistent before submitting the document. Attention to detail pays big dividends in terms of building a reputation for quality legal work.

To beginning law students and others, it may be hard to believe that experienced legal writers rou-tinely engage in the above-described citation process without consulting the relevant citation manual. As experts, they have learned this process through practice, emulation, and feedback.

This book facilitates learning legal citation in several ways. First, it provides a succinct exposition of the basic principles of legal citation in its first eighty-eight pages (Chapter 1). These basic principles operate regardless of the particular system of citation ultimately used for a particular project. Second, Chapters 2 through 4 comparatively present the detailed rules of the two leading citation systems used in the United States. Chapter 2 covers case citations. It uses, *inter alia*, visual illustrations from actual cases to help with learning one of the most difficult tasks: what to include, what to omit, and what to abbreviate in the names of cases. Chapter 3 covers legislative, administrative, and related citations. Chapter 4 covers secondary source citations. Third, the remainder of the book consists of twelve appendices containing reference material useful in constructing actual citations. Fourth, throughout the text and appendices are hundreds of examples of citations for emulation.

Chapters 2-4 should be not be read for the purpose of mastering their detail. Instead, they should be read quickly for the purpose of learning how to spot the "issues" involved in citation: what should be recorded during the research process, where variations occur between the systems, and what must be looked up. Those chapters can be used for later reference.

If you are a novice learning legal citation, you are likely to feel a degree of frustration. Some of that frustration is the result of how the leading citation manuals have approached the subject of legal citation. Even if those sources avoided "hypertrophy" (see Chapter 1(A)(2)), unfortunately, the underlying difficulties would still remain. First and foremost are the complexities and multitude of legal and nonlegal sources that lawyers cite in the documents they prepare and courts rely upon in making their decisions. Second, lawyers, law journals, and publishers are under the pressure to conserve space. Limiting the space citations use is a key method of doing so. Third, legal citation was developed, and still is developing, by adaption and accretion. When form develops in this way, there is necessarily an inherent "fluidness" of evolving conventions. Fourth, readers expect consistency in citation. When multiple legal professionals do legal work or multiple students work on the same journal, pressure builds to create a "common denominator" in terms of citation form.

In conclusion, I hope that this book helps make the process of learning citation less frustrating. I welcome suggestions on how this book can be improved, including correction of errors, need for better explanations, etc. I also apologize in advance for any inconvenience resulting from any inaccuracies, changes in legal sources, or new developments.

Larry L. Teply
Omaha, Nebraska
February 2008
lteply@post.harvard.edu

ACKNOWLEDGMENTS

Because of the absence of footnoting and citation in this series, I have not been able to provide full references to specific sources. Nevertheless, I want to recognize the large number of sources that played a role in the writing of this book.

First of all, I want to acknowledge the substantive contributions of the two leading legal citation manuals: *The Bluebook: A Uniform System of Citation* (Columbia Law Review Ass'n et al. eds., 18th ed. 2005) [*BB*] and Ass'n of Legal Writing Directors & Darby Dickerson, *ALWD Citation Manual: A Professional System of Citation* (3d ed., Aspen Publishers 2006) [*ALWD*]. (For purposes of citation neutrality and to provide additional examples, I have alternated the form used in citing the sources in the following paragraphs.)

I want to acknowledge the following research sources which, *inter alia*, provided excellent underlying reference material and background information: [*ALWD*] Morris L. Cohen & Kent C. Olson, *Legal Research in a Nutshell* (9th ed., Thomson/West 2007); Robert C. Berring & Elizabeth A. Edinger, *Finding the Law* (12th ed., Thomson/West 2005); *Black's Law Dictionary* (Bryan A. Garner ed., 8th ed., West 2004); Roy M. Mersky & Donald J. Dunn, *Fundamental of Legal Research* (8th ed., Found. Press 2002); Miles O. Price et al., *Effective Legal Research* (4th ed., Little, Brown & Co. 1979); Mary Miles Prince, *Prince's Dictionary of Legal Citations* (7th ed., Williams S. Hein & Co. 2006); Amy E. Sloan, *Basic Legal Research: Tools and Strategies* (3d ed., Aspen Publishers 2006); Larry L. Teply, *Legal Research and Citation* (5th ed., West 1999); and Larry L. Teply, *Legal Research and Citation Exercises* (West 1999).

I want to acknowledge the following excellent writing and stylistic resources which, *inter alia,* have served as sources of substantive material and background information: [*BB*] Linda Holdeman Edwards, *Legal Writing and Analysis* (2d ed. 2007); Bryan A. Garner, *The Redbook: A Manual of Legal Style* (2d ed. 2006); Laurel Currie Oates & Anne Enquist, *The Legal Writing Handbook: Analysis, Research, and Writing* (4th ed. 2006); Richard K. Neuman, *Legal Reasoning and Legal Writing: Structure, Strategy, and Style* (5th ed. 2005); Mark Painter, *The Legal Writer: 40 Rules for the Art of Legal Writing* (2d ed. 2003); Marjorie D. Rombauer, *Legal Problem Solving: Analysis, Research & Writing* (5th ed. 1991); Nancy L. Schultz & Louis J. Sirico, Jr., *Legal Writing and Other Lawyering Skills* (4th ed. 2004); Larry L. Teply, *Legal Writing, Analysis, and Oral Argument* (1990); and Eugene Volokh, *Academic Legal Writing:*

Law Review Articles, Student Notes, Seminar Papers, and Getting on Law Review (2d ed. 2005).

I want to acknowledge the influence of ideas or the use of brief quotations or paraphrased material from the following articles: [*ALWD*] Albert W. Alschuler, *Rediscovering Blackstone*, 145 U. Pa. L. Rev. 1 (1996); Paul Axel-Lute, *Legal Citation Form: Theory and Practice*, 75 L. Libr. J. 148 (1982); Michael Bacchus, Student Author, *Strung Out: Legal Citation, the Bluebook, and the Anxiety of Authority*, 151 U. Pa. L. Rev. 245 (2002); Thomas E. Baker, *A Postscript on Precedent in the Divided Fifth Circuit*, 36 Sw. U. L.J. 725 (1982); Jason B. Binimow, *Precedential Effect of Unpublished Opinions*, 105 A.L.R.5th 499 (2003); Jennifer L. Corde, *ALWD Citation Manual: A Grammar Guide to the Language of Legal Citation*, 26 UALR L. Rev. 573 (2004); K.K. DuVivier, *String Citations* (pts. 1 & 2), 29 Colo. Law. 83 (July 2000), 29 Colo. Law. 67 (Sept. 2000); Darby Dickerson, *Professionalizing Legal Citation: The ALWD Citation Manual*, 47 Fed. Law. 20 (Nov./Dec. 2000); Joseph L. Gerken, *A Librarian's Guide to Unpublished Opinions*, 96 L. Libr. J. 475 (2004); Alex Glashausser, *Citation and Representation*, 55 Vand. L. Rev. 59 (2002); Craig Joyce, *Keepers of the Flame, Prosser and Keeton on the Law of Torts (Fifth Edition) and the Prosser Legacy*, 39 Vand. L. Rev. 851 (1986); Ellen Platt, *Unpublished vs. Unreported: What's the Difference?* 5 Persps. 26 (Fall 1996);

Richard A. Posner, *Goodbye to the Bluebook*, 53 U. Chi. L. Rev. 1343 (1986); Ira P. Robbins, *Semiotics, Analogical Legal Reasoning, and the Cf. Signal: Getting Our Signals Uncrossed*, 48 Duke L.J. 1043 (1999); Andrew T. Soloman, *Making Unpublished Opinions Precedential: A Recipe for Ethical Problems & Legal Malpractice?* 26 Miss. C. L. Rev. 185 (2007); Student Author, *Manual Labor, Chicago Style*, 101 Harv. L. Rev. 1323 (1988); Charles A. Sullivan, *On Vacation*, 40 Hous. L. Rev. 1143 (2006); and Marie Wallace, *Practice Pointer: Looseleaf Services*, 2 Persps. 63 (Jan. 1993).

Finally, I want to acknowledge ideas from numerous other sources and conference presentations that I have absorbed over years of teaching, but I have not attributed directly.

With regard to others, I want to acknowledge the support, assistance, and encouragement provided by my colleagues, students, and family. Particular mention should be made of my son, Robert J. Teply. As a practicing lawyer and former editor of the *Harvard Negotiation Law Review*, Robert has provided many invaluable insights and suggestions. I also want to acknowledge the helpful suggestions offered by Professor Nancy L. Schultz of Chapman University School of Law.

I appreciate the efficient and cheerful secretarial assistance and proofreading provided by Pat Andersen and Vickie Rule. I also want to recognize the cheerful and efficient copying services provided by Colleen Kelly-Firmature in our Copy Center. In addition, I want to thank Erin E. Manion, an outstanding student at Creighton Law School, for her excellent comments from a student's perspective on an earlier draft of this book. I want to thank our Law Library Director, Professor Kay L. Andrus, for his support and comments as well as his staff for their excellent assistance. At the top of the list is Ann C. Kitchel, the Associate Director of our Law Library, who tracked down answers to all kinds of questions about legal sources. I also appreciate the efforts of Legal Reference Librarian George Butterfield and Reference/Electronic Services Librarian Troy Johnson. I also owe thanks to former Reference Librarian Patrick Charles, who indirectly provided the genesis of the idea for this book.

Finally, I want to recognize the research support for this project provided by Creighton Law School.

Larry L. Teply
Omaha, Nebraska
February 2008
lteply@post.harvard.edu

OUTLINE

OUTLINE

TABLE OF CASE CITATION EXAMPLES

C. UNITED STATES DISTRICT COURTS

D. SPECIALIZED AND ABOLISHED FEDERAL COURTS

E. STATE COURTS AND DISTRICT OF COLUMBIA COURTS

TABLE OF CASE CITATION EXAMPLES

TABLE OF CASE CITATION EXAMPLES

TABLE OF CASE CITATION EXAMPLES

TABLE OF LEGISLATIVE RELATED SOURCES CITATION EXAMPLES

Page

A. CONSTITUTIONS

B. FEDERAL AND STATE STATUTES

C. LEGISLATIVE HISTORY SOURCES

D. UNIFORM LAWS, MODEL CODES, MODEL ACTS, AND MODEL RULES OF PROFESSIONAL RESPONSIBILITY

E. ADMINISTRATIVE REGULATIONS AND EXECUTIVE ORDERS

F. RULES OF PROCEDURE
AND EVIDENCE

G. TREATIES AND OTHER
INTERNATIONAL
AGREEMENTS

TABLE OF SECONDARY SOURCE CITATION EXAMPLES

D. INTERNET SOURCES

E. LOOSELEAF SERVICES

F. NEWSPAPERS

G. PERIODICALS

H. RESTATEMENTS OF THE LAW

I. TEXTS AND TREATIES

LEGAL WRITING CITATION

IN A NUTSHELL

*

CHAPTER 1

OVERVIEW OF LEGAL CITATION

A. INTRODUCTION

1. DEVELOPMENT OF CITATION CONVENTIONS

In the early days of the common law in England, judges announced their decisions—and the reasons for them—orally in open court. Over time, prior cases involving similar circumstances came to be regarded as an appropriate basis or authority for deciding subsequent similar cases. The basic underlying concept was that, as a matter of fairness, "like cases should be decided alike."

To facilitate arguments by analogy and the use of prior decisions as precedents, reports of judicial opinions making new or otherwise useful points began to be published by reporters. As the practice developed, any reported opinion (when signed or initialed by any barrister who was present in court) could be cited to the court as a precedent.

Between 1535 and 1865, judicial opinions in England often appeared in more than one published report. In addition, the text of the opinions in the same case varied in different reports. Because lawyers and judges needed a convenient and commonly

1

understood way to refer to these reported judicial
decisions as well as statutes or legal texts, they
developed basic conventions. These conventions are
still followed today.

2. CITATION SYSTEMS, MANUALS, STYLE SHEETS, AND GUIDES

Citation conventions developed through customary
"accretion," and minor variations were often seen. In
light of this evolving customary citation practice,
student-edited law journals faced a significant practical problem: harmonizing citations and form throughout the law journal when multiple authors were
writing (and multiple students were editing) the
content. The solution was the creation of *A Uniform
System of Citation*, known today as *The Bluebook*, the
first comprehensive system of citation rules (hereinafter "*The Bluebook*" or "*BB*"). *The Bluebook* originated
at the Harvard Law School in 1926, and it built on
the traditional patterns of citation in existence at that
time. *The Bluebook* is revised and updated by the
editors of the *Columbia Law Review*, the *Harvard
Law Review*, the *University of Pennsylvania Law
Review*, and the *Yale Law Journal*.

Compared to *The Bluebook* of today, the first
edition was a modest undertaking. The entirety of its
abbreviations and forms of citation were stated in
twenty-six pages. *The Bluebook* has evolved through
ever-expanding, more detail-oriented editions. *The
Bluebook* now has extensive reference tables as well
as a separate set of rules ("Bluepages") specifically

focusing on citation form for practitioners and students..

Over time, *The Bluebook* became the dominant source for citation rules in the United States—although lawyers, the courts, and lawbook publishers never fully adopted those rules. Furthermore, many law journals using *The Bluebook* developed their own additional style manuals or style sheets to supplement or vary *The Bluebook's* rules. Nevertheless, the influence of *The Bluebook* on citation practice in law schools, law firms, and the courts was, and still is, substantial.

In the mid-1980s, a citation "revolt" developed at the journals and in the writing program at the University of Chicago. In an essay supporting the new *University of Chicago Manual of Legal Citation* (popularly called *The Maroon Book*), Judge Richard Posner observed that "[a]nthropologists use the word 'hypertrophy' to describe the tendency of human beings to mindless elaboration of social practices. The pyramids in Egypt are the hypertrophy of burial. The hypertrophy of law is [*The Bluebook*]." Thus, it was said that "form is prescribed for the sake of form, not of function" with a result that "a large structure is built up, all unconsciously, through accretion."

In very few pages, *The Maroon Book* attempted to provide flexible "guidelines" on citation that left "a fair amount of discretion" to legal writers and editors "because it is neither possible [n]or desirable to write a particular rule for every sort of citation problem that might arise." *The Maroon Book*, however, departed too radically from traditional conventions and practice. As a result, *The Maroon Book* failed to gain widespread acceptance, but it continues to be updated in the form of "restatements" as part of the *University of Chicago Law Review's* "Style Sheet."

In the 1990s, the Association of Law Libraries began working on a guide for courts, legislatures, and others considering the creation of "universal" citations for legal sources. Universal citations are designed to be equally usable in both print and electronic media and are not tied to any single publisher. In 2004, this effort culminated in the publication of the second edition of its *Universal Citation Guide*. This guide has significantly impacted the development of "public domain" citations.

In 2000, the Association of Legal Writing Directors published its *ALWD Citation Manual: A Professional System of Citation* (hereinafter "*ALWD Manual*" or "*ALWD*"). Instead of focusing primarily on citation in law journals, the *ALWD Manual* created a single system of citation for law students, legal scholars, and practitioners. Its "more user friendly" format employs contrasting colored text, example boxes, and color-coded symbols to mark spaces within citations.

Like *The Bluebook*, the *ALWD Manual* has a series of rules governing citation form and many useful appendices. The *ALWD Manual* has also now had multiple editions. Many of the rules in the *ALWD Manual* are identical to those in *The Bluebook* while others reflect differences in opinion on what information should be given to the reader. However, some of the differences seem to be just more hypertrophy.

Many other citation guides and manuals also exist. Some focus on legal citation within a government agency (e.g., the U.S. Department of Justice Tax Division Citation and Style Manual; *NLRB Style Manual: A Guide for Legal Writing in Plain English*; the Solicitor General's citation format; etc.). Others are cooperative efforts in a specialized field (e.g., *Tax Cite: A Federal Tax Citation and Reference Manual*, a joint effort by the *Virginia Tax Review*, the N.Y.U.'s *Tax Review*, the ABA Section of Taxation, and the editors of Georgetown's *The Tax Lawyer*).

Many courts have internal style manuals covering, *inter alia*, legal citation. In addition, some states have state-specific style manuals governing citation in local court documents and instate legal publications (e.g., *California Style Manual: A Handbook for Legal Style for California Courts and Lawyers*; *North Dakota Citation Manual*; *Texas Rules of Form*; etc.).

Some law school classes will specify the use of a particular citation manual, usually *The Bluebook* or the *ALWD Manual*. Undoubtedly, law journals will prefer a particular citation system and will require the use of that system on all student submissions. Some courts may also strictly require lawyers to use a specific citation system. Furthermore, court rules may impose a variety of specific citation requirements. For example, Rule 13(a)(6) of the Arizona Rules of Civil Appellate Procedure provides that "[c]itations of authorities shall be to the volume and page number of the official reports [*Arizona Reports*] and also when possible to the unofficial reporters."

In any event, *The Bluebook*, the *ALWD Manual*, and all of the other citation manuals and style guides reflect the traditional conventions discussed in the following sections of this chapter.

B. CASE CITATION CONVENTIONS

1. NAMES OF CASES

Very early, lawyers and judges began to refer to cases by the names of the parties to the action. The Latin *"versus"* (meaning "against")—or the equivalent Law-French term *"vers"*—was used to indicate the relationship of the parties in the "style" (name) of the case—with the plaintiff in the action being named first (e.g., *Turnbridge versus Teather* or *Mildway vers Standish*). Over time, "versus" or "vers" came to be abbreviated to "vs." and then simply "**v.**"

[BB & ALWD] Wolfe v. Shelley

Sometimes, cases were referred to and cited by a popular name rather than the names of the parties:

[BB & ALWD] Shelley's Case

In addition, many early admiralty actions were "in rem" (against a thing). In other words, these actions were technically against the ship itself or some other "res" (thing) connected with a ship like the cargo rather than against the actual owners of the ship or cargo. Reporters styled these (and later other) in rem actions by the name of the ship or a description of the property involved:

[*BB & ALWD*] *The Pensher*

Today, cases are still cited in these three ways:

(1) the names of the parties on each side of the action, separated by **v.**;

(2) the popular name of the case; or

(3) the property involved in an "in rem" action.

2. PROCEDURAL PHRASES

Courts, lawyers, and reporters also used various procedural phrases. Uncontested cases in which formal adverse parties did not exist were designated in various ways, such as "Matter of," "Petition of," or "Application of" and the party's name or the subject matter of the action (e.g., In the Matter of Wharton, a Lunatic). Over time, such procedural phrases came to be cited by the Latin term "*In re*":

[*BB & ALWD*] *In re Wharton*
[*BB & ALWD*] *In re Mores' Trust*

Some proceedings were brought for, by, on behalf of only one side of a lawsuit. Such proceedings were often conducted without notice to, or argument from, the other side of the action. Reports of such proceedings were introduced by "*Ex parte*" (the Latin meaning "from the part"), followed by the name of the relevant party:

[*BB & ALWD*] *Ex parte Morgan*

Some other proceedings were brought by the government or another appropriate person at the instance or application of a private party (called the "relator") who was interested in the outcome. Reporters indicated such actions by a wide variety of terms, including "on the relation of" (or the Latin "*ex relatione*"), "for the use of," "on behalf of," "on the information of," "as next friend of," or simply "by." Over time, all versions of these phraseologies came to be indicated by "*ex rel.*," the widely recognized abbreviation of *ex relatione*. Note that "*ex*" does not have a period after it in any of its uses.

[*BB* & *ALWD*] *State ex rel. Mander v. Pearson*

Today, these three procedural phrases (*In re*, *Ex parte*, and *ex rel.*) are used in the same way.

3. CITATION OF PUBLISHED REPORTS

As the reporting and publication of cases developed in England, lawyers and judges needed some way to indicate where the case could be found. A convention quickly developed. Reports began to be cited by some form of the reporter's last name. For example, cases in Thomas Vernon Esquire's volumes containing "Cases Argued and Adjudged in the High Court of Chancery" came to be routinely cited by an abbreviated version of his last name: **Vern.** Hence, they were called nominative reports.

Because nominative reports were often published in a series, it quickly became customary to precede the reporter designation with the volume number (e.g., **1 Vern.**) when more than one volume was published. Furthermore, because a reporter volume contains many cases, lawyers and courts indicated the page on which the actual report of the case began (e.g., **1 Vern. 346**). This basic approach established the pattern for citing a reporter that has been carried forward to today:

[Vol.] [Reporter Abbrev.] [Beginning Page]

Not surprisingly, early case reporting in the United States followed the English practice. Nominative reports of state court decisions began to appear in 1789. Nominative reports in the United States were cited in the same way as English reports (e.g., **5 Pick. 146** was a citation to the *Gibson v. Crehore* case beginning on page 146 of volume 5 of *Pickering's Reports* of Massachusetts cases). Unlike English practice, however, opinions of the courts in the United States were read from the bench instead of being delivered orally and the nominative reporters often were officially sanctioned by statute.

In the middle of the nineteenth century, nominative reports were replaced by jurisdiction-named, official reporter series (e.g., *Massachusetts Reports*) in the states. In addition, *United States Reports* became the official reports for U.S. Supreme Court cases. Opinions in these new, jurisdiction-named, official reporter series were cited using the same basic pattern used to cite nominative reports—with the abbreviated name of the official report substituted for the abbreviated name of the nominative reporter (e.g., **97 Mass. 302** was a citation to the *Estabrook v. Earle* case beginning on page 302 of volume 97 of *Massachusetts Reports*, and **91 U.S. 37** was, of course, a citation to page 37 of volume 91 of *United States Reports*).

When this change in nomenclature took place, earlier officially sanctioned, nominative reports were renumbered consecutively and incorporated into the jurisdiction-named series. For example, the early nominative reporter volumes became the first 96 volumes of *Massachusetts Reports*. Similarly, nominative reports became the first 90 volumes of *United States Reports*.

Even after the incorporation of these early reports into the jurisdiction-named series occurred, however, lawyers and judges still tended to continue to cite the earlier incorporated cases in their traditional, nominative form. Even today, the practice is not uniform. For example, current U.S. Supreme Court opinions published in the official *United States Reports* series still cite early U.S. Supreme Court opinions to the original nominative report rather than the relevant renumbered volume of *United States Reports*.

One reason for not immediately citing early nominative reports to only the renumbered volume number of the official, jurisdiction-named series may have been the fact that all of the opinions antedating renumbering had cited the renumbered cases by their old form—as nominatives. Other reasons may have been unguided inertia, familiarity with the tradition, and the cost of purchasing the renumbered reporter series.

Furthermore, a common editorial feature may also have contributed significantly to the practice: star paging—using stars, brackets, or indented page numbers to indicate where the exact page breaks occurred in the reprinted report. For example, when the early nominative Massachusetts reporters were reprinted as the first ninety-six volumes of the *Massachusetts Reports*, star paging was used to indicate the pagination of the nominative reporter volumes when it differed, which, of course, greatly facilitated citing the original.

As discussed in Chapter 2(C)(2)(*a*) & (*d*), *The Bluebook* still requires a reference to the original nominative reporter in citations to cases in the first ninety volumes of *United States Reports* and early state reports, but the *ALWD Manual* prohibits it.

4. JUMP, PINPOINT, OR PINCITE REFERENCES

As case reporting became more sophisticated and reports become lengthier, lawyers and judges began to include what is now known as jump, pinpoint, or pincite references in their citations to make it easier for the reader to find quoted material or specific discussion within a case. Early on, it became customary to indicate these specific references by adding the relevant page number(s) to the citation, separated from the initial page number on which the case began by a comma. Thus, a citation to **3 Cranch 267, 269** was a citation to discussion on page 269 (in this instance, *Strawbridge v. Curtiss*) that began on page 267 of volume 3 of *Cranch's Reports*. If the specific reference was to the first page, the page number was repeated: **3 Cranch 267, 267**.

5. PARALLEL CITATIONS

Another convention that developed was the method of providing parallel citations when the same case was printed in two or more different reports. To provide references to more than one source, the references were simply added one after the other, separated by a comma. For example, after *English Reports, Full Reprint* comprehensively reprinted about 100,000 English cases decided between 1220 and 1865 in 176 volumes, an early English case could be cited to both the original nominative reporter (e.g., Meeson & Welsby's *Exchequer Reports*) and *English Reports, Full Reprint* (e.g., **3 Mees. & Wels. 1, 150 Eng. Rep. 1030**).

The practice of parallel citation, however, was not always followed when early reports were reprinted. For example, prior to 1880, more than 230 different reporters at various times had reported lower federal court decisions. Between 1894 and 1897, 18,313 of these lower federal court cases were reprinted in a unique series, *Federal Cases*. Unlike other reporters, the arrangement of the cases in this set was not chronological. Instead, the cases were organized alphabetically and assigned an arbitrary case number—beginning with Case No. 1, *The Aalesund*, and ending with Case No. 18,222, *In re Zug*. When the last volume was ready for printing, ninety-one additional cases had been found and were added to the end of the last volume, continuing the consecutive numbering from 18,223 to 18,313. *Federal Cases* came to be cited to exclusion of the original reports it reprinted, and, therefore, no parallel citations to the original nominative reports were given.

The need for parallel citations was greatly accelerated by the development of the National Reporter System. In 1879, John B. West began publishing the full text of selected state court decisions in the *Northwestern Reporter* on a regional basis. West expanded this undertaking to cover the entire United States through additional regional reporters (*Atlantic, North Eastern, Pacific, South Eastern, South Western,* and *Southern Reporters*).

By grouping several states, West was able to publish opinions far more frequently than the official, jurisdiction-named series. The system also had the advantage of common editorial features. One of the most useful features was West's editorial summary of points of law in each case (headnotes), which were indexed into a comprehensive topic and key number system. This system allowed lawyers and judges to find relevant discussions of particular points of law by subject through West's accompanying Digests (separately publish collections of West's headnotes organized by a subject system—namely, topics and key numbers).

West also developed reporters covering the federal courts (West's *Supreme Court Reporter, Federal Reporter, Federal Supplement,* and *Federal Rules Decisions*). In addition, its National Reporter System includes localized reporters for New York and California (West's *New York Supplement* and West's *California Reporter*) and other specialized reporters (*Federal Claims Reporter, Military Justice Reporter, Bank-*

ruptcy Reporter, and *Veterans Appeals Reporter*). In 1996, West Publishing Co. was acquired by the Thomson Corp. (hereinafter "Thomson/West").

From a citation perspective, the important point is that the National Reporter System quickly became the dominant way to find and read American case law. Thus, it was extremely useful to have the Thomson/West citation. However, Thomson/West's reporters were unofficial—in other words, not sanctioned by statute or court rule to be an official reporter and a citation to the official report was often required. As a result, parallel citations to both the official report and Thomson/West's reporter were often used. When parallel citations were provided to both official and unofficial reports, it became customary always to provide the official citation first (e.g., **39 Wyo. 285, 270 P. 1077**).

Despite Thomson/West's dominance, several other unofficial reporters were produced by other publishers—the most prominent of which are *United States Supreme Court Reports, Lawyers' Edition* (known as the *Lawyers' Edition*) and the *American Law Reports* ("*A.L.R.*") series. The *Lawyers' Edition* reports U.S. Supreme Court decisions from the inception of its publication in 1882. Unlike Thomson/West's *Supreme Court Reporter*, however, it also retrospectively reprinted all prior Supreme Court cases. The editorial features of the *Lawyers' Edition* differ from Thomson/West's, such as the selected inclusion of summaries of the briefs of counsel and annotations (explanatory discussions with extensive case citations).

Because of the popularity of Thomson/West's *Supreme Court Reporter* and the *Lawyers' Edition*, lawyers often provided parallel citations to all three reporters when citing U.S. Supreme Court cases. By tradition, the citation of *United States Reports* appeared first, Thomson/West's *Supreme Court Reporter* second, and the *Lawyers' Edition* last (e.g., parallel citations to the famous case of *Erie Railroad Co. v. Tompkins* would be given as follows: **304 U.S. 64, 58 S. Ct. 817, 82 L. Ed. 1188**). Both Thomson/West's *Supreme Court Reporter* and the *Lawyers' Edition* have star paging, so *United States Reports* can be cited without actually consulting that source.

The *Lawyers' Edition* connects with the *A.L.R.* series. The various *A.L.R.* series (*A.L.R.*, *A.L.R. Federal*, *A.L.R. Second Series*, etc.) contain only a few cases—followed by an extensive annotation on a subject involved in each reported case. Parallel references to cases appearing in the *A.L.R.* series and its historical predecessor (*Lawyers' Reports Annotated* ("*L.R.A.*") series) may be seen during the course of research. However, lawyers ordinarily do not include parallel citations in their legal writing to cases appearing in *A.L.R.* series because the principal value of these series is their annotations, not the text of the reported cases.

6. DESIGNATION OF REPORTER SERIES

Some reports, like *A.L.R.* (discussed in the preceding paragraph) and most of Thomson/West's reporters in its National Reporter System, now have multiple series. When a reporter begins a second series, the volume numbering begins again with one. To prevent confusion with the first series, **2d** must be added to the citation of the reporter (e.g., **S.W.2d** for citations to Thomson/West's *South Western Reporter, Second Series*). Designation of additional series is indicated in the same way (e.g., **P.3d** for citations to Thomson/West's *Pacific Reporter, Third Series* and **A.L.R.6th** for citations to *American Law Reports, Sixth Series*).

7. THE DATE OF DECISION AND THE NAME OF THE COURT

In early citations in England and the United States, the date of the decision was frequently omitted from citations. For example, the early U.S. Supreme Court cases in the first 107 volumes of *United States Reports* did not usually provide the specific dates of decision. Nor was the date given in most instances for cases cited by lawyers or the courts in their opinions.

Nevertheless, as practice evolved, the date of decision came to be included as part of every modern case citation. In the United States, the now universally accepted convention is to place the date, enclosed by parentheses, after the abbreviated reporter designation. When citing cases published in traditional reporters, that date is the year of decision:

[*BB & ALWD*] *Hanna v. Plumer*, 380 U.S. 460 (1965).

With regard to the name of the court in the citation, three universally recognized citation conventions developed. First, the appropriately abbreviated
name of the court, including its geographic jurisdiction, must be indicated in the parenthetical containing the date. Second, when the highest court of a
jurisdiction is cited, the abbreviated name of the
court is omitted. Third, when the abbreviated name
of the reporter in the citation unambiguously indicates the geographic jurisdiction, the geographic
jurisdiction is omitted.

To illustrate how these three important conventions ordinarily operate in the context of U.S.
Supreme Court cases, consider the citation to the
Hanna case on the preceding page. Because the U.S.
Supreme Court **(U.S. Sup. Ct.)** is the highest federal
court in the United States and the abbreviation for
United States Reports is the same as the Court's
geographic jurisdiction **(U.S.)**, neither the abbreviated name of the Court nor its geographic jurisdiction
is included in citations to this reporter. That only
leaves the date in the parenthetical **(1965)**.

The rules operate in the same way in citing cases
decided by the highest court of a state. For example,
on October 16, 1928, the Wyoming Supreme Court
(Wyo. Sup. Ct.) decided the case of *Lawer v. Kline.*
This case was officially reported in volume 39 of
Wyoming Reports. It was also unofficially reported in
volume 270 of the *Pacific Reporter,* Thomson/West's
regional reporter that covers Wyoming. If the *Lawer*
case were cited to only *Wyoming Reports*, it would be
cited as follows:

[*BB & ALWD*] *Lawer v. Kline*, **39** Wyo. **285 (1928).**

If a parallel citation to the *Pacific Reporter* were also included in the citation, it would be cited as follows:

[*BB & ALWD*] *Lawer v. Kline*, **39** Wyo. **285, 270 P. 1077 (1928).**

In both instances, because the Wyoming Supreme Court is the highest state court in Wyoming and the abbreviation for *Wyoming Reports* is the same as the court's geographic jurisdiction **(Wyo.)**, neither the abbreviated name of the court nor its geographic jurisdiction is included in the parenthetical at the end of the citation. That only leaves the date in the parenthetical **(1928)**.

In contrast, however, assume that the *Lawer* case were cited only to Thomson/West's *Pacific Reporter*. It would be cited as follows:

[*BB & ALWD*] *Lawer v. Kline*, **270 P. 1077 (Wyo. 1928).**

The geographic jurisdiction must now be indicated in the parenthetical containing the date because the *Pacific Reporter* contains decisions from several states, not just Wyoming. Therefore, because the abbreviated name of the reporter **(P.)** in the citation does not unambiguously indicate the geographic jurisdiction **(Wyo.)**, the geographic jurisdiction cannot be omitted. As indicated in the preceding paragraph, however, the Wyoming Supreme Court is the highest state court. Thus, because the highest court of a jurisdiction is cited, the abbreviated name of the court **(Sup. Ct.)** is omitted. Finally, the exact date of decision, October 16, 1928, was not used in the above citations because, when traditional published reporters are cited, it is universally accepted that the year of decision **(1928)** is sufficient.

It should be noted that about twenty states have now ceased publishing their official, jurisdiction-named reporter series. For example, Wyoming discontinued *Wyoming Reports* in 1959. Those states now rely on Thomson/West reporters as the official source of their decisions.

8. CITATION SENTENCES AND CLAUSES

Another convention arose very early in citation practice. Citations were treated like separate sentences, concluding with a period at the end of the citation.

[*BB* & *ALWD*] *Smith v. Doe*, **538 U.S. 84 (2003).**

When two or more different cases were cited in support of a proposition, the citations were typically separated by semi-colons, with the last citation ending with a period. When several cases or other sources were cited, it was called a string citation.

[*BB* & *ALWD*] *Smith v. Doe*, **538 U.S. 84 (2003);** *Guthrie v. Harkness*, **199 U.S. 148 (1905);** *Wells Fargo Bank N.A. v. Boutris*, **419 F.3d 949 (9th Cir. 2005);** *Haynes v. Williams*, **279 F.3d 478 (D.C.**

Cir. 2004); *Riley v. Jones*, 476 F. Supp. 2d 696 (E.D. Mich. 2007); *State ex rel. Carmichael v. Jones*, 41 So. 2d 280 (Ala. 1949); *Manchin v. Browning*, 296 S.E.2d 909 (W. Va. 1982).

As the practice developed, citations were also placed within a textual sentence when a citation was used in conjunction with *only part of the sentence*. In this latter situation, the citations were treated as a phrase and set off with commas.

[*BB & ALWD*] The Third Circuit has recognized the possibility of a due process right to effective assistance of counsel in immigration removal proceedings, *Chmakov v. Blackman*, 266 F.3d 210, 213 (3d Cir. 2001), but the Eighth Circuit has pointedly questioned the existence of such a right, *Obleshchenko v. Ashcroft*, 392 F.3d 970, 971-72 (8th Cir. 2004).

This general pattern of using and punctuating citation sentences and clauses has carried forward to today.

The following illustration summarizes the operation of the citation conventions discussed above. This illustration is drawn from a case decided in the United States District Court in the Eastern District of Pennsylvania. It is reported in volume 342 of the *Federal Supplement Second*, beginning on page 338 of that volume.

338   **342** FEDERAL SUPPLEMENT, 2d SERIES

assessments of Dr. Berenson or Dr. Uk-
lonsky. The Third Circuit has held that
the ALJ "must give some indication of the
evidence which he rejects and his reason(s)
for discounting such evidence." *Burnett v.
Commissioner of Social Security,* 220 F.3d
112, 119 (3d Cir.2000). *See also Schau-
deck v. Commissioner of Social Security,*
181 F.3d 429, 433 (3d Cir.1999) ("[T]he
ALJ must indicate in his decision which
evidence he has rejected and which he is
relying on as the basis for his finding").
Without an assessment of the two medical
opinions, the ALJ's opinion is both difficult
for the court to review for legal error and
in contravention of the prevailing law of
this Circuit. Upon review of the two medical opinions and the testimony reproduced
in the record, this court finds that the
ALJ's decision, is not supportable by reasonable evidence. The court declines to
delay the plaintiff's award of benefits by
remanding the case to the Commissioner
for a rehearing. *See* 42 U.S.C. § 405(g).

Tara SEGAL, Plaintiff

v.

Jo Anne B. BARNHART, Commissioner of the Social Security Administration, Defendant.

No. Civ.A. 04–2589.

United States District Court,
E.D. Pennsylvania.

Oct. 29, 2004.

Background: Administrative Law Judge
(ALJ) denied claimant's application for Social Security disability benefits. Claimant
petitioned for review. Claimant brought
motion for summary judgment.

Holding: The United States District
Court for the District of the Eastern District of Pennsylvania, Katz, Senior District
Judge, held that substantial evidence did
not support decision of ALJ.

Motion granted.

Segal v. Barnhart, 342 F. Supp. 2d 338 (E.D. Pa. 2004).
  [1]   **[2]**   **[3]**   **[4]**   **[5]**   **[6] [7]**

[1] the **case name** (*Segal v. Barnhart*);

[2] the **volume number** of the reporter (**342**);

[3] the abbreviated **name of the reporter**, which
is the *Federal Supplement Second* (**F. Supp. 2d**);

[4] the **page number** on which the opinion begins
(**338**) (and a "pinpoint" citation added to identify
specific material cited within the opinion, as appropriate);

[5] the abbreviated **name of the court**, including
its geographic jurisdiction (**E.D. Pa.**) (that information is not clearly indicated from the reporter cited);

[6] the **date** (year) of the decision (**2004**); and

[7] the citation sentence ends with a period (.).

9. CITATION SIGNALS

Another early, and ultimately very important, development in legal citation is the use of introductory "signals." *Black's Law Dictionary* defines a citation signal as "an abbreviation or notation supplied to indicate some basic fact about an authority." These signals are *see*; *see also*; *see, e.g.*; *see generally*; *but see*; *contra*; *cf.*; *but cf.*; *compare . . . with*; and *accord*.

Using one of these introductory signals contrasts with directly citing an authority ("**no signal**"):

[*BB* & *ALWD*] *Lawer v. Kline*, 270 P. 1077 (Wyo. 1928). [This is a direct "no signal' citation.]

Such "direct" or "no signal" citations were routinely (and still are) used to identify one of the following: (1) legal authority that has been referred to by name in the text; (2) a source that has been directly quoted; or (3) authority that states the proposition for which it was cited.

a. See

One of the earliest uses of a citation signal was "*see*." Because early English nominative reports included what might be termed explanatory commentary in reporting the oral proceedings, early reporters began to use "*see*" to introduce a citation. " *See*" became a shorthand means of indicating a reference to a case that the lawyers or judges referred to, but did not cite. In addition, these early reporters used "*see*" to introduce cross-references. Sometimes, "*see*" also functioned as the verb of a textual sentence providing a cross-reference.

As practice further developed, lawyers and judges used "*see*" to identify authority that "indirectly" or "implicitly" supported the proposition for which the authority was cited. Others used "*see*" to mean that the proposition for which the authority was cited could be viewed as being "suggested" by the cited authority. Still others (including the first (1926) edition of *The Bluebook*) used "*see*" to indicate that the cited authority contained "dictum" supporting the proposition for which the authority was cited. (Dictum is a judicial comment made during the course of opinion which is unnecessary in relation to the decision in the case.) Even today, not everyone agrees on the meaning of this signal. In any event, the following illustrates how "*see*" appears in a citation:

[*BB & ALWD*] *See Lawer v. Kline*, 270 P. 1077 (Wyo. 1928).

   b. See also

Relatively early in development of citation signals was the addition of "*also*" to the "*see*" signal:

[*BB & ALWD*] *See also Lawer v. Kline*, 270 P. 1077 (Wyo. 1928).

"*See also*" signified that the cited authority constituted further support for the proposition for which the authority was cited. In addition, it was apparently used by some reporters to draw the reader's attention to a source similar to one(s) cited immediately before it, but was perhaps distinguishable in some way. For that reason, it was generally regarded as a "weaker" signal than "*see*" alone. Furthermore, because "*see also*" included the basic signal "*see*," it was subject to all the attendant nuances of meaning that "*see*" alone had.

   c. *See, e.g.*

Early reporters and other legal writers sometimes added "*e.g.*" (the abbreviation of the Latin *"exempli gratia"*) immediately after the "*see*" signal, as shown in the following illustration (although not always punctuated in this way):

[BB] *See, e.g., Lawer v. Kline,* 270 P. 1077 (Wyo. 1928).

The generally accepted meaning attributed to the addition of "*e.g.*" was that other authorities "stood for" the proposition in the same way as *Lawer v. Kline* did. Thus, the addition of "*e.g.*" was widely regarded as indicating that the cited authority was "illustrative" of many authorities that could be cited to support the stated proposition in the same manner as the one cited. Furthermore, it was often interpreted as implying that actually citing those additional authorities would not be "useful" to the reader or was otherwise "unnecessary."

As practice developed, "*e.g.*" came to be combined with other signals, serving the same purpose.

d. See generally

The combination of "*see*" with "*generally*" was a relatively late addition. The first use of this signal in a U.S. Supreme Court opinion (*Whitney v. Dick*) did not occur until 1906. This signal is universally understood that the cited material is "helpful" background material or information. Often, when "*see generally*" was used to introduce a case, something like "and cases cited in the opinion" was added (as was done in the *Whitney* case). It is a very weak signal in terms of support for a proposition. The following is an illustration of how this signal appears in legal writing:

[BB & ALWD] *See generally Lawer v. Kline,* **270 P. 1077 (Wyo. 1928).**

e. But see

Early on, legal writers added the term "*But*" in front of "*see*" to create the signal "*But see*" ("*Sed vide*" in Latin). The essence of this signal was, as stated by *Black's Law Dictionary*, to direct "the reader's attention to an authority or a statement that conflicts or contradicts the statement or principle just given," as shown in the following illustration:

[BB & ALWD] *But see Lawer v. Kline,* **270 P. 1077 (Wyo. 1928).**

However, because "*But see*" incorporated the signal "*see*," it was subject to all the same nuances of meaning that "*see*" had.

f. Contra

"*Contra*" means "against or contrary to" and was used to cite a case that had laid down a proposition or rule directly contrary to the one stated:

[*BB & ALWD*] *Contra Lawer v. Kline*, 270 P. 1077 (Wyo. 1928).

Very early, English nominative reporters used "*contra*" as a signal (sometimes followed by a comma, but most often without one). "*Contra*" also found early use in reporters in the United States and has continued to the present.

g. Cf.

"*Cf.*" is derived from the Latin "*confer*" and means "compare." In a citation, it would appear as follows:

[*BB & ALWD*] *Cf. Lawer v. Kline*, 270 P. 1077 (Wyo. 1928).

This signal developed much later than signals like "*see*" and "*contra*." For example, "*cf.*" as a signal began to be used by the U.S. Supreme Court with some frequency only around 1915.

In many respects, this signal is the least precise in terms of accepted meaning. *Black's Law Dictionary* indicates that this signal "directs the reader's attention to another authority or section of the work in which contrasting, analogous, or explanatory statements may be found." Because "contrasting," "analogous," and "explanatory" may be very different things, it is often difficult to tell what a judge or lawyer had in mind when this signal was used (unless the citation is accompanied by further explanation).

Frequently however, (but, of course, not always), judges and other legal writers use "*cf.*" in a more limited sense than suggested by *Black's*. For example, some writers would be intending to indicate that authority introduced by "*cf.*" supports the proposition for which it is cited "only by analogy." Still others would be intending to indicate that authority introduced by the "*cf.*" signal supports a "different proposition" than the one for which it is cited (the "main proposition"); however, the cited authority introduced by "*cf.*" is viewed to be "sufficiently analogous" to the main proposition "to lend support" to it.

Certainly, almost all legal writers would agree that authority introduced by "*cf.*" is not to be read as a citation of controlling authority that "dictates" the result by being directly on point with regard to both the facts and the law. Instead, many readers are likely to view authority introduced by "*cf.*" as, at most, supporting the main proposition only by way of dictum or analogy.

h. But cf.

The signal "***but cf.***" functions much like "***but see***." Subject to permutations of meaning inherent in "*cf.*," "***but cf.***" is generally used to introduce authorities that support propositions that are analogously contrary to the "main proposition" to which the citation refers. It appears as follows:

[BB & ALWD] *But cf. Lawer v. Kline,* **270 P. 1077 (Wyo. 1928).**

i. Compare . . . with

In the early part of the twentieth century, "***compare***" and "***with***" began to be used together to facilitate a comparison of authorities. Some legal writers used this signal to identify two or more authorities that reached "different results" in relation to the cited proposition. Others, however, used it to cite two or more authorities that, when compared, would provide "support for" or "illuminate" the cited proposition.

[BB] *Compare Lawer v. Kline,* **270 P. 1077 (Wyo. 1928)** *with Ellis v. Mihelis,* **26 Cal. Rptr. 71 (Ct. App. 1962).** [The signal usage here would be the same for an *ALWD* citation, but (as discussed below) the citation of the California case differs.]

When multiple authorities were cited with a "**compare . . . with**" signal, they were typically treated as a series, separated by commas with an "**and**" before the last item in the series, which is the practice followed by *The Bluebook* today.

j. Accord

Early United States court opinions frequently described authorities or the law of two or more jurisdictions to be in "***accord***" with one another (e.g., "This decision is in accord with [another cited case]," "[T]he American and English courts are in entire accord in holding that a contract which the master has been corruptly or recklessly induced to sign will be wholly disregarded . . . ," etc.).

"*Accord*" as a signal, however, was not used with frequency in U.S. Supreme Court opinions until the middle of the twentieth century. *Black's Law Dictionary* indicates that "**accord**" is used "to introduce a case clearly supporting a proposition for which another case is being quoted directly." Case citations using "*accord*" appear as follows:

[*BB & ALWD*] *Accord Lawer v. Kline*, 270 P. 1077 (Wyo. 1928).

10. ADDING PARENTHETICAL INFORMATION TO CITATIONS

Much of the ambiguity inherent in the use of signals can be resolved by adding parenthetical information to a citation (so-named because the information appears in parentheses at the end of the citation). For example, an explanatory parenthetical can be used to indicate how a particular authority is relevant to the proposition for which it is cited:

[*BB & ALWD*] *Cf. Lawer v. Kline*, 270 P. 1077, 1077-78 (Wyo. 1928) (holding that a five-year lease, executed by a partner without written authority, did not violate the Statute of Frauds).

Sometimes, a short phrase may be all that is needed if the meaning of the notation is apparent:

[*BB* & *ALWD*] *Cf. Lawer v. Kline,* **270 P. 1077 (Wyo. 1928) (Statute of Frauds).**

Another frequent use of a parenthetical is to provide a quotation from the cited source—usually to demonstrate to the reader that the case does indeed stand for what it was cited:

[*BB* & *ALWD*] *Lawer v. Kline,* **270 P. 1077, 1079 (Wyo. 1928) ("[T]he decided weight of authority is to the effect that a partner has implied authority to execute leases . . . when they are necessary and appropriate to carry on the business of the partnership, and that such leases are binding upon it, unless, of course, the partner who signs has no actual authority, and the want thereof is known to the lessor.").** [Note that the quotation is a complete sentence; thus, the final punctuation of the sentence (the period) was retained; a pinpoint reference (**1079**) identifies the specific page where the quotation may be found.]

A parenthetical is also typically used to indicate the cited source has quoted another source:

[*BB* & *ALWD*] *Buckley v. Valeo,* **424 U.S. 1, 43 (1976) (quoting** *Thomas v. Collins,* **323 U.S. 516, 535 (1945)).**

Still another frequent use of a parenthetical is to indicate the weight of authority (e.g., dictum) or the portion of the opinion cited (e.g., a concurring, dissenting, or plurality opinion).

[*BB & ALWD*] *Terry v. Adams*, **345 U.S. 461, 484 (1953) (Clark, J., concurring) (declaring that a private party may not control "the uncontested choice of public officials" without complying with state-action safeguards).** [Abbreviations for titles of judges and other officials are set out in **Appendix 10** of this book.]

A second parenthetical is used to indicate alterations in quoted material (e.g., "**emphasis added**" or "**citations omitted**"):

[*BB & ALWD*] *Terry v. Adams*, **345 U.S. 461, 484 (1953) (Clark, J., concurring) (declaring that a private party may not control "the *uncontested choice* of public officials" without adhering to state action safeguards) (emphasis added).**

Similarly, a parenthetical may be used to indicate other information about the nature of the opinion, as shown in the following examples.

[*BB & ALWD*] *Buckley v. Valeo*, **424 U.S. 1 (1976) (per curiam).**

In the above example, "**per curiam**" indicates that the opinion is a summary one that an appellate court has handed down without identifying the individual judge who wrote the opinion. Typically, this type of opinion simultaneously grants certiorari and disposes of the merits (discussing both the facts and the issues involved), usually resulting in at least a partial reversal of the judgment below.

[*BB* & *ALWD*] *Arcoren v. Peters*, 829 F.2d 671 (8th Cir. 1987) (en banc).

"**En banc**" is used to indicate that all the judges, and not just a smaller panel, were present and participating. This Law-French term means "on the bench" and is spelled "**in banc**" in some opinions.

[*BB* & *ALWD*] *Brown v. Belmontes*, 544 U.S. 945 (2005) (mem.).

In the above example, "**mem.**" is the recognized abbreviation of "memorandum." It is used to indicate a unanimous appellate opinion that succinctly states the decision of the court or briefly reports the court's conclusion, usually without elaboration because the decision follows a well-established legal principle or does not relate to any point of law.

[*BB* & *ALWD*] *Bragdon v. Abbott*, 524 U.S. 624 (1998) (affirming 5-4).

Sometimes, the division of the judges deciding the case is also indicated parenthetically.

11. ADAPTATION OF TRADITIONAL CITATION CONVENTIONS TO NEW DEVELOPMENTS: ELECTRONIC DATABASES AND PUBLIC DOMAIN CITATIONS

a. *Citing Cases on WESTLAW and LEXIS*

WESTLAW, LEXIS, and other databases provide extensive full-text coverage of judicial opinions. When an opinion has been printed in a traditional reporter, the overwhelming preference of lawyers is to cite the case to the printed source only. However, many opinions in databases will never appear in a traditional reporter. In such a situation, WESTLAW, LEXIS, or some other electronic source must be cited.

The traditional print citation rules have been adapted for purposes of citing cases available through WESTLAW, LEXIS, and other electronic sources. In general, such cases are cited by case name, specific information identifying the database, and a parenthetical identifying the court and exact date. The following are examples:

[*ALWD*] *Tilyou v. Carroll*, **1992 WL 170916 (E.D.N.Y. July 2, 1992).**

[*ALWD*] *Pfeiffer v. Insty Prints*, **1993 U.S. Dist. LEXIS 15317 (N.D. Ill. Oct. 29, 1993).**

Some authorities and many lawyers would add the docket number (assigned by the clerk of the court) to the citation, as shown below:

[*BB*] *Tilyou v. Carroll*, **No. CV-92-0705 (CPS), 1992 WL 170916 (E.D.N.Y. July 2, 1992).**

When screen numbers or pages within electronic sources are cited for the purpose of giving a pinpoint citation, asterisks or paragraph symbols, as appropriate, are used:

[*BB*] *Tilyou v. Carroll*, **No. CV-92-0705 (CPS), 1992 WL 170916, at *5 (E.D.N.Y. July 2, 1992)**

(rejecting the argument that the estate was an indispensable party).

[*ALWD*] *Tilyou v. Carroll*, 1992 U.S. Dist. LEXIS 10204, at **14-16 (E.D.N.Y. July 2, 1992) (rejecting the argument that the estate was an indispensable party).

The conventions regarding deletion of information about the court discussed in subsection 7, above, are applied in this context as well. Thus, if the information identifying the database clearly indicates which court decided the case, all or part of the abbreviated name of the court (including its geographic jurisdiction) may be eliminated:

[*BB*] *Kasl v. Bristol Care, Inc.*, No. WD 54543, 1998 Mo. App. LEXIS 954 (May 26, 1998).

b. *Public Domain Citations*

A growing number of jurisdictions have developed so-called public domain, medium neutral, or universal citations. Public domain citations are made possible when the court assigns a chronological accession number to each case and numbers the paragraphs in the opinion. As a result, the data elements of this type of citation retain their meaning in any format in which cases are published. Thus, these cases are equally usable in both print and electronic media.

The format for the chronological accession number varies. It often consists of the year (e.g., **2004**), identification of the court (e.g., **WI App** for the

Wisconsin Court of Appeals), and the number of the opinion (e.g., **129**, indicating that it is the 129th opinion issued by the court that year). When the public domain citation is given, lawyers ordinarily add parallel citations, as appropriate.

Because the court is usually indicated by the chronological accession number, the court is not identified in a parenthetical at the end of the citation. Furthermore, if the year of decision is included in the chronological accession number, the year is also omitted from the parenthetical at the end of the citation. Thus, in most instances, there will be no parenthetical at the end of the citation. Pinpoint citations are usually to paragraph numbers assigned by the court (e.g., ¶ **44**), but other designations may be used (e.g., **p.5**). Peculiar punctuation may also be used. Here are some examples of citations meeting the requirements of particular jurisdictions:

Koepsell's Olde Popcorn Wagons, Inc. v. Koepsell's Festival Popcorn Wagons, Ltd., **2004 WI App 129, ¶ 44, 275 Wis. 2d 397, 416, 685 N.W.2d 853, 862.**

Dunham v. Dunham, **2006 WY 1, ¶ 9, 125 P.3d 1015, 1017-18.**

Watson v. Watson, **2001-CA-01178-SCT (Miss. 2004).**

Terry v. Terry, **2006-1406, p.5 (La. App. 3 Cir. 3/28/07); 954 So. 2d 790, 794.**

C. CONVENTIONS FOR CITING STATUTES AND RELATED SOURCES

Traditionally, early English statutes were cited by name (e.g., **Statute of Westminster II**), regnal year (e.g., **13**), abbreviated name of the monarch (e.g., **Edw. 1** for Edward I), chapter (e.g., **c. 24** or **ch. 24** for chapter 24)—with the actual year of enactment added parenthetically to assist the reader (e.g., **1285**, which was the thirteenth year after Edward I began reigning on November 20, 1272). Thus, a typical citation would appear as follows:

Statute of Westminster II, 13 Edw. 1, ch. 24 (1285) *or* **[BB] Statute of Westminster II, 13 Edw. 1, c. 24 (1285).**

This format was not, of course, well suited for statutes in the United States.

1. FEDERAL STATUTES

a. Citing Federal Statutes in the Statutes at Large

In the United States, the source for the authoritative text of federal laws is the *United States Statutes at Large*. The publication of this set began in 1846 (and superceded two earlier chronological publications of federal laws). It published all federal legislation enacted up to 1846 retrospectively, and it has continued to publish federal legislation as it is enacted to the present. The title for this work appears to have been influenced by a similar project undertaken in England in 1587. The *Statutes at Large* of England consisted of eighteen hundred folio pages. It attempted to set forth retrospectively all English statutory law enacted since the Magna Carta.

Laws in the *United States Statutes at Large* are known as session laws and are arranged *chronologically*. The U.S. Supreme Court initially began to cite this source by volume number, the abbreviated name of the work (most often "Stat. at Large"), followed by the relevant page number(s). Later, **Stat.** became the widely used abbreviation (e.g., **83 Stat. 852**).

Prior to the 85th Congress (1957), laws in the *Statutes at Large* were organized by chapter number. Thereafter, they were organized by public law number. The chapter number or the public law number became an integral part of the citation, along with either an official name, a popular name, or a name constructed from **Act of** and its full date of enactment. Traditionally, the year of enactment would be appended parenthetically at the end of the citation *unless it was included in the name of the statute*, which is the practice followed by *The Bluebook*. However, the *ALWD Manual* requires the date to be appended in a parenthetical at the end of every citation and creates a public law number for statutes prior to the 85th Congress.

[*BB*] Rural Development Act of 1972, Pub. L. No. 92-419, 86 Stat. 657.

[*BB* & *ALWD*] National Environmental Policy Act of 1969, Pub. L. No. 91-190, 83 Stat. 852 (1970).

[*ALWD*] **Rules Enabling Act of 1934, Pub. L. No. 73-415, 48 Stat. 1064 (1934).**

[*BB*] **Law & Equity Act, ch. 90, 38 Stat. 956 (1915).**

[*BB*] **Act of June 1, 1872, ch. 255, 17 Stat. 196.**

The original section number (e.g., **§ 17**) was often added to facilitate identification of a particular provision, along with a pinpoint citation to it in the *Statutes at Large* (e.g., **83**):

[*BB*] **Judiciary Act of 1789, ch. 20, § 17, 1 Stat. 73, 83.**

[*ALWD*] **Judiciary Act of 1789, Pub. L. No. 1-20, § 17, 1 Stat. 73, 83 (1789).**

b. *Codification of Federal Statutes*

One significant disadvantage of session laws like the *United States Statutes at Large* is their very nature: they are published chronologically in order of enactment rather than organized by subject. Thus, to determine the current text of a law using only the *Statutes at Large* volumes, the volume where the original law first appears would need to be examined, and then all subsequent volumes in which any amendments to it appear.

To remedy that situation, statutory codifications were undertaken. Today, as explained below, federal laws currently in force are cited to the current statutory codification of federal laws, the *United States Code*. Laws as they appear in the *Statutes at Large* are now ordinarily cited only to indicate historical fact, such as enactment, repeal, or amendment.

The first codification of the *United States Statutes at Large* resulted in the 1875 publication of the *Revised Statutes of the United States*. A commission rewrote all public laws and all of their amendments that were still in force and were of general and permanent application. They were then arranged by subject (titles). Prior to publication, Congress enacted the revision into law, repealing all prior public laws that were incorporated into the revision. Thus, the *Revised Statutes of 1875* became what is known as positive law. As a result, it was the appropriate source to cite (rather than the *Statutes at Large*).

The first edition of the *Revised Statutes of the United States Passed at the First Session of the Forty-Third Congress, 1873-74* (1875) contained significant errors. A second edition published in 1878 corrected them. Changes in the text were indicated in the second edition by brackets and italics. Unlike the first edition, however, Congress never enacted the second edition into positive law, so that the text was technically regarded as only prima facie evidence of the law. Lawyers and courts routinely cited the *Revised Statutes*—most often as **Rev. Stat.** or **R.S.**, followed by the section number (e.g., **Rev. Stat. § 5198** or **R.S. § 5198**). It is unlikely that the *Revised Statutes* will ever be cited today, but references to that source still remain in the reported cases as well as in the historical notes for federal statutes.

In 1926, the first edition of the *United States Code* (**U.S.C.**) was published. The 1926 edition of the

United States Code identified all sections of the
Revised Statutes which had not been repealed and all
subsequently enacted public laws from the *Statutes at
Large*. This body of law was compiled into fifty titles,
arranged by *subject*. The Government Printing Office
currently produces a new edition of the *United States
Code* every six years. During the intervening years,
cumulative supplements are issued annually. The
United States Code is the official codification of
federal statutes.

c. *Citing Statutes* in the *United States Code*

The basic structure of a citation of a federal
statute in the official *United States Code* is universally accepted:

[Title] U.S.C. [Section] [Date]

For example, the following citation would be
immediately recognized as referring to **§ 1652** appearing in **Title 28** (covering the "Judiciary and
Judicial Procedure") of the **2006** edition of the *United
States Code*.

[*BB & ALWD*] 28 U.S.C. § 1652 (2006).

The U.S. Supreme Court typically adds "ed." after
the date (e.g., 2006 ed.). The name of the provision
may be added at the beginning of the citation:

[*BB & ALWD*] Rules of Decision Act, 28 U.S.C. § 1652 (2006).

Citations to statutes appearing in the official, annual supplements indicate that fact (**Supp.**) in the parenthetical with the date. However, the practice is not uniform among lawyers and the courts. For example, the U.S. Supreme Court typically cites the supplement as follows: 29 U.S.C. § 633a (1970 ed., Supp. IV) (citing only the supplement); 16 U.S.C. § 1801 (1982 ed. & Supp. III) (citing both the main volume and the supplement). Others more often use one of the following forms:

[*ALWD*] 29 U.S.C. § 633a (Supp. 1974).

[*BB*] 29 U.S.C. § 633a (Supp. IV 1974).

[*ALWD*] 16 U.S.C. § 1801 (1982 & Supp. 1985).

[*BB*] 16 U.S.C. § 1801 (1982 & Supp. III 1985).

d. Citing Statutes in Annotated Versions of the United States Code

Instead of using the official *United States Code* published by the U.S. Government Printing Office, lawyers almost always use one of the two annotated versions of the *United States Code*: Thomson/West's *United States Code Annotated* (**U.S.C.A.**) or LexisNexis' *United States Code Service* (**U.S.C.S.**). These privately published annotated versions contain several extremely useful editorial features not found in the official version, such as annotations of cases that have interpreted particular sections of the *Code*. The annotated versions also include extensive historical notes, tables, cross-references, and citations to other sources discussing the provision.

Even though the text of the statutes in all versions of the *United States Code* is almost always the same, technically only the version published by the U.S. Government Printing Office is official should any differences arise. Furthermore, if the text of a statute differs in the *United States Code* and the *United States Statutes at Large* (which has happened on occasion), the text in the *Statutes at Large* will prevail over that in the *United States Code*—unless Congress has enacted the *Code* provisions into positive law. To date, Congress has done so for about half of the fifty titles in the *United States Code* (the enacted titles are listed, among other places, following § 204(a) of Title 1 in the annotated versions of the *Code*).

Federal statutes in the *United States Code Annotated* and the *United States Code Service* are cited in the same basic way as the official version of the *United States Code*, except that the publisher is indicated parenthetically:

[Title] U.S.C.A. [Section] [Publisher] [Date]

[Title] U.S.C.S. [Section] [Publisher] [Date]

With regard to the date, the copyright date of the annotated volume or the supplement is used. The publisher designation has, of course, varied over time (reflecting the ownership of the annotated codes at the time of publication or preferred designation):

[*BB & ALWD*] Rules of Decision Act, 28 U.S.C.A. § 1652 (West 2003).

[*BB*] **Rules of Decision Act, 28 U.S.C.S. § 1652 (LexisNexis 2003).**

[*ALWD*] **Rules of Decision Act, 28 U.S.C.S. § 1652 (Lexis 2003).**

[*BB & ALWD*] **16 U.S.C.A. § 801 (West 1985).**

[*BB*] **15 U.S.C.S. § 1801 (Law. Co-op. 1984).**

2. STATE STATUTES

State legislatures enact state statutes in much the same way as Congress does. Publication of those statutes parallels publication of federal legislation: chronologically and organized by subject. Like the *United States Statutes at Large*, state session laws are published after the completion of regular or special legislative sessions (e.g., *Session Laws of Hawaii, Session Laws of South Dakota*, etc.). Sometimes, legislative services also provide rapid publication of newly enacted state statutes.

While there is considerable variation among the fifty states in publishing state session laws, the following citations would be immediately recognized as citations to such laws (which are typically cited by year and page number):

[*BB & ALWD*] **2007 Ga. Laws 334**

[*BB & ALWD*] **1997 Ill. Laws 88**

Lawyers and courts rarely need to cite state session laws, however, because the preferred citation for currently in force state statutory provisions is to the state code or some other subject-matter organized set of consolidated, revised, or compiled statutes or their supplements. Nevertheless, session laws might be cited, like the *United States Statutes at Large*, for very recent enactments or to support a statement of historical fact relating to a state statutory provision.

a. Citing State Statutory Provisions

Because fifty state jurisdictions are involved, considerable variation exists in the titular designation of state statutory collections (e.g., *General Laws of Rhode Island, Revised Statutes of Nebraska, Idaho Code Annotated*, etc.). Likewise, the organization of the provisions within a statutory collection also varies substantially (e.g., sections, titles, chapters, etc.). The pattern of publication also varies. Some state statutory collections are published both officially and privately. Sometimes, official versions are annotated while others are not. Privately published versions almost always are.

In general, state statutory collections are cited by indicating the following:

(1) the abbreviated name of the statutory collection, beginning with the abbreviated name of the state (e.g., **Ark. Code Ann.**);

(2) the cited section(s), title(s), chapter(s), etc. (e.g., **§ 18.30.300**; **tit. 19, § 494**; **ch. 151B, § 1**; **art. 5221k**; **ch. 68, ¶ 2-201**);

(3) the name of the publisher or compiler (e.g., **West**, **Lexis**, **Vernon**, etc.); and

(4) the year of the statutory collection, depending on how the set is dated (e.g., **2008**). [Items (3) and (4) appear together in a parenthetical.]

The following citations would be universally recognized as citations of state statutory collections:

[*BB*] **Ark. Code Ann. § 23-78-114 (LexisNexis Supp. 2007).**

[*BB & ALWD*] **Conn. Gen. Stat. Ann. § 33-844 (West 2005).**

[*BB & ALWD*] **Haw. Rev. Stat. § 577.3.5 (2004).**

[*BB*] **N.D. Cent. Code § 14.02.4-03 (Mitchie 2002).**

[*BB*] **Wis. Stat. Ann. § 704.07 (West 2001 & Supp. 2006).**

With regard to the year used in citing published state statutory collections, the widely accepted preference is to use the year that appears on the spine of the volume in the citation. If there is none, not everyone is in agreement about which date should be used. As discussed in Chapter 3(B)(4), some prefer the date on the copyright page while others prefer the year that appears on the title page.

b. *Citing State Statutory Subject-Matter Codes*

Some state statutory collections (e.g., those in California, New York, and Texas) are organized into individual subject-matter codes. These subject-matter codes are cited as follows:

[*BB* & *ALWD*] Cal. Penal Code § 12025.5 (West 2000).

[*BB* & *ALWD*] N.Y. Lab. Code § 201-D (McKinney 2002).

[*BB* & *ALWD*] Tex. Educ. Code Ann. § 54.052 (Vernon 2006).

3. UNIFORM STATE LAWS

The National Conference of Commissioners of Uniform State Laws is responsible for encouraging the drafting and adoption of uniform state legislation on a variety of subjects. Uniform laws are published, along with a variety of research resources, in *Uniform Laws Annotated Master Edition* (**U.L.A.**). The following would be widely recognized as citations to uniform laws in this source:

[*BB* & *ALWD*] Unif. Parentage Act, 9B U.L.A. 364 (2001).

[*BB* & *ALWD*] Unif. Anatomical Gift Act § 1(b), 8A U.L.A. 94, 99 (1993).

When a uniform act is cited as the law of a particular jurisdiction, however, it should be cited as a state statute.

[*BB* & *ALWD*] Mont. Code Ann. §§ 40-6-101 to 40-6-135 (1995) (adopting a version of the Uniform Parentage Act).

4. MUNICIPAL ORDINANCES AND CHARTERS

On the local level, charters regulate city councils, county boards, and other subordinate political divisions of a state government. These entities enact ordinances governing local matters, such as zoning, noise levels, etc.

Municipal ordinances are cited by analogy to statutes, but variances frequently occur. The specifics of the format vary according to the nature of the source cited and the jurisdiction. Local practice plays an important role in what is viewed as an appropriate citation.

D. CITATION CONVENTIONS FOR OTHER PRIMARY AUTHORITY

In addition to cases and statutes discussed in the preceding two sections, the following are additional sources of primary authority (i.e., law emanating directly from a lawmaking governmental body): (1) federal and state constitutions; (2) administrative regulations; (3) rules of procedure and evidence; and (4) treaties and other international agreements. These sources are discussed in this section.

1. FEDERAL AND STATE CONSTITUTIONS

The United States Constitution is cited by the abbreviated form: **U.S. Const.** This abbreviation is then followed by the specific reference to the relevant article, section, clause, or amendment.

However, practice concerning the capitalization and abbreviation of the references to the particular article, section, clause, or amendment is not uniform. Nor is the use of ordinal (e.g., **6**) versus Roman numbers (e.g., **VI**) to designate specific numerical provisions. Most often, the following abbreviations will be used. **Appendix 1(D)** lists *The Bluebook* and *ALWD* abbreviations for subdivision designations.

   art. for Article *[BB & ALWD]*
   § for Section *[BB & ALWD]*
   cl. for Clause *[BB & ALWD]*
   amend. for Amendment *[BB & ALWD]*
   pmbl. for Preamble *[BB* **only]** [Not abbreviated under the *ALWD Manual*]

It is universally accepted that citations to constitutional provisions appear without a date when the provision is currently in force. The following are widely recognized and accepted citations of constitutions, using Roman numerals to designate particular articles or amendments, but not sections or clauses:

   [BB & ALWD] **U.S. Const. art. I, § 8, cl. 8.**

   [BB & ALWD] **U.S. Const. amend. V.**

State constitutions are typically cited in a similar manner:

   [BB & ALWD] **R.I. Const. art. X, § 4.**

   [BB & ALWD] **N.J. Const. art. I, ¶ 10.**

2. ADMINISTRATIVE REGULATIONS

Since 1936, federal administrative rules and regulations have been published chronologically in the *Federal Register* (**Fed. Reg.**). The *Federal Register* is published daily (except Saturday, Sunday, and official holidays). It is analogous to the *United States Statutes at Large*. Citations to the *Federal Register* include the following conventional components:

[Vol.] Fed. Reg. [Page] [Exact Date]

The title may be added when it would assist readers or would serve some other purpose. Thus, a typical citation to a regulation in the *Federal Register* would appear as follows:

[*BB & ALWD*] Bank Activities & Operations, 69 Fed. Reg. 1895 (Jan. 13, 2004). [Abbreviations for the months are shown in **Appendix 1(C)**.]

Rules and regulations published in the *Federal Register* are codified in the *Code of Federal Regulations* (**C.F.R.**), which is analogous to the *United States Code*. Citations to the *Code of Federal Regulations* include the following components:

[Title] C.F.R. [Section] [Year]

Thus, a typical citation to a rule or regulation in the *Code of Federal Regulations* would appear as follows:

[*BB & ALWD*] 12 C.F.R. § 7.4000 (2006).

The title may be added when it would assist readers or would serve some other purpose:

[*BB & ALWD*] Bank Activities & Operations, 12 C.F.R. § 7.4000 (2006).

Finally, note that citations to rules and regulations in the *Federal Register* routinely indicate parenthetically where those rules or regulations will appear in the *Code of Federal Regulations*, as illustrated below:

[*BB & ALWD*] Bank Activities and Operations, 69 Fed. Reg. 1895 (Jan. 13, 2004) (codified at 12 C.F.R. § 7.4000 (2006)).

Many states now officially codify and publish state administrative regulations in state registers similar to the *Code of Federal Regulations*. In other states, each agency issues its own regulations. They are cited in a manner that is analogous to citation of federal rules and regulations.

3. RULES OF PROCEDURE AND EVIDENCE

Rules of procedure govern the form and mode of litigation. The Federal Rules of Civil Procedure were promulgated by the U.S. Supreme Court in 1938 pursuant to the Rules Enabling Act of 1934. These rules are used in all U.S. District Courts. In addition, over half of the states have adopted rules modeled on the Federal Rules of Civil Procedure. Pursuant to the Rules Enabling Act, the U.S. Supreme Court subsequently promulgated the Federal Rules of Criminal Procedure and the Federal Rules of Appellate Procedure. The following are widely recognized citations to these currently-in-force rules:

[*BB & ALWD*] Fed. R. Civ. P. 12(b).

[*BB & ALWD*] Fed. R. Crim. P. 11.

[*BB & ALWD*] Fed. R. App. P. 3(c).

The Federal Rules of Evidence govern proof at trial in both civil and criminal cases in the federal courts. They were enacted by Congress in 1975 and can be amended (within certain limits) by the U.S. Supreme Court. Rules modeled on the Federal Rules of Evidence have been adopted, in whole or in part, by a large number of states. The widely recognized citation for the Federal Rules of Evidence currently in force is as follows:

[*BB & ALWD*] Fed. R. Evid. 703.

State rules of procedure and evidence are cited analogously.

4. TREATIES AND OTHER INTERNATIONAL AGREEMENTS ENTERED INTO BY THE UNITED STATES

Treaties can be thought of as written agreements between nations based on mutual consent. Under Article VI of the U.S. Constitution, treaties made under the authority of the United States are declared the supreme law of the land. State laws inconsistent with such treaties are invalid. The U.S. Constitution provides that the President has the authority to make treaties with the advice and consent of Congress and two-thirds approval by the Senate. In addition, the President may enter into international agreements or executive agreements under the President's own constitutional authority or under authority granted by an act of Congress.

All treaties before 1950 to which the United States was a party were published officially in the *United States Statutes at Large* (**Stat.**). Since 1950, treaties and other international agreements have been officially published in *U.S. Treaties and Other International Agreements* (**U.S.T.**). The State Department has also published treaties and other international agreements in several series: *Treaty Series* (**T.S.** to 1945), *Executive Agreement Series* (**E.A.S.** to 1945), and *Treaties and Other International Acts Series* (**T.I.A.S.** from 1945 to date). Other sources for international agreements include the *League of Nations Treaty Series* (**L.N.T.S.** from 1920 to 1945), the *United Nations Treaty Series* (**U.N.T.S.**) from 1945 to date, the *Pan American Union Treaty Series* (**Pan.-Am. T.S.**), and the *European Treaty Series* (**[*BB*] Europ. T.S.** *or* **[*ALWD*] European T.S.**).

In general, treaties are cited using (1) the title of the treaty, (2) a pinpoint reference, if any, (3) the date of signing, and (4) treaty source or sources. Some lawyers and courts also separately identify the parties to the agreement if there are three or less. However, the particulars vary. The following are examples of citations of treaties and other agreements:

[*BB*] Convention on the Taking of Evidence Abroad in Civil or Commercial Matters, opened for signature, Mar. 18, 1970, 23 U.S.T. 2555.

[*BB*] United Nations Convention Relating to the Status of Refugees, July 28, 1951, 19 U.S.T. 6259.

[*ALWD*] *Treaty Defining Relations with Cuba* (May 29, 1934), 48 Stat. 1683.

E. CITATION CONVENTIONS FOR SECONDARY AUTHORITY

Secondary authority explains the law. However, such authority does not itself establish it. Thus, it is, at most, persuasive. In other words, it may have some weight, but it is never binding. This section discusses the accepted conventions, such as they are, with respect to the five most important types of secondary authority: (1) legal texts and treatises; (2) legal periodicals; (3) legal encyclopedias; (4) restatements of the law; and (5) *A.L.R.* annotations.

1. TEXTS AND TREATISES

In a legal context, treatises are works that systematically examine a subject. They are often multivolume works. Texts differ from treatises in that they are generally shorter and are oriented to formal study of a subject. Texts are primarily designed for student use and quick reference by lawyers. On occasion, other types of books may be cited. The citation of these publications has slowly evolved.

In England and the formative years of the United States, only a few texts and treatises on the law existed. One of them was Sir William Blackstone's *Commentaries on the Laws of England,* which is widely regarded as the most influential treatise in the history of Anglo-American law. It was printed by the Clarendon Press between 1765 and 1769 at Oxford in four volumes. It was the basis of legal education in England and America for years, and it greatly influenced the American colonists and Western settlers, who used it as their chief source of law.

Interestingly, this famous work was cited by early courts and lawyers in a variety of ways. Here are some variations taken from early U.S. Supreme Court opinions: "2 Bl. Comm. 37," "2 Black. Com. 318," "Blackstone, 1 Comm. 71, 72," "4 Blackstone Com., page 27," and "1 Bl. Com. 91." Despite the variations, several critical items were included in these citations: (1) an indication of the author (**Blackstone**); (2) the identification of the name of the work (**Commentaries**), although it is abbreviated in various ways); (3) the volume number; and (4) the page. Noticeably absent was the year of publication, which was much like the absence of dates for cases cited in the early nominative reporters.

Over time, as other texts and treatises were cited, the year of publication came to be regarded an essential element of such a citation (although even today Blackstone's *Commentaries* are still routinely cited without a date or full title). Take, for example, the evolution of the citation of one of the arguably best texts ever written on American law: William Prosser's single volume hornbook, *The Law of Torts*. In 1943, two years after it was published, the U.S. Supreme Court cited it, using the year of publication in a parenthetical: "Prosser on Torts (1941), § 37, p. 243." On other occasions, the Court cited only page numbers, without indicating the section.

Three years after Prosser's second edition was published, the Court cited this work as follows: "Prosser, Torts (2d ed. 1955), § 34." This citation illustrates another universally accepted convention for citing texts and treatises—the edition must be indicated in a parenthetical containing the year of publication if the work cited is not the first edition.

In a U.S. Supreme Court case decided after the fourth edition appeared, the Court cited this edition of Prosser's hornbook as follows: "W. Prosser, Law of Torts § 112 (4th ed. 1971)." Prosser's initial and the formal title of the book were now used. The Court's citation of the fifth edition reflected the addition of several authors and a change in the title: "W. Keeton, D. Dobbs, R. Keeton, & D. Owen, Prosser and Keeton on the Law of Torts § 39, p. 243 (5th ed. 1984)."

Thus, as illustrated by the citation of Prosser's hornbook, a reasonable expectation developed that the following items should be included in citation of texts, treatises, or books in some way:

(1) the name of the author(s);

(2) the title of the text, treatise, or book (using capitalization rules described in Chapter 1(F)(3)(*m*) below);

(3) the volume number if the work encompasses more than one volume (like Blackstone's);

(4) the relevant section(s) or page(s);

(5) the edition if the edition cited is not the first one; and

(6) the year of publication.

Beyond these essential items, complete agreement about the details does not exist. For example, is it sufficient to use only the author's last name? Should the author's initials or full name be used? If the number of authors is large, should all of them be listed? Where should the volume number be placed in the citation? Should a subtitle be included? When should pages be cited rather than section numbers? Does the publisher need to be included in the citation? Should the name of the editor be included in the citation, and if so, how?

These issues are discussed in Chapter 4(A), but for now, the following citations illustrate some of the typical variations that one can expect to see:

[*BB*] W. Page Keeton et al., *Prosser and Keeton on Law of Torts* **§ 39, at 243 (5th ed. 1984).**

[*ALWD*] W. Page Keeton, Dan B. Dobbs, Robert E. Keeton & David G. Owen, *Prosser and Keeton on Law of Torts* **§ 39, 243 (5th ed., West 1984).**

[*BB*] 2 Ronald D. Rotunda & John E. Nowak, *Treatise on Constitutional Law: Substance and Procedure* **§ 14.6 (3d ed. 1999).**

[*ALWD*] Ronald D. Rotunda & John E. No-wak, *Treatise on Constitutional Law: Substance and Procedure* **vol. 2, § 14.6 (3d ed., West 1999).**

2. LEGAL PERIODICALS

Articles in legal periodicals are another important type of persuasive secondary authority. Although the specific details sometimes vary, it is well accepted that the following information should be included in citations of articles in legal periodicals:

(1) name of the author;

(2) title of the article (using capitalization rules described in Chapter 1(F)(3)(*m*) below);

(3) volume number;

(4) abbreviated periodical name;

(5) beginning page of the article;

(6) specific internal page references, if any; and

(7) date.

The following is an illustration of such a citation:

[*BB & ALWD*] Ralph H. Folsom & Larry L. Teply, *Surveying "Genericness" in Trademark Litigation,* **70 Trademark Rep. 243, 250 (1982).**

Special circumstances require adjustments in how articles are cited. For example, some legal periodicals do not have volume numbers. Using the year instead of the volume number and dropping the date at the end of the citation is a well-accepted practice:

[*BB & ALWD*] Richard McMillan, Jr. & Todd D. Peterson, *The Permissible Scope of Hearings,*

Discovery, and Additional Fact-Finding During Judicial Review of Informal Agency Action, 1982 Duke L.J. 333, 349.

Several periodicals paginate each issue separately. As discussed and illustrated in Chapter 4(C)(4) below, such articles are typically cited by the full date or period of publication. But how that information is shown varies substantially. For example, some authors put that information in a parenthetical. The placement of the page number also varies.

Another special situation in which citation form varies substantially involves student-written works. Other special situations include the citation of book reviews, symposia, colloquia, surveys, and multipart articles. All of these variations are discussed and illustrated in Chapter 4(C) below.

3. LEGAL ENCYCLOPEDIAS

Legal encyclopedias discuss broad legal topics, and their text is supported by extensive citations to cases and other research sources. Lawyers and courts sometimes cite legal encyclopedias for basic legal rules and propositions. The two legal encyclopedias that are national in scope are *Corpus Juris Secundum* (**C.J.S.**) and *American Jurisprudence Second* (**Am. Jur. 2d**).

The following are the universally accepted conventions for citing these two encyclopedias:

[Vol.] C.J.S. [Topic] [Section] [Year]

[Vol.] Am. Jur. 2d [Topic] [Section] [Year]

The following illustrate citations to these encyclopedias:

[*BB* & *ALWD*] 43 C.J.S. *Infants* § 20 (2007).

[*BB* & *ALWD*] 23 Am. Jur. 2d *Deeds* § 274 (2007).

Locally oriented legal encyclopedias are available for some jurisdictions (e.g., *Florida Jurisprudence Second, Ohio Jurisprudence Third*, etc.). They generally use a format similar to that of the national legal encyclopedias. They are also cited in the same basic way as national legal encyclopedias.

4. RESTATEMENTS OF THE LAW

Restatements of the Law are drafted by committees of leading legal scholars and lawyers under the auspices of the American Law Institute. Restatements cover basic (mostly common-law) areas of the law. Most of them now have multiple series. This type of authority is unique to the law. Restatements are very well respected persuasive secondary authorities. Other than typeface variations, the basic format for citing restatements is widely accepted:

[Restatement Title] [Subdivision] [Date]

The title consists of "**Restatement of**" and the subject covered. If the restatement is now in a series (e.g., **Second** or **Third**), that information is included immediately after **Restatement** (e.g., **Restatement (Second)**, etc.). The date is the year of publication, not adoption. The subdivision cited is ordinarily a section. A comment (**cmt.**) or an illustration (**illus.**) is also frequently cited. The following show widely accepted citations to restatements, but note the typeface differs:

[*ALWD*] *Restatement of Conflict of Laws* § 377 (1934).

[*BB*] Restatement (Second) of Torts § 520 (1977).

[*BB*] Restatement (Second) of Agency § 388 cmt. a, illus. 3 (1957).

[*ALWD*] *Restatement (Third) of Unfair Competition* § 39 cmt. d (1995).

5. *A.L.R.* ANNOTATIONS

As noted in section B(5) above, the *American Law Reports* ("**A.L.R.**") series contain selected cases and annotations. Although they are used primarily for research purposes, annotations in *American Law Reports* are sometimes cited. The format for citing these annotations, however, has varied over the years. In general, the elements of a citation include the following:

(1) the name of the author (unless the annotation was unsigned);

(1a) the word, **Annotation** (included in *Bluebook* citations);

(2) the title (using capitalization rules described in Chapter 1(F)(3)(*m*) below);

(3) the volume number;

(4) the abbreviated name of the *A.L.R.* series (e.g., **A.L.R. Fed. 2d**);

(5) the page number on which the annotation begins;

(6) the pinpoint citation (if any); and

(7) the year of publication.

The examples below illustrate the likely variations:

[*BB*] Kristine Cordier Karnezis, Annotation, *Insured's Right to Recover from Insurer Pre-judgment Interest on Amount of Fire Loss*, 5 A.L.R.4th 126 (1981).

[*ALWD*] Kristine Cordier Karnezis, *Insured's Right to Recover from Insurer Prejudgment Interest on Amount of Fire Loss*, 5 A.L.R.4th 126 (1981).

F. THE PROCESS OF LEGAL CITATION

This Preface introduced the following five key steps in the process of citing sources during the course of legal writing:

(1) Identifying the basic information needed to construct the citation;

(2) Applying the detailed requirements of a system of citation or otherwise refining the citation to (a) comply with the requirements imposed by the recipient of the writing, (b) meet reader expectations, or (c) conform to local customary practice;

(3) Incorporating the citation into the document, using appropriate signals, citation sentences or

phrases, appropriate citation order, explanatory parentheticals, short forms, typeface, etc.;

(4) Double-checking to make sure that the authorities cited have not overruled, amended, or superseded and that any subsequent history has been appropriately indicated; and

(5) Proofreading the document carefully and making sure, *inter alia*, that the citation form is correct and internally consistent.

1. IDENTIFY THE BASIC INFORMATION NEEDED TO CONSTRUCT THE CITATION

The conventions discussed in the preceding sections indicate the basic information that will be needed to cite the principal sources used in legal writing. For example, assume that notes on a case from the *Pacific Reporter* are being taken during the course of legal research. It is readily apparent that the information about the first-listed parties on each side of a case, the reporter, the court, and the year of the decision should be recorded. In addition, the notes should identify the pinpoint location of quotations or other substantive matters within the opinion that may be needed to be cited later.

Sometimes, in determining the answer to a legal issue or developing appropriate background on a legal subject, the research path may be lead to relatively unfamiliar or infrequently cited sources, such as foreign cases, international sources, editorials, news articles, broadcasts, canon law, collected works, interim orders, interviews, popular magazines, bills and resolutions, legislative committee reports, services, topical reporters, e-mails, etc. In such circumstances, it may be necessary to record as much information as possible. When it is later determined what exactly is needed to cite the source properly, the detailed information will have been recorded so that the source will not have to be relocated.

2. APPLY THE DETAILED REQUIREMENTS OF A SYSTEM OF CITATION OR OTHERWISE APPROPRIATELY REFINE THE CITATION

Is compliance with a particular system of citation, citation manual, or style sheet required or preferred? What specific court-imposed citation requirements, if any, exist? These determinations might require some research. If specific requirements or preferences do exit, they should be followed (but violated for good reasons).

Even if a writer is not laboring under the requirement of using rules of a citation system or a state-specific citation manual, care should be taken to conform the citations to the generally accepted conventions discussed in the preceding section or local customary practice. For example, local custom may prefer citation of the state statutes using Thomson/West's abbreviation (e.g., **A.R.S.**) rather than *The Bluebook* and the *ALWD Manual's* form (i.e., **Ariz. Rev. Stat.**). Otherwise, the writer may end up frustrating the reader's expectations and creating questions of doubt about the writer's professional competence.

3. PROPERLY INCORPORATE THE CITATIONS INTO THE DOCUMENT

Legal writers must take care when they incorporate citations into a document.

a. Consistency

Whatever system is used, the same source should be cited consistently throughout the document.

b. Hierarchy of Authority

A writer should constantly be sensitive to the "hierarchy of authority." Merely persuasive authority from other jurisdictions is always "trumped" by mandatory authority—unless a court decides in the rare instance to overrule existing precedent in the jurisdiction. Nor does it make sense to cite lower courts when the issue has been authoritatively resolved by a higher court within the jurisdiction. Likewise, it is useless to cite statutes that have no application in the relevant jurisdiction.

c. Freshness of Authority

As one well-respected commentator has aptly pointed out, "[t]he older the authority, the less authority it may have" because older authority may have been eroded by changes in related areas or social attitudes. Thus, recent decisions tend to have a greater persuasive impact ("freshness of authority"). Nevertheless, if a landmark or seminal case is directly on point, most commentators recommend citing that case "more prominently than its progeny."

One important exception exists concerning the "freshness of authority." If the decision was one of statutory interpretation, its value as a precedent ordinarily is *increased* by the age of the decision. Consider the following example. In the 1922 *Federal Baseball* case, the U.S. Supreme Court held that professional baseball was merely a "sport" and not interstate "commerce," and therefore, it was not subject to the federal antitrust laws. In 1953, the Court reaffirmed this holding in the *Toolson* case. Again in 1972, even though all other professional sports had subsequently been held to involve interstate commerce and had been subjected to the federal antitrust laws, the Court refused to overrule its prior decisions in the *Flood* case.

In *Flood*, the Court stated that "we adhere once again to *Federal Baseball* and *Toolson*." The Court pointed out that "[i]f there is any inconsistency and illogic in all this, it is an inconsistency of long standing that is to be remedied by the Congress and not by this Court." The Court added that "[i]f we were to act otherwise, we would be withdrawing from the conclusion as to congressional intent made in *Toolson* and from the concerns of retrospectivity therein expressed."

d. String Citations

After thoroughly researching an issue, some legal writers are tempted to demonstrate that they have exhaustively researched the cases by citing them in long string citations. Furthermore, as aptly pointed out by one commentator, some legal writers think that "if enough cases are tossed [out], [the reader] will simply capitulate under the sheer burden of authority." Such approaches are "unnecessary" and often "counterproductive."

Despite these temptations, several reasons exist why string citations should be avoided. First, when it is important to demonstrate to the reader that several jurisdictions have adopted a particular rule or analysis, a citation to a secondary authority will often be sufficient for that purpose. Second, string citations (that are not adequately integrated into persuasive writing) squander precious space. Third, string citations can interrupt the flow of an argument, which might cause the reader to lose the thread of the argument entirely. Fourth, the same effect can often be obtained by using the signal, "*see, e.g.*," to introduce one or two of the best cases on point.

Some commentators suggest that using brief explanatory parenthetical phrases with each case in a string citation might be an effective means of distinguishing several cases in a limited space so that the reader can easily see "simple comparisons." Even then, however, as one commentator aptly states, one must be careful because "[r]eaders may miss key information if it is shrouded in a forest of citations

and squirreled away in what appears to be a parenthetical aside."

e. Order of Signals

The Bluebook and the *ALWD Manual* prescribe the
order in which various types of signals should appear.
The following listing shows the order in which signals
should appear in citation sentences or clauses. *The
Bluebook* and *ALWD Manual* ascribe slightly different meanings to these signals, but ordinary readers
will not be able to recognize those nuances. Instead,
they will likely ascribe the more ambivalent customary meanings set out in section B(9), above.

Signals Indicating "Support"

The Bluebook	*ALWD*
[No Signal]	[No Signal]
E.g.,	[*E.g.*] (no comma)
Accord	*See*
See	*Accord*
See also	*See also*
Cf.	*Cf.*

Signals Indicating a "Comparison"

The Bluebook	*ALWD*
Compare . . .	*Compare . . . with*
[*and*] *. . .*	
with . . .	
[*and*] *. . .*	

Signals Indicating a "Contradiction"

The Bluebook	*ALWD*
Contra	*Contra*
But see	*But see*
But cf.	*But cf.*

Signals Indicating "Background Material"

The Bluebook	*ALWD*
See generally	*See generally*

f. General Rules Regarding Use of Signals

Both *The Bluebook* and the *ALWD Manual* have several related rules regarding the use of signals. Unless differences are indicated, *The Bluebook* and the *ALWD Manual* are the same.

● When a signal begins a citation sentence, the signal should be capitalized.

[*BB & ALWD*] At least one circuit appears to have recognized the possibility of a due process right to effective assistance of counsel in immigration removal proceedings. *See Chmakov v. Blackman*, 266 F.3d 210 (3d Cir. 2001).

● When a signal begins a citation clause, the signal should not be capitalized.

[*BB & ALWD*] One circuit has recognized the possibility of a due process right to effective assistance of counsel in immigration removal proceedings, *see Chmakov v. Blackman*, 266 F.3d 210 (3d Cir. 2001), but at least one other

circuit has questioned the existence of such a right, *see Obleshchenko v. Ashcroft*, 392 F.3d 970 (8th Cir. 2004).

• "*E.g.*" may be used alone when many authorities stand for the same proposition, but they are not cited; *The Bluebook* always uses a comma after "*e.g.*" The *ALWD Manual* never does with any of its signals.

[*BB*] *E.g., Shane v. Fauver*, 213 F.3d 113 (3d Cir. 2000).

[*ALWD*] *E.g. Shane v. Fauver*, 213 F.3d 113 (3d Cir. 2000). [No comma used after *e.g.*]

• "*E.g.*" may be combined with any other signal; *The Bluebook* always sets off "*e.g.*" with commas, but the *ALWD Manual* never does.

[*BB*] **Most circuits have recognized the possibility of a due process right to effective assistance of counsel in immigration removal proceedings.** *See, e.g., Chmakov v. Blackman*, **266 F.3d 210 (3d Cir. 2001).**

[*ALWD*] **Most circuits have recognized the possibility of a due process right to effective assistance of counsel in immigration removal proceedings.** *See e.g. Chmakov v. Blackman*, **266 F.3d 210 (3d Cir. 2001).**

• The same signal should not be repeated when more than one authority provides the same degree and type of support. In other words, as the *ALWD Manual* states, "[t]he signal 'carries through' until a different signal is used."

[BB & ALWD] See Shane v. Fauver, 213 F.3d
113 (3d Cir. 2000); *Lopez v. Smith*, 203 F.3d 1122
(9th Cir. 2000).

● The *ALWD Manual* separates different signals
and their accompanying citations with a semicolon
(and one space). In contrast, *The Bluebook* requires
that signals of the same type (i.e., "supportive,"
"comparative," "contradictory," or "background," as
shown above) be "strung together" in a single citation
sentence, separated by colons. Signals of different
types must be grouped separately in different citation
sentences. However, within a citation clause, signals
of more than one type may be used, separated by
semicolons.

[BB] See Shane v. Fauver, 213 F.3d 113 (3d
Cir. 2000); *Lopez v. Smith*, 203 F.3d 1122 (9th Cir.
2000). *Contra McGore v. Wrigglesworth*, 114 F.3d
601 (6th Cir. 1997) (holding leave to amend no
longer allowed).

[ALWD] See Shane v. Fauver, 213 F.3d 113 (3d
Cir. 2000); *Lopez v. Smith*, 203 F.3d 1122 (9th Cir.
2000); *contra* McGore v. Wrigglesworth, 114 F.3d
601 (6th Cir. 1997).

● *The Bluebook* uses "*and*" to join multiple
authorities on each "side" of a "*compare*" and "*with*"
signal. The *ALWD Manual* joins them with semi-
colons.

[BB] Compare Blake v. Wright, 179 F.3d 1003,
1012 (6th Cir. 1999) (holding that public officials
may assert qualified immunity) *and Tapley v.*

Collins, 211 F.3d 1210, 1216 (11th Cir. 2000) (stating that "the qualified immunity defense is so well-rooted in our jurisprudence that only a specific and unequivocal statement of Congress can abolish the defense") *with Berry v. Funk*, 146 F.3d 1003, 1013 (D.C. Cir. 1998) (holding that the existence of a statutory good faith defense in Wiretap Act shows congressional intent not to allow qualified immunity in Wiretap Act cases).

[*ALWD*] *Compare Blake v. Wright*, 179 F.3d 1003, 1012 (6th Cir. 1999) (holding that public officials may assert qualified immunity); *Tapley v. Collins*, 211 F.3d 1210, 1216 (11th Cir. 2000) (stating that "the qualified immunity defense is so well-rooted in our jurisprudence that only a specific and unequivocal statement [by] Congress can abolish the defense") *with Berry v. Funk*, 146 F.3d 1003, 1013 (D.C. Cir. 1998) (holding that the existence of a statutory good faith defense in Wiretap Act shows congressional intent not to allow qualified immunity in Wiretap Act cases).

• *The Bluebook* drops "**but**" from "**but see**" and "**but cf.**" when either of these signals follows another negative signal.

[*BB*] Statements made by parties in pleadings in other cases may be admitted against them in federal court. *See Vincent v. Louis Marx & Co.*, 874 F.2d 36 (1st Cir. 1989) (holding that the judge had discretion under Federal Rule of

Evidence 403 to admit plaintiff's inconsistent complaint in prior state case against third party). *But see Schneider v. Lockheed Aircraft Corp.*, 658 F.2d 835, 843 (D.C. Cir. 1981) (per curiam) (holding that statements made in hypothetical pleadings in third-party proceedings are not admissible); *cf. Martel v. Stafford*, 992 F.2d 1244, 1248 (1st Cir. 1993) (holding that statements made in briefs by party's counsel in one case cannot routinely be used in another case as admission of party).

[*ALWD*] Statements made by parties in pleadings in other cases may be admitted against them in federal court. *See Vincent v. Louis Marx & Co.*, 874 F.2d 36 (1st Cir. 1989) (holding that the judge had discretion under Federal Rule of Evidence 403 to admit plaintiff's inconsistent complaint in prior state case against third party); *but see Schneider v. Lockheed Aircraft Corp.*, 658 F.2d 835, 843 (D.C. Cir. 1981) (per curiam) (holding that statements made in hypothetical pleadings in third-party proceedings are not admissible); *but cf. Martel v. Stafford*, 992 F.2d 1244, 1248 (1st Cir. 1993) (holding that statements made in briefs by party's counsel in one case cannot routinely be used in another case as admission of party).

• Although not absolutely required in every instance, explanatory parenthetical explanations should be used to assist the reader, particularly for comparative citations.

[*BB & ALWD*] *Cf. Merrill v. Sherburne*, 1 N.H. 199, 217 (1818) (concluding that a statute depriving a private litigant of rights vested by a past judgment constituted a forbidden attempt by the legislature to exercise "judicial" power); *G. & D. Taylor & Co. v. Place*, 4 R.I. 324, 332 (1856) (agreeing that "to open judgments or decrees obtained in a court, and to allow the substitution of a new . . . sworn answer . . . for the purpose and with the effect of reversing the relative condition of the parties to a pending suit, dependent upon the effect of that answer, is an exercise of judicial power").

● When signals are used as verbs in ordinary sentences, they should not be italicized.

[*BB*] For a discussion of the prohibition of the judicial creation of criminal defenses, see James McCauley Landis, *Statutes and the Sources of Law*, in *Harvard Legal Essays* 213 (Roscoe Pound ed., 1934). [In this context, "see" is used as a verb in an ordinary sentence.]

● Within a citation clause or sentence, the signals should appear in the order listed above.

g. *Citation Order Within a Signal*

The Bluebook and the *ALWD Manual* add detailed rules concerning the order of citation *within* a single signal. These rules are set out in **Appendix 9**. However, Judge Richard Posner persuasively asserted that "[t]here is no need to have rules about the

order in which authorities are cited in a string citation [because] [t]here is a natural order that depends
on the purpose of the string citation and the contents
of the cited works." Thus, "[i]f [an] author wants to
show the evolution of a body of law . . . , [then the
author] will cite them in chronological order."

As Judge Posner also aptly points out, "[i]f [an
author] is citing cases from the same jurisdiction to
provide authority for a proposition, [the author] will
cite them in reverse chronological order because,
other things being equal, a recent case is more
authoritative than an old one." Furthermore, "[w]hen
other things are not equal, as where one citation is of
a decision from a higher court than the other, the
author will cite the decision of the higher court first
even if that decision is older." Therefore, "[a]ll that
rules can do is distract the author from thinking
about the logical ordering of [the] citations."

Perhaps as a result of such criticism, *The Bluebook*
now specifically gives authors license to deviate from
the "citation ordering" rules for a good reason. The
latest editions of *The Bluebook* recognize that authorities may be cited in a different order than the one
prescribed when one or more authorities are "more
helpful or authoritative than the other authorities
cited within a signal."

h. *Citing Multiple Pages, Passim, and Et Seq.*

When material spanning multiple pages is cited,
The Bluebook provides that "inclusive page numbers"

be given. In doing so, the last two digits must be retained:

[*BB*]   **85-86**
                    212-26
                    1330-38

The *ALWD Manual* makes dropping those digits optional:

[*ALWD*]   **85-86**
                    212-26 *or* **212-226**
                    1330-38 *or* **1330-1338**

Both *The Bluebook* and the *ALWD Manual* provide that "nonconsecutive" "scattered" pages should be cited by listing the individual pages, separated by commas.

[*BB*]   **85-86, 212-26, 1330-38**

[*ALWD*]   **85-86, 212-26, 1330-38** *or* **85-86, 212-226, 1330-1338**

In addition, both *The Bluebook* and the *ALWD Manual* permit the use of **passim** (Latin for "here and there" or "throughout") in lieu of citing pinpoint page numbers when the point is made throughout a source.

[*BB & ALWD*] *See* **1920 Haw. Spec. Sess. Laws 30 (requiring special licensing of schools that taught in a language other than English, requiring English school attendance until third grade, and otherwise regulating foreign language schools, which is extensively discussed in**

Farrington v. Tokushige, **273 U.S. 284 passim (1927).**

The Bluebook requires inclusive page or section numbers be given in citations. It specifically prohibits the use of "*et seq.*," which is the abbreviation of the Latin "*et sequens*" (for "and the following one") and "*et sequentes*" or "*et sequentia*" (masculine and neuter, respectively, for "and the following ones"). In contrast, the *ALWD Manual* indicates that the use of "*et seq.*" "is not encouraged," but its use is not prohibited outright.

i. Multiple Sections or Paragraphs

When a cited source is divided into sections or paragraphs, the relevant subdivision should be cited:

[*BB & ALWD*] 43 C.J.S. *Infants* § 20 (2007).

[*BB & ALWD*] *Dunham v. Dunham*, 2006 WY 1, ¶ 9, 125 P.3d 1015, 1017-18.

When consecutive paragraphs or sections are cited, two paragraph (¶¶) or section symbols (§§) are used:

[*BB & ALWD*] 43 C.J.S. *Infants* §§ 14-16, 20 (2007).

[*BB & ALWD*] *Dunham v. Dunham*, 2006 WY 1, ¶¶ 9-10, 125 P.3d 1015, 1017-18.

Additional rules concerning multiple sections and paragraphs are discussed in Chapter 3(B)(3) below in the context of statutes. As will be seen there, these subdivisions can be designated in peculiar ways.

j. Citing Footnotes

Sometimes, material in footnotes is specifically cited. When a single footnote is cited, it is indicated a "**n.**" Multiple notes are indicated by "**nn.**" *The Bluebook* omits any space between "**n.**" or "**nn.**" and the footnote number. In contrast, the *ALWD Manual* inserts one space between them. The following is a citation to material in footnote 16 on page 679:

[BB] *Morrison v. Olson*, 487 U.S. 654, 679 n.16 (1988) (noting that courts may appoint court officials).

[ALWD] *Morrison v. Olson*, 487 U.S. 654, 679 n. 16 (1988) (noting that courts may appoint court officials).

The Bluebook and the *ALWD Manual* both contain additional detailed (sometimes varying) rules concerning citing footnotes. For example, if the material cited was in both the text and in footnote 16, *The Bluebook* would indicate that fact as follows:

[BB] *Morrison v. Olson*, 487 U.S. 654, 679 & n.16 (1988) (noting that federal courts may appoint court officials).

Other various rules in *The Bluebook* and the *ALWD Manual* cover scattered footnotes on a singe page, multiple consecutive footnotes on different pages, etc. In these rare situations, those sources should be consulted.

k. Using Short Forms

"Short forms" are used to save space when citing a source that has been previously fully cited. The following illustrate commonly seen short forms using "*id.*" (the abbreviation of the Latin "*idem*" meaning the same and used to refer the immediately preceding authority) and other short forms:

[*BB & ALWD*] *Lawer v. Kline*, 270 P. 1077 (Wyo. 1928). [Initial citation]

[*BB & ALWD*] *Lawer*, 270 P. at 1077-78.

[*BB & ALWD*] 270 P. at 1077-78.

[*BB & ALWD*] *Id.* at 1077-78.

When parallel citations are used, the format changes slightly:

[*BB & ALWD*] *Lawer v. Kline*, 39 Wyo. 285, 270 P. 1077 (1928). [Initial citation]

[*BB & ALWD*] *Lawer*, 39 Wyo. at 289-90, 270 P. at 1077-78.

[*BB & ALWD*] 39 Wyo. at 289-90, 270 P. at 1077-78.

[*BB & ALWD*] *Id.* at 289-90, 270 P. at 1077-78.

Both *The Bluebook* and the *ALWD Manual* provide sound basic guidelines for using such short forms. Generally speaking, it is recommended that such forms be used as follows:

● when it is clear to the reader to what the short form refers;

● the earlier reference falls in the same section or otherwise meets the recipient's preferred usage; and

● the reader can easily locate the full reference.

Further restrictions on the use of "*id.*" are applied when "*id.*" is used in an article, memorandum, or paper with footnotes or endnotes:

● "*id.*" cannot be used if the immediately preceding footnote or endnote contains citations to multiple sources.

In addition to "*id.*," lawyers sometimes use "*supra*" (Latin meaning "above" and "earlier in this text") and "*infra*" (Latin meaning "below" and "later in this text") to refer earlier or later cited authority. *Supra* and *infra* are often used for cross-references.

[*BB*] See *infra* Part III and notes 92-94.

[*ALWD*] See *infra* pt. III and notes 92-94.

Supra and *infra* can also be used as part a short form. For example, assume that the following article has been cited.

[*BB & ALWD*] Ralph H. Folsom & Larry L. Teply, *Trademarked Generic Words*, 89 Yale L.J. 1323, 1328 (1980). [Initial citation]

A later reference to this article using "*supra*" would appear as follows:

[*BB & ALWD*] Folsom & Teply, *supra*, at 1322.

If the first reference to this article had been in a footnote (e.g., **28**), then it would be referenced as follows:

[*BB*] Folsom & Teply, *supra* note 28, at 1322.

[*ALWD*] Folsom & Teply, *supra* n. 28, at 1322.

"*Supra*" and "*infra*" should not be used when "*id.*" would be appropriate. In addition, they should not be used when the reader will likely find it difficult to locate the full citation. Furthermore, *The Bluebook* and the *ALWD Manual* prohibit the use of "*supra*" with the following types of cited sources:

The Bluebook	*ALWD*
Cases	Cases
Statutes	Statutes
Constitutions	Constitutions
Restatements	Session laws
Model codes	Ordinances
Regulations	Regulations
Legislative materials (except hearings)	Legislative materials (except hearings)

A "**hereinafter**" form for an authority (e.g., "**CITES**") can also be established (using the same typeface as it would appear in the full citation).

[*BB*] **Convention on International Trade in Endangered Species of Wild Fauna and Flora,** *opened for signature* **Mar. 3, 1973, 27 U.S.T. 1087, 993 U.N.T.S. 243 [hereinafter CITES].**

The shortened form is substituted in the "***supra***" or "***infra***" reference.

[*BB*] CITES, *supra*, art. 14.

Like "**supra**" and "**infra**," the use of "**hereinafter**" form is restricted. *The Bluebook* prohibits the use of "**hereinafter**" with the above-listed types of authorities. However, both for "**supra**" and "**hereinafter**," *The Bluebook* does allow for exceptions in "extraordinary circumstances, such as when the name of the authority is extremely long."

The *ALWD Manual* limits the use of "**hereinafter**" to three situations: (1) when the authority does not have an author and the title is lengthy; (2) when the ordinary shortened form would cause confusion; and (3) when a footnote contains more than one source by the same author, so that the shortened reference to the author's name would not sufficiently identify the source cited in the subsequent reference.

l. Typeface Adjustments

When citations are incorporated into a document, adjustments may have to be made to the typeface. Except for journal articles appearing in *Bluebook* form, the typeface shown in the examples in this chapter is widely accepted. In handwritten or typed documents), underscoring should be substituted for italics. The comma after a case name or at the end of a signal (<u>**see, e.g.,**</u>) should not be underscored. However, underscoring does extend under periods (e.g., <u>**id.**</u> or <u>**cf.**</u>).

The following summarizes the material that should be italicized:

● case names (in both full and short-form citations), including procedural phrases;

● titles of books, articles, essays, legislative materials, the title or topic in a citation to a legal encyclopedia, and other titles;

● introductory signals, cross-references (e.g., *id.*, *supra*, etc.), and words or phrases introducing subsequent history or related authority (discussed below).

The Bluebook typeface in journal articles uses three types of typeface: Roman type, italics, and large and small caps. Supporting authorities are cited only in footnotes. In footnotes, large and small caps are used for the authors and titles of books and names of periodicals. In text, titles of books and the names of periodicals appear in italics. Case names in full citations in footnotes appear in ordinary Roman typeface, but short form references and textual references are italicized.

[*BB* Journal] W. PAGE KEETON ET AL., PROSSER AND KEETON ON LAW OF TORTS § 39, at 243 (5th ed. 1984).

[*BB* Journal] Ralph H. Folsom & Larry L. Teply, *Trademarked Generic Words*, 89 YALE L.J. 1323, 1328 (1980).

[*BB* Journal] Lawer v. Kline, 270 P. 1077 (Wyo. 1928).

[*BB* Journal] RESTATEMENT (SECOND) OF
CONTRACTS § 228 cmt. a (1981).

m. *Capitalization of Titles*

Capitalization must also sometimes be adjusted.
For example, the actual titles of *A.L.R.* annotations
are not capitalized (except for the first letter of the
first word). However, *The Bluebook* and the *ALWD
Manual* change the capitalization (or the lack thereof)
in citations of titles of annotations, law journal
articles, and books for purposes of citations.

The Bluebook capitalizes "the initial word and any
word that immediately follows a colon." In addition,
"[a]rticles, conjunctions, and prepositions when there
are four or fewer letters" should not be capitalized
"unless they begin the heading or title, or immediately follow a colon."

The *ALWD Manual* provides a slightly different
rule. It capitalizes the initial letter of the following:

(1) the first word in the title;

(2) the first word of any subtitle;

(3) the first word after a colon or dash;

(4) all other words except articles, prepositions, the
word "**to**" when it is used as part of an infinitive, and
coordinating conjunctions, such as "**and**," "**or**," "**but**,"
"**nor**," "**for**," etc.; and

(5) both words of a hyphenated word in the title
(e.g., *Waiver of Physician-Patient Privilege*); but
do not capitalize the second word when (a) it is an
article, preposition, or conjunction (e.g., *Hit-and-
Run Accidents*) or (b) the first word is a *prefix* and

the word after the hyphen is *not* a proper noun or proper adjective (e.g., **Pre-Erie Decisions** [*Erie* is a proper noun], **Quasi-contract Theory of Liability, Self-employment Status, Application for Re-employment, Anti-poverty Program,** etc.). [But many authorities on grammar and style recognize that usage varies in situation (b) and would permit capitalization of the second word after words like "quasi-," "anti-," and "self-" in the above situations (e.g., **A Comparative Analysis of Self-Incrimination by Corporations**).]

4. DOUBLE-CHECK TO MAKE SURE THAT CITED AUTHORITIES HAVE NOT BEEN OVERRULED, AMENDED, OR SUPERSEDED AND THAT SUBSEQUENT HISTORY HAS BEEN INDICATED

As part of the last steps in the citation process, a legal writer should double-check to make sure that (1) the authorities cited have not overruled, amended, or superseded and (2) any subsequent history has been appropriately indicated, when appropriate. Assume, for example, a case has been cited that was subsequently affirmed or reversed on appeal. That fact would be shown as follows:

[*BB & ALWD*] *Panetti v. Dretke*, 401 F. Supp. 2d 702 (W.D. Tex. 2004), *aff'd*, 448 F.3d 815 (5th Cir. 2006).

The following are the most frequently used indications of subsequent history. The designation of subsequent history should be italicized, but not the comma before nor the one after it (when there is one).

affirmed = *aff'd,*
reversed = *rev'd,*
certiorari granted = *cert. granted,*
certiorari denied = *cert. denied,*
certiorari dismissed = *cert. dismissed,*
modified = *modified,*
overruled = **[BB]** *overruled by* **[ALWD]** *overruled,*

Inclusion of subsequent history has no effect on the use of "*id.*" and it is not shown in short-form citations. Additional explanation can be added to the above terms and others, as appropriate:

affirmed by an equally divided court = *aff'd by an equally divided court,*
reversed on other grounds = *rev'd on other grounds,*
reversed per curiam = *rev'd per curiam,*

When the case name differs in the prior or subsequent history, both case names must be given in the citation. However, the second name should not be given when the parties' names are merely reversed or when the difference occurs in a citation to a denial of review by writ of certiorari or a rehearing. *The Bluebook* specifically adds two additional exceptions. Differences in the names need not be indicated when (1) the private party's name is unchanged in the appeal of an administrative action and (2) the difference is merely stylistic (e.g., **State** to **Florida**).

When different cases are shown in a citation, "***sub nom.***" (the abbreviation of the Latin "*sub nomine*" meaning "under the name") is used:

[*BB & ALWD*] *Louis v. Nelson*, 544 F. Supp. 973 (S.D. Fla. 1982), *rev'd on other grounds sub nom. Jean v. Nelson*, 711 F.2d 1455 (11th Cir. 1983), *aff'd*, 472 U.S. 846 (1985).

The Bluebook includes a date only with the last cited decision when a case with several decisions in the same year is cited. In contrast, the *ALWD Manual* requires the year be given for each decision.

[*BB*] *Fielding v. Allen*, 181 F.2d 163 (2d Cir.), *cert. denied*, 340 U.S. 817 (1950).

[*ALWD*] *Fielding v. Allen*, 181 F.2d 163 (2d Cir. 1950), *cert. denied*, 340 U.S. 817 (1950).

Both the *ALWD Manual* and *The Bluebook* do not require denials of certiorari or other similar discretionary review be shown unless the denial occurred within the last two years or it is [*BB*] "particularly relevant" or [*ALWD*] "particularly important." Likewise, prior history, denial of rehearings, and the history on remand are normally not given unless it is relevant in some way. The prior history of a case is indicated by phrases such as the following:

affirming = ***aff'g***
enforcing = ***enforcing***
modifying = ***modifying***
reversing = ***rev'g***
vacating as moot = ***vacating as moot***

[*BB & ALWD*] *Halls v. Beals*, 396 U.S. 45 (1969), *vacating as moot* 292 F. Supp. 610 (D. Colo. 1968).

5. PROOFREAD THE DOCUMENT MAKING SURE THAT THE CITATIONS ARE CORRECT AND INTERNALLY CONSISTENT

Finally, proofread the document, making sure, *inter alia*, that the citation form is correct before submitting the document. Special attention should be given to quotations accompanying citations. It is expected that quotations be verbatim. The following summarizes the generally accepted practice:

● When letters or words substituted or alterations are made, those changes should be shown by enclosing them in brackets (e.g., **"We do not suggest that jurisdictional doctrines other than those discussed in [the] text, such as particularized rules governing adjudications of status, are inconsistent with the [*International Shoe*] standard of fairness."**).

● Omission of letters from a "common root word" should be indicated by empty brackets ("[ ]") (e.g., **"arise[ ] out of or relate[ ] to the defendant's activities in the forum state"**).

● Omissions of a word or words are ordinarily indicated by the insertion of three periods (ellipses), separated and set off by spaces (e.g., **"The superior courts shall have original jurisdiction of . . . [c]ases and proceedings in which exclusive** jurisdiction is not vested by law in another court.").

• When the quoted language is used *as part of a phrase or a clause*, omissions before or after the quotation are not shown (e.g., **Under this test, a corporation's principal place of business is the state where the "bulk of the corporate activity" occurs.**).

• When the quoted language is used *as a full sentence* and the beginning of the quoted sentence is omitted, the first letter should be capitalized and enclosed in brackets (e.g., **"[T]he court shall dismiss the supplemental claim unless it was joined before removal of the action, in which case the district court shall remand the claim to the [s]tate court from which it was removed."**).

• When the quoted language is used *as a full sentence* and the end of the quoted sentence is omitted, insert an ellipsis between the last work quoted word and the final punctuation mark of the sentence (e.g., **"When a district court lacks or declines to exercise supplemental jurisdiction, the court shall dismiss the supplemental claim unless it was joined before removal of the action . . . ."**).

• Finally, when mistakes have occurred in the quoted material, they should be retained in the quotation but followed by "**[sic]**" (Latin for "so, thus") (e.g., **"[A]ny contract in which sexual services serve as consideration are [sic] unenforceable and void as against public policy."**)

CHAPTER 2

CITING CASES IN *BLUEBOOK* OR *ALWD* FORM

Chapter 1 indicated case citations contain several basic elements: (1) the case name; (2) the volume number of the reporter; (3) the abbreviated name of the reporter; (4) the page number on which the opinion begins; (5) a "jump" or "pinpoint" citation, as appropriate; (6) the abbreviated name of the court, including its geographic jurisdiction (unless that information is clearly indicated from the reporter cited); and (7) the date of the decision. *The Bluebook* and the *ALWD Manual* provide further rules for citing cases, which are discussed in this chapter.

A. CASE NAMES: INCLUSIONS AND DELETIONS

The total number of pages in an issue of a law journal is limited. Lawyers also must often comply with strict page limits for appellate briefs and other legal documents. Faced with these restrictions, *The Bluebook* and the *ALWD Manual*, building on traditional conventions, have two basic types of rules to maximize space available for "substantive" discussion: (1) rules governing *inclusions and deletions* in case names; and (2) rules dealing with *abbreviations*.

At the same time, law journals and law firms face another challenge. Members of law journals often simultaneously write or edit articles. Lawyers within law firms often do the same thing with regard to firm work products. It would look strange if case names and other aspects of case citations varied substantially within a single article or document. This need for reasonable consistency is made especially difficult because case names vary widely. If left on their own, writers would come up with widely varying citations. The solution adopted by *The Bluebook* and the *ALWD Manual* is to provide very detailed rules covering virtually every possible situation.

In contrast, the *Maroon Book* defers to the case name conventions already reflected in the Tables of Cases and running heads in the reporters. The *Maroon Book* directs authors to use the case name as it appears "in the Table of Cases Reported in the first reporter cited, dropping or abbreviating words at the end of each party's name if necessary to keep the case name reasonably short." Furthermore, "[t]he running head may be used if it is sufficiently descriptive of the case that the reader will be able to locate the case through the Table of Cases Reported, a case name citator, or a law digest in the event of miscitation." Commonly known initials are to be used when it is more familiar than the name in the running head. This innovative approach assures reasonable consistency within an article or document by establishing a common reference point and makes an extensive, detailed set of rules extensively discussed in this and the next section unnecessary.

1. TERMS DESCRIBING A PARTY
ALREADY NAMED

Titles of cases typically include terms describing a party already named, such as "defendant," "appellant," "warden," "executrix," "superintendent," etc. **Descriptions of a party already named should be omitted.**

MAD RIVER BOAT TRIPS, INC.
Appellant (Defendant),

v.

JACKSON HOLE WHITEWATER, INC.,
Appellee (Plaintiff).

[*BB & ALWD*] *Mad River Boat Trips, Inc. v. Jackson Hole Whitewater, Inc.*

In the above example, the terms "**Appellant (Defendant)**" and "**Appellee (Plaintiff)**" describe parties already named and should be deleted.

2. GIVEN NAMES AND INITIALS
OF INDIVIDUALS

Traditionally, **parties are cited by their surnames (last or family names).** The general rule is that the given names or initials should be omitted (e.g., a party listed in the reporter as "Jane S. Smith" would be cited as "Smith"). Furthermore, no part of a surname consisting of more than one word should be omitted (e.g., Garcilaso de la Vega, Von Der Linden, etc.). When in doubt, the index in the reporter can provide guidance on what should be included. There are three situations, however, when given names and initials of individuals should be retained in the citation.

• First, **given names and initials should be retained when the party's surname has been abbreviated in the report** (e.g., Jane S., J.S., or J.S.S.).

Robert STALNAKER, Administrator of the Public Employees' Retirement System, Appellant and Cross-Appellee,

v.

M.L.D., Appellee and Cross-Appellant.

[*BB* & *ALWD*] *Stalnaker v. M.L.D.*

In the above example, the given name "**Robert**" is omitted pursuant to the general rule, but the initials "**M.L.**" are retained because M.L.'s surname has been abbreviated to "**D.**" Again, the additional descriptive terms should be omitted.

• Second, **given names or initials of individuals should be retained when they are part of the name of a "business firm" (*BB*) or "organization" (*ALWD*)** (e.g., Jane S. Smith Pest Control, Inc.).

JOHN R. SEXTON & CO.

v.

Betsy Y. JUSTUS, Secretary of the North Carolina Department of Revenue.

[BB & ALWD] John R. Sexton & Co. v. Justus

In the above example, "**John R.**" is retained because it is part of the name of a "business firm"/ "organization," but "**Betsy Y.**" is omitted because "Betsy Y. Justus" is an individual. The description of Justus as the "**Secretary of the North Carolina Department of Revenue**" should be omitted, as discussed in subdivision 1 above.

● Third, **given names or initials of individuals should be retained (a) when they are part of a foreign name and the name is** *entirely* **in a foreign language or (b) when given names follow a foreign surname**, as in Korean, Chinese, or Vietnamese names (e.g., Le Bup Thi Dao, Chom Cho Ha, etc.).

James K. WONG, Plaintiff-Appellant,

v.

Henry Ho WONG and Colene Smith Wong, husband and wife, individually, and as tenants by the entirety, Defendants-Appellees.

[*BB & ALWD*] *Wong v. Wong*

Given names should be included only when the name is *entirely* in a foreign language. Here, they are not (i.e., "James K." Wong and "Henry" Ho Wong). In contrast, consider the following case name:

MANG SUN WONG, Appellee,

v.

CHI HONG LAM, Appellant.

[*BB & ALWD*] *Mang Sun Wong v. Chi Hong Lam*

In the above example, the given names are included because the names are entirely in a foreign language—in this instance, Chinese.

3. WORDS INDICATING MULTIPLE PARTIES

Words indicating multiple parties should be omitted. Examples include *et al.* ("and others" from the Latin "*et alii*" and "*et alia*"), *et vir* (Latin for "and husband"), and *et ux.* ("and wife" from the Latin "*et uxor*").

Barry ROMM et al.

v.

Lawrence L. FLAX et ux.

[*BB & ALWD*] *Romm v. Flax*

In the above example, "*et al.*" and "*et ux.*" should be omitted because they are indications of multiple parties.

4. ALTERNATIVE PARTY NAMES

Alternative names for a party should be omitted.

Richard and Susan ZEID, Appellants,
v.
Dr. William PEARCE, d/b/a Coronado
Animal Clinic, Appellee.

[*BB & ALWD*] *Zeid v. Pearce*

In the above example, "**d/b/a**" stands for "doing business as"; thus, "**Coronado Animal Clinic**" is omitted because it is an alternative name for the party already cited. Another designation requiring the same treatment is "**a/k/a**" for "also known as."

5. TWO NAMES FOR ONE CASE
AND CONSOLIDATED CASES

Only the first listed case should be cited when the case is a consolidation of two or more actions. Bankruptcy cases, discussed in subsection 18 below, are a possible exception.

SECRET DESIRES LINGERIE, INC., et al.
v.
CITY OF ATLANTA et al.

GAMBILL, d/b/a L & L Ltd.
v.
CITY OF ATLANTA.

[*BB & ALWD*] *Secret Desires Lingerie, Inc. v. City of Atlanta*

In the above example, the second action, *Gambill v. City of Atlanta* was consolidated with the first-listed action; the second action should be omitted. As noted in subdivision 3 above, "*et al.*" (and others) is omitted because it is an indication of multiple parties.

6. ADDITIONAL PARTIES ON EACH SIDE OF THE CASE

All parties other than the first listed on each side of the case should be omitted. However, the first-listed "relator" should be retained in the citation.

Sally Inez ADAMS, on Behalf of her niece, Jamill C. BOYSAW
v.
HERCULES, INC. and Insurance Company of North America.

[BB & ALWD] *Adams ex rel. Boysaw v. Hercules, Inc.*

In the above example, "**Adams**" has brought the action on behalf of another person, "**Boysaw**," who is the relator. Thus, the relator is also included in the citation. Because "**Insurance Company of North America**" is an additional party on the defendant's side of the case, it is omitted. As discussed in Chapter 1(B)(2) above, "**on behalf of**" becomes "***ex rel.***"

7. MULTIPLE PROCEDURAL PHRASES

Recall from Chapter 1(B)(2) above, that some cases do not have traditional adversarial parties or are not contested. In these types of cases, the title is often styled as "petition of," "matter of," or "application of" and the party's name. These phrases are abbreviated as "***In re***" in *Bluebook* and *ALWD* citations. Likewise, "*Ex parte*" is used to designate actions done for, on behalf of, or on the application of only one party.

The Bluebook and the *ALWD Manual* provide that **all procedural phrases after the first should be omitted.** For purposes of this rule, the *ALWD Manual* specifically states that **"Will of" and "Estate of" are not treated as procedural phrases** and should thus be retained in the name of the case. *The Bluebook* states this exception more broadly, indicating that all similar terms (e.g., "**Succession of**," "**Marriage of**," "**Accounting of**," etc.) are not treated as procedural phrases and should be retained in the citation. *The Bluebook* also specifically provides that all procedural phrases, except *ex rel.*, should be omitted when adversarial parties are named.

In re Ex parte Willie BOLDEN

[*BB & ALWD*] *In re* Bolden

In the above example, only the first procedural phrase is included in the citation. In the example below, "**Will of**" is not treated as a procedural phrase and is retained.

In re Will of ALEXANDER

[*BB & ALWD*] *In re* Will of Alexander

8. ARTICLES AND PREPOSITIONS

"The" is often the first word of the name of a party in a reporter and should be omitted from the citation (subject to three exceptions). The *ALWD Manual* also specifically provides that articles and prepositions may be omitted from the names of organizations that are not needed for clarity.

THE RIVAL CO., Plaintiff,
v.
SUNBEAM CORP. et al., Defendants.

[BB & ALWD] **Rival Co. v. Sunbeam Corp.**

The Bluebook and the *ALWD Manual* recognize three exceptions to the general rule (discussed above) that "the" should be omitted.

● First, **"the" should be retained in the citation when it begins the name of the res in an "in rem" action.**

**Gary Allan KOPCZYNSKI,
Plaintiff-Appellee,**

v.

**THE JACQUELINE, Documentation
Number 519060, Her Engine, Tackle,
Appurtenances, etc., Defedant-Appellant.**

[BB & ALWD] **Kopczynski v. The Jacqueline**

In the above example, "**The**" is retained in the citation because it is the name of a ship (the object of the "in rem" action).

● Second, **"The" should be retained in the citation when it begins the popular name of the case.**

THE LEGAL TENDER CASES

[BB & ALWD] **The Legal Tender Cases**

When referring to the popular name of the case beginning with "the" *in textual discussion*, however, it is generally the accepted practice (as specifically recognized by *The Bluebook*) not to include "the" as part of the case name. In the following example, note the difference in typefaces used for "**the**."

> **The *Legal Tender Cases* recognized that the power of Congress to emit bills of credit as well as to incorporate national banks was clearly established. *See The Legal Tender Cases*, 110 U.S. 421, 444 (1884).**

● Third, **"the" should be retained in the citation when "The Queen" or "The King" is the cited party.** This rule obviously applies to foreign cases. The following example is based on a case in *English Reports, Full Reprint*.

The King *against* Airey

[*BB & ALWD*] *The King v. Airey*

9. PROPERTY IN AN "IN REM" ACTION

Only the first-listed item (or group of items) should be cited when multiple items are the subject of an "in rem" action. Furthermore, when real property is the object of such an action and the first item listed is a **street address** for that property, the *ALWD Manual* provides the street address should be cited and larger geographic designations can be omitted.

The Bluebook states this same basic rule, but in a slightly different way. *The Bluebook* provides that when real property is the cited party, the common street address, if available, should be cited and all other descriptions of the property should be omitted, including larger geographic designations.

George B. **TELLEVIK**, Chief, Washington State Patrol, and Gregory J. **Webb**, Chief, Carnation Police Department, Appellants,

v.

31641 MILLROSE LANE LOCATED IN the CITY OF CARNATION, WASHINGTON and All Appurtenances and Improvements Thereon, $5,644,540.00 in U.S. Currency, 450 One-Ounce Gold Canadian Maple Leaf Coins, 500 One-Ounce Platinum Ingots, Defendants.

[BB & ALWD] Tellevik v. 31641 Millrose Lane

In the above example, the real property is listed first and is cited; the remaining objects of the "in rem" action (i.e., all appurtenances and improvements, the currency, gold coins, and platinum ingots) are omitted because only the first listed item should be cited. The street address is used. As an option, the *ALWD Manual* allows the larger geographic designation to be included, but *The Bluebook* does not. Pursuant to the rules stated above, the additional party ("**Gregory J. Webb**"), the given names and initials of the individuals, and their descriptions are also omitted.

10. TWO BUSINESS DESIGNATIONS IN THE NAME OF A "BUSINESS FIRM" OR AN "ORGANIZATION"

A large variety of business firm designations (sometimes with or without periods in their abbreviations) appear in reporters. Examples of business firm designations include the following:

Aktiengesellshaft or A.G.
Federal Savings Bank or F.S.B.
Incorporated or Inc.
Limited or Ltd.
Limited Liability Corporation or L.L.C.
Limited Liability Partnership or L.L.P.
Limited Partnership or L.P.
National Association or N.A.
Professional Association or P.A.
Professional Corporation or P.C.
Sociedad Anónima or S.A.

Both *The Bluebook* and the *ALWD Manual* provide for the deletion of "double business names" in citations. However, they state the rule in slightly different ways, but the end result is usually the same. *The Bluebook* deletes the above-listed and similar terms when the cited case name also contains a word such as **Ass'n**, **Bros.**, **Co.**, **Corp.**, and **R.R.** *The Bluebook* cautions that it must be clear that the party is a business firm, and it adds that such a deletion should take place only when the business name "could not *possibly* be mistaken for the name of some other entity, such as a natural person."

The *ALWD Manual's* approach is to provide a list of "business designations." When a cited party's name includes two of the below-listed designations, the *ALWD Manual* deletes the second one from the citation.

> **Association or Assn.**
> **Company or Co.**
> **Corporation or Corp.**
> **Federal Savings Bank or F.S.B.**
> **Incorporated or Inc.**
> **Limited or Ltd.**
> **Limited Liability Corporation or LLC**
> **Limited Liability Partnership or LLP**
> **Limited Partnership or LP**
> **National Association or N.A.**
> **Professional Association or P.A.**
> **Professional Corporation or P.C.**
> **Railroad or R.R.**
> **Railway or Ry.**
> **Sociedad Anónima or S.A.**

Arnaud ALBERT, Petitioner,

v.

STARBUCKS COFFEE CO., INC.,
Respondent.

As noted above, the result is usually the same under either set of rules (the second "**Inc.**" is deleted):

[*BB* & *ALWD*] Albert v. Starbucks Coffee Co.

11. "LONG" [*ALWD*] AND "EXTREMELY LONG" [*BB*] CASE NAMES

With regard to "long" names of "organizations," the *ALWD Manual* permits, but does not require, shortening such a name "in a sensible way" by means of deleting words from the end of the name of the organization. Long names are defined as ones containing "more than five words."

The Bluebook **applies a similar rule to all case names, not just organizations. It states that words unnecessary for identification of the case should be omitted in "extremely long case names."** The *Bluebook* notes, however, that the first word in each party's name, including a relator, should always be retained "in full." *The Bluebook* suggests that the running head located at the top of each page in the reporter may serve as a guide for this purpose.

The SUNBEAM-OSTER CO., INC. GROUP BENEFITS PLAN FOR SALARY AND NON-BARGAINING HOURLY EMPLOYEES,
Plaintiff and Appellants,

v.

Leonard WHITEHURST,
Defendant and Appellee.

[*BB* & *ALWD*] *Sunbeam-Oster Co. Group Benefits Plan v. Whitehurst*

In the above example, the case name was shortened in a way that would be acceptable under either the *ALWD Manual* or *The Bluebook* standards for lengthy case names. "**The**" was dropped (see subdivision 8, above). In addition, the second business designation ("**Inc.**") was deleted because of the presence of "**Co.**" (see subdivision 10, above).

Note that *The Bluebook* specifically requires that no portion of a partnership name be omitted from a case name.

12. "WIDELY RECOGNIZED" OR "COMMONLY KNOWN" INITIALS

Another optional way of shortening a case name is to use the "widely recognized" [*BB*] or "commonly known" [*ALWD*] initials in lieu of a party's name. *The Bluebook* and the *ALWD Manual* indicate that no periods should be used when such initials are used in a case name. The *ALWD Manual* cautions that they should be used when "no danger of confusion" exists. As a guide, *The Bluebook* suggests focusing on whether the entity is commonly referred to by its initials "in spoken language."

American Broadcasting Co. = ABC
American Civil Liberties Union = ACLU
American Federation of Labor = AFL
American Association of Retired Persons = AARP

Civil Aeronautics Board = CAB
Central Intelligence Agency = CIA
Congress of Industrial Organizations = CIO
Environmental Protection Agency = EPA
Equal Employment Opportunity
    Commission = EEOC
Federal Aviation Administration = FAA
Federal Communications Commission = FCC
Federal Election Commission = FEC
Food and Drug Administration = FDA
Federal Deposit Insurance Corp. = FDIC
Federal Housing Authority = FHA
Federal Trade Commission = FTC
International Business Machines Corp. =
    IBM
Interstate Commerce Commission = ICC
Mothers Against Drunk Driving = MADD
National Association for the Advancement of
    Colored People = NAACP
National Broadcasting Co. = NBC
National Labor Relations Board = NLRB
Securities and Exchange Commission = SEC
Tennessee Valley Authority = TVA
United Mine Workers = UMW

13. LABOR UNIONS

Special rules apply to labor unions as parties.

● First, *The Bluebook* and the *ALWD Manual* both provide that **only the "smallest unit"** (*BB*) or the **"local unit"** (*ALWD*) should be cited.

**SACRAMENTO FIRE FIGHTERS LOCAL 798,
INTERNATIONAL ASSOCIATION OF FIRE
FIGHTERS, AFL-CIO, Plaintiff and
Respondent,**

v.

**William S. PAXTON et al.,
Defendants and Appellants.**

---

*[BB & ALWD] Sacramento Fire Fighters Local
798 v. Paxton*

In the above example, only the local unit was
cited; the "higher" designations of the union
("**International Association of Fire Fighters,
AFL-CIO**") were omitted.

• Second, **both** *The Bluebook* **and the** *ALWD
Manual* **allow "widely recognized"** (*BB*) **or
"commonly known"** (*ALWD*) **initials to be used
in lieu of the name of the union.**

Richard WEBSTER, Petitioner,

v.

**UNITED AUTO WORKERS, LOCAL 51, et al.,
Respondent.**

---

*[BB & ALWD] Webster v. United Auto Workers,
Local 51 or Webster v. UAW, Local 51*

In the above example, "**United Auto Workers**" could be cited by its name or by the widely recognized or commonly known abbreviation ("**UAW**"). In addition, the local unit was retained in the citation.

● Third, the *ALWD Manual* and *The Bluebook* require further adjustments. **The *ALWD Manual* treats a labor union as an "organization."** As noted above, under the general rules applying to all organizations, the full name of the organization should be used, but "long" names (defined as more than five words) may be shortened "in a sensible way" by deleting "some words from the end of the name." Nonessential geographic terms, prepositions, and articles may be deleted as well.

In contrast, *The Bluebook* **provides the following specific rules: (1) all craft and industry designations, except the first full one, should be omitted; and (2) all prepositional phrases of location should be omitted.** Despite the differences in these rules, the overall result is generally the same.

Richard J. Srein, Plaintiff-Appellee,

v.

SOFT DRINK & BREWERY WORKERS LOCAL 812, also known as Teamsters AFL-CIO Local 812, Defendant-Appellees.

[BB & ALWD] Srein v. Soft Drink & Brewery Workers Local 812

In the above example, the first full craft designation used ("**Soft Drink & Brewery Workers**") was retained pursuant to *The Bluebook* rules. Nor was "**& Brewery**" deleted pursuant to the *ALWD Manual* rules because it did not appear at the end of a long case name. Furthermore, the local unit ("**Local 812**") was retained pursuant to the rules discussed above. The reference to the "**Teamsters**" was deleted because it is an alternative name for a party, as discussed in subdivision 4, above.

14. "STATE OF" AND SIMILAR PHRASES

"**State of,**" "**People of,**" and "**Commonwealth of**" should be omitted from a citation when the state, people, or commonwealth is litigating *in courts of other jurisdictions.* Assume the following case was decided by the U.S. Supreme Court and was reported in the Supreme Court reporters:

> **James G. WATT, Secretary of the Interior, et al., Petitioners,**
> **v.**
> **State of ALASKA et al., Respondents.**

[*BB & ALWD*] *Watt v. Alaska*

In the above example, "**State of**" was omitted because this case was *not* decided by an Alaska *state* court. In addition, "**Secretary of the Interior**" was omitted because it describes a party already named.

In contrast, **only "State," "People," and "Commonwealth" should be used when citing decisions by courts in those respective jurisdictions.** Assume the following case was decided by the Utah Supreme Court and appears in, among other places, the *Pacific Reporter, Third Series* as follows:

STATE of Utah, Plaintiff, Appellant, and Cross-Appellee,

v.

Sean GRAHAM, Defendant, Appellee, and Cross-Appellant.

[*BB & ALWD*] *State v. Graham*

In the above example, only "**State**" is used in the case name because this case was decided by a *Utah state court.*

15. "CITY OF" AND SIMILAR PHRASES

When "City of," "Town of," "Village of," "Borough of," and similar phrases *begin* a party's name, these phrases are included in the citation.

Steven RADLOFF, Appellant,

v.

CITY OF OELWEIN, IOWA, Appellee.

[BB & ALWD] *Radloff v. City of Oelwein, Iowa*

In the above example, because the name of the party *begins* with "**City of**," that phrase is retained in the citation. *The Bluebook* states that all geographic designations not introduced by a preposition (in this instance, "**Iowa**") should be retained in the citation. In contrast, the *ALWD Manual* specifically states that larger geographic references (in this instance, "**Iowa**") may be omitted, but, otherwise, the full name of the local governmental unit should be included. Thus, the following would also be permissible under the *ALWD Manual*:

[ALWD] *Radloff v. City of Oelwein*

When "City of" and similar phrases *do not begin the name of a party* (e.g., Mayor of the City of Oelwein), ***The Bluebook* specifically provides that "City of" and similar phrases should be omitted** (e.g., Mayor of Oelwein).

16. "UNITED STATES OF AMERICA" AND THE "UNITED STATES" AS A PARTY

"Of America" should be omitted when it appears after "United States." The *ALWD Manual* requires "United States" always to be cited simply as "U.S." In contrast, *The Bluebook* prohibits abbreviation of "United States" when it is the party cited ("United States").

UNITED STATES OF AMERICA, Appellee,
v.
William R. TIBOLT, Appellant.

[BB] United States v. Tibolt

[ALWD] U.S. v. Tibolt

17. GEOGRAPHIC TERMS

Treatment of geographic terms in case names has been discussed in several of the above subsections. For example, according to *The Bluebook*, all prepositional phrases of location except "of America" should be omitted in union names. Both *The Bluebook* and the *ALWD Manual* omit "of America" after "United States." Geographic terms were also obviously involved in citing cities and states as parties.

The Bluebook and the *ALWD Manual* take different approaches to more generally defining what geographic terms should be included or deleted. Those approaches, however, do not often result in different citations.

The *ALWD Manual* simply provides that "only the first geographic[ ] location in a party's name" should be retained. Furthermore, as noted above, it permits, but does not require, omission of geographic terms that do not make up an essential part of the name of an "organization."

In contrast, *The Bluebook* provides three specific rules with regard to geographic terms:

(1) **Terms indicating national or larger locations should be included in the case name** (except when they occur in union names and when "of America" follows "United States");

(2) **Other prepositional phrases of location (i.e., those of less than national geographic areas) should be omitted, unless only one word would be left in the party's name;** and

(3) **All geographic words that are not introduced by a preposition should be retained.**

Gloria HARLAN, Petitioner,

v.

FIRST INTERSTATE BANK OF UTAH,

Respondent.

[BB] Harlan v. First Interstate Bank

[ALWD] Harlan v. First Interstate Bank or Harlan v. First Interstate Bank of Utah

As indicated in (2) above, in *Bluebook* citations, prepositional phrases of location of less than national geographic areas ("**of Utah**" in this example) should be omitted unless only one word would be left in the party's name. Because more than one word is remains in the case name, "**of Utah**" should thus be omitted from the citation.

As noted above, the *ALWD Manual* provides that only the first geographic location in a party's name should be retained. That means "**of Utah**" (being the first) should be retained. However, the *ALWD Manual* permits the omission of geographic terms not making up an essential part of the name of an organization. Because "**of Utah**" is unlikely to be considered essential, it can be (but is not required to be) omitted.

EIE GUAM CORP., Petitioner,

v.

LONG TERM CREDIT BANK OF JAPAN,

Respondent.

[BB & ALWD] Eie Guam Corp. v. Long Term Credit Bank of Japan

In the above example, "**Guam**" is included in the citation for purposes of a *Bluebook* citation because, as noted in (3) above, all geographic words that are not introduced by a preposition should be retained. "**Of Japan**" is retained because, as noted in (1) above, terms indicating national or larger locations should be included (except when they occur in union names and when "**of America**" follows "**United States**"). In the *ALWD* citation, "**Guam**" and "**of Japan**" are included because they both are the first geographic location in a party's name. However, "of Japan" could be omitted if it is considered to be unessential.

18. BANKRUPTCY AND SIMILAR CASES

When an opinion is styled with both adversary and nonadversary parties, such as in many

bankruptcy cases, the adversary parties should be cited, even if the nonadversary name is listed first. *The Bluebook* indicates that the nonadversary name should be added parenthetically and introduced by an appropriate procedural phrase (or phrases), depending on the circumstances. The *ALWD Manual* makes adding the nonadversary name parenthetically optional.

In re Gary Lee WATERS.

Roger W. MOISTER, Jr., Trustee, Plaintiff,
v.
Deborah M. WATERS, Defendant.

[BB] *Moister v. Waters (In re Waters)*

[ALWD] *Moister v. Waters or Moister v. Waters (In re Waters)* [Optional to add (*In re Waters*)]

In this example, the adversary parties (i.e., **Roger W. Moister, Jr.** and **Deborah M. Waters**) are cited—not the nonadversarial party (i.e., **Gary Lee Waters**)—even though they are not listed first. The *ALWD Manual* makes the parenthetical indication of the nonadversarial party optional. In general, if party names or other phrases will aid in identifying a case, that information may be appended parenthetically:

[BB & ALWD] *The Legal Tender Cases (Julliard v. Greenman)*, 110 U.S. 421 (1884).

B. CASE NAMES: ABBREVIATIONS

In addition to omitting parts of case names, the other principal method of saving space is through abbreviations. Writers must be careful to match the following particular situations with the appropriate rules.

1. CASE NAME ABBREVIATIONS IN TEXTUAL SENTENCES WITHOUT IMMEDIATELY ACCOMPANYING CITATIONS

When case names appear in the text *without* an immediately accompanying citation, the traditional approach has been not to abbreviate words in the case name. *The Bluebook* and *ALWD Manual* follow this approach by providing that only a few words in the case name should be abbreviated. **The *ALWD Manual* makes the abbreviation of the following words *optional*, but *The Bluebook* rules make their abbreviation *mandatory*.**

	Bluebook	*ALWD*
And	&	&
Association	Ass'n	Assn.
Brothers	Bros.	Bros.
Company	Co.	Co.
Corporation	Corp.	Corp.
Incorporated	Inc.	Inc.
Limited	Ltd.	Ltd.
Number	No.	No.
United States	**Not Abbreviated**	U.S.

[*BB & ALWD* Text] In *Klaxon Co. v. Stentor Electric Manufacturing Co.*, the Supreme Court held that *Erie* required federal courts in diversity cases to follow the conflict-of-laws rules prevailing in the states in which the courts sit. 313 U.S. 487, 496 (1941).

In the above example, under *ALWD* rules, "**Company**" *may* (but does not have to) be abbreviated to "**Co.**" in the case name, but no other words should be abbreviated. On the other hand, *The Bluebook* requires abbreviation of "**Company**." This *Bluebook* rule applies to case names used as grammatical parts of textual sentences without citations, whether in the main text or footnotes in law journals.

2. "EMBEDDED" CASE CITATIONS

In addition to case names appearing in text without accompanying citations in legal writing (discussed in preceding subdivision), a case citation may be **"embedded" in a textual sentence**. In other words, it may be used as a *grammatical part* of a textual sentence (i.e., as the subject of a sentence, a direct object, an object of a preposition).

This use contrasts with a citation clause, which is to set the citation off from the sentence by commas. Recall from Chapter 1(B)(8) that citation clauses are used when the cited source relates to only part of a sentence. The difference is significant because abbreviations in embedded case citations follow the rules set out in the preceding subsection, while abbreviations in citation clauses follow the rules set out in the next section. The following shows the application of the rules from the immediately preceding section to an embedded citation:

[*BB & ALWD*] In *Klaxon Co. v. Stentor Electric Manufacturing Co.*, 313 U.S. 487 (1941), the Supreme Court held that *Erie* required federal courts in diversity cases to follow the conflict-of-laws rules prevailing in the states in which the courts sit. *Id.* at 496.

In the above example, "**Company**" *must* be abbreviated to "**Co.**" in the case name under *Bluebook* rules. However, no other words are abbreviated because the case and citation are an integral part of a textual sentence (here, an object of a preposition). It is optional to abbreviate "**Co.**" under *ALWD* rules.

3. CASE NAME ABBREVIATIONS IN CITATION CLAUSES AND SENTENCES

Under *ALWD* rules with regard to case name abbreviations in citation sentences and clauses, the name of an individual person should never be abbreviated. For "organizations," however, the *ALWD Manual* provides an extensive list of abbreviations in its General Abbreviations Appendix 3, which covers (A) general abbreviations; (B) geographic locations (states, territories, cities, countries, and regions); (C) months and days; (D) subdivisions of publications; and (E) publishing terms. Those abbreviations are presented in **Appendix 1(A)-(E)** of this book.

Use of these abbreviations in case names is *optional*. If any word included in the *ALWD* "General Abbreviations" Appendix (see **Appendix 1(A)-(E)** in this book) has been abbreviated, however, all words included in that Appendix must also be abbreviated, including the first word of a case name. The *ALWD* abbreviations are exclusive. These abbreviations "override" any abbreviations used in the style of the case, the running head, or Table of Cases in the reporter. Furthermore, if a word is abbreviated in the reporter but it is not designated for abbreviation in the ALWD "General Abbreviations" Appendix, it should not be abbreviated.

The *ALWD Manual* cautions that abbreviations in its "General Abbreviations" Appendix should not be used if the "abbreviation would cause confusion." Accordingly, that rationale prohibits abbreviation of case names that consist of only one name, but *state names* are not included in this restriction.

Like the *ALWD Manual*, **The Bluebook has an extensive set of abbreviations for case names in citation sentences and clauses set out in two tables. One is specifically for case name abbreviations ("T.6") and the other is for geographic terms ("T.10").** These abbreviations are set out comparatively in **Appendix 1(A)-(B)** of this book. **If a word retained in a case name appears in either of these tables, it must be abbreviated.** Many times, the abbreviations set out by the *ALWD Manual* and *The Bluebook* are the same, but not always. The following are typical abbreviations. They are used in the examples below.

And = &
Association = [*BB*] Ass'n [*ALWD*] Assn.
Board = Bd.
California = Cal.
Company = Co.
Industr[y, ies, ial] = Indus.
Insurance = Ins.
International = Int'l [*BB*] Intl. [*ALWD*]
Jamaica = Jam.
Labor = Lab. [*ALWD*] [*BB* not abbreviated]
Manufacturer = Mfr.
Mississippi = Miss.
Mutual = Mut.
National = [*BB*] Nat'l [*ALWD*] Natl.
Relations = [*ALWD*] Rel. [*BB* not listed]
System[s] = Sys.

Unlike the *ALWD Manual*, which limits abbreviations to the ones listed in its appendices, ***The Bluebook*** also permits any other word with at least eight letters not appearing in its tables to be abbreviated "if *substantial* space is thereby saved and the result is unambiguous in context."

Unless otherwise specifically indicated in their respective tables or appendices, both *The Bluebook* and the *ALWD Manual* form the plural in an abbreviation by adding "s" to the end of the abbreviation. The specific exceptions are comparatively noted in **Appendix 1(A)-(B)** of this book.

The following citations illustrate how these additional abbreviations apply in citation sentences and clauses.

**HARDWARE DEALERS MUTUAL FIRE
INSURANCE CO. v. MISSISSIPPI
POWER & LIGHT CO.**

[*BB* & *ALWD* **Citation Sentences or Clauses**]
*Hardware Dealers Mut. Fire Ins. Co. v. Miss.
Power & Light Co.*

In the above example, "**Mutual**," "**Insurance**," "**Company**," "**Mississippi**," and "**And**" are on the lists in *The Bluebook* and *ALWD Manual* and are abbreviated in exactly the same way. Under the rules in the *ALWD Manual*, it is technically possible not to abbreviate *any* words in the above case name: *Hardware Dealers Mutual Fire Insurance Company v. Mississippi Power and Light Company*. However, once one abbreviation is made (e.g., "**Co.**"), then *all* words on the lists in the *ALWD Manual* must be abbreviated. The same will be true for all of the following examples as well.

**BODELL CONSTRUCTION COMPANY, a Utah
Corporation, Plaintiff and Appellant,**

v.

**UNITED STATES TITLE GUARANTY
COMPANY, a Texas Corporation, et al.,
Defendants and Appellees.**

[*BB* & *ALWD* Citation Sentences or Clauses] *Bodell Constr. Co. v. U.S. Title Guar. Co.*

In the above example, "**Construction**," "**Company**," "**United States**," and "**Guaranty**" are on the lists in *The Bluebook* and *ALWD Manual* and are abbreviated in exactly the same way. As noted in the preceding section, the *ALWD Manual* specifically requires "**United States**" always be cited simply as "**U.S.**" In contrast, *The Bluebook* prohibits abbreviation of "**United States**" when it is the party cited ("**United States**"). However, the United States is not a party and, therefore, it should be abbreviated.

CALIFORNIA DENTAL ASSOCIATION *v.* ALUMINA MANUFACTURERS OF JAMAICA

[*BB* Citation Sentences or Clauses] *Cal. Dental Ass'n v. Alumina Mfrs. of Jam.*

[*ALWD* Citation Sentences or Clauses] *Cal. Dental Assn. v. Alumina Mfrs. of Jam.*

In the above example, "**California**," "**Manufacturer**," and "**Jamaica**" are listed both in *The Bluebook* tables and the *ALWD* appendices and are abbreviated in the same way, but *The Bluebook* and the *ALWD Manual* abbreviate "**Association**" differently. The addition of the "**s**" to "**Mfr.**" illustrates how plurals are indicated (unless the designated abbreviation includes both the singular and the plural).

PAYFLEX SYSTEMS, INC., et al., Appellants,
v.
Roscoe L. EGGERS, Commissioner, Internal Revenue Service, et al., Appellees.

[*BB* & *ALWD* Citation Sentences or Clauses]
PayFlex Sys., Inc. v. Eggers

In the above example, "**Systems**" is abbreviated as "**Sys.**" because *The Bluebook* and the *ALWD Manual* in their respective tables and appendices include both the singular and the plural within the abbreviation of "**Sys.**" Had the appellee in the above example been the "**Commissioner of Internal Revenue**" rather than an individual governmental official ("**Roscoe L. Eggers**"), then a special rule applies. Both *The Bluebook* and the *ALWD Manual* provide that only "**Commissioner**" should be cited:

[*BB* Citation Sentences or Clauses] *PayFlex Sys., Inc. v. Comm'r*

[*ALWD* Citation Sentences or Clauses] *PayFlex Sys., Inc. v. Commr.*

INTERNATIONAL UNION OF PETROLEUM & INDUSTRIAL WORKERS, Petitioner,
v.
NATIONAL LABOR RELATIONS BOARD, Respondent.

[*BB* Citation Sentences or Clauses]—

(1) *Int'l Union of Petroleum & Indus. Workers v. Nat'l Labor Relations Bd.*

(2) *Int'l Union of Petrol. & Indus. Workers v. Nat'l Labor Rel. Bd.* [abbreviating words containing eight or more letters (i.e., "**Petroleum**" and "**Relations**"); abbreviating them, however, is optional; "**Labor**" is also not included in *The Bluebook* tables, but it cannot be abbreviated because it is fewer than eight letters.]

(3) *Int'l Union of Petrol. & Indus. Workers v. NLRB* [substituting the widely recognized initials of the "**National Labor Relations Board**"]

[*ALWD* Citation Sentences or Clauses]—

(1) *Intl. Union of Petroleum & Indus. Workers v. Natl. Lab. Rel. Bd.* ["**National**," "**Labor**," "**Relations**," and "**Board**" are all included in *ALWD* appendices; "**Petroleum**" cannot be abbreviated because it is not listed in *ALWD* appendices; abbreviation of words not listed is specifically prohibited.]

(2) *Intl. Union of Petroleum & Indus. Workers v. NLRB* [substituting the commonly known initials of the "**National Labor Relations Board**"]

C. CITING REPORTERS

As discussed in Chapter 1, another element in case citation is the reporter.

1. ABBREVIATION OF REPORTERS

The Bluebook and the *ALWD Manual* list abbreviations of reporters in their respective tables and appendices. Most of the time, the abbreviations seen in various publications match up with those required by *The Bluebook* and the *ALWD Manual* (e.g., **S.W.**, **N.W.2d**, **N.M.**, **Fla.**, **P.3d**, **Mass.**, **N.E.2d**, etc.).

One significant variation on traditional abbreviations is the spacing of certain reporters. *The Bluebook* and the *ALWD Manual* insert **one space** between any two abbreviations when *either* one is not a single capital letter. Ordinal contractions, such as "**2d**" or "**4th**," are treated as single capital letters. The following are some examples:

Arizona Appeals Reports = **Ariz. App.**
California Reporter = **Cal. Rptr.**
California Reporter Second = **Cal. Rptr. 2d**
Federal Supplement = **F. Supp.**
Federal Supplement Second = **F. Supp. 2d**
Federal Supplement Third = **F. Supp. 3d**
New York Miscellaneous Reports Second =
     Misc. 2d
Southern Reporter Second = **So. 2d**
United States Supreme Court Reports,
     Lawyers' Edition = **L. Ed.**
United States Supreme Court Reports,
     Lawyers' Edition Second = **L. Ed. 2d**
Virginia Court of Appeals Reports =
     Va. App.
West's Supreme Court Reporter = **S. Ct.**

Appendix 2 of this book comparatively sets out the abbreviations that *The Bluebook* and *ALWD* provide for reporters. On occasion, there are rare minor variations, as illustrated below.

Bluebook	*ALWD*
F. App'x	**Fed. Appx.**
Pa. Commw.	**Pa. Cmmw.**
Tex. Ct. App.	**Tex. App.**
Navajo Rptr.	**Navajo**
Mass. App. Ct.	**Mass. App.**
Am. Samoa 2d	**Am. Sam. 2d**

2. REPORTERS THAT SHOULD BE CITED

As discussed in Chapter 1, cases often appear in multiple reporters. The following summarizes the basic requirements mandated by *The Bluebook* and the *ALWD Manual* in absence of court rules requiring otherwise.

a. *U.S. Supreme Court Cases*

Both The Bluebook *and the* ALWD Manual *prefer* that U.S. Supreme Court cases be cited only to *United States Reports*. If a citation to that reporter is unavailable, the clear second choice is Thomson/West's *Supreme Court Reporter*, followed by *United States Supreme Court Reports, Lawyers' Edition*, in that order of preference. *United States Law Week* (**U.S.L.W.**) is the next choice, followed by online or other sources.

[*BB & ALWD*] *Coopers & Lybrand v. Livesay,* **437 U.S. 463 (1978).**

In the above example, only *United States Reports* is cited pursuant to *Bluebook* and *ALWD* preferences. Also, "**Coopers & Lybrand**" is a partnership, and its name was fully retained in the above citation pursuant to the specific *Bluebook* rule requiring that no portion of a partnership name be omitted, noted at the end of section A(11), above. Nor is any change made in the name under the *ALWD* rules regarding "organizations" because the name does not have more than five words (discussed in the same section).

As indicated and illustrated in Chapter 1, many lawyers prefer to include parallel citations to all three of these reporters. While not permitted by *The Bluebook,* the *ALWD Manual* recognizes such a citation as an "alternate format" which is "not preferred [but] is permitted."

[*ALWD* Alternate Format] *Coopers & Lybrand v. Livesay,* **437 U.S. 463, 98 S. Ct. 2454, 57 L. Ed. 2d 351 (1978).**

For the first 90 volumes of *United States Reports, The Bluebook* requires the parenthetical addition of the nominative reporter's name and volume of his series. The names of these early nominative reporters and their abbreviations are shown in **Appendix 3(A)** of this book. Thus, the *Strawbridge v. Curtiss* would be cited as follows:

[*BB*] *Strawbridge v. Curtiss,* **7 U.S. (3 Cranch) 267 (1806).**

In contrast, the *ALWD Manual* provides that these early nominative reporters should not be cited. Thus, the proper citation to the *Strawbridge* case would be:

[*ALWD*] Strawbridge v. Curtiss, 7 U.S. 267 (1806).

b. Lower Federal Courts

As their tables and appendices respectively indicate, *The Bluebook* and the *ALWD Manual* prefer Thomson/West's reporters (especially its *Federal Reporter* and *Federal Supplement*) be cited as well as other specialized Thomson/West reporters (such as *Federal Rules Decisions* (**F.R.D.**), the *Bankruptcy Reporter* (B.R.), the *Federal Claims Reporter* (**Fed. Cl.**), the *Military Justice Reporter* (**M.J.**), etc.). For documents submitted to a federal court, all citation requirements in local rules must be followed.

[*BB & ALWD*] Alamo v. Clay, 137 F.3d 1366 (D.C. Cir. 1998).

[*BB & ALWD*] Parker v. Rowland Express, Inc., 492 F. Supp. 2d 1159 (D. Minn. 2007).

[*BB* Citation] In re PolyMedica Corp. Sec. Litig., 224 F.R.D. 27 (D. Mass. 2004). ["Sec." includes the plural in *Bluebook* citations.]

[*ALWD* Citation] In re PolyMedica Corp. Secs. Litig., 224 F.R.D. 27 (D. Mass. 2004). ["Sec." does not include the plural in *ALWD* citations; thus, "**s**" was added to the abbreviation. See **Appendix 1(A)** of this book.]

[*BB & ALWD*] *Calvin v. Siegel* (*In re Siegel*), **190 B.R. 639 (Bankr. D. Ariz. 1996).** [In *ALWD* citations, the addition of "(*In re* **Siegel**)" is optional.]

[*BB* Citation] *Palm Beach Isles Assocs. v. United States,* **42 Fed. Cl. 340 (1998).** ["**United States**" is not abbreviated in *Bluebook* citations when it is a party.]

[*ALWD* Citation] *Palm Beach Isles Assocs. v. U.S.,* **42 Fed. Cl. 340 (1998).** ["**United States**" is always abbreviated to "**U.S.**" in *ALWD* citations.]

[*BB & ALWD*] *Mittleider v. West,* **11 Vet. App. 181 (1998).**

[*BB*] *United States v. Gallo,* **55 M.J. 418 (C.A.A.F. 2001).** [As discussed below, the abbreviation for the U.S. Court of Appeals for the Armed Forces for *Bluebook* citations differs from that in the *ALWD Manual;* compare the citation below.]

[*ALWD*] *U.S. v. Gallo,* **55 M.J. 418 (App. Armed Forces 2001).** ["**United States**" is always abbreviated in *ALWD* citations, but it is not in *Bluebook* citations when it is the party; compare the citation above.]

Recall from Chapter 1(B)(5) that 18,313 of the nominative lower federal court cases were reprinted in a unique set, *Federal Cases* (**F. Cas.**). These cases were organized alphabetically and assigned an arbitrary "case number." *Federal Cases* came to be cited to the exclusion of the original reports it reprinted. This same approach is also followed by *The*

Bluebook and the *ALWD Manual*. The Federal Case Number is appended to *Bluebook* citations to *Federal Cases*, but it is not in *ALWD* citations:

[BB] *M'Grath v. Candalero*, **16 F. Cas. 128 (D.S.C. 1794) (No. 8180).** [*The Bluebook* inserts commas in numbers containing five or more digits; 8180 only has four and thus no comma is used.]

[ALWD] *M'Grath v. Candalero*, **16 F. Cas. 128 (D.S.C. 1794).**

c. State Courts

Recall from Chapter 1(B)(5) that the two principal sources for state court opinions are (1) official reports (e.g., *Maine Reports*) and (2) Thomson/West's unofficial regional reporters (e.g., *Atlantic Reporter*). Although use and citation of Thomson/West's reporters is widespread, the official report is technically the authoritative text. Some states have ceased publishing their official reports (e.g., Iowa in 1968); thus, other reporters (e.g., *Northwestern Reporter*) are the only published sources for judicial opinions in those states. The status of official state court reports is shown in **Appendix 4** of this book.

Today, most reporters are designated by (1) the court (e.g., *California Appellate Reports*); (2) the geographic jurisdiction (e.g., *Nebraska Reports*); or (3) the geographic region (e.g., *Southern Reporter*). Recall also when more than one reporter is cited, a "parallel citation" is being provided. Both *The Bluebook* and the *ALWD Manual* give specific guidance when those parallel citations must be given and when they can be omitted.

When submitting documents to a state court, all of its requirements must be followed. Normally, that often means that parallel citations to both the official and unofficial West regional reporters must be given. The official report is cited first.

[*BB* & *ALWD* in documents submitted to a state court requiring parallel citation of its court decisions] *State v. Mead*, **230 Iowa 1217, 300 N.W. 523 (1941).** [Only "**State**" is used (and not "Iowa" or "State of Iowa") when decisions by the state courts of Iowa are cited.]

In all other documents, including law journal articles and "ordinary legal memoranda," only Thomson/West's regional reporter should be cited:

[*BB* & *ALWD* in all other documents than those submitted to an Iowa state court] *State v. Mead*, **300 N.W. 523 (Iowa 1941).**

California state court decisions can be found in multiple reporters. Just as some lawyers prefer to provide parallel citations to all three U.S. Supreme Court reporters, some lawyers prefer to give "full" parallel citations for California cases. For example, there are three major reporters in which California Supreme Court decisions may currently be found: (1) the official *California Reports*; (2) the *Pacific Reporter*; and (3) the *California Reporter*. Some lawyers omit the citation to the *Pacific Reporter*, but cite the other two. Others cite only the *Pacific Reporter*.

In absence of local custom or court requirements, the rules in both *The Bluebook* and the *ALWD Manual* direct that the *Pacific Reporter* be cited:

[BB & ALWD] *Kasky v. Nike, Inc.,* **45 P.3d 243 (Cal. 2002).**

A citation to all three reporters would appear as follows: **[BB]** *Kasky v. Nike, Inc.,* **27 Cal. 4th 939, 45 P.3d 243, 119 Cal. Rptr. 2d 296 (2002)** *or* **[ALWD]** *Kasky v. Nike, Inc.,* **27 Cal. 4th 939, 119 Cal. Rptr. 2d 296, 45 P.3d 243 (2002).** [Reflecting the different preferences in terms of order]

Like California, New York state court decisions may be found in multiple reporters. For example, New York Court of Appeals decisions can be found in (1) the official *New York Reports*, (2) the *North Eastern Reporter*, and (3) the *New York Supplement*. The citation patterns are similar to those for California decisions. In absence of local custom or court requirements, the rules in both *The Bluebook* and the *ALWD Manual* direct that the *North Eastern Reporter* be cited:

[BB & ALWD] *People v. Brown,* **769 N.E.2d 1266 (N.Y. 2002).** [Only **"People"** is used (and not "N.Y." or "People of the State of N.Y.") when decisions by the state courts of New York are cited.]

A citation to all three reporters would appear as follows: **[BB]** *People v. Brown,* **97 N.Y.2d 500, 769 N.E.2d 1266, 743 N.Y.S.2d 374 (2002)** *or* **[ALWD]** *People v. Brown,* **97 N.Y.2d 500, 743 N.Y.S.2d 374, 769 N.E.2d 1266 (2002).**

d. Early State Court Cases

Recall from earlier discussions that up to the late nineteenth century, reporters were ordinarily designated by the last name of the individual who prepared the reporter and that these reporters were subsequently incorporated into the court-named or jurisdiction-named reporter series. As set out in **Appendix 3(D)** of this book, *The Bluebook* still requires an indication of those early nominative reporters, but the *ALWD Manual* does not.

[BB] *Moore v. Turbeville*, 5 Ky. (2 Bibb) 602 (1812).

[ALWD] *Moore v. Turbeville*, 5 Ky. 602 (1812).

e. Public Domain (Neutral or Universal) Citations

Recall from Chapter 1 that a growing number of jurisdictions have developed so-called public domain (or medium neutral or universal) citations. Such citations are made possible by the court assigning a "chronological accession number" to each case and numbering the paragraphs of the opinion. However, the format varies. See **Appendix 4** for specific information and examples.

The Bluebook requires that when public domain citations exist, they must be included in the citation. The *ALWD Manual* makes their inclusion optional in absence of a court requirement. When a public domain citation is given, a parallel citation to the ordinarily cited source is also given.

[BB] *Poteet v. White*, **2006 UT 63, 147 P.3d 439.**

[ALWD] *Poteet v. White*, **2006 UT 63, 147 P.3d 439** *or Poteet v. White*, **147 P.3d 439 (Utah 2006).**

f. Citing Cases Available Through WESTLAW, LEXIS, and Other Databases

Recall from Chapter 1 that WESTLAW, LEXIS, and other databases provide extensive full-text coverage of judicial opinions. When an opinion has been printed in a traditional reporter and is also available on WESTLAW or LEXIS, *The Bluebook* and the *ALWD Manual* require citation of the traditional print sources.

When cases available on WESTLAW and LEXIS are cited, as indicated in Chapter 1, the following format is used. *The Bluebook* includes the docket number. The *ALWD Manual* does not.

[BB] *Boosey & Hawkes Music Publishers, Ltd. v. Walt Disney Co.*, **No. 93 CIV. 0373 KTD, 2000 WL 204524 (S.D.N.Y. Feb. 8, 2000).**

[BB] *Sedio, N.V. v. Bell, Kalnick, Klee & Green*, **No. 91 C 3691, 1992 U.S. Dist. LEXIS 874 (N.D. Ill. Jan. 28, 1992).** ["Bell, Kalnick, Klee & Green" is a partnership; under *Bluebook* rules, no portion of a partnership name should be omitted in the citation.]

[ALWD] *Boosey & Hawkes Music Publishers, Ltd. v. Walt Disney Co.*, **2000 WL 204524 (S.D.N.Y. Feb. 8, 2000).**

[ALWD] *Sedio, N.V. v. Bell, Kalnick, Klee & Green*, **1992 U.S. Dist. LEXIS 874 (N.D. Ill. Jan. 28, 1992).** [A partnerships is treated as an "organization" under *ALWD* rules; the entire name is retained because it is not lengthy.]

g. Cases in Reporter Tables

Some dispositions of cases (without opinions) are only listed in a reporter table. Those dispositions are cited to the reporter with a parenthetical indication of that fact ("table")—usually as part of showing the subsequent history of a case. The following are typical *Bluebook* and *ALWD* citations referring to a table:

[BB] *Holt v. Lewis*, **955 F. Supp. 1385 (N.D. Ala. 1995),** *aff'd*, **109 F.3d 771 (11th Cir. 1997) (unpublished table decision).**

[ALWD] *Holt v. Lewis*, **955 F. Supp. 1385 (N.D. Ala. 1995),** *aff'd*, **109 F.3d 771 (11th Cir. 1997) (table).**

When the opinion is available on WESTLAW or LEXIS that only otherwise appears in a reporter table, the table should be cited—followed by a parallel citation to the full opinion on WESTLAW or LEXIS.

h. Cases in the Federal Appendix

Thomson/West began publishing the Federal Appendix in 2001. It contains *unpublished* opinions from several of the federal courts of appeals that are

willing to provide them to Thomson/West. Because
they were not "selected" by the court for publication,
unpublished opinions are ordinarily not considered to
be "binding precedent." Furthermore, many courts
prohibit lawyers from citing such cases, and it makes
no difference that they appear in the *Federal Appendix*. See Chapter 4(K)(1) for further discussion. The
following are examples of citations to cases in the
Federal Appendix:

[BB Citation] *Teleflex, Inc. v. KSR Int'l Co.,*
119 Fed. App'x 282 (Fed. Cir. 2005). [*The Bluebook*
abbreviates "Appendix" as "**App'x**" and "International" as "**Int'l**" in citation sentences and clauses.]

[ALWD Citation] *Teleflex, Inc. v. KSR Intl.
Co.,* **119 Fed. Appx. 282 (Fed. Cir. 2005) (unpublished).** [The *ALWD Manual* abbreviates "Appendix"
as "**Appx.**" and "International as "**Intl.**" in citation
sentences and clauses when abbreviation is elected.]

i. Special-Subject Reporters

Many special-subject reporters contain cases
relating to particular topics. These reporters are
generally connected with looseleaf topical services.
Parallel citations are not given to these specialty
reporters when the case appears in an official or the
preferred *Bluebook* or *ALWD* reporter. Otherwise,
specialty reporters are cited following the basic
format for citing cases (using the service publisher
abbreviation shown in **Appendix 8** of this book).

[BB] *Sunbelt Television, Inc. v. Jones Intercable, Inc.*, 7 Trade Reg. Rep. (CCH) ¶ 69,645 (C.D. Cal. 1991).

[ALWD] *Klein v. Boyd*, [1997-98 Transfer Binder] Fed. Sec. L. Rep. (CCH) ¶ 90,136 (3d Cir. Feb. 12, 1998).

j. English Cases

Of foreign cases, by far the most frequently cited are English cases, particularly early ones. They have played an important role in legal scholarship and are cited as persuasive authority in American courts. As indicated in Chapter 1(B)(5), prior to 1865, numerous unofficial "nominative" reporters were published in England, many of which were duplicative and varied in quality. A large number of cases from 1220 to 1865 were reprinted from a large number of reports in the 176-volume set, *English Reports, Full Reprint*. Early English cases should be cited to this set, if they are reprinted in it:

[BB & ALWD] *The King v. Davis*, 89 Eng. Rep. 609 (K.B. 1585). ["K.B." is the abbreviation of "King's Bench"; although "**the**" is ordinarily omitted from citations, it is retained when "**The King**" or "**The Queen**" is cited. Some traditional citations added the original nominative report to the citation: *The King v. Davis*, 1 Show. K.B., 89 Eng. Rep. 609 (1585).]

After 1864, the semi-official *Law Reports* now comprise the primary body of English reporters. Eleven different series of *Law Reports* have been

issued in the past, reflecting the various organiza-
tions of the judicial system in the United Kingdom.
Currently, they are issued in monthly parts in four
series: *Appeal Cases* (**A.C.** covering the House of
Lords and Privy Council), *Queens Bench Division*
(**Q.B.**), *Chancery Division* (**Ch.**), and the *Family
Division* (**Fam.**). In addition to *Law Reports*, there
are several unauthorized reports: *All England Law
Reports*, *Law Times Reports*, *Law Journal Reports*,
and *Times Law Reports*. The following is a typical
Bluebook citation to the *Law Reports* series.

[BB] *The Queen v. Thompson*, **[1893] 2 Q.B. 12.**
["**The**" is retained because "**The Queen**" is cited; in
the *Queens Bench Division Reports*, the volumes are
numbered in a new series each year; therefore, the
volume year (**[1893]**) in brackets should be given,
followed by the volume number (**2**) within that year].

D. DESIGNATION OF THE COURT

Recall from Chapter 1(B)(7) that the abbreviated
name of the court, including its geographic jurisdiction, must be given parenthetically in case citations.
The Bluebook and the *ALWD Manual* both follow the
universally recognized citation conventions concerning the designation of the court: (1) when the highest
court of a jurisdiction is cited, the abbreviated name
of the court is omitted; and (2) when the abbreviated
name of the reporter in the citation unambiguously
indicates the geographic jurisdiction, the geographic
jurisdiction is omitted.

1. STATE INTERMEDIATE AND TRIAL COURTS

One area of significant variation between *The Bluebook* and the *ALWD Manual* is how intermediate and trial courts are indicated. In general, the *ALWD Manual* requires a more detailed identification of the court in a slightly different format. In *Bluebook* citations, the department, district, or division should be included only if "that information is of particular relevance." In the vast majority of situations, it will not be. A comparative list of court designations is provided in **Appendix 5** of this book. The following citations illustrate the basic differences:

[BB] *State ex rel. Romley v. Fields*, **35 P.3d 82 (Ariz. Ct. App. 2001).** ["**State**" (rather than "**Arizona**") is used because the case was decided by an Arizona state court; the jurisdiction ("**Ariz.**") must be included in the parenthetical because the *Pacific Reporter* contains decisions from many states and the abbreviated name of the reporter thus does not identify the geographic jurisdiction.]

[ALWD] *State ex rel. Romley v. Fields*, **35 P.3d 82 (Ariz. App. 1st Div. 2001).** [The division must be given in the *ALWD* citation.]

[BB] *In re Frank S.*, **47 Cal. Rptr. 3d 320 (Ct. App. 2006).** [The given name ("**Frank**") is retained in the citation because the individual's last name has been reduced to a single initial (usually to protect the identity of the party); under such circumstances, both the given name and the initial that represents the party's surname are used; the indication of the geographic jurisdiction is omitted because the jurisdiction is unambiguously apparent from the name of the reporter—the *California Reporter* only contains California cases.]

[*ALWD*] *In re Frank S.*, 47 Cal. Rptr. 3d 320 (App. 1st Dist. 2006). [The *ALWD Manual* requires the particular district be given in the citation.]

[*BB*] *Bush v. Holmes*, 886 So. 2d 340 (Fla. Dist. Ct. App. 2004). [The *Southern Reporter* contains cases from several states; thus, the name of the reporter does not identify the jurisdiction and "**Fla.**" must be included in the citation.]

[*ALWD*] *Bush v. Holmes*, 886 So. 2d 340 (Fla. 1st Dist. App. 2004). [The *ALWD Manual* requires the particular district be given in the citation.]

[*BB*] *In re Holley*, 729 N.Y.S.2d 128 (App. Div. 2001). [The *New York Supplement* contains cases only from New York; thus, the name of the reporter identifies the jurisdiction and "**N.Y.**" should not be included in the citation; however, this reporter contains cases from several courts, so the court must be identified.]

[*ALWD*] *In re Holley*, 729 N.Y.S.2d 128 (App. Div. 1st Dept. 2001). [The *ALWD Manual* requires the particular department be given in the citation.]

[*BB*] *Rees v. Cochran*, 40 Fla. Supp. 2d 185 (Cir. Ct. 1990). [The *Florida Supplement* published opinions from the Florida circuit courts, county courts, and other courts of record; "**Fla.**" should be omitted from the parenthetical because the geographic jurisdiction is readily apparent from the abbreviated name of the reporter.]

[*ALWD*] *Rees v. Cochran*, **40 Fla. Supp. 2d 185 (6th Cir. 1990).** [The *ALWD Manual* requires the particular circuit be given in the citation.]

2. DESIGNATING THE FEDERAL COURTS OF APPEALS

The Bluebook and the *ALWD Manual* both cite the numbered circuits of the United States Courts of Appeals as follows, regardless of the year: **1st Cir., 2d Cir., 3d Cir., 4th Cir., 5th Cir., 6th Cir., 7th Cir., 8th Cir., 9th Cir., 10th Cir., and 11th Cir.** The United States Court of Appeals for the District of Columbia Circuit *and its variously named predecessors* are cited as **D.C. Cir.** The United States Court of Appeals for the Federal Circuit is cited as **Fed. Cir.**

[*BB & ALWD*] *Boumediene v. Bush*, **476 F.3d 981 (D.C. Cir. 2007).**

3. DESIGNATING THE FEDERAL DISTRICT COURTS

The United States District Courts are organized by district and division. Every state has at least one district, and many states have two or more. *The Bluebook* and the *ALWD Manual* cite the federal district, but not the division with the district.

Adjacent capital letters are closed up (e.g., **E.D.N.Y.**), but single capitals with longer abbreviations are not (e.g., **E.D. Pa.** or **D. Neb.**).

[ALWD] ***United Teachers of Dade v. Stierheim, 213 F. Supp. 2d 1368 (S.D. Fla. 2002).*** [The first geographic location ("**of Dade**") is retained in the citation. See subsections A(13) and A(17) above.]

[BB] ***United Teachers v. Stierheim, 213 F. Supp. 2d 1368 (S.D. Fla. 2002).*** [Prepositional phrases of location less than national geographic areas are omitted, including union names. See subsections A(13) and A(17) above.]

4. DESIGNATING THE EARLY FEDERAL CIRCUIT COURTS

The circuit courts were an important part of the early federal court system. These courts were abolished in 1912. Opinions from those courts can be found in the *Federal Cases* set and the *Federal Reporter*. The old circuit courts are cited by district, but not division (e.g., **C.C.W.D. Mo. = the Circuit Court of the Western District of Missouri**).

[BB] ***Wilson v. Rousseau, 30 F. Cas. 162 (C.C.N.D.N.Y. 1845) (No. 17,832).***

[ALWD] ***Wilson v. Rousseau, 30 F. Cas. 162 (C.C.N.D.N.Y. 1845).***

[BB & ALWD] ***Hamilton v. McClaughry, 136 F. 445 (C.C.D. Kan. 1905).***

5. THE FIFTH CIRCUIT SPLIT

On October 1, 1981, the former United States Court of Appeals for the Fifth Circuit was split into two autonomous circuits: a new Fifth Circuit (composed of the District of the Canal Zone, Louisiana, Mississippi, Texas) and a new Eleventh Circuit (composed of Alabama, Florida, and Georgia). However, the Fifth Circuit continued to exist for matters submitted for decision before October 1st. As part of this change, the Fifth Circuit divided itself into two administrative units, one called Unit A (corresponding to the new Fifth Circuit) and the other called Unit B (corresponding to the new Eleventh Circuit).

This division raised novel (and confusing) issues of precedent. With regard to binding precedent in the new Fifth Circuit, decisions of the former Fifth Circuit are binding in the new Fifth Circuit, *regardless of date and unit*. This approach was based on the fact that the new Fifth Circuit saw itself as a continuation of the old Fifth Circuit.

With regard to binding precedent in the new Eleventh Circuit, the rules are more complicated. *Former Fifth Circuit cases decided on or before September 30, 1981*, are binding precedent in the Eleventh Circuit (unless they have been overruled by the Eleventh Circuit judges sitting en banc).

That left in "litigatory limbo" the decisions of the former Fifth Circuit handed down after September 30, 1981. *Unit B decisions of the former Fifth Circuit and en banc decisions of the former Fifth Circuit decided after September 30, 1981*, are binding precedent in the Eleventh Circuit (unless they have been overruled by the Eleventh Circuit judges sitting en banc).

Unit A en banc decisions and Unit A panel decisions decided after September 30, 1981, are persuasive precedent in the Eleventh Circuit.

Because of this effect on precedent, cases decided during this transition period must indicate "**Unit A**" or "**Unit B**" in the citation. *The Bluebook* requires the month to be listed while the *ALWD Manual* does not. The basic citation pattern for these peculiar cases is illustrated below:

[**BB**] *McGowen v. Faulkner Concrete Pipe Co.*, **659 F.2d 554 (5th Cir. Unit A Oct. 1981).** [This case would be binding precedent in the new Fifth Circuit, but it would only be a persuasive precedent in the new Eleventh Circuit.]

[*ALWD*] *McGowen v. Faulkner Concrete Pipe Co.*, **659 F.2d 554 (5th Cir. Unit A 1981).**

[**BB**] *LaBanca v. Ostermunchner*, **664 F.2d 65 (5th Cir. Unit B Dec. 1981).** [This case would be binding precedent in the new Fifth Circuit and in the Eleventh Circuit; *The Bluebook* requires the month be given, but the *ALWD Manual* does not.]

[*ALWD*] *LaBanca v. Ostermunchner*, **664 F.2d 65 (5th Cir. Unit B 1981).**

Finally, some cases rendered after September 30, 1981 (but submitted for decision prior to that date) are labeled in the *Federal Reporter* as a "Former Fifth Circuit case" without indicating unit information.

These (often en banc) cases have an asterisk noting that the statute splitting the court provided that further proceedings "shall be had in the same manner and with the same effect" had the split not occurred. Cases labeled in this way should be identified as "**Former 5th Cir.**"

[*BB* & *ALWD*] *Kite v. Marshall*, **661 F.2d 1027 (Former 5th Cir. 1981).**

6. BANKRUPTCY COURTS AND BANKRUPTCY APPELLATE PANELS

The Bluebook and the *ALWD Manual* both provide that bankruptcy courts should be indicated by "**Bankr.**" They differ, however, on how bankruptcy appellate panels should be indicated. *The Bluebook* uses "**B.A.P.**" while the *ALWD Manual* uses "**Bankr. App.**"

[*BB* & *ALWD* Citation] *In re Harnischfeger Indus., Inc.*, 294 B.R. 47 (Bankr. D. Del. 2003).

[*BB* Citation] *Payne v. Clarendon Nat'l Ins. Co. (In re Sunset Sales, Inc.)*, 222 B.R. 914 (B.A.P. 10th Cir. 1998).

[*ALWD* Citation] *Payne v. Clarendon Natl. Ins. Co. (In re Sunset Sales, Inc.)*, **222 B.R. 914 (B.A.P. 10th Cir. 1998).** [The abbreviation of "**National**" differs from *The Bluebook*, and the inclusion of the nonadversary party's name is optional.]

7. MULTIDISTRICT LITIGATION

The Judicial Panel on Multidistrict Litigation was created in 1968. It consists of seven circuit and district court judges chosen by the Chief Justice of the U.S. Supreme Court. The panel is empowered to transfer to any federal district court "civil actions involving one or more common questions of fact . . . for coordinated and consolidated pretrial proceedings." *The Bluebook* cites the panel as "**J.P.M.L.**," and the *ALWD Manual* cites it as "**M.D.L.**"

[BB] *In re Plumbing Fixtures Cases*, **298 F. Supp. 484 (J.P.M.L. 1968).**

[ALWD] *In re Plumbing Fixtures Cases*, **298 F. Supp. 484 (M.D.L. 1968).**

E. YEAR OR DATE OF THE DECISION

As discussed in Chapter 1, the usual practice is that the year of decision for published cases must be given in case citations. Likewise, the usual practice is to give the exact date of decision for unreported cases as well as for cases appearing in electronic databases such as WESTLAW and LEXIS, slip opinions (individually issued court opinions at the time of decision before the opinion appears in advance sheets and reporters), and other similar sources.

The Bluebook and the *ALWD Manual* follow these same requirements. The format for giving the exact date is "month-day-year." The abbreviations for the month are the same for both *The Bluebook* and the

ALWD Manual. Those abbreviations are shown in **Appendix 1(C)** of this book.

[BB] *Parks v. Hayward's Pit, Inc.,* **No. 93-2387-JWL, 1993 WL 545231 (D. Kan. Dec. 21, 1993).**

[ALWD] *Parks v. Hayward's Pit, Inc.,* **1993 U.S. Dist. LEXIS 18529 (D. Kan. Dec. 21, 1993).**

As discussed in Chapter 1(F)(4), *The Bluebook* and the *ALWD Manual* differ with regard to the dates given in citations of multiple decisions within a single year. *The Bluebook* includes a date only with the last cited decision when a case with several decisions in the same year is cited. In contrast, the *ALWD Manual* requires that the year be given for each decision.

[BB] *Pollock v. Farmers' Loan & Trust Co.,* **157 U.S. 429,** *modified,* **158 U.S. 601 (1895).**

[ALWD] *Pollock v. Farmers' Loan & Trust Co.,* **157 U.S. 429 (1895),** *modified,* **158 U.S. 601 (1895).**

In citations of English cases, when the date differs from the volume year, *The Bluebook* requires that the actual year of decision be indicated at the end of the citation.

[BB] *Wise v. Kaye,* **[1962] Q.B. 606 (C.A. 1961).** ["**C.A.**" is the abbreviation for the "Court of Appeal"; there is no Court of Appeal series of *Law Reports*; instead, Court of Appeal opinions are reported in the series to which the appeal relates.]

CHAPTER 3

CITING LEGISLATIVE, ADMINISTRATIVE, AND RELATED SOURCES IN *BLUEBOOK* OR *ALWD* FORM

This chapter focuses primarily on the variations in citation form of legislative sources based on the requirements of *The Bluebook* and the *ALWD Manual*. It discusses some sources not introduced in Chapter 1(C) and (D), such as legislative history. It also contains discussion that can be skimmed (e.g., citing superseded constitutional provisions, statutes no longer in force, etc.). This material can be consulted as needed to construct a specific citation.

A. CONSTITUTIONS

1. BASIC RULES

In the United States, constitutions are the most basic written source of law. As illustrated in Chapter 1(D)(1), *The Bluebook* and the *ALWD Manual* provide the following rules for citing constitutions:

(1) The name of the constitution should be formed by the abbreviation of the jurisdiction, followed by the word, "**Const.**" The **U.S. Const.** should be cited by (a) **article**, (b) **section**, and (c), if appropriate, **clause**;

"article" should be abbreviated to **art.**, section to **§**, and "clause" to **cl.**; "**art.**" and "**cl.**" should not be capitalized in conformity with the abbreviations set out in the tables and appendices of *The Bluebook* and the *ALWD Manual*, respectively. These abbreviations are comparatively set out in **Appendix 1(D)** of this book.

[*BB* & *ALWD*] U.S. Const. art. III, § 3, cl. 1.

(2) "Amendment" is abbreviated to **amend.** and the abbreviation is not capitalized. Amendments to the U.S. Const. are cited by **Roman number**.

[*BB* & *ALWD*] U.S. Const. amend. VII.

(3) Constitutional provisions currently in force are cited without a date.

[*BB* & *ALWD*] W. Va. Const. art. 7, § 4.

2. CITING REPEALED OR SUPERSEDED CONSTITUTIONAL PROVISIONS

If the cited constitutional provision has been *repealed* or *superseded*, *The Bluebook* and the *ALWD Manual* require that fact to be indicated parenthetically in the pattern shown below. *The Bluebook* also permits the citation of the repealing provision.

[*BB*] U.S. Const. art. 1, § 2, cl. 3 (repealed 1868) *or* **U.S. Const. art. 1, § 2, cl. 3,** *repealed by* **U.S. Const. amend. XIV, § 2.**

[*ALWD*] U.S. Const. art. 1, § 2, cl. 3 (repealed 1868 by U.S. Const. amend. XIV, § 2).

The *ALWD Manual* also provides that the year in which the repealed provision was enacted can be included in the citation:

[*ALWD*] Mont. Const. art. III, § 6 (1889) (superseded 1972 by Mont. Const. art. II, § 16).

The Bluebook provides that if the cited provision was *adopted in a different year than the one in which the constitution was adopted*, the year of adoption must be indicated. *The ALWD Manual* makes that indication optional but encourages it when it would "assist readers." Thus, *subsequently amended provisions* are indicated in the same basic way as shown above.

[*BB*] U.S. Const. art. I, § 3 (amended 1913) *or* **U.S. Const. art. I, § 3,** *amended by* **U.S. Const. amend. XVII.**

[*ALWD*] U.S. Const. art. I, § 3 (amended 1913). [Optional parenthetical included to "assist readers."]

Finally, if the entire constitution has been *totally superseded*, *The Bluebook* provides that the year of the adoption should be included in the citation. The *ALWD Manual* requires that a parenthetical be used to indicate "why [it] is no longer in force" and "includ[ing] the year in which it lost [its] effect."

[*BB*] Tenn. Const. art. I, § 17 (1796).

[*ALWD*] Tenn. Const. art. I, § 17 (superseded 1835).

3. SHORT-FORM CITATIONS

The Bluebook and the *ALWD Manual* both indicate that no short-form citations should be used with constitutions other than *id.*

[*BB & ALWD*] Mass. Const. pt. I, art. XI. [Full citation]

[*BB & ALWD*] *Id.* art. X. [Short-form citation]

4. TEXTUAL REFERENCES

In accord with traditional practice, the *ALWD Manual* points out that textual references to constitutions should be spelled out (rather than given in citation form). In addition, it is traditional practice to spell out "**section**" (and "**paragraph**") references to constitutional provisions.

[*BB & ALWD* Text] An "open courts" provision was first adopted in section 17 of Article I of Tennessee Constitution of 1796.

5. TYPEFACE

In citations in law journal articles, *The Bluebook* places the name of the constitution in large and small capital letters. In all other instances, constitutions are cited in ordinary Roman type.

[*BB* Journal] U.S. CONST. amend. I.

B. STATUTORY SOURCES

The legislative branch of government is responsible for enacting statutes. Conventions for citing state and federal statutes, uniform acts, and municipal ordinances were extensively discussed in Chapter 1(C)(1)-(3). This section focuses primarily on differences between *The Bluebook* and the *ALWD Manual* with regard to these sources. In doing so, it also reviews the general format for citing these and related sources.

1. DESIGNATION OF STATE SUBJECT-MATTER CODES

Abbreviations of state statutory collections are shown in **Appendix 6(B)** of this book. These abbreviations are essentially the same for both *The Bluebook* and the *ALWD Manual*. Furthermore, as discussed and illustrated in Chapter 1(C)(2)(*b*), a few states have organized their statutes into individual "subject-matter" codes. *The Bluebook* and the *ALWD Manual* abbreviate a few of the names of those subject-matter codes differently. The abbreviations are also comparatively shown in **Appendix 6(B)** of this book.

The following example is representative of the minor differences—generally along the same lines that abbreviations differ for case names.

[*BB*] N.Y. Gen. Ass'ns Law § 16 (McKinney 1994). ["**Ass'ns**" is *The Bluebook* abbreviation for "**Associations.**"]

[*ALWD*] N.Y. Gen. Assns. Law § 16 (McKinney 1994). [The *ALWD* abbreviation is "**Assns.**"]

2. DESIGNATION OF THE NAME OF THE PUBLISHER OR COMPILER

With a few exceptions for official statutes such as the *United States Code*, citations to statutory collections include the name of the publisher or compiler in the parenthetical containing the year. **Appendix 6** of this book shows abbreviations of federal and state statutory collections as they are listed by *The Bluebook* and the *ALWD Manual*.

The tables and appendices in *The Bluebook* and the *ALWD Manual* become out of date between editions. As a result, they may not reflect the changing names of publishers as a result of mergers or corporate "branding." For example, one might list the publisher as "**Lexis**" while the other lists the publisher as "**LexisNexis**." In general, the publisher as it is listed in the publication should be used.

3. CITING MULTIPLE SUBDIVISIONS

The general methods for citing multiple sections and paragraphs were discussed in Chapter 1(F)(*i*). Statutory compilations often have complicated numbering schemes, sometimes using title, chapters, sections, letters, and peculiar punctuation. *The Bluebook* and the *ALWD Manual* provide detailed rules to help avoid ambiguities when multiple statutory subdivisions are cited.

a. Citing a "Span" of Consecutive Statutory Paragraphs or Sections

The *ALWD Manual's* approach is to retain all digits and letters of the "span" of paragraphs or sections when they are cited. *The Bluebook* allows, but does not require, omission of repetitious (identical) digits or letters preceding a punctuation mark if the omission would not cause confusion.

[*BB*] §§ 19.10-19.20 *or* **§§ 19.10-.20** ["19" can optionally be omitted because they are identical digits preceding a punctuation mark.]

[*ALWD*] §§ 19.10-19.20 [All digits are retained.]

However, when in doubt, the simplest approach is to retain all the digits.

The Bluebook and the *ALWD Manual* also both provide that "**to**" can be used to avoid ambiguities.

[*BB*] §§ 56-7-1 to -10 *or* **§§ 56-7-1 to 56-7-10** ["To" is used to avoid ambiguity.]

[*ALWD*] §§ 56-7-1 to 56-7-10 ["To" is used to avoid ambiguity.]

b. Citing "Scattered" Paragraphs or Sections

When "scattered" multiple paragraphs or sections are cited, they are separated by commas without the use of "and" or an ampersand. *Two* section or paragraph symbols are used.

[*BB & ALWD*] ¶¶ 19(a), 25, 34(d)(1)

c. Citing "Scattered" Subdivisions Within a Single Paragraph or Section

When "scattered" multiple subdivisions *within a single paragraph or section*, the same general rules are followed, but only *one* section or paragraph symbol is used.

[*BB & ALWD*] § 19(a), (d), (h)

4. YEAR USED IN CITATIONS OF STATUTORY COLLECTIONS

When citing published statutory collections, *The Bluebook* and the *ALWD Manual* both require the use of the date on the spine of the volume. However, some sets do not have a date on the spine. In such circumstances, *The Bluebook* and the *ALWD Manual* differ on the preferred date. *The Bluebook* requires the year on the title page be used and, if there is none, then the copyright year. The *ALWD Manual* reverses this order of preference—with the copyright year given preference over the year on the title page. The following example from *Maine Revised Statutes Annotated* of 1964 shows the difference:

[*BB*] Me. Rev. Stat. Ann. tit. 10, § 3258 (1964). [The year on the title page used because there is no date on the spine of the volume.]

[*ALWD*] Me. Rev. Stat. Ann. tit. 10, § 3258 (1997). [The copyright date of the volume is used because there is no date on the spine of the volume.]

Recall also from Chapter 1(C)(1) that the official *United States Code* is issued every six years (e.g., **2006**) and that date should be used in citations. In contrast, when citing statutes in the unofficial *United States Code Annotated* and *United States Code Service*, the copyright date of the volume containing the provision is used.

In addition, recall from Chapter 1(C)(1)(*a*) with regard to session laws such as the *United States Statutes at Large*, *The Bluebook* follows the traditional approach of appending the year of enactment in a parenthetical at the end of the citation *unless it was included in the name of the statute*. However, the *ALWD Manual* requires the date to be appended in a parenthetical in every citation.

5. CITING STATUTORY SUPPLEMENTS

The methods for citing the official supplements of the official *United States Code* were also detailed in Chapter 1(C)(1)(*c*), above, and that materials should be referenced for this purpose. With regard to citing all other statutory supplements for material appearing only in the supplement, the copyright date of the supplement is used.

[*BB* & *ALWD*] Fair Credit Reporting Act, Me. Rev. Stat. Ann. tit. 10, §§ 1312-1329 (West Supp. 2006).

When the statutory material cited is contained in both the main volume and a supplement, the year of the main volume and the supplement are given.

6. CITING STATUTORY SOURCES AVAILABLE IN ELECTRONIC DATABASES

Electronic databases are convenient sources for statutory compilations and session laws. *The Bluebook* and the *ALWD Manual* provide that when online sources are cited, two modifications are required. First, the name of the database and its currency should be included in the citation. Thus, instead of using the date of the statutory compilation, the information regarding the currency of the database (as provided in the database) should be used in a parenthetical.

Second, the name of the publisher, compiler, or editor should be included the parenthetical (unless state or federal officials are responsible for the compilation of the code). Within the parenthetical, months should be abbreviated according to the standard abbreviations listed in **Appendix 1(C)** of this book. The *ALWD Manual* also provides that publisher names and other words appearing in the parenthetical should be abbreviated as well (as listed in **Appendix 1(A)-(E)** of this book).

[*BB & ALWD*] Cal. Civ. Proc. Code § 410.10 (West, Westlaw through ch. 470 of 2007 Reg. Sess.).

7. STATUTES NO LONGER IN FORCE

The *ALWD Manual* provides that statutes no longer in force are cited like statutes currently in force, but with a parenthetical indication that the provision is no longer in force, along with the year in which it ceased to be in force.

[*ALWD*] 28 U.S.C. § 1471 (repealed 1984).

The Bluebook gives a more complicated formula for citing statutes no longer in force: (1) the current official or unofficial code should be cited if the provision still appears in it; (2) if it no longer is included in the current code, then the last edition of the official or unofficial code in which the provision appeared should be cited; if that is impossible, then the session laws should be cited; finally, the last resort is a secondary source. Like the *ALWD Manual*, a parenthetical must be used to alert the reader that the provision has been repealed, amended, or otherwise no longer in force.

[*BB*] 15 U.S.C. § 77r (1994) (repealed 1996). [citing the last edition of the official code in which the section appeared]

8. *INTERNAL REVENUE CODE*

In accord with traditional practice, *The Bluebook* and the *ALWD Manual* provide that the *Internal Revenue Code* can be cited as a separate code (**I.R.C.**) (rather than to Title 26 of the *United States Code* where it is codified). In practitioner documents, it is recognized that the date as well as the publisher can be omitted, but the *ALWD Manual* "encourage[s]" the use of a date and the publisher must be included if an unofficial version is cited (e.g., *United States Code Annotated*).

[BB] **I.R.C. § 501(c)(3).** [In practitioner documents discussing only the current version of the *Code*; official code cited.]

[ALWD] **I.R.C. § 501(c)(3).** [A "date is encouraged"; official code cited.]

In law journal citations, *The Bluebook* requires a date of the official code or supplement in which the provision appears. Unofficial sources require the publisher as well. Both *The Bluebook* and the *ALWD Manual* (when the publisher and date are given) use the same format.

[*BB* Journal, *BB* Practitioner Optional & *ALWD* Optional] I.R.C. § 501(c)(3) (2006). [Date of the current official *Code* is given.]

[*BB* & *ALWD*] I.R.C. § 501(c)(3) (West Supp. 2007). [Publisher and date of the unofficial *United States Code Annotated* volume are given.]

9. SHORT-FORM CITATIONS

After a statute has been fully cited, both *The Bluebook* and the *ALWD Manual* permit the use of a variety of short forms. Generally speaking, any form that clearly identifies the statute can be used. Thus, it might be sufficient to mention the name of the act (e.g., **Sherman Act**), a shortened version of a lengthy name (e.g., **USA Patriot Act** instead of the "United and Strengthening America by Providing Appropriate Tools Required to Intercept and Obstruct Terrorism Act"), a code citation (e.g., **15 U.S.C. § 1**), or just the section (e.g., **§ 1**). *Id.* can be used to cite the immediately preceding source.

The *ALWD Manual* has a special rule for documents with footnotes rather than having citations in the body of the text. If "*id.*" is not appropriate, then the full citation must be given, but the date should be omitted. Likewise, *The Bluebook* has special restrictions on the use of short forms for law journal articles. It limits the use of the short forms in the preceding paragraph to the readily identifiable references within same footnote or the preceding five footnotes. Otherwise, the full citation must be used.

10. TEXTUAL REFERENCES TO STATUTES

Traditionally, in textual references to statutory provisions, "**section**" is spelled out, and it is not capitalized unless it begins the sentence. That is the rule followed by *The Bluebook* in law review text and footnote text, except when the author is referring to a section of the *United States Code*; in that case, the section symbol should be used.

[*BB* Text] Section 1 of title 15 declares illegal "[e]very contract, combination in the form of trust or otherwise, or conspiracy, in restraint of trade or commerce among the several States, or with foreign nations." In § 2 of title 15, monopolization is prohibited. [When it is the first word of the sentence, "**Section**" must be spelled out and capitalized. When it is not and it refers to a section of the *United States Code*, a symbol is used.]

The *ALWD Manual* also requires that section (and paragraph) be spelled out if it begins a textual sentence, but the use of a symbol is an option. However, "**title**," "**chapter**," and other subdivisions that cannot be designated by means of a symbol must be spelled out.

[*ALWD* Text] **The first federal antitrust law to restrict monopolization was § 2 of the Sherman Act**. [Section could be spelled out: **The first federal antitrust law to restrict monopolization was section 2 of the Sherman Act.**]

Furthermore, the name of the statutory compilation, except for the *United States Code*, should be spelled out.

[*BB* & *ALWD* Text] **This provision was removed from the *Code of Laws of South Carolina* in 2008**.

11. TYPEFACE

In citations in law journal articles, *The Bluebook* places the abbreviated name of the statutory compilation in large and small capital letters. In all other instances, constitutions are cited in ordinary Roman type.

[*BB* Journal] **WIS. STAT. ANN. § 945.02 (West 2005).**

C. LEGISLATIVE HISTORY SOURCES

Legislative intent is often regarded as the controlling factor in interpreting legislation. The legislative process generates various sources that can be consulted and cited. For example, on the federal level, legislative history can include Presidential messages that accompany proposed legislation, differences in congressional bills, testimony presented at hearings, congressional committee reports, debates on the floor of the House and Senate, proposed or adopted amendments, and other documents.

Legislative history of state legislation is ordinarily difficult to obtain because many items constituting legislative history are rarely published. However, when available, those items are generally cited in the same manner as federal legislative history (with the addition of the abbreviated name of the state if it is not apparent from other parts of the citation).

This section discusses the citation of the three most important sources of legislative history: (1) debates; (2) committee reports and documents; and (3) hearings. Federal materials are used as the model for this purpose. This section also provides examples of citations to other sources of legislative materials.

1. CONGRESSIONAL DEBATES

Congressional legislative debates are reported verbatim (subject to revision by members of Congress) in the *Congressional Record* (**Cong. Rec.**) (1873 to date). For congressional debates in the

Congressional Record, The Bluebook and the *ALWD Manual* cite them in the same way: by volume, page, and year, as shown below:

[*BB & ALWD*] 34 Cong. Rec. 2948 (1901).

The *Congressional Record* is first issued in a "daily edition" and it is repaginated when it is bound. If the daily edition of the *Record* is being cited, "**daily ed.**" must be inserted before the full date. The daily edition should be used for matter that has not yet appeared in the permanent edition. "**S**" is inserted before the page number when a Senate debate is being cited; and "**H**" is inserted for a House debate. The month is abbreviated as shown in **Appendix 1(C)** of this book.

[*BB & ALWD*] 152 Cong. Rec. S10419 (daily ed. Sept. 28, 2006) (statement of Sen. Reid).

The *Congressional Record's* two immediate predecessors were the *Congressional Globe* (**Cong. Globe**) (1833-1873) and *Register of Debates* (**Reg. Deb.**) (1824-1837).The following are examples of the format for citations to the *Congressional Globe* and *Register of Debates*.

[*BB & ALWD*] Cong. Globe, 41st Cong., 2d Sess. 1503 (1870).

[*BB & ALWD*] 10 Reg. Deb. 1187 (1834) (statement of Henry Clay).

The first Congress through the first session of the 18th Congress are covered by the *Annals of Congress* (**Annals of Cong.**) (1789-1824). The *Annals* were not published contemporaneously, but were compiled between 1834 and 1856 from the best records available (primarily newspaper accounts). Debates are paraphrased rather than presented verbatim. The *Annals* are paginated and cited by *column number* (two columns per page). The pattern for citing the *Annals* is shown below.

[*BB* & *ALWD*] 17 Annals of Cong. 874 (1807). [This citation is to **column 874**.]

The first volume of the *Annals of Congress*, which is cited more frequently than other volumes, requires special attention. *The Bluebook* specifically requires that the name of the editor or editors be included in the parenthetical with the date for citations to volume 1 of the *Annals of Congress*. This requirement reflects the fact that there are two different versions of this volume: one edited by Joseph Gales and the other edited by Joseph Gales, Jr. and William W. Seaton. The important point here is to be sure to provide enough information in the citation that the reader can identify the version cited.

[*BB*] 1 Annals of Cong. 767 (Joseph Gales, Jr. & William W. Seaton eds., 1789) (statement of James Madison).

In *Bluebook* journal citations, large and small capital letters are used for the abbreviated references to all these sources for debates.

[*BB* Journal] 55 CONG. REC. 1763 (1917).

2. CONGRESSIONAL COMMITTEE REPORTS AND DOCUMENTS

The Bluebook provides that numbered congressional committee reports and documents are cited by the following:

(1) the House (**H.**) or Senate (**S.**) report number, with the number of the Congress connected by a hyphen to the number of the report (e.g., **S. Rep. No. 95-185**, **H.R. Rep. No. 95-263**, etc.);

(2) the part and/or page number(s) where the cited material appears, if any; page numbers are introduced by "**at**";

(3) the year of publication in a parenthetical;

(4) the session (**1st Sess.** or **2d Sess.**) should be added in the parenthetical before the year for certain early reports and documents: (a) House Reports published before the 47th Congress (1881); (b) Senate Reports published before the 40th Congress (1867); and (c) House and Senate documents published before the 60th Congress (1907); in addition, in a rare instance that Congress has held a third session, that information should be included (**3d Sess.**);

(5) **(Conf. Rep.)** should be added in a separate parenthetical if the report cited is a conference report; and

(6) the parallel citation to the permanent edition of the *United States Code Congressional and Administrative News* (**U.S.C.C.A.N.**), whenever possible (e.g., **1962 U.S.C.C.A.N. 2844, 2846**), introduced by "*as reprinted in*."

[*BB*] S. Rep. No. 98-225, at 51 (1983), *as reprinted in* 1984 U.S.C.C.A.N. 3182, 3234.

[*BB*] H.R. Rep. No. 107-609, pt. 1, at 6566 (2002), *as reprinted in* 2002 U.S.C.C.A.N. 1352, 1355.

[*BB*] H.R. Rep. No. 104-864, at 39 (1996) (Conf. Rep.), *as reprinted in* 1996 U.S.C.C.A.N. 3920, 3920.

Titles of numbered reports can also be given. Words of seven or more letters can be abbreviated if the result is unambiguous. Suggested abbreviations are shown in **Appendix 11** of this book. If the title is given, the author should also be given. Case name abbreviations are applied to institutional authors "if the result will be completely unambiguous." The two most common ones are "**Comm.**" for "Committee" and "**Subcomm.**" for "Subcommittee."

[*BB*] House Comm. on the Judiciary, Rep. on the Civil Rights Act of 1963, H.R. Rep. No. 88-914, pt. 2, at 8, 17, 26, 29 (1963).

This general pattern is followed for all congressional documents:

[*BB*] House Select Comm. on Small Bus., Congress and the Monopoly Problem: Fifty-Six Years of Antitrust Dev., 1900-1956, H.R. Doc. No. 85-240, at 659 (1957).

The *ALWD Manual* modifies the above elements in six distinct ways. First, it abbreviates "Senate" to "**Sen.**" instead of "S." Second, it requires the exact date that the document "was ordered to be printed" instead of only the year—providing the month, day, and year, if available. Third, it places the reference to the *United States Code Congressional and Administrative News* in a parenthetical. The same is done when the report has been reprinted in the *Congressional Record*. Fourth, "report" is abbreviated "**Rpt.**" rather than "**Rep.**" Fifth, a conference report is cited as "**H.R.** [or **Sen.**] **Conf. Rpt.**" instead of being indicated parenthetically. Sixth, the title of the report, if given, is italicized, and the name of institutional authors may be abbreviated with the abbreviations set out in **Appendix 1(A)-(E)** and **Appendix 11** of this book.

[*ALWD*] **Sen. Rpt. 99-541 at 2 (Oct. 17, 1986) (reprinted in 1986 U.S.C.C.A.N. 3555, 3556).**

[*ALWD*] **H. Select Comm. on Small Bus.,** *Congress and the Monopoly Problem: Fifty-Six Years of Antitrust Development,* **1900-1956, H.R. Doc. No. 85-240, at 659 (Aug. 29, 1957).**

In *Bluebook* journal citations, large and small capital letters are used for the abbreviated references to the abbreviated report or document name, authors, and titles.

[BB Journal] HOUSE SELECT COMM. ON SMALL BUS., CONGRESS AND THE MONOPOLY PROBLEM: FIFTY-SIX YEARS OF ANTITRUST DEV., 1900-1956, H.R. DOC. NO. 85-240, at 659 (1957).

3. CONGRESSIONAL HEARINGS

For legislative history purposes, congressional hearings are much less frequently relied upon than committee reports. The formats for *The Bluebook* and the *ALWD Manual* are shown below.

[BB] *Methamphetamine Epidemic Elimination Act: Hearing on H.R. 3889 Before the Subcomm. on Crime, Terrorism, and Homeland Security of the H. Comm. on the Judiciary,* **109th Cong. 24 (2006) (statement of Joseph T. Rannazzisi, Deputy Chief, Office of Enforcement Operations, U.S. Drug Enforcement Administration).**

[*ALWD*] H.R. Educ. & Lab. Comm., *The Crime Awareness and Campus Security Act of 1989: Hearings on H.R. 3344,* **101st Cong. 27 (Mar. 14, 1990).** [The *ALWD* format consists of the abbreviated name of the committee, title and bill number, Congress number, session number for older hearings, pinpoint reference, and exact date.]

4. BILLS AND RESOLUTIONS

Enacted bills and joint resolutions are cited as statutes. Unenacted federal bills are cited by the name of the bill (if relevant), the abbreviated name of the house, the bill number, the number of the Congress, the provision within the bill (if any), and the year of publication (*Bluebook*) or the exact date for the version cited (*ALWD*). As indicated in subsection

2, the session number must be added for earlier years. *The Bluebook* adds this information in a parenthetical with the date at the end of the citation. The *ALWD Manual* inserts this information immediately after the number of the Congress (e.g., **38th Cong., 1st Sess.**). Unenacted resolutions are cited analogously. The same is true for simple and concurrent resolutions that bind only one or both houses of Congress. This type of citation (in this instance, an unenacted bill) is shown as follows:

[*BB*] Federal Constitutional Convention Procedures Act, S. 1272, 93d Cong. § 10 (1973).

[*ALWD*] Fed. Constitutional Conv. Procs. Act, S. 1272, 93d Cong. § 10 (July 9, 1973). [Using abbreviations from Appendix 1 in the title.]

D. TREATIES AND OTHER INTERNATIONAL AGREEMENTS

The basic elements for citing treaties and other international agreements were set out in Chapter 1(D)(4). Such citations contain (1) the title of the treaty; (2) a pinpoint reference, if any; (3) the date of signing; and (4) treaty source or sources. However, as discussed below, *The Bluebook* and the *ALWD Manual* differ on citation format and details. In part, those differences stem from the fact that *The Bluebook* cites treaties with three or fewer parties differently than treaties with four or more parties. The following examples (with accompanying explanations) illustrate the specific differences.

[*BB*] Extradition Treaty, May 4, 1978, U.S.-Mex., 31 U.S.T. 5059. [Because this Extradition Treaty is a bilateral one, the parties should be listed using their abbreviated names as shown in **Appendix 1(B)** of this book; if the United States is one of the parties, it should be listed first; the exact date of signing is used; if two parties signed on different dates, then the first and last dates of signing are used, separated by a hyphen (e.g., **May 4-May10, 1978**); "**U.S.T.**" refers to the official *United States Treaties and Other International Agreements* series, which began in 1950 and is the preferred *Bluebook* source for agreements between the United States and one or two other parties; only one source should be cited; finally, months should be abbreviated as shown in **Appendix 1(C)** of this book.]

[*ALWD*] *Extradition Treaty* (May 4, 1978), 31 U.S.T. 5059. [The *ALWD Manual* indicates that "**one** source" should be cited and that source "may be an official source or unofficial source, including an Internet location"; months should be abbreviated as shown in **Appendix 1(C)** of this book; parties are not identified; if the parties signed on different dates, then the last date should be used; the exact title as it appears on the title page is used along with the first form of the description (e.g., "**Treaty**").]

[*BB*] Treaty of Amity, Commerce, and Navigation, Nov. 19, 1794, U.S.-Gr. Brit., 8 Stat. 116. [The *United States Statutes at Large* is the preferred *Bluebook* source for agreements between the United States and one or two other parties prior to 1950.]

[BB] **International Convention for the Prevention of Pollution of the Sea by Oil, May 12, 1954, 12 U.S.T. 2989, 327 U.N.T.S. 3.** [For agreements with more than three parties to which the United States is a party, one U.S. domestic source should be cited and one source published by an international organization; here, *United Nations Treaties Series* (**U.N.T.S.**) is cited; in contrast, any one source may be cited under the *ALWD* rules.]

[BB] **Geneva Convention Relative to the Protection of Civilian Persons in Time of War of Aug. 12, 1949, art. 79,** *opened for signature* **Aug. 12, 1949, 6 U.S.T. 3517, 3568, 75 U.N.T.S. 287, 338.** [When a multiparty convention like this one was not signed on a single date, the date on which the treaty "was opened for signature, done, approved, or adopted" should be indicated in italics; the date the treaty entered into force or another date may be added parenthetically when "it is of particular relevance;" the subject-matter description that appears on the title page along with the first designation of the form of the agreement should be used in the title.]

[ALWD] *Geneva Convention Relative to the Protection of Civilian Persons in Time of War of Aug. 12, 1949,* **art. 79 (entered into force Oct. 21, 1950), 6 U.S.T. 3517, 3568.** [The *ALWD Manual* provides that when the date of signing is not available, one of the following dates should be used (in the following order of preference): (1) "the effective date"; (2) "the date on which ratifications were exchanged between or among the signatories; (3) "the date of ratification by the President of the United States"; (4) "the date of ratification by the Senate"; or (5) "any other date," such as the date when the treaty was opened for signature; only one treaty source is cited; the exact subject-matter description that appears on the title page along with the first designation of the form of the agreement should be used in the title.]

E. ADMINISTRATIVE REGULATIONS AND EXECUTIVE ORDERS

1. ADMINISTRATIVE REGULATIONS

The citation of administrative regulations was discussed in Chapter 1(D)(2), above. When the regulations in the *Code of Federal Regulations* (**C.F.R.**) are cited to unofficial electronic databases such as WESTLAW and LEXIS, the *ALWD Manual* requires that the parenthetical "include the name of the database provider and the specific date ([abbreviated] month-day-year) through which the [*C.F.R.*] is current on the database."

[*ALWD*] FDIC Standards for Establishing Safety and Soundness, 12 C.F.R. § 364.100 (2007) (Westlaw current through Jan. 3, 2008).

[*ALWD*] FDIC Standards for Establishing Safety and Soundness, 12 C.F.R. § 364.100 (2007) (Lexis current through Oct. 18, 2007).

The Bluebook handles this situation by using the normal citation and a parallel provision of the search information that could be used to "find" the provision in the electronic database. Thus, *The Bluebook* requires that the name of the database be given along with "any identifying codes or numbers that uniquely identify the material." *The Bluebook* adds that "[i]f the name of the data is not clear from the database identifier," it should be included parenthetically at the end of the citation.

[*BB*] FDIC Standards for Establishing Safety and Soundness, 12 C.F.R. § 364 (2007), WL 12 CFR s 364.100.

[*BB*] FDIC Standards for Establishing Safety and Soundness, 12 C.F.R. § 364 (2007), LEXIS 12 CFR 364.100.

The differing approaches of *The Bluebook* and the *ALWD Manual* emphasize different functions of the citation. The *ALWD Manual* focuses on providing currentness because WESTLAW and LEXIS constantly (and conveniently) incorporate changes from the *Federal Register* into the relevant databases. Thus, these databases may be more current than (and differ from) the official print version and the electronic version available from the federal government's websites. In contrast, *The Bluebook* focuses on providing the reader assistance with the search for finding the actual text of the regulation on an electronic source (e.g., using "Find" or "Get a Document").

2. EXECUTIVE ORDERS

As the head of the executive branch, commander-in-chief of the armed forces, and the officer in charge of foreign relations, the President of the United States issues executive orders and proclamations. These documents announce policy and direct action by federal agencies and officials and have the force of law. Presidential proclamations, executive orders, and reorganization plans are published in the *Federal Register* and are compiled in Title 3 of the *Code of Federal Regulations*. Some are included in the *United States Code*.

The Bluebook cites these documents by *page* number to the *Code of Federal Regulations*, with a parallel citation to the *United States Code* if they have been reprinted therein. The *Federal Register* should be cited if they are not in the *C.F.R.*

[*BB*] Exec. Order No. 13,132, 3 C.F.R. 206 (1999), *reprinted in* **5 U.S.C. § 601 (2000).**

The *ALWD Manual* varies the form as follows:

[*ALWD*] Exec. Or. 13,132, 3 C.F.R. 206 (1999) (reprinted in 5 U.S.C. § 601 (2000)). [The parallel citation to the *United States Code* or other sources is optional.]

The *Public Papers of the President* (**Pub. Papers**) publishes Presidential papers, speeches, and other documents (since 1945). There is also a *Weekly Compilation of Presidential Documents* available.

F. RULES OF PROCEDURE AND EVIDENCE

The citation of rules of procedure and evidence is fully discussed in Chapter 1(D)(3), above. In *Bluebook* journal citations, large and small capital letters are used for the abbreviated references to all these sources, as shown in the following example:

[*BB* Journal] FED. R. CIV. P. 60(b).

G. UNIFORM STATE LAWS, MODEL CODES, AND RULES AND CODES OF PROFESSIONAL RESPONSIBILITY

1. UNIFORM STATE LAWS

The citation of uniform state laws is discussed in Chapter 1(C)(3), above. *The Bluebook* and the *ALWD Manual* apply the abbreviations set out in **Appendix 1** of this book to the title of a uniform act.

[*BB*] Unif. P'ship Act § 38(2)(b), 6 U.L.A. 487 (2001).

[*ALWD*] Unif. Partn. Act § 38(2)(b), 6 U.L.A. 487 (2001).

In *Bluebook* journal citations, large and small capital letters are used to cite such laws:

[*BB* Journal] UNIF. P'SHIP ACT § 38(2)(b), 6 U.L.A. 487 (2001).

2. MODEL CODES, MODEL ACTS, AND RULES AND CODES OF PROFESSIONAL RESPONSIBILITY

Model codes and acts are promulgated by various organizations. They are cited by analogy to statutes.

The Bluebook indicates that the year of the version cited and the abbreviated name of the author should be indicated parenthetically unless the author was the American Bar Association, the American Law Institute, or the National Conference of Commissioners on Uniform State Laws. Titles are abbreviated pursuant to the abbreviations set out in **Appendix 1** of this book.

[*BB*] Model Penal Code § 2.02(2)(c) (1985).

[*BB*] Rev. Model Bus. Corp. Act § 8.01 (1984).

In contrast, in addition to the year, the *ALWD Manual* requires that all organizational authors be given in the citation.

[*ALWD*] Model Penal Code § 2.02(2)(c) (ALI 1985). [The abbreviated name of the organizational author (the American Law Institute) is given.]

[*ALWD*] Rev. Model Bus. Corp. Act § 8.01 (ABA 1984). [The abbreviated name of the organizational author (the American Bar Association) is given.]

When a tentative or proposed draft is cited, that fact along with the date of the draft must be indicated parenthetically.

[*BB*] Model Penal Code § 201.5 cmt. 1 (Tent. Drft. No. 9, 1959). [*The Bluebook* abbreviates "**tentative**" to "**tent.**" and "**draft**" to "**drft.**" See **Appendix 1(E)**.

[*ALWD*] Model Penal Code § 201.5 cmt. 1 (ALI Tent. Dft. No. 9, 1959). [The *ALWD Manual* abbreviates "tentative" to "**tent.**" and "draft" to "**dft.**" See **Appendix 1(E)**. If the draft information does not end with a numeral, the *ALWD Manual* specifies that no comma should be used. "**ALI**" is also indicated.]

Rules or codes of professional conduct are cited in the same way as model codes and acts. The *ALWD Manual* abbreviates "Rules" to "**R.**," "Professional" to "**Prof.**," and "Responsibility" to "**Resp.**" *The Bluebook* abbreviates "Professional" to "**Prof'l.**"

[*BB*] Model Rules of Prof'l Conduct R. 1.2 & cmt. 1 (1983). [Both Rule 1.2 and the accompanying comment are cited; "comment" is abbreviated to "**cmt.**"]

[*ALWD*] Model R. Prof'l Conduct 1.2 & cmt. 1 (ABA 1983). [The *ALWD Manual* permits the omission of articles and prepositions from titles of model codes, acts, and rules; unlike *The Bluebook*, "**R.**" for rule is omitted before "**1.2.**"]

In *Bluebook* journal citations, large and small capital letters are used to cite model codes, model acts, and rules or codes of professional conduct:

[*BB* Journal] MODEL PENAL CODE § 2.02(2)(c) (1985).

[*BB* Journal] REV. MODEL BUS. CORP. ACT § 8.01 (1984).

[*BB* Journal] MODEL RULES OF PROF'L CONDUCT R. 1.2 & cmt. 1 (1983).

CHAPTER 4

CITING SECONDARY AND INTERNET SOURCES IN *BLUEBOOK* OR *ALWD* FORM

Texts, treatises, law review articles, dictionaries, legal encyclopedias, restatements, annotations, and other materials are secondary authority. In absence of primary authority on point, secondary authority may persuade courts to adopt a suggested resolution of an issue. Secondary authority may be cited for the purpose of clarifying ambiguities in primary authority. In addition, it may be cited to a court in an attempt to convince the court that a prior decision should be limited, distinguished, or overruled.

Chapter 1(E) discussed the basic conventions for citing secondary sources. This chapter primarily focuses on the variations in citation form based on the requirements of *The Bluebook* and the *ALWD Manual*. Some of this material may be skimmed and consulted when constructing specific citations. In addition, citation of Internet sources is discussed.

A. TEXTS AND TREATISES

The Bluebook and the *ALWD Manual* vary considerably with regard to the citation of texts, treatises, and other books. The following sequential examples (with accompanying explanations) illustrate the specific differences. Titles are capitalized in the manner described in Chapter 1(F)(3)(*m*).

1. SINGLE AUTHOR, FIRST EDITION, SINGLE PUBLISHER, AND DATE

[BB] Larry L. Teply, *Law School Competitions in a Nutshell* **(2003).** [The full name of an author is given, including any designation such as "**Jr.**" or the "**III**" ("inserting a comma before the designation only if the author does"); "**Prof.**," "**Dr.**," and similar titles are not used; the title appears in italics, but information that would be in italics if it appeared in text (such as case names) should not be in italics; if the book is in its first edition like this one, the edition is not given the parenthetical; the publisher is also not given in *Bluebook* citations; the year of publication is cited.]

[*ALWD*] Larry L. Teply, *Law School Competitions in a Nutshell* **(West Group 2003).** [The full name of an author is given "exactly as [it] appear[s] on the front cover or title page"); like *The Bluebook*, "**Jr.**" or the "**III**" are included, but not "degree information" or titles of respect (such as "**Hon.**"); the name of the publisher is included in the parenthetical, but a first edition is not indicated in the parenthetical; in the publisher's name, words appearing in **Appendix 1** of this book may be abbreviated and prepositions and articles may be omitted if they are "not needed for clarity"; however, words in the title should not be abbreviated unless they are in the cited source, and all articles and prepositions in the title must be included.]

2. MULTIPLE EDITIONS AND PRINTINGS

[*BB*] Larry L. Teply, *Legal Negotiation in a Nutshell* **(2d ed. 2005).** [Any edition after the first is listed in the parenthetical containing the year of publication (e.g., "**2d ed.**," "**3d ed.**," "**4th ed.**," etc.); use the publisher's description of the edition (e.g., "**rev. ed.**" for "revised edition"); the particular printing of the same edition is not cited unless it is relevant for some purpose (e.g., an important difference between two printings exists); then, the date of the printing should be cited (e.g., "**4th prtg. 2008**").]

[*ALWD*] Larry L. Teply, *Legal Negotiation in a Nutshell* **(2d ed., Thomson/West 2005).** [The indication of the edition after the first or original edition in the parenthetical is followed by a comma; if the title page had identified two or more publishers (and not just multiple offices or divisions of the same publisher), then all of the publishers are given, including the date of publication for each, separated by commas; the same rule for printings (as indicated above) is followed.]

3. TWO AUTHORS AND PINPOINT CITATIONS

[*BB*] Larry L. Teply & Ralph U. Whitten, Civil Procedure 1021 (3d ed. 2004). [When there are two authors (as in this example), they are listed in the order in which they appear in the title page, separated by an ampersand; if an alternative relationship is indicated on the title page, that relationship should be shown (such as "**with**" or "**as told to**"); "**1021**" is a pinpoint reference to page 1021 of the book; use "**at**" preceded by a comma to avoid confusion with another part of the citation, such as "when the title of a work ends with an Arabic numeral or when the work uses Roman numerals for pagination."]

[*ALWD*] **Larry L. Teply & Ralph U. Whitten,** *Civil Procedure* **1021 (3d ed., Found. Press 2004).** [Two authors should be separated by an ampersand; "**1021**" is a pinpoint reference to page 1021 of the book; use "**at**" preceded by a comma"[i]f the title ends in a numeral."]

4. THREE OR MORE AUTHORS AND SUBTITLES

[*BB*] **Larry L. Teply et al.,** *Civil Procedure* **(2007)** *or* **Larry L. Teply, Ralph U. Whitten & Denis F. McLaughlin,** *Civil Procedure: Cases, Text, Notes, and Problems* **(2007).** [When a work has three or more authors and "saving space is desired" and in short forms, the name of the first author is used followed by "**et al.**" to indicate "and others"; in the alternative, all the names of the authors can be given; all authors' names should be given "when doing so is particularly relevant"; in this instance, that might be useful to distinguish this book from the preceding example; the subtitle should be given "only if it is particularly relevant"; again, in this instance, that might be useful to make clear that the cited work is a casebook, not the *Civil Procedure* text cited in the preceding example.]

[*ALWD*] Larry L. Teply, Ralph U. Whitten & Denis F. McLaughlin, *Civil Procedure: Cases, Text, Notes, and Problems* **(Carolina Academic Press 2007)** *or* **Larry L. Teply et al.,** *Civil Procedure* **(Carolina Academic Press 2007).** [Works with three or more authors are shown in the same way as described for *The Bluebook* citation above; a subtitle "may" be included; a colon is used to introduce the subtitle "unless the main title ends with a question mark or exclamation point."]

5. "INSTITUTIONAL" OR "ORGANIZATIONAL" AUTHORS

[*BB*] Criminal Justice Standards Comm., Am. Bar Ass'n, *ABA Standards for Criminal Justice Prosecution Function and Defense Function* **(3d ed. 1993).** [When no author is credited as in this example, "the smallest subdivision that prepared the work" should be cited, followed by the "overall body of which that subdivision is a part"; if there had been an individual author, that person's name would be used, followed by "only the largest institutional division, unless the smaller unit is particularly relevant"; the institutional author name may be abbreviated using the abbreviations set in **Appendix 1(A)-(B)** of this book, provided "the result will be completely unambiguous" (e.g., "Committee" to "**Comm.**," "American" to

"**Am.**," and "Association" to "**Ass'n**"; in other instances, "United States" should be abbreviated to
"**U.S.**," and (as with case names), "**Inc.**," "**Ltd.**," and
similar terms should be omitted if the name also
contains "**Ass'n**," "**Bros.**," "**Co.**," or "**Corp.**" indicating the institutional author is a business firm.]

[*ALWD*] ABA Crim. Just. Stands. Comm.,
Crim. Just. Sec., *ABA Standards for Criminal
Justice Prosecution Function and Defense
Function* (3d ed., ABA 1993). [The full name of the
organizational author should be given "as it appears
on the front page or title page"; abbreviations set out
in **Appendix 1** of this book or those used for law
journals set out in **Appendix 7** of this book may be
used for the institutional author, and prepositions
may be omitted if they are not needed for clarity (e.g.,
"Criminal" to "**Crim.**," "Justice" to "**Just.**," "Standards" to **Stands.**, "Committee" to "**Comm.**," "Section" to "**Sec.**," and "American Bar Association" to
"**ABA**"); if there had been an individual author in
addition to the organization, they would be cited
together as work with two authors.]

6. MULTIPLE VOLUMES

[*BB*] 5A Charles Alan Wright & Arthur R.
Miller, *Federal Practice and Procedure* § 1313,
at 367 (3d ed. 2004). [The volume number of a
multivolume work should be given at the beginning
of the citation; when a single volume of a multivolume work with varying authors for each volume
(as in this instance), use only the author or authors of

the volume that is being cited; the date of the actual volume cited is used.]

[*ALWD*] Charles Alan Wright & Arthur R. Miller, *Federal Practice and Procedure* **vol. 5A, § 1313, 367 (3d ed., West 2004).** [The volume number appears after the title, as shown above; the date of the actual volume cited is used; "**at**" may be inserted when the reader might be confused about which is the section number and which is the section number (e.g., **§ 1313, at 1367**].

7. EDITORS, TRANSLATORS, AND MULTIPLE PUBLISHERS

[*BB*] 4 *Thompson on Real Property* **§ 37.11(b) (David A. Thomas ed., 2d ed. 2004).** [The full name of the editor (**ed.**) should be identified in the parenthetical with the edition and date, as shown above; two or more editors are indicated by "**eds.**"; three or more editors can be indicated by giving the first, followed by "**et al.**" See **Appendix 1(E)**.]

[*ALWD*] *Thompson on Real Property* **vol. 4, § 37.11(b) (David A. Thomas ed., 2d ed., Matthew Bender & Co. 2004).** [The full name(s) of the editor ("**ed.**"), editors ("**eds.**") or translator ("**trans.**") or translators ("**trans.**") should be identified in the parenthetical with the edition and date, as shown above; if there is more than one publisher, all publishers should be cited. See **Appendix 1**.]

[*BB & ALWD*] Jean Bodin, *On Sovereignty* **11 (Julian H. Franklin ed. & trans., Cambridge**

Univ. Press 1992) (1576). [*The Bluebook* provides that pre-1900 works should be cited to a modern scholarly edition, if possible; when no modern citation is possible, then *The Bluebook* adds the place of publication and the name of the publisher, separated by a comma, before the date; the *ALWD Manual* provides that either the original or modern edition may be cited; the date of the original publication may be given in a separate parenthetical.]

8. COLLECTED WORKS

The format for collected works varies slightly depending on whether it is the collected works of a single author or several.

[*BB*] Robert M. Baum, *Compensating Defense Witnesses, in* **Criminal Justice Section, Am. Bar Ass'n,** *Ethical Problems Facing the Criminal Defense Lawyer* **311, 313 (Rodney J. Uphoff, ed., 1995).** [This citation is an example of a shorter work within a larger collection by several different authors; the page on which the shorter work begins should be given (i.e., **311**) and a reference to the specific material, if any (e.g., **313**); "*in*" is italicized.]

[*ALWD*] Robert M. Baum, *Compensating Defense Witnesses,* **in Crim. Just. Sec., Am. Bar Ass'n,** *Ethical Problems Facing the Criminal Defense Lawyer* **311, 313 (Rodney J. Uphoff, ed., ABA 1995).** [In *ALWD* citations, "**in**" is not italicized.]

[BB] 3 Oliver Wendell Holmes, *The Profession of the Law*, *in The Collected Works of Justice Holmes* 471, 472-73 (Sheldon M. Novick ed., 1995). [This citation is an example of a collection of a single author's works.]

[ALWD] Oliver Wendell Holmes, *The Profession of the Law*, *in The Collected Works of Justice Holmes* vol. 3, at 471 (Sheldon M. Novick ed., U. Chi. Press 1995).

9. WORKS IN A SERIES

[BB] Alan Scott, *Ideology and the New Social Movements* 103 (Controversies in Sociology Series No. 24, 1990). [When a book is part of a series issued by someone other than the author, the series and the number should be indicated parenthetically; institutional entities may be abbreviated.]

[ALWD] Alan Scott, *Ideology and the New Social Movements* 103 (Controversies in Sociology Series No. 24, Unwin Hyman 1990). [If the publisher's name is included in the series title, the name of the publisher should not be repeated; the series description may be abbreviated using the abbreviations set out in **Appendix 1** of this book.]

10. STAR EDITIONS

As indicated in Chapter 1(E)(1), Sir William Blackstone's *Commentaries on the Laws of England* (1765-1769) greatly influenced the development of the law in both England and the United States. It was reprinted often, but the original pagination was shown by means of "star" paging, using an asterisk (either in the text or the margin). Today, both *The Bluebook* and the *ALWD Manual* use a special form for this frequently cited work.

[BB] **William Blackstone, 4** *Commentaries* ***22.** [Multiple star pages are shown as *22-23.]

[ALWD] **William Blackstone,** *Commentaries* **vol. 4, *22.** [Multiple star pages are shown as **22-23.]

11. SPECIAL WORKS

In addition to Blackstone, *The Bluebook* provides special forms for a few works, most importantly: (1) *The Federalist* papers; (2) the *Manual for Complex Litigation*; (3) *The Bible*; and (4) William Shakespeare's plays. The *ALWD Manual* has its own list: (1) *The Bible*; (2) *The Koran*; and (3) *The Talmud*.

12. TYPEFACE

In citations in law journal articles, *The Bluebook* places the author and the title in large and small capital letters. The format varies for collected works, as illustrated below. In all other instances, the typeface shown above is used.

[BB Journal] **5A CHARLES ALAN WRIGHT & ARTHUR R. MILLER, FEDERAL PRACTICE AND PROCEDURE § 1313, at 367 (3d ed. 2004).**

[*BB* Journal] 3 Oliver Wendell Holmes, *The Profession of the Law*, *in* THE COLLECTED WORKS OF JUSTICE HOLMES 471, 472-73 (Sheldon M. Novick ed., 1995).

13. SHORT-FORM CITATIONS

The general use of short forms was discussed in Chapter 1(F)(3)(*k*) above. After a text or treatise has been fully cited, "*id.*" can be used to refer to the same work in an immediately following citation (e.g., *Id. or Id.* at 89-90 *or* [*BB*] *Id.* § 1313, at 367 *or* [*ALWD*] *Id.* § 1313, 367.) For shorter works in a collection, if the first citation refers only to a shorter work contained in the collection, "*id.*" should not be used to refer to the entire collection. Instead, "*supra*" should be used.

In *Bluebook* citations, the author's last name (or the full institutional author's name) is generally used with *supra* (e.g., **Wright & Miller**, *supra*, § 1313, at 367.) Note the same typeface is retained (e.g., in law journal citations, WRIGHT & MILLER, *supra*, § 1313, at 367.) In documents with footnotes, the note number is added (e.g., **Wright & Miller**, *supra* **note 24, § 1313, at 367.**)

In *ALWD* citations, the author's last name and the title are generally used (e.g., **Wright & Miller**, *Federal Practice and Procedure*, *supra*, § 1313, 367.) In documents with footnotes, the note number is added, but the title is omitted (e.g., **Wright & Miller**, *supra* **n. 24, § 1313, 367.**) A space is left between "**n.**" and the number.

B. DICTIONARIES

Dictionaries are cited like books, but many do not have identified authors or editors. The following are some examples of citations to dictionaries:

[BB] *Black's Law Dictionary* **892 (7th ed. 1999);** *Ballentine's Law Dictionary* **52 (3d ed. 1969);** *Webster's Third New International Dictionary* **1182 (1986).** [These above editions of *Black's* and *Ballentine's* do not have a named author or editor and are cited using a "special citation form."]

[ALWD] *Black's Law Dictionary* **402 (Bryan A. Garner ed., 8th ed., West 2004);** *Black's Law Dictionary* **892 (7th ed., West 1999);** *Webster's Ninth New Collegiate Dictionary* **937 (10th ed., Merriam-Webster 2000).**

In citations in law journal articles, *The Bluebook* places the citations of dictionaries in large and small capital letters.

[BB Journal] WEBSTER'S NEW TWENTIETH CENTURY DICTIONARY OF THE ENGLISH LANGUAGE **1035 (2d unabr. ed. 1979).** [Abbreviations for publishing terms such as "unabridged" are set out in **Appendix 1(E)** of this book.]

C. PERIODICALS

The basic format for citing articles in legal periodicals was set out in Chapter 1(E)(3) above. This section discusses a variety of additional considerations and special situations.

1. NAME OF THE AUTHOR AND MULTIPLE AUTHORS

The names of authors of articles in legal periodicals are cited in the same manner as books. In *Bluebook* citations, the full name of an author is given, including any designation such as "**Jr.**" or the "**III**" ("inserting a comma before the designation only if the author does"). "**Prof.**," "**Dr.**," and similar titles are not used. Similarly, in *ALWD* citations, the full name of an author is given exactly as it is given on the title page of the article. "**Jr.**" or the "**III**" are included, but not "degree information" or titles of respect (such as "**Hon.**").

[*BB & ALWD*] Larry L. Teply, *Antitrust Immunity of State and Local Governmental Action*, 48 Tul. L. Rev. 272 (1974). ["**Tul. L. Rev.**" is the abbreviation of the *Tulane Law Review*.]

Two authors are listed in the order in which they appear on the title page, separated by an ampersand.

[*BB & ALWD*] Nancy W. Perry & Larry L. Teply, *Interviewing, Counseling, and In-Court Examination of Children: Practical Approaches for Attorneys*, 18 Creighton L. Rev. 1369 (1985).

In *Bluebook* citations, when an article has three or more authors and "saving space is desired" and in short forms, the name of the first author is used followed by "**et al.**" to indicate "and others." However, all the names of the authors can be given, and they should be given "when doing so is particularly relevant." In *ALWD* citations, the *ALWD Manual* provides the option of including all of the authors' names or using the "**et al.**" form.

[*BB* & *ALWD*] Catherine M. Brooks et al., ***Child Abuse and Neglect Reporting Laws: Understanding Interests, Understanding Policy,* 12 Behav. Sci. & L. 49 (1994) or Catherine M. Brooks, Nancy W. Perry, Stephen D. Starr & Larry L. Teply,** ***Child Abuse and Neglect Reporting Laws: Understanding Interests, Understanding Policy,* 12 Behav. Sci. & L. 49 (1994).** ["**Behav. Sci. & L.**" is the abbreviation for *Behavioral Sciences and the Law*.]

2. ABBREVIATED NAME OF THE JOURNAL

The abbreviated name of the journal is used in the citation. In some instances, as shown in **Appendix 7** of this book, *The Bluebook* and *ALWD* abbreviations are the same. However, there are many minor differences, as illustrated in the following two examples:

[*BB*] Ralph H. Folsom & Larry L. Teply, *A Comparative View of the Law of Trademarked Generic Words,* **6 Hastings Int'l & Comp. L. Rev. 1 (1982).** ["**Int'l**" is the abbreviation for "International"; the journal is the *Hastings International and Comparative Law Review*.]

[*ALWD*] Ralph H. Folsom & Larry L. Teply, *A Comparative View of the Law of Trademarked Generic Words*, 6 Hastings Intl. & Comp. L. Rev. 1 (1982). ["Intl." is the abbreviation for "International."]

If an article appears in multiple sources, the "**reprinted in**" format can be used, as shown below.

[*BB*] Ralph H. Folsom & Larry L. Teply, *Trademarked Generic Words*, 89 Yale L.J. 1323 (1980), *reprinted in* 70 Trademark Rep. 243 (1980) & 1 Nat'l L. Rev. Rep. 765 (1981). [The journals are the *Yale Law Journal*, the *Trademark Reporter*, and the *National Law Review Reporter*.]

[*ALWD*] Ralph H. Folsom & Larry L. Teply, *Trademarked Generic Words*, 89 Yale L.J. 1323 (1980) (reprinted in 70 Trademark Rep. 243 (1980) & 1 Natl. L. Rev. Rep. 765 (1981)).

The same approach can be taken for other "related authority," such as reviews, translations, microfilmed versions, etc.

[*BB*] Larry L. Teply, *Antitrust Immunity of State and Local Governmental Action*, 48 Tul. L. Rev. 272 (1974), *reviewed at Journey to the No Man's Land of Antitrust Immunity*, 60 A.B.A. J. 864 (1974). ["Tul. L. Rev." is the abbreviation for *Tulane Law Review* and "A.B.A. J." is *The Bluebook's* abbreviation for the American Bar Association's *ABA Journal*.]

[*ALWD*] Larry L. Teply, *Antitrust Immunity of State and Local Governmental Action*, 48 Tul. L. Rev. 272 (1974) (reviewed at *Journey to the No Man's Land of Antitrust Immunity*, 60 ABA J. 864 (1974)). [ABA J. is the *ALWD Manual's* abbreviation for the American Bar Association's *ABA Journal*.]

3. STUDENT WORKS

Law journals contain a variety of student-authored works. These works are designated by a wide variety of names, including "**Note**," "**Comment**," "**Project**," "**Commentary**," "**Recent Development**," "**Case Note**," "**Recent Case**," etc. The name of the student is sometimes given on the first page of the work, on the last page, or in the table of contents.

In general, student-authored works are cited in the same manner as articles written by authors who are not students, as illustrated in the examples above. To distinguish them, the *ALWD Manual* inserts the words, "**Student Author(s)**," after the student author's name, set off by commas, before the title. In contrast, *The Bluebook* inserts the description of the student work (e.g., "**Commentary**") after the student author's name, set off by commas, before the title.

[*BB*] **Larry L. Teply & Richard L. Williams, Commentary,** *Interruption of User: A Prescription for Prescription*, **25 U. Fla. L. Rev. 204 (1973).** [The journal is the *University of Florida Law Review*.]

[*ALWD*] Larry Teply & Martin Kessler, Student Authors, *Jetport: Planning and Politics in the Big Cypress Swamp*, 25 U. Miami L. Rev. 713 (1971). [The journal is the *University of Miami Law Review.*]

With regard to shorter comments or notes on recent cases, recent statutes, or other recent developments, *The Bluebook* indicates that a "digest-like heading" should be omitted. Instead, the work should be cited by the author's name, followed by the designation of the work (e.g., **Case Comment**, etc.).

[*BB*] Larry L. Teply, Case Comment, *Excess Liability: Judicial Creation of Direct Action Against Liability Insurers*, 24 U. Fla. L. Rev. 572 (1972).

Unsigned student works begin with [*ALWD*] "**Student Author**" or [*BB*] the appropriate designation (e.g., "**Note**," "**Comment**," etc.). *The Bluebook* specifically notes that student works signed only with initials are treated as unsigned works. When no separable designation has been made, italicize the entire title.

[*BB*] Note, *Foreign Affairs Preemption and State Regulation of Greenhouse Gas Emissions*, 119 Harv. L. Rev. 1877 (2006).

[*BB*] *Developments in the Law—International Criminal Law*, 114 Harv. L. Rev. 1943 (2001).

4. SEPARATELY PAGINATED ISSUES

Some law journals and other periodicals (such as magazines) are paginated separately within each issue. In such as case, *The Bluebook* provides that "[full] date of issue as it appears on the cover" should be cited. The beginning page is introduced with "**at**." If no author is listed, the citation should begin with the title. Months are abbreviated as shown in **Appendix 1(C)** of this book.

[BB] Larry L. Teply, *Client Counseling Competition: Lou Brown's "Baby" Goes International to Spread the Message of Preventive Law*, 11 **Preventive L. Rep., June 1992, at 39.** [The journal is the *Preventive Law Reporter*.]

[BB] Daniel A. Martinez, Jennifer Tanck & Alyson George, *E-Discovery Primer: New Rules, New Trends*, Trial Advoc. Q., Summer 2007, at 10, 12-16 *or* Daniel A. Martinez et al., *E-Discovery Primer: New Rules, New Trends*, Trial Advoc. Q., Summer 2007, at 10, 12-16.

The *ALWD Manual* follows a similar rule, but it places the date in a parenthetical (e.g., **Jan. 31, 2008**). In addition, it does not use "**at**" to introduce the page number. Furthermore, it specifically notes if the periodical does not contain a date, the issue number should be inserted before the year (e.g., **No. 1, 2008**). Months are abbreviated as shown in **Appendix 1(C)** of this book.

[*ALWD*] **Daniel A. Martinez, Jennifer Tanck & Alyson George,** *E-Discovery Primer: New Rules, New Trends,* **23 Tr. Advoc. Q. 10, 12-16 (Summer 2007)** *or* **Daniel A. Martinez et al.,** *E-Discovery Primer: New Rules, New Trends,* **23 Tr. Advoc. Q. 10, 12-16 (Summer 2007).** [Note the *Trial Advocacy Quarterly* is abbreviated differently in *The Bluebook* and the *ALWD* citations.]

[*ALWD*] **Larry L. Teply,** *Client Counseling Competition: Lou Brown's "Baby" Goes International to Spread the Message of Preventive Law,* **11 Preventive L. Rep. 39 (June 1992).**

5. SYMPOSIA, COLLOQUIA, AND SURVEYS

When symposia, colloquia, and surveys are cited as a unit, *The Bluebook* and the *ALWD Manual* provide that the appropriate designation should be cited. The first page should be the cited page. *The Bluebook* adds that the designation can be omitted if "it is made clear by the title."

[*BB*] **Symposium,** *Elder Law Across the Curriculum,* **30 Stetson L. Rev. 1265 (2001).**

As specifically noted by *The Bluebook*, articles within a symposium, colloquium, or survey should be cited "in the same manner as any other article."

[*BB & ALWD*] **Larry L. Teply,** *The Elderly and Civil Procedure: Service and Default, Capacity Issues, Preserving and Giving Testimony, and*

Compulsory Physical or Mental Examinations,
30 Stetson L. Rev. 1273 (2001).

However, if it "is part of a survey of the law of one jurisdiction, the title of the article should incorporate the title of the survey."

6. BOOK REVIEWS

For *ALWD* citations, book reviews are cited like any other article. If the review does not have a title, the designation in the journal should be used (e.g., "**Book Review**"). The title of the book being reviewed can be given parenthetically.

[*ALWD*] Yale Kamisar, *Book Review,* **78 Harv. L. Rev. 478 (1964) (reviewing** *Gideon's Trumpet***).**

For *Bluebook* citations, book reviews are cited by the full name of the reviewer and title of the review. If it is not clear from the title of the review, the author, title, and publication date of the book reviewed is given in a second parenthetical. If it is, simply indicate "**book review**" in the second parenthetical. Student-authored book reviews are cited as "**Book Note**" even if it is designated in the journal in some other way. Unsigned book reviews are cited in the manner of other unsigned student works, as illustrated below.

[*BB*] Michael Sullivan & Daniel J. Solove, *Can Pragmatism Be Radical? Richard Posner and Legal Pragmatism,* **113 Yale L.J. 687, 714 (2003) (book review).**

[*BB*] Book Note, *Getting to Fair Trade for All*, 119 Harv. L. Rev. 2252 (2006) (reviewing Joseph E. Stiglitz, *Fair Trade for All: How Trade Can Promote Development* (2005)).

7. MULTIPART ARTICLES

Some articles are published in parts. To cite an entire article published in this way in *Bluebook* or *ALWD* form, the parts should be identified in parentheses at the end of the main title of the article, followed by the publication information for each part.

[*BB* & *ALWD*] Roscoe Pound, *The Scope and Purpose of Sociological Jurisprudence* (pts. 1-3), 24 Harv. L. Rev. 591 (1911), 25 Harv. L. Rev. 140 (1912), 25 Harv. L. Rev. 489 (1912).

The Bluebook uses a shortened form if all the parts appear in a single volume.

[*BB*] Vern Countryman, *The Use of State Law in Bankruptcy Cases* (pts. 1 & 2), 47 N.Y.U. L. Rev. 407, 631 (1972).

A specific part would be cited as follows:

[*BB* & *ALWD*] Roscoe Pound, *The Scope and Purpose of Sociological Jurisprudence* (pt. 2), 25 Harv. L. Rev. 140 (1912).

8. TYPEFACE

As indicated above, titles of articles are shown in italics. However, if the title contains information that would be in italics if it appeared in text (such as case names), that information should not be in italics.

[*BB* & *ALWD*] **Curtis A. Bradley, Jack L. Goldsmith & David H. Moore, Sosa,** *Customary International Law, and the Continuing Relevance of* **Erie, 120 Harv. L. Rev. 869 (2007)** *or* **Curtis A. Bradley et al., Sosa,** *Customary International Law, and the Continuing Relevance of* **Erie, 120 Harv. L. Rev. 869 (2007).** [The references to the *Sosa* and *Erie* cases appear in ordinary Roman type in the title.]

In law journal citations, *The Bluebook* places the abbreviated name of the periodical in large and small capital letters.

[*BB* **Journal] Ralph H. Folsom & Larry L. Teply,** *Surveying "Genericness in Trademark Litigation,* **70 Trademark Rep. 243, 250 (1982).**

9. SHORT-FORM CITATIONS

In most respects, the same rules regarding short-form citations for books discussed in section A(13) of this chapter are used for periodicals. As noted there and in Chapter 1(F)(3)(*l*) , after an article in a periodical has been fully cited, *"id."* can be used to refer to the same work in an immediately following citation (e.g., *Id. or Id.* **at 252.**).

In *Bluebook* citations, the author's last name is generally used with *supra* (e.g., **Kamisar,** *supra,* **at 479.**) If there is no author, then the title of the work is used (e.g., **Book Note,** *supra,* **at 2254.**) In documents with footnotes, the note number is added (e.g., **Kamisar,** *supra* **note 18, at 479.**).

In *ALWD* citations, in documents without footnotes, the author's last name is used along with volume number, periodical abbreviation, and pinpoint reference(s) (e.g., **Pound, 25 Harv. L. Rev. at 148.**). In documents with footnotes, the note number is used (e.g., **Pound,** *supra* **n. 197, at 148.**). A space is left between "**n.**" and the number.

D. NEWSPAPERS

In general, newspaper articles are cited like nonconsecutively paginated periodicals discussed in the preceding section, but with several modifications.

1. NEWS ARTICLES

Compared to the *ALWD Manual*, *The Bluebook* has more specific rules oriented to citing news articles. In contrast, the *ALWD Manual* primarily relies on the general periodical rules for this purpose. See **Appendix 7** of this book. *The Bluebook* cites news articles in nonconsecutively paginated newspapers as follows:

(1) the full name of the author (if any) (cited in the manner that it would be for a periodical, as discussed and illustrated in section C(1) of this chapter);

(2) the title of the article (in italics);

(3) the abbreviated name of the newspaper (adding the place of publication if it is not clear from the name of the newspaper);

(4) the exact date (month/day/year) (to the extent that it is given);

(5) the section (if any); and

(6) the page as needed ([*BB*] preceded by **at**).

Consecutively paginated newspapers are cited by volume number and page. The following examples illustrate how this format works. Examples of *ALWD* citations are also provided.

[*BB*] Felicity Barringer & Andrew C. Revkin, *Measures on Global Warming Move to Spotlight in the New Congress*, N.Y. Times, Jan. 18, 2007, at A24.

[*BB*] Hamil R. Harris & Michael Abramowitz, *Bush Signs Voting Rights Act Extension*, Wash. Post, July 28, 2006, at A3.

[*BB*] Frances Gibb, *Libel Ruling Heralds New Era for British Investigative Journalism*, Times (London), Oct. 12, 2006, at 16.

[*ALWD*] Kaja Whitehouse, *Beneficiary Designation Form Is Key to Passing on Your Assets*, Wall St. J. D3 (June 4, 2002).

[*ALWD*] Wes Smith, *Airboat Wars: Yuppies vs. Crackers in High-Decibel Showdown*, Orlando Sent. A1 (June 26, 2005).

[*ALWD*] Eric Lichtblau, *F.B.I. Abandons Disputed Test for Bullets from Crime Scenes*, N.Y. Times A12 (Sept. 2, 2005).

2. EDITORIALS, OP-ED. PIECES, AND LETTERS TO THE EDITOR

Editorials, op-ed pieces, and letters to the editors are specially identified as shown below. Again, the format varies between *The Bluebook* and the *ALWD Manual*.

[*BB*] Mary Ann Glendon, Op-Ed., *Judicial Tourism*, Wall St. J., Sept. 16, 2005, at A14.

[*BB*] Carl B. Feldbaum, Letter to the Editor, *A Lincolnesque Moment*, S.F. Chron., June 5, 2004, at B8.

[*ALWD*] Rhonda Chriss Lokeman, Editorial, *Public Housing Problems Persist*, Kan. City Star C6 (July 8, 1993).

[*ALWD*] Shari Sendman, Ltr. to the Ed., *Police Lineups and Eyewitnesses*, N.Y. Times A18 (Apr. 24, 2006).

3. TYPEFACE

Titles of articles are shown in italics. However, if the title contains information that would be in italics if it appeared in text (such as case names) should not be in italics. In citations in law journal articles, *The Bluebook* places the abbreviated name of the periodical in large and small capital letters.

[*BB* Journal] Peter Wong, *High Court Upholds Measure 37*, STATESMAN J. (Salem, Or.), Feb. 22, 2006, at 1A. [The place of publication was added because it is not clear from the name of the newspaper.]

E. LEGAL ENCYCLOPEDIAS

The format for citing legal encyclopedias was discussed in Chapter 1(E)(3). The *ALWD Manual* specifically points out that the complete name of the topic or title name should be used and it should not be abbreviated. Titles of individual subdivisions are not cited. The topic or title is shown in italics.

[*BB* & *ALWD*] 90 C.J.S. *Trover and Conversion* § 96 (2002).

In citations in law journal articles, *The Bluebook* places the abbreviated name of the legal encyclopedia in large and small capital letters.

[*BB* Journal] 4 AM. JUR. 2D *Alteration of Instruments* § 57 (2007). [To cite a specific material within a section that covers more than one page, *The Bluebook* uses the "**at**" form (e.g., **§ 57, at 47**).]

F. RESTATEMENTS OF THE LAW

Citation of restatements of the law was discussed in Chapter 1(E)(4). *The Bluebook* provides for abbreviations of restatement titles and subtitles using the abbreviations set out in **Appendix 1(A)** of this book. In addition, **Appendix 1(D)** of this book contains a list of abbreviations for subdivisions used in citations. In particular, the following are frequently used:

Comment(s) = **cmt., cmts.** [*BB* & *ALWD*]
Illustration(s) = **illus.** [*BB*] **illus.,** [*ALWD*] **illuss.**

As pointed out in Chapter 1, the typeface differs in citations of restatements. In addition, a third typeface is used in citations in law journal articles. These differences are illustrated below:

[*BB*] **Restatement (Third) of Prop.: Servitudes § 2.17 cmt. i, illus. 31-34 (2000).**

[*ALWD*] *Restatement (Third) of Property: Servitudes* § **2.17 cmt. i, illuss. 31-34 (2000).** [Unlike *The Bluebook*, "**illus.**" only covers the singular in *ALWD* citations, and the plural abbreviation is formed by adding an "**s**" to "**illus.**"]

[*BB* **Journal**] RESTATEMENT (THIRD) OF PROP.: SERVITUDES § **2.17 cmt. i, illus. 31-34 (2000).**

G. *A.L.R.* ANNOTATIONS

Chapter 1(E)(5) set out the format for citing *A.L.R.* annotations. Additional illustrations are given below.

[*BB*] **William M. Howard, Annotation,** *Statute of Limitations Under Federal Arbitration Act on Filing of Motion to Confirm Award,* **3 A.L.R. Fed. 2d 419 (2005).** [Because "**under**" is a preposition with more than four letters, it is capitalized. See Chapter 1(F)(3)(*m*) above.]

[*ALWD*] **William M. Howard,** *Statute of Limitations under Federal Arbitration Act on Filing of Motion to Confirm Award,* **3 A.L.R. Fed. 2d 419**

(2005). [Because "**under**" is a preposition, it is not capitalized. See Chapter 1(F)(3)(*m*) above.]

Some early annotations are unsigned. Citations to those annotations follow the same format as signed ones (but, of course, no author is given).

[*BB*] Annotation, *Effect of Unauthorized Delivery or Fraudulent Procurement of Escrow on Title or Interest in Property,* **48 A.L.R. 405 (1927).**

[*ALWD*] *Effect of Unauthorized Delivery or Fraudulent Procurement of Escrow on Title or Interest in Property,* **48 A.L.R. 405 (1927).**

In citations in law journal articles, *The Bluebook* places the abbreviated name of the annotation in large and small capital letters.

[*BB* Journal] William M. Howard, Annotation, *Statute of Limitations Under Federal Arbitration Act on Filing of Motion to Confirm Award,* **3 A.L.R. FED. 2D 419 (2005).**

H. LOOSELEAF SERVICES

Citation of cases reported in special-subject (often looseleaf) services has been discussed in Chapter 2(C)(2)(*i*). Material other than cases also appears in looseleaf services. A typical citation to such material is shown below:

[*BB* & *ALWD*] A.A. Sommer, Jr., *"Going Private": A Lesson in Corporate Responsibility,*

[1974-1975 Transfer Binder] Sec. Reg. & L. Rep. (BNA) No. 278, at D-3 (Nov. 20, 1974). [See also **Appendix 8** of this book.]

I. INTERNET SOURCES

1. DESIRABILITY OF CITATION

The generally accepted view is that a traditional print source or a widely available commercial database (such as Westlaw and Lexis) should be cited in preference to Internet sources. With regard to cases, the *ALWD Manual* is specific: "Do not cite the Internet if the case is available in a reporter, an online database such as Westlaw or LexisNexis, or a looseleaf service." *The Bluebook* has a similar strong preference for print sources. Thus, it would be extremely rare that a case would be cited to the Internet (and even then a public domain or neutral citation is likely to be used). This same preference for print sources carries over to secondary sources. The fundamental underlying reason is that Internet sites and web pages can change frequently.

2. ELECTRONIC ADDRESSES

The key to finding items on the Internet is the Uniform Resource Locator ("URL"). For example, the electronic home page of Federal Trade Commission is **http://www.ftc.gov/**. However, it is preferable that the reference point the reader directly to the resource cited. If multiple URLs exist, only one should be cited.

The Bluebook adds that the primary URL should be used rather than links to an alternate server.

In general, it is important to give the reader as much help as possible with regard to the ability to find the web site from the information given. The safest approach is simply to paste the entire URL from the browser window into the draft of the document that is being prepared. The *ALWD Manual* suggests removing the automatic underlining of the URL unless the document is being submitted electronically and the hyperlink would be easy for the reader to use.

Unfortunately, many URLs are often unwieldy. The *ALWD Manual* aptly suggests that a URL should be broken "at a logical point, preferably after a slash [or] *before* a period." In addition, remember that the URL is often case sensitive and that inserting a hyphen into a URL is likely to cause difficulties in retrieving the web page because it may look as if it is part of the web address.

Even if the full web address is given, however, that still might not be sufficient to lead the reader to the relevant page. It may turn out better to give the reader a shorter name and to identify the keystrokes. *The Bluebook* suggests using a parenthetical after identifying the root URL explaining how to access the information. Instead of using a parenthetical, the *ALWD Manual* indicates that a semicolon after the URL, followed by the keystroke identifiers in italics (e.g., ***search***, ***select***, **drop-down menu**, etc.) and the relevant keystrokes.

3. DOCUMENT FORMAT

The Bluebook explicitly prefers the citation of a format that preserves the original pagination and other features of the printed work (e.g., Adobe's portable document format or "PDF") over the HTML format when there is a choice between the two.

4. "AVAILABLE AT" PARALLEL CITATIONS

When the source exists in print form, but it is not widely available, *The Bluebook* indicates that "a parallel citation may be provided if it will substantially improve access to the source cited." *The Bluebook* uses the explanatory phrase "*available at*" to introduce the Internet citation. The *ALWD Manual* places this information in a parenthetical. The following citations illustrate these formats:

[*BB*] Cass R. Sunstein, *Second-Order Perfectionism* (Univ. of Chi. John M. Olin Law & Econ. Working Paper No. 319, 2006), *available at* http://ssrn.com/abstract=948788.

[*ALWD*] U.S. Dept. of Just., *Forensic Sciences: Review of Status and Needs* 4 (Feb. 1999) (available at http://www.ncjrs.gov/pdffiles1/173412 .pdf).

5. "DIRECT" CITATIONS TO INTERNET SOURCES

The Bluebook provides that if a resource "is unavailable in a traditional printed format [n]or on a widely available commercial database," then an Internet source may be cited. The *ALWD Manual* is more liberal in a few instances. For example, as noted in Chapter 3(D) above, it specifically permits the complete substitution of an Internet citation for a bound treaty source (as opposed to a parallel citation). The better approach, however, is to use the **"available at"** parallel citation, if possible.

Direct Internet citations must include a date. *The Bluebook* indicates that the date should be formatted analogously to that given for printed materials. If the web page or document "has no close print analogue, it should be treated as an unpublished source and the date should be provided as it appears on the Internet site." *The Bluebook* notes that the date used should be related to the material cited, not the "last updated," "last modified," or "copyright designations" referring to the entire site. If such a date is not available, then the date on which the web site was "last visited" should be indicated parenthetically after the URL. The following are examples:

[BB] Jonathan W. Emord, *Contrived Distinctions: The Doctrine of Commercial Speech in First Amendment Jurisprudence*, Cato Institute Policy Analysis No. 161, Sept. 23, 1991, http://www.cato.org/pubs/pas/pa-161.html.

[*BB*] **James M. Anderson,** *The Missing Theory of Variable Selection in the Economic Analysis of Tort Law* **3 (Aug. 1, 2006), http://ssrn.com/abstract=921767.**

[*BB*] **Int'l Criminal Court, Establishment of the Court, http://www.icc-cpi.int/about/ataglance/establishment.html (last visited Apr. 6, 2007).**

The *ALWD Manual* sets out the following preferences: (1) "[t]he exact date [month-day-year] of the document being cited"; (2) "[t]he exact date of the document being cited, followed by the specific time of the cited posting" (used for news articles updated over time); (3) "[t]he date on which the site was last updated or modified"; and (4) "[t]he date on which [it was] accessed." The following are examples of direct *ALWD* citations to the Internet:

[*ALWD*] **Carl Haub, Global and U.S. National Population Trends, tbl. 4, http:// www. gcrio .org/CONSEQUENCES/summer95/table4.html (updated Nov. 11, 2004).**

[*ALWD*] **World Bank, Data Collection Methods, http:// www1.worldbank.org/prem/poverty/ impact/methods/datacoll.htm (last updated Sept. 12, 2002).**

[*ALWD*] **U.S. Conf. Mayors,** *Hunger Homelessness Survey Summary: January 10, 2005*, **http:// www.usmayors.org/uscm/us_mayor_newspaper/ documents/01_10_05/hunger_survey.asp (accessed Dec. 29, 2006).**

J. PRACTITIONER AND COURT DOCUMENTS, TRANSCRIPTS, AND APPELLATE RECORDS

In legal writing, references sometimes are made to court documents. In published legal writing, *The Bluebook* provides that the full name of the document (as it appears on the filing) should be identified first, followed a pinpoint citation (if any). If an opinion has been published in the case, the ordinary citation to the case is used, followed by the docket number. Most often, a citation to an electronic database is then given. The following are examples:

[*BB*] Brief for Petitioner, N.Y. Times Co., at 31, *N.Y. Times Co. v. United States*, 403 U.S. 713 (1971) (Nos. 1873, 1885), 1971 WL 134368.

[*BB*] Reply Brief for Petitioners at 4, *Stenberg v. Carhart*, 530 U.S. 914 (2000) (No. 990-830), 2000 WL 432363.

[*BB*] Complaint at 20-25, *El-Masri v. Tenet*, 437 F. Supp. 2d 530 (E.D. Va. 2006) (No. 1:05-cv-01417).

[*BB*] Petition for Writ of Habeas Corpus at 2, 16, *Omar v. Harvey*, 416 F. Supp. 2d 19 (D.D.C. 2006) (No. Civ. A 05-2374 RMU).

The *ALWD Manual* use a similar pattern, inserting the "title of the document [shown] on the front cover, followed by [any] pinpoint reference[, and then] a citation to the case to which it relates." The abbreviations set out in **Appendix 1** and **Appendix 12** of

the book are used in the title. The following is an
example of this pattern:

**[*ALWD*] Respt.'s Br. on Merits at 25, *Town of
Castle Rock v. Gonzales*, 545 U.S. 748 (2005).**

In documents submitted to a court (as opposed to
published legal writing) such as complaints, answers,
motions, briefs, memoranda of law, interrogatories,
disclosures, affidavits, stipulations, transcripts,
orders, judgments, etc., it is common practice to
abbreviate references to these documents. The basic
components of a citation to these documents are (1)
the name of the document; (2) the jump or pinpoint
reference; and (3) the date.

The Bluebook indicates that the date should be
given for references to the following: (1) depositions;
(2) hearing and trial transcripts; (3) judgments or
orders; (4) two or more documents bear the same
name; or (5) the date is significant or needed to avoid
confusion. In addition, local court rules must be
complied with at all times. Abbreviations for documents are found in **Appendix 12** of this book.
Articles and prepositions may be eliminated when
they are not needed for clarity. The following are
some examples:

[*BB*] Compl. ¶ 57.

[*BB*] Petr's Br. 12.

[*BB*] Def.'s Mem. Supp. Mot. Dismiss 16.

[*BB*] Pl.'s. Aff. ¶ 2 (Jan. 6, 2008).

[*BB*] R. at 16.

The *ALWD Manual* points out that some lawyers prefer not to abbreviate the name of a court document when it is initially cited. Otherwise, abbreviations may be used in every instance unless a local court rule provides differently. The abbreviations are set out in **Appendix 1** and **Appendix 12** of this book.

For all documents other than the record, the *ALWD Manual* requires a date. The date is (1) the filing date (abbreviated month/day/year) for documents filed with the court or (2) the exact date of service (abbreviated month/day/year) for documents served on the opposing lawyer(s) but were not filed with the court. Otherwise, the *ALWD Manual* uses the exact date on which the document was prepared. If no date can be determined, then "**n.d.**" is used for "no date." The following are some examples:

[*ALWD*] **Def.'s Answer ¶ 2 (Jan. 15, 2008).**

[*ALWD*] **Pl.'s Interrog. No. 4 (Nov. 12, 2007).**

[*ALWD*] **Def.'s Memo. Support Motion Dismiss 16 (Feb. 10, 2007).**

[*ALWD*] **Resp.'s. Br. 12 (July 8, 2007).**

[*ALWD*] **R. 8** *or* **R. at 8** *or* **R. 8)** *or* **(R. at 8)** *or* **[R. 8]** *or* **[R. at 8.]**

To indicate a line number in a transcript or record, the page number is used, followed by a colon, and then the line number (e.g., **8:4** is a reference to line 4 on page 8). In absence of court rules that provide otherwise, the *ALWD Manual* recommends that the entire citation be put in bold typeface or in parentheses, or both, in a memorandum, brief, or similar document to facilitate the reader's easy identification of the source.

Finally, short-citations are not ordinarily used for record citations, but short citations can be used for other documents once they have been fully cited.

K. UNPUBLISHED, UNREPORTED, VACATED, AND DEPUBLISHED OPINIONS

1. UNPUBLISHED OPINIONS

As noted in the discussion of the *Federal Appendix* in Chapter 2(C)(2)(*h*), it has become common practice for courts to designate certain opinions as "unpublished" or "not for publication." Traditionally, court rules have prohibited citation of these unpublished opinions or using them as precedent in the courts of the jurisdiction in which they originate (except for the limited purpose of supporting an assertion of claim preclusion, issue preclusion, or law of the case.) In other words, such opinions bind only the particular parties before the court in which they are issued.

The prohibition of citing unpublished opinions has attracted an enormous amount of scholarship criticizing these "no citation" rules as well as debate among judges themselves. The trend is now clearly toward allowing citation of unpublished decisions. In 2006, Federal Rule of Appellate Procedure 32.1 was adopted. It requires all federal appellate courts to allow citation of unpublished federal judicial opinions issued on or after January 1, 2007. The rule further provides that if a party cites an unreported opinion or order that is unavailable in a publicly accessible electronic database, a copy of that opinion or order must be filed with the court and served on the other parties.

In response, the four federal circuits absolutely prohibiting citations of unpublished opinions have revised their local rules to comply with the new rule. However, these circuits still prohibit citation of unpublished opinions issued prior to January 1, 2007, and all unpublished opinions, regardless of the date of issuance, remain non-precedential. The nine circuits that allowed citation of unpublished opinions prior to Federal Rule 32.1 have modified their rules so as to fully comply with the new federal rule, but appear to otherwise continue prior practices.

State courts have also continued to struggle with the issue of citing unpublished opinions. Virtually all states have addressed this issue through court rules, statutes, or court decisions. About half of the states still prohibit citation of unpublished opinions, but the trend among the states is likewise to allow citation of unpublished opinions as persuasive precedents.

Given the state of flux on the issue of citing unpublished opinions, care must be taken not to violate a court rule. Thus, when submitting a document (such as an appellate brief or a memorandum in support of a motion) to a court, the applicable rules concerning the citation of unpublished opinions must be checked.

When unpublished opinions are cited in permissible contexts, that fact should be noted parenthetically or textually.

[BB] ***United States v. Paul*, No. 06-30506, 2007 WL 2384234 (9th Cir. Aug. 17, 2007) (unpublished opinion).**

In a public domain citation of an unpublished decision, *The Bluebook* adds a capital "U" after the chronological accession number to indicate that the opinion is unpublished. However, some jurisdictions use a "N" (noncitable/unpublished) for this purpose:

[BB] ***Poindexter v. Kagan*, 2000 WI App 233U.**

***State v. Kallowat*, 2000 MT 354N.**

2. "UNREPORTED" OPINIONS

In contrast to opinions specifically designated "not for publication," a wealth of other "unreported" opinions are available through WESTLAW, LEXIS, looseleaf services, legal newspapers, and the internet. For example, only a small portion of federal district court opinions are selected for publication in the *Federal Supplement* or one of the other specialized reporters in the National Reporter System.

Unreported opinions can be especially helpful when they (1) state explicitly what reported cases have stated only implicitly, (2) make a point vividly because of the particular facts, (3) engage in a cogent analysis, or (4) are the only authority available.

3. "DEPUBLISHED" OPINIONS

In addition to being careful with regard to un-published opinions, care must be taken not to cite an opinion that has been "depublished." Typically, a depublished opinion will involve an intermediate appellate court opinion that a higher court has stricken from the official reports, usually as part of a denial of review (often without a reported order). The fact of depublication should be noted parenthetically and, if an order has been reported, it should be indicated as subsequent history:

[BB] *Hernandez v. Hillsides, Inc.*, **48 Cal. Rptr. 3d 780 (Cal. App. 2006),** *depublished by* **53 Cal. Rptr. 3d 801 (2007).**

4. VACATED OPINIONS

An opinion is often "vacated" by a higher court as a result of appellate review and an order of reversal. Again, one must be careful not to inadvertently cited an opinion that has been vacated. Such an opinion is said to have "no precedential value, and for all intents and purposes [it] never existed." Interestingly, however, an opinion vacated on one ground may be regarded as remaining persuasive as to other, nonvacated grounds.

*

APPENDIX 1

CASE NAME AND OTHER ABBREVIATIONS

<u>GENERAL INSTRUCTIONS</u>:

For *Bluebook* abbreviations of case names, use Appendix 1(A) and (B) below.

For *ALWD* abbreviations, use Appendix 1(A)-(E) below.

A. *BLUEBOOK* "CASE NAME" ABBREVIATIONS AND *ALWD* "GENERAL ABBREVIATIONS"

ALWD = *ALWD Citation Manual*
BB = *Bluebook*

Unless otherwise indicated below, the *ALWD* and *BB* abbreviations are the same.

Unless otherwise indicated below, plurals are formed by adding the letter "s" to the abbreviation.

WORD OR PHRASE IN SOURCE	ABBREVIATION (IF ANY)
Academy	Acad.
Accounting	Acctg. [*ALWD*]
Acquisition	Acq. [*ALWD*]
Administration	Admin. [*BB*]
Administrative	Admin.

WORD OR PHRASE IN SOURCE	ABBREVIATION (IF ANY)
Administrative Law Judge	A.L.J. [*ALWD*]
Administrator	Adm'r [*BB*]
	Adminstr. [*ALWD*]
Administratrix	Adm'x [*BB*]
	Admx. [*ALWD*]
Admiralty	Admir. [*ALWD*]
Admission	Admis. [*ALWD*]
Advance	Adv. [*ALWD*]
Advanced	Adv. [*ALWD*]
Advertising	Adver. [*BB*]
	Advert. [*ALWD*]
Advocate	Advoc. [*ALWD*]
Advocacy	Advoc. [*ALWD*]
Affidavit	Aff. [*ALWD*]
Against [in case name]	v.
Agriculture	Agric.
Agricultural	Agric.
Air Force	A.F. [*ALWD*]
Alcoholic Beverage	Alcoh. Bev. [*ALWD*]
Alternative	Alt. [*ALWD*]
Alternative Dispute Resolution	ADR [*ALWD*]
Ambulance	Ambul. [*ALWD*]
Amended	Amend. [*ALWD*]
Amendment	Amend. [*ALWD*]
America	Am.
American	Am.
American Bar Association	ABA [*ALWD*]
American Law Institute	ALI [*ALWD*]
Amusement	Amuse. [*ALWD*]
And [and]	&
Annotated	Ann. [*ALWD*]
Answer	Ans. [*ALWD*]

WORD OR PHRASE IN SOURCE	ABBREVIATION (IF ANY)
Answers	Ans. *[ALWD]*
Apartment	Apt. *[ALWD]*
Appeal	App. *[ALWD]*
Appellate	App. *[ALWD]*
Arbitrator	Arb. *[ALWD]*
Arbitration	Arb. *[ALWD]*
Assistant	Asst. *[ALWD]*
Associate	Assoc.
Association	Ass'n *[BB]*
	Assn. *[ALWD]*
Association of Legal Writing Directors	ALWD *[ALWD]*
Atlantic	Atl. *[BB]*
	A. *[ALWD]*
Attorney	Atty. *[ALWD]*
Authority	Auth.
Automobile	Auto. *[BB]*
Automotive	Auto. *[BB]*
Avenue	Ave.
Bankruptcy	Bankr.
Bar	B. *[ALWD]*
Benevolent	Benv. *[ALWD]*
Beverage	Bev. *[ALWD]*
Board	Bd.
Book	Bk. *[ALWD]*
Boulevard	Blvd. *[ALWD]*
Brief	Br. *[ALWD]*
Broadcast	Broad.
Broadcasting	Broad.
Brother	Bro. *[ALWD]*
Brotherhood	Bhd.
Brothers	Bros.
Building	Bldg.

WORD OR PHRASE IN SOURCE	ABBREVIATION (IF ANY)
Bulletin	Bull. *[ALWD]*
Business	Bus.
Casualty	Cas.
Center	Ctr.
Centre	Ctr.
Central	Cent. *[BB]*
	C. *[ALWD]*
Century	Cent. *[ALWD]*
Certiorari	Cert. *[ALWD]*
Chancellor	Chan. *[ALWD]*
Chancery	Ch. *[ALWD]*
Chemical	Chem.
Chief Judge	C.J. *[ALWD]*
Chief Justice	C.J. *[ALWD]*
Chronicle	Chron. *[ALWD]*
Circuit	Cir. *[ALWD]*
Civil	Civ. *[ALWD]*
Coalition	Coal. *[BB]*
College	Coll. *[BB]*
Commission	Comm'n *[BB]*
	Commn. *[ALWD]*
Commissioner	Comm'r *[BB]*
	Commr. *[ALWD]*
Committee	Comm.
Commerce	Com. *[ALWD]*
Commercial	Com. *[ALWD]*
Common	Com. *[ALWD]*
Commonwealth	Cmmw. *[ALWD]*
Communication	Commc'n *[BB]*
	Commun. *[ALWD]*
Communications	Commc'ns *[BB]*
	Commun. *[ALWD]*
Community	Cmty. *[BB]*

WORD OR PHRASE IN SOURCE	ABBREVIATION (IF ANY)
Company	Co.
Comparative	Comp. [*ALWD*]
Compensation	Comp. [*BB*]
	Compen. [*ALWD*]
Compilation	Comp. [*ALWD*]
Complaint	Compl. [*ALWD*]
Compliance	Compl. [*ALWD*]
Concurrent	Con. [*ALWD*]
Condemnation	Condemn. [*ALWD*]
Condominium	Condo.
Conference	Conf. [*ALWD*]
Congress	Cong.
Congressional	Cong.
Conservation	Conserv. [*ALWD*]
Consolidated	Consol.
Constitution	Const. [*ALWD*]
Construction	Constr.
Continental	Cont'l [*BB*]
	Contl. [*ALWD*]
Continuing Legal Education	CLE [*ALWD*]
Convention	Conv. [*ALWD*]
Cooperative	Coop.
Coordinator	Coord. [*ALWD*]
Copyright	Copy. [*ALWD*]
Corporate	Corp. [*ALWD*]
Corporation	Corp.
Correction	Corr. [*BB*]
	Correct. [*ALWD*]
Corrections	Corr. [*BB*]
	Corrects. [*ALWD*]
Correctional	Corr. [*BB*]
County	Co. [*ALWD*]

WORD OR PHRASE IN SOURCE	ABBREVIATION (IF ANY)
Court	Ct. [*ALWD*]
Criminal	Crim. [*ALWD*]
Cumulative	Cum. [*ALWD*]
Customs	Cust. [*ALWD*]
Decision	Dec. [*ALWD*]
Declaration	Decl. [*ALWD*]
Defendant	Def. [*ALWD*]
Defense	Def.
Demurrer	Demr. [*ALWD*]
Department	Dep't [*BB*]
	Dept. [*ALWD*]
Deposition	Depo. [*ALWD*]
Deputy	Dep. [*ALWD*]
Detention	Det. [*BB*]
Determination	Determ. [*ALWD*]
Development	Dev.
Digest	Dig. [*ALWD*]
Director	Dir.
Discipline	Disc. [*ALWD*]
Disciplinary	Disc. [*ALWD*]
Discount	Disc. [*BB*]
Distribution	Distrib. [*ALWD*]
Distributive	Distrib. [*ALWD*]
Distributor	Distrib. [*BB*]
Distributing	Distrib. [*BB*]
	Distribg. [*ALWD*]
District	Dist.
District Attorney	D.A. [*ALWD*]
District Court [federal]	D. [*ALWD*]
Division	Div.
Docket	Dkt. [*ALWD*]
Doctor	Dr. [*ALWD*]
Document	Doc. [*ALWD*]

WORD OR PHRASE IN SOURCE	ABBREVIATION (IF ANY)
Domestic	Dom. [*ALWD*]
East	E.
Eastern	E.
Economic	Econ.
Economics	Econ.
Economical	Econ.
Economy	Econ.
Education	Educ.
Educational	Educ.
Electric	Elec. [*BB*]
Electrical	Elec.
Electricity	Elec.
Electronic	Elec.
Emergency	Emerg. [*ALWD*]
Eminent Domain	Em. Dom. [*ALWD*]
Employment	Empl. [*ALWD*]
Employment Retirement Income Security Act	ERISA [*ALWD*]
Encyclopedia	Ency. [*ALWD*]
Engineer	Eng'r [*BB*]
	Engr. [*ALWD*]
Engineering	Eng'g [*BB*]
	Engr. [*ALWD*]
Enterprise	Enter.
Entertainment	Entm't [*BB*]
	Ent. [*ALWD*]
Environment	Env't [*BB*]
	Env. [*ALWD*]
Environmental	Envtl.
Equality	Equal.
Equipment	Equip.
Equity	Eq. [*ALWD*]
Equitable	Eq. [*ALWD*]

WORD OR PHRASE IN SOURCE	ABBREVIATION (IF ANY)
Esquire	Esq. [*ALWD*]
Establishment	Estab. [*ALWD*]
Estate	Est. [*ALWD*]
Evidence	Evid. [*ALWD*]
Examination	Exam. [*ALWD*]
Examiner	Exam'r [*BB*]
	Examr. [*ALWD*]
Exchange	Exch.
Executive	Exec. [*ALWD*]
Executor	Ex'r [*BB*]
Executrix	Ex'x [*BB*]
	Execx. [*ALWD*]
Exhibit	Ex. [*ALWD*]
Export	Exp. [*BB*]
Exporter	Exp. [*BB*]
Exportation	Exp. [*BB*]
Family	Fam. [*ALWD*]
Federal	Fed. [*BB*]
	F. *or* Fed. [*ALWD*]
Federal Savings Bank	F.S.B. [*ALWD*]
Federation	Fed'n [*BB*]
	Fedn. [*ALWD*]
Fidelity	Fid.
Finance	Fin.
Financial	Fin.
Financing	Fin. [*BB*]
Foreign	For. [*ALWD*]
Fort	Ft. [*ALWD*]
Foundation	Found.
Franchise	Fran. [*ALWD*]
Francising	Fran. [*ALWD*]
Gasoline	Gas. [*ALWD*]
Gazette	Gaz. [*ALWD*]

WORD OR PHRASE IN SOURCE	ABBREVIATION (IF ANY)
General	Gen.
Government	Gov't [*BB*]
	Govt. [*ALWD*]
Governmental	Govtl. [*ALWD*]
Governor	Gov. [*ALWD*]
Guaranty	Guar.
Headquarters	H.Q. [*ALWD*]
Hearing	Hrg. [*ALWD*]
Highway	Hwy. [*ALWD*]
Honorable	Hon. [*ALWD*]
Hospital	Hosp.
House	H. [*ALWD*]
House of Representatives	H.R. [*ALWD*]
Housing	Hous.
Human Resources	Hum. Res. [*ALWD*]
Immigration	Immig. [*ALWD*]
Import	Imp. [*BB*]
Importer	Imp. [*BB*]
Importation	Imp. [*BB*]
Incorporated	Inc.
Indemnity	Indem.
Independence	Indep. [*ALWD*]
Independent	Indep.
Industrial	Indus.
Industries	Indus.
Industry	Indus.
Information	Info.
Injunction	Inj. [*ALWD*]
Institute	Inst.
Institution	Inst. [*BB*]
	Instn. [*ALWD*]
Instruction	Instr. [*ALWD*]
Insurance	Ins.

WORD OR PHRASE IN SOURCE	ABBREVIATION (IF ANY)
Intellectual	Intell. [*ALWD*]
Interdisciplinary	Interdisc. [*ALWD*]
Interior	Int. [*ALWD*]
Internal Revenue Service	IRS [*ALWD*]
International	Int'l [*BB*]
	Intl. [*ALWD*]
Interrogatory	Interrog. [*ALWD*]
Intramural	Intra. [*ALWD*]
Investment	Inv.
Island	Is. [*ALWD*]
Islands	Is. [*ALWD*]
Joint	Jt. [*ALWD*]
Joint Appendix	Jt. App. *or* J.A. [*ALWD*]
Journal	J. [*ALWD*]
Judge	J. [*ALWD*]
Judges	JJ. [*ALWD*]
Judge Advocate General's Corps	JAG [*ALWD*]
Judgment	Judm. [*ALWD*]
Judicial	Jud. [*ALWD*]
Judiciary	Jud. [*ALWD*]
Juris Doctor	J.D. [*ALWD*]
Jurisdiction	Jxn. [*ALWD*]
Jurisprudence	Jur. [*ALWD*]
Justice	J. [*ALWD*]
Justices	JJ. [*ALWD*]
Justice (other than a person)	Just. [*ALWD*]
Juvenile	Juv. [*ALWD*]
Labor	Lab. [*ALWD*]
Laboratory	Lab. [*BB*]
Language	Lang. [*ALWD*]
Law	L. [*ALWD*]

WORD OR PHRASE IN SOURCE	ABBREVIATION (IF ANY)
Lawyer	Law. *[ALWD]*
Legal	Leg. *[ALWD]*
Legislature	Legis. *[ALWD]*
Legislative	Legis. *[ALWD]*
Legislation	Legis. *[ALWD]*
Letter	Ltr. *[ALWD]*
Liability	Liab.
Librarian	Libr. *[ALWD]*
Library	Lib. *[ALWD]*
Limited	Ltd.
Limited Liability Company	LLC *[ALWD]*
Limited Liability Partnership	LLP *[ALWD]*
Limited Partnership	LP *[ALWD]*
Litigation	Litig.
Litigator	Litig. *[ALWD]*
Local	Loc. *[ALWD]*
Machine	Mach.
Machinery	Mach.
Magazine	Mag. *[ALWD]*
Magistrate	Mag. *[ALWD]*
Maintenance	Maint.
Management	Mgmt. *[BB]*
	Mgt. *[ALWD]*
Manual	Man. *[ALWD]*
Manufacturer	Mfr.
Manufacturing	Mfg.
Maritime	Mar.
Market	Mkt.
Marketing	Mktg.
Mechanic	Mech. *[BB]*
Mechanics	Mechs. *[BB]*
	Mech. *[ALWD]*

<u>WORD OR PHRASE IN SOURCE</u>	<u>ABBREVIATION (IF ANY)</u>
Mechanical	Mech.
Mediator	Med. [*ALWD*]
Medical	Med.
Medical Doctor	M.D. [*ALWD*]
Medicine	Med.
Memorandum	Memo. [*ALWD*]
Memorial	Mem'l [*BB*]
	Meml. [*ALWD*]
Merchant	Merch. [*BB*]
Merchandise	Merch. [*BB*]
Merchandising	Merch. [*BB*]
Metropolitan	Metro.
Military	Mil. [*ALWD*]
Miscellaneous	Misc. [*ALWD*]
Monthly	Mthly. [*ALWD*]
Morning	Morn. [*ALWD*]
Mortgage	Mortg. [*ALWD*]
Mortgagee	Mtgee. [*ALWD*]
Mortgagor	Mtgor. [*ALWD*]
Motion	Mot. [*ALWD*]
Mount	Mt. [*ALWD*]
Mountain	Mt. [*ALWD*]
Municipal	Mun.
Mutual	Mut.
National	Nat'l [*BB*]
	Natl. [*ALWD*]
Nature	Nat. [*ALWD*]
Natural	Nat. [*ALWD*]
Navigation	Nav. [*ALWD*]
Negligence	Negl. [*ALWD*]
Negotiation	Negot. [*ALWD*]
Newsletter	Newsltr. [*ALWD*]
Newspaper	Newsp. [*ALWD*]

WORD OR PHRASE IN SOURCE	ABBREVIATION (IF ANY)
North	N.
North America	N.A. *[ALWD]*
	N. Am. *[BB]*
Northeast	Ne. *[BB]*
	N.E. *[ALWD]*
Northeastern	Ne. *[BB]*
	N.E. *[ALWD]*
Northern	N.
Northwest	Nw. *[BB]*
	N.W. *[ALWD]*
Northwestern	Nw. *[BB]*
	N.W. *[ALWD]*
Northwestern [Univ.]	Nw. *[ALWD]*
Number	No.
Obligation	Oblig. *[ALWD]*
Obligations	Oblig. *[ALWD]*
Occupation	Occ. *[ALWD]*
Occupations	Occ. *[ALWD]*
Office	Off. *[ALWD]*
Official	Off. *[ALWD]*
Opinion	Op. *[ALWD]*
Order	Or. *[ALWD]*
Ordinance	Ord. *[ALWD]*
Organization	Org.
Organizing	Org. *[BB]*
Pacific	Pac. *[BB]*
	P. *[ALWD]*
Partial Summary Judgment	P.S.J. *[ALWD]*
Partnership	P'ship *[BB]*
	Partn. *[ALWD]*
Patent	Pat. *[ALWD]*
Pension	Pen. *[ALWD]*
Performing	Perf. *[ALWD]*

<u>WORD OR PHRASE IN SOURCE</u>	<u>ABBREVIATION (IF ANY)</u>
Permanent	Perm. [*ALWD*]
Person	Pers. [*BB*]
Personal	Pers. [*BB*]
Personnel	Pers. [*BB*]
Perspective	Persp. [*ALWD*]
Petition	Pet. [*ALWD*]
Petitioner	Petr. [*ALWD*]
Pharmaceutics	Pharm. [*BB*]
Pharmaceutical	Pharm.
Pharmacy	Pharm. [*ALWD*]
Philosophical	Phil. [*ALWD*]
Philosophy	Phil. [*ALWD*]
Photograph	Photo. [*ALWD*]
Photography	Photo. [*ALWD*]
Physician	Phys. [*ALWD*]
Physicians	Phys. [*ALWD*]
Plaintiff	Pl. [*ALWD*]
Planning	Plan. [*ALWD*]
Pleading	Pldg. [*ALWD*]
Politics	Pol. [*ALWD*]
Popular	Pop. [*ALWD*]
Practical	Prac. [*ALWD*]
Practice	Prac. [*ALWD*]
Practising Law Institute	P.L.I. [*ALWD*]
Practitioner	Pract. [*ALWD*]
Preliminary	Prelim. [*ALWD*]
Preparation	Prep. [*ALWD*]
Preparatory	Prep. [*ALWD*]
Preserve	Pres. [*BB*]
Preservation	Pres. [*BB*]
President	Pres. [*ALWD*]
Presidential	Pres. [*ALWD*]
Privacy	Priv. [*ALWD*]

WORD OR PHRASE IN SOURCE	ABBREVIATION (IF ANY)
Private	Priv. *[ALWD]*
Probate	Prob. *[ALWD]*
Probation	Prob. *[BB]*
Procedure	P. *or* Proc. *[ALWD]*
Proceeding	P. *or* Proc. *[ALWD]*
Proclamation	Procl. *[ALWD]*
Procurement	Procure. *[ALWD]*
Product	Prod.
Production	Prod.
Professional	Prof'l *[BB]*
	Prof. *[ALWD]*
Professional Association	P.A. *[ALWD]*
Professional Corporation	P.C. *[ALWD]*
Professor	Prof. *[ALWD]*
Property	Prop.
Protection	Prot. *[BB]*
	Protec. *[ALWD]*
Psychiatry	Psych. *[ALWD]*
Psychology	Psychol. *[ALWD]*
Psychological	Psychol. *[ALWD]*
Public	Pub.
Publication	Publ'n *[BB]*
Publishing	Publ'g *[BB]*
	Publg. *[ALWD]*
Quarterly	Q. *[ALWD]*
Railroad	R.R.
Railway	Ry.
Record [on appeal]	R. *[ALWD]*
Record [other]	Rec. *[ALWD]*
Reference	Ref. *[ALWD]*
Refining	Ref. *[BB]*
Regional	Reg'l *[BB]*
	Regl. *[ALWD]*

WORD OR PHRASE IN SOURCE	ABBREVIATION (IF ANY)
Regular	Reg. [*ALWD*]
Regulation	Reg. [*ALWD*]
Regulatory	Reg. [*ALWD*]
Rehabilitation	Rehab.
Relations	Rel. [*ALWD*]
Religious	Relig. [*ALWD*]
Remedies	Rem. [*ALWD*]
Remedy	Rem. [*ALWD*]
Reorganization	Reorg. [*ALWD*]
Report	Rpt. *or* Rep. [*ALWD*]
Reporter	Rptr. *or* Rep. [*ALWD*]
Representative	Rep. [*ALWD*]
Reproduction	Reprod.
Reproductive	Reprod.
Request	Req. [*ALWD*]
Resolution	Res. [*ALWD*]
Resolutions	Res. [*ALWD*]
Resource	Res. [*BB*]
Resources	Res. [*BB*]
Respondent	Respt. [*ALWD*]
Responsibility	Resp. [*ALWD*]
Restaurant	Rest.
Retirement	Ret.
Review	Rev. [*ALWD*]
Revised	Rev. [*ALWD*]
Revision	Rev. [*ALWD*]
Road	Rd.
Rule	R. [*ALWD*]
Rules	R. [*ALWD*]
Ruling	Rul. [*ALWD*]
Saint	St. [*ALWD*]
Savings	Sav.
Schedule	Sched. [*ALWD*]

WORD OR PHRASE IN SOURCE	ABBREVIATION (IF ANY)
Scheduling	Sched. [*ALWD*]
School	Sch.
Schools	Sch. [*BB*]
	Schs. [*ALWD*]
Science	Sci.
Sciences	Scis. [*BB*]
	Sci. [*ALWD*]
Scientific	Sci. [*ALWD*]
Secretary	Sec'y [*BB*]
	Sec. [*ALWD*]
Section [other than a	
subdivision of a source]	Sec. [*ALWD*]
Security	Sec.
Securities	Sec. [*BB*]
	Secs. [*ALWD*]
Selective	Sel. [*ALWD*]
Senate	Sen. [*ALWD*]
Senator	Sen. [*ALWD*]
Sentencing	Senten.
Service	Serv.
Session	Sess. [*ALWD*]
Settlement	Settle. [*ALWD*]
Shareholder	S'holder [*BB*]
Shipping	Ship. [*ALWD*]
Social	Soc.
Society	Soc'y [*BB*]
	Socy. [*ALWD*]
Solicitor	Sol. [*ALWD*]
South	S.
Southern [other than	
Southern Reporter]	S.
Southeast	Se. [*BB*]
	S.E. [*ALWD*]

WORD OR PHRASE IN SOURCE	ABBREVIATION (IF ANY)
Southeastern	Se. *[BB]*
	S.E. *[ALWD]*
Southern Reporter	So. *[ALWD]*
Southwest	Sw. *[BB]*
	S.W. *[ALWD]*
Southwestern	Sw. *[BB]*
	S.W. *[ALWD]*
Southwestern [Univ.]	Sw. *[ALWD]*
Special	Spec. *[ALWD]*
Standard	Stand. *[ALWD]*
State	St. *[ALWD]*
Statement	State. *[ALWD]*
Statute	Stat. *[ALWD]*
Statutes	Stat. *[ALWD]*
Steamship	S.S.
Steamships	S.S. *[BB]*
	S.Ss. *[ALWD]*
Stipulate	Stip. *[ALWD]*
Stipulation	Stip. *[ALWD]*
Street	St.
Studies	Stud. *[ALWD]*
Subcommittee	Subcomm.
Subpoena	Subp. *[ALWD]*
Summary Judgment	S.J. *[ALWD]*
Superior	Super. *[ALWD]*
Supplement [N.Y.]	S. *[ALWD]*
Supplement [other]	Supp. *[ALWD]*
Supplemental	Supp. *[ALWD]*
Supreme Court [U.S. Supreme Court]	S. Ct. *[ALWD]*
Supreme [other]	Sup. *[ALWD]*
Surety	Sur.
Surrogacy	Surrog. *[ALWD]*

WORD OR PHRASE IN SOURCE	ABBREVIATION (IF ANY)
Surrogate	Surrog. [*ALWD*]
System	Sys.
Systems	Sys.
Taxation	Taxn. [*ALWD*]
Technology	Tech.
Telecommunication	Telecomm. [*BB*]
Telecommunications	Telecomms. [*BB*]
	Telecomm. [*ALWD*]
Telephone	Tel.
Telegraph	Tel. [*BB*]
Television	TV [*ALWD*]
Temporary	Temp.
Temporary Restraining Order	T.R.O. [*ALWD*]
Territorial	Terr. [*ALWD*]
Testimony	Test. [*ALWD*]
Township	Twp. [*BB*]
Transcontinental	Transcon.
Transcript	Transcr. [*ALWD*]
Transnational	Transnatl. [*ALWD*]
Transport	Transp. [*BB*]
Transportation	Transp.
Treasurer	Treas. [*ALWD*]
Treasury	Treas. [*ALWD*]
Trial	Tr. [*ALWD*]
Tribune	Trib. [*ALWD*]
Tribunal	Trib. [*ALWD*]
Trustee	Tr. [*BB*]
Turnpike	Tpk. [*BB*]
Unauthorized	Unauth. [*ALWD*]
Unconsolidated	Unconsol. [*ALWD*]
Unemployment	Unempl. [*ALWD*]
Uniform	Unif.

<u>WORD OR PHRASE IN SOURCE</u>	<u>ABBREVIATION (IF ANY)</u>
Uniform Commercial Code	U.C.C. *[ALWD]*
Uniform Laws Annotated	U.L.A. *[ALWD]*
United Nations	UN *[ALWD]*
United States	U.S.
University	Univ. *[BB]*
	U. *[ALWD]*
Urban	Urb. *[ALWD]*
Utility	Util.
Vehicle	Veh. *[ALWD]*
Versus, against [in case name]	v.
Veteran	Vet. *[ALWD]*
Vice President	V.P. *[ALWD]*
Village	Vill. *[BB]*
Volunteer	Vol. *[ALWD]*
Weekly	Wkly. *[ALWD]*
West	W.
Western	W.
Year Book	Y.B. *[ALWD]*
Yearbook	Y.B. *[ALWD]*

B. GEOGRAPHIC DESIGNATIONS

ALWD = *ALWD Citation Manual*
BB = *Bluebook*

Unless otherwise indicated below, the *ALWD* and *BB* abbreviations are the same.

As indicated below, some geographic designations are not abbreviated.

<u>Geographic Designation</u>	<u>Abbreviation (if any)</u>
Afghanistan	Afg.
Africa	Afr.
Alabama	Ala.
Alaska	Alaska
Albania	Alb.
Alberta [Canada]	Alta. *[BB]*
	Alb. *[ALWD]*
Algeria	Alg.
America	Am.
American Samoa	Am. Sam.
Andorra	Andorra *[BB]*
	And. *[ALWD]*
Angola	Angl.
Anguilla	Anguilla
Antarctica	Ata. *[ALWD]*
Antigua & Barbuda	Ant. & Barb.
Argentina	Arg.
Arizona	Ariz.
Arkansas	Ark.
Armenia	Arm.
Australia	Austl. *[BB]*
	Austrl. *[ALWD]*
Australian Capital Territory	Austl. Cap. Terr. *[BB]*
Austria	Austria
Azerbaijan	Azer.
Bahamas	Bah. *[BB]*
Bahrain	Bahr.
Baltimore	Balt. *[ALWD]*
Bangladesh	Bangl.
Barbados	Barb.
Belarus	Belr.
Belgium	Belg.

GEOGRAPHIC DESIGNATION	ABBREVIATION (IF ANY)
Belize	Belize
Benin	Benin
Bermuda	Berm.
Bhutan	Bhutan
Bolivia	Bol.
Bosnia & Herzegovina	Bosn. & Herz.
Boston	Bos. [*ALWD*]
Botswana	Bots.
Brazil	Braz.
British Columbia	B.C. [*BB*]
	Brit. Colum. [*ALWD*]
Brunei	Brunei
Bulgaria	Bulg.
Burkina Faso	Burk. Faso
Burundi	Burundi
California	Cal.
Cambodia	Cambodia [*BB*]
	Camb. [*ALWD*]
Cameroon	Cameroon [*BB*]
	Camer. [*ALWD*]
Canada	Can.
Canal Zone	C.Z.
Cape Verde	Cape Verde
Cayman Islands	Cayman Is. [*BB*]
	Cay. Is. [*ALWD*]
Central African Republic	Cent. Afr. Rep. [*BB*]
	C. Afr. Rep. [*ALWD*]
Ceskoslovensko	Cesk. [*ALWD*]
Chad	Chad
Channel Islands	Channel Is. [*ALWD*]
Chicago	Chi.
Chile	Chile
China, People's Republic of	P.R.C.

GEOGRAPHIC DESIGNATION	ABBREVIATION (IF ANY)
Christmas Island	Christ. Is. [*ALWD*]
Colombia	Colom.
Colorado	Colo.
Comoros	Comoros
Congo, Republic of the	Congo
Congo, Democratic Republic of the	Dem. Rep. Congo [*BB*]
Connecticut	Conn.
Cook Islands	Cook Is. [*ALWD*]
Costa Rica	Costa Rica
Côte d'Ivoire	Côte d'Ivoire
Croatia	Croat.
Cuba	Cuba
Cyprus	Cyprus
Czechoslovakia	Czech. [*ALWD*]
Czech Republic	Czech Rep.
Delaware	Del.
Denmark	Den.
Detroit	Det. [*ALWD*]
District of Columbia	D.C. [*BB*]
Djibouti	Djib.
Dominica	Dominica
Dominican Republic	Dom. Rep.
East Timor	E. Timor
Ecuador	Ecuador [*BB*]
	Ecu. [*ALWD*]
Egypt	Egypt
	Egy. [*ALWD*]
El Salvador	El Sal.
England	Eng.
Equatorial Guinea	Eq. Guinea [*BB*]
	Eq. Guin. [*ALWD*]
Eritrea	Eri.

GEOGRAPHIC DESIGNATION	ABBREVIATION (IF ANY)
Estonia	Est.
Ethiopia	Eth.
Europe	Eur.
Falkland Islands	Falkland Is. [*BB*]
	Falk. Is. [*ALWD*]
Fiji	Fiji
Finland	Fin.
Flordia	Fla.
France	Fr.
Gabon	Gabon
Gambia	Gam.
Georgia (state)	Ga.
Georgia	Geor.
Germany	Ger. [*ALWD*]
Germany, Federal Republic of	F.R.G. [*BB*]
Ghana	Ghana
Gibraltar	Gib.
Great Britain	Gr. Brit.
Greece	Greece
Greenland	Green.
Grenada	Gren.
Guadeloupe	Guad.
Guam	Guam
Guatemala	Guat.
Guinea	Guinea [*BB*]
	Gin. [*ALWD*]
Guinea-Bissau	Guinea-Bissau [*BB*]
	Gin.-Bis. [*ALWD*]
Guyana	Guy.
Haiti	Haiti
Hawaii	Haw.
Heard & McDonald Islands	H. & McD. Is. [*ALWD*]

GEOGRAPHIC DESIGNATION	ABBREVIATION (IF ANY)
Holland	Hol. [*ALWD*]
Honduras	Hond.
Hong Kong	H.K.
Hrvatska	Hrv. [*ALWD*]
Hungary	Hung. [*BB*]
	Hun. [*ALWD*]
Iceland	Ice.
Idaho	Idaho
Illinois	Ill.
India	India
Indiana	Ind.
Indonesia	Indon.
Iowa	Iowa
Iran	Iran
Iraq	Iraq
Ireland	Ir.
Israel	Isr.
Italy	Italy
Jamaica	Jam.
Japan	Japan
Jordan	Jordan [*BB*]
	Jor. [*ALWD*]
Kansas	Kan.
Kazakhstan	Kaz.
Kentucky	Ky.
Kenya	Kenya
Kiribati	Kiribati
Korea, North	N. Korea [*BB*]
	N. Kor. [*ALWD*]
Korea, South	S. Korea [*BB*]
	S. Kor. [*ALWD*]
Kuwait	Kuwait
Kyrgyzstan	Kyrg.

GEOGRAPHIC DESIGNATION	ABBREVIATION (IF ANY)
Labrador	Labr. [*ALWD*]
Laos	Laos
Latvia	Lat.
Lebanon	Leb.
Lesotho	Lesotho [*BB*]
	Les. [*ALWD*]
Liberia	Liber. [*BB*]
Libya	Libya
Liechtenstein	Liech.
Lithuania	Lith.
Los Angeles	L.A.
Louisiana	La.
Luxembourg	Lux.
Macau	Mac. [*BB*]
Macedonia	Maced.
Madagascar	Madag.
Maine	Me.
Malawi	Malawi
Malaysia	Malay.
Maldives	Maldives
Mali	Mali
Malta	Malta
Manitoba	Man.
Marshall Islands	Marsh. Is. [*BB*]
	Marshall Is. [*ALWD*]
Martinique	Mart.
Maryland	Md.
Massachusetts	Mass.
Mauritania	Mauritania
Mauritius	Mauritius
Mayotte	May. [*ALWD*]
Mexico	Mex.
Michigan	Mich.

GEOGRAPHIC DESIGNATION	ABBREVIATION (IF ANY)
Micronesia	Micr.
Minnesota	Minn.
Mississippi	Miss.
Missouri	Mo.
Moldova	Mold. [*BB*]
	Mol. [*ALWD*]
Monaco	Monaco
Mongolia	Mong.
Montana	Mont.
Montenegro	Monten. [*ALWD*]
Montserrat	Montserrat
Morocco	Morocco [*BB*]
	Mor. [*ALWD*]
Mozambique	Mozam.
Myanmar	Myan.
Namibia	Namib. [*BB*]
	Nam. [*ALWD*]
Nauru	Nauru
Nebraska	Neb.
Nepal	Nepal
Netherlands	Neth.
Netherlands Antilles	Neth. Ant. [*ALWD*]
Nevada	Nev.
New Brunswick	N.B. [*BB*]
	N. Bruns. [*ALWD*]
New Caledonia	N. Caled. [*ALWD*]
Newfoundland	Newfl. [*ALWD*]
Newfoundland & Labrador	Nfld. [*BB*]
New Hampshire	N.H.
New Jersey	N.J.
New Mexico	N.M.
New South Wales	N.S.W. [*BB*]
New York	N.Y.

GEOGRAPHIC DESIGNATION	ABBREVIATION (IF ANY)
New York City	N.Y.C. [*ALWD*]
New Zealand	N.Z.
Nicaragua	Nicar.
Niger	Niger
Nigeria	Nig. [*BB*]
North America	N. Am. [*BB*]
	N.A. [*ALWD*]
North Carolina	N.C.
North Dakota	N.D.
Northern Ireland	N. Ir.
Northern Territory	N. Terr. [*BB*]
North Mariana Is.	N. Mar. I. [*BB*]
	N. Mar. Is. [*ALWD*]
Northwest Territories	N.W.T. [*BB*]
Norway	Nor.
Nova Scotia	N.S. [*BB*]
	N. Sco. [*ALWD*]
Nunavut	Nun. [*BB*]
Ohio	Ohio
Oklahoma	Okla.
Oman	Oman
Ontario	Ont.
Oregon	Or.
Pakistan	Pak.
Palau	Palau
Panama	Pan.
Papua New Guinea	Papua N.G. [*BB*]
	Papua N. Guin. [*ALWD*]
Paraguay	Para. [*BB*]
	Parag. [*ALWD*]
Pennsylvania	Pa.
Peru	Peru
Philadelphia	Phila.

GEOGRAPHIC DESIGNATION	ABBREVIATION (IF ANY)
Philippines	Phil. [*BB*]
	Philip. [*ALWD*]
Pitcairn Island	Pitcairn Is.
Pittsburgh	Pitt. [*ALWD*]
Poland	Pol.
Portugal	Port.
Prince Edward Island	P.E.I. [*BB*]
Puerto Rico	P.R.
Qatar	Qatar
Québec	Que.
Queensland	Queensl. [*BB*]
Réunion	Réunion
Rhode Island	R.I.
Romania	Rom.
Russia	Russ. [*BB*]
	Rus. [*ALWD*]
Rwanda	Rwanda [*BB*]
	Rwa. [*ALWD*]
St. Helena	St. Helena
St. Kitts & Nevis	St. Kitts & Nevis
St. Lucia	St. Lucia
St. Pierre and Miquelon	St. Pierre & Miquelon [*ALWD*]
St. Vincent & the Grenadines	St. Vincent
San Francisco	S.F.
San Marino	San Marino
São Tomé and Príncipe	São Tomé & Príncipe
Saskatchewan	Sask.
Saudi Arabia	Saudi Arabia
Scotland	Scot.
Senegal	Sen. [*BB*]
Serbia	Serb. [*ALWD*]

GEOGRAPHIC DESIGNATION	ABBREVIATION (IF ANY)
Serbia & Montenegro	Serb. & Mont. *[BB]*
Seychelles	Sey.
Sierra Leone	Sierra Leone
Singapore	Sing.
Slovakia	Slovk.
Slovenia	Slovn.
Solomon Islands	Solom. Is. *[BB]*
	Sol. Is. *[ALWD]*
Somalia	Somal. *[BB]*
	Som. *[ALWD]*
South Africa	S. Afr.
South America	S. Am. *[BB]*
	S.A. *[ALWD]*
South Australia	S. Austl. *[BB]*
South Carolina	S.C.
South Dakota	S.D.
Soviet Union	U.S.S.R. *[ALWD]*
Spain	Spain
Sri Lanka	Sri Lanka
Sudan	Sudan
Suriname	Surin.
Swaziland	Swaz.
Sweden	Swed.
Switzerland	Switz.
Syria	Syria
Taiwan	Taiwan
Tajikistan	Taj.
Tanzania	Tanz.
Tasmania	Tas. *[BB]*
Tennessee	Tenn.
Texas	Tex.
Thailand	Thail. *[BB]*
	Thai. *[ALWD]*

GEOGRAPHIC DESIGNATION	ABBREVIATION (IF ANY)
Togo	Togo
Tonga	Tonga
Trinidad & Tobago	Trin. &Tobago [BB]
	Trin. & Tob. [ALWD]
Tunisia	Tunis. [BB]
	Tun. [ALWD]
Turkey	Turk.
Turkmenistan	Turkm.
Turks & Caicos Islands	Turks & Caicos Is. [BB]
Tuvalu	Tuvalu
Uganda	Uganda
Ukraine	Ukr.
United Arab Emirates	U.A.E.
United Kingdom	U.K.
United States of America	U.S.
Uruguay	Uru.
Utah	Utah
Uzbekistan	Uzb.
Vanuatu	Vanuatu
Vatican City	Vatican [BB]
Venezuela	Venez. [BB]
	Venz. [ALWD]
Vermont	Vt.
Victoria	Vict. [BB]
Vietnam	Vietnam
Virginia	Va.
Virgin Islands, U.S.	V.I.
Virgin Islands, British	Virgin Is. [BB]
Wales	Wales
Washington	Wash.
Washington, D.C.	D.C. [ALWD]
Western Australia	W. Austl. [BB]
Western Samoa	W. Samoa [BB]

GEOGRAPHIC DESIGNATION	ABBREVIATION (IF ANY)
West Virginia	W. Va.
Wisconsin	Wis.
Wyoming	Wyo.
Yemen	Yemen
Yugoslavia	Yugo.
Yukon Territory	Yukon [*BB*]
	Yukon Ter. [*ALWD*]
Zambia	Zambia
Zimbabwe	Zimb. [*BB*]
	Zim. [*ALWD*]

C. MONTHS / CALENDAR DESIGNATIONS

ALWD = *ALWD Citation Manual*
BB = *Bluebook*

Unless otherwise indicated below, the *ALWD* and *BB* abbreviations are the same.

As indicated below, some calendar designations are not abbreviated.

MONTHS OF THE YEAR	ABBREVIATION (IF ANY)
January	Jan.
February	Feb.
March	Mar.
April	Apr.
May	May
June	June
July	July
August	Aug.
September	Sept.
October	Oct.

MONTHS OF THE YEAR	ABBREVIATION (IF ANY)
November	Nov.
December	Dec.

DAYS OF THE WEEK	ABBREVIATION (IF ANY)
Monday	Mon. [*ALWD*]
Tuesday	Tues. [*ALWD*]
Wednesday	Wed. [*ALWD*]
Thursday	Th. [*ALWD*]
Friday	Fri. [*ALWD*]
Saturday	Sat. [*ALWD*]
Sunday	Sun. [*ALWD*]

D. SUBDIVISION DESIGNATIONS

ALWD = *ALWD Citation Manual*
BB = *Bluebook*

Unless otherwise indicated below, the *ALWD* and *BB* abbreviations are the same.

Unless otherwise indicated below, plurals are formed by adding the letter "s" to the abbreviation.

As indicated below, some subdivision designations are not abbreviated (e.g., "Preamble" is abbreviated by *The Bluebook*, but it is not by the *ALWD Manual*).

SUBDIVISION DESIGNATIONS	ABBREVIATION (IF ANY)
addendum	add. [*BB*]
amendment	amend.
annotation	annot. [*BB*]
appendix	app.
article	art.
bibliography	bibliog.

SUBDIVISION DESIGNATIONS	ABBREVIATION (IF ANY)
book	bk.
chapter	ch.
clause	cl.
column	col.
commentary	cmt. [*BB*]
comment	cmt.
decision	dec. [*BB*]
department	dept. [*BB*]
division	div.
endnote	n. [*ALWD*]
endnotes	nn. [*ALWD*]
example	ex.
figure	fig.

    [Note: No space between fig. and the following number or letter in *BB* citations]

folio	fol.
footnote	
in cross-references	note [*BB*]
in textual sentences	note [*ALWD*]
in other references	n. [*BB*]
in citations	n. [*ALWD*]

    [Note: No space between n. and the following number or letter in *BB* citations]

footnotes	
in cross-references	notes [*BB*]
in textual sentences	notes [*ALWD*]
in other references	nn. [*BB*]
in citations	nn. [*ALWD*]

    [Note: No space between nn. and the following number or letter in *BB* citations]

historical note	hist. n.

    [Note: No space between hist. n. and the following number or letter in *BB* citations]

SUBDIVISION DESIGNATIONS	ABBREVIATION (IF ANY)
historical notes	hist. nn.

[Note: No space between hist. nn. and the following number or letter in *BB* citations]

hypothetical	hypo.
illustration	illus.
illustrations	illus. [*BB*]
	illuss. [*ALWD*]
introduction	intro.
line	l.
lines	ll.
number	No. [*BB*]
	n. [*ALWD*]
numbers	Nos. [*BB*]
	nn. [*ALWD*]
page	
in cross-references	p. [*BB*]
in other references	[at] [*BB*]
pages	
in cross-references	pp. [*BB*]
in other references	[at] [*BB*]
paragraph	
if symbol appears in	
source	¶ [*BB*]
if otherwise	para. [*BB*]
in all instances	¶ *or* para. [*ALWD*]
paragraphs	
if symbol appears in	
source	¶¶ [*BB*]
if otherwise	paras. [*BB*]
in all instances	¶¶ *or* paras. [*ALWD*]
part	pt.
preamble	pmbl. [*BB*]
principle	princ. [*BB*]

<u>SUBDIVISION DESIGNATIONS</u>	<u>ABBREVIATION (IF ANY)</u>
publication	pub. [*BB*]
record	rec. [*ALWD*]
reporter's note	rptr. n. [*ALWD*]
reporter's notes	rptr. nn. [*ALWD*]
rule	R. [*BB*]
schedule	sched.
section	
in amending act	sec. [*BB*]
in all other contexts	§ [*BB*]
in all instances	§ *or* sec. [*ALWD*]
sections	
in amending act	secs. [*BB*]
in all other contexts	§§ [*BB*]
in all instances	§§ *or* secs. [*ALWD*]
serial	ser. [*BB*]
serials	ser. [*BB*]
series	ser.
subdivision	subdiv.
subparagraph	subpara. [*ALWD*]
subsection	subsec.
supplement	supp.
table	tbl.

     [Note: No space between tbl. and the following number or letter in *BB* citations]

title	tit.
volume	vol.

E. PUBLISHING TERMS

ALWD = *ALWD Citation Manual*
BB = *Bluebook*

Unless otherwise indicated below, the *ALWD* and *BB* abbreviations are the same.

As indicated below, some publishing terms are not abbreviated.

PUBLISHING TERM	ABBREVIATION (IF ANY)
abridged	abr.
abridgement	abr.
annotated	ann.
anonymous	anon.
compilation	comp.
compiled	comp.
compiler	comp. [*ALWD*]
copyright	copy. [*BB*]
	copy. *or* © [*ALWD*]
draft	drft. [*BB*]
	dft. [*ALWD*]
edition	ed.
editor	ed.
manuscript	ms.
mimeograph	mimeo.
new series	n.s.
no date	n.d.
no place	n.p.
no publisher	n. pub. [*BB*]
	n.p. [*ALWD*]
old series	o.s.
permanent	perm. [*BB*]
photoduplicated reprint	photo. reprint [*BB*]

<u>PUBLISHING TERM</u>	<u>ABBREVIATION (IF ANY)</u>
printing	prtg.
replacement	repl.
reprint	repr. [*ALWD*]
reprinted	repr. [*ALWD*]
revised	rev.
revision	rev.
special	spec.
temporary	temp.
tentative	tent.
translated	trans. [*ALWD*]
translation	trans.
translator	trans.
unabridged	unabr.
volume	vol.

APPENDIX 2

ABBREVIATIONS OF STATE, FEDERAL, AND U.S. TERRITORIAL COURT REPORTERS

ALWD = *ALWD Citation Manual*
BB = *Bluebook*

Unless otherwise indicated below, the *ALWD* and *BB* abbreviations are the same. This appendix does not include specialized tax reporters or services.

REPORTER	ABBREVIATION
Abbott's New Cases (See App. 3(D) (N.Y.))	Abb. N. Cas. [*BB*]
Abbott's Practice Reports (See App. 3(D) (N.Y.))	Abb. Pr., Abb. Pr. (n.s.) [*BB*]
Addison (See App. 3(D) (Pa.))	Add. [*BB*]
Aikens (See App. 3(D) (Vt.))	Aik. [*BB*]
Alabama Appellate Court Reports	Ala. App.
Alabama Reports	Ala.
Alaska Federal Reports	Alaska Fed. [*BB*]
Alaska Reports	Alaska [*BB*]
Alden (See App. 3(D) (Pa.))	Ald. [*BB*]
Allen (See App. 3(D) (Mass.))	Allen [*BB*]
American Samoa Reports	Am. Samoa [*BB*] Am. Sam. [*ALWD*]
American Samoa Reports Second Series	Am. Samoa 2d [*BB*] Am. Sam. 2d [*ALWD*]

REPORTER	ABBREVIATION
American Samoa Reports Third Series	Am. Samoa 3d [*BB*] Am. Sam. 3d [*ALWD*]
Anderson's Unreported Ohio Appellate Court Cases	Ohio App. Unrep. [*BB*]
Anthon's Nisi Prius Cases (See App. 3(D) (N.Y.))	Ant. N.P. Cas. [*BB*]
Appeals Cases, District of Columbia	App. D.C. [*BB*]
Arizona Appeals Reports	Ariz. App.
Arizona Reports	Ariz.
Arkansas Appellate Reports	Ark. App.
Arkansas Reports	Ark.
Atlantic Reporter	A.
Atlantic Reporter Second Series	A.2d
Avazadas del Colegio de Abogados de Puerto Rico	C.A. [*ALWD*]
Bailey (See App. 3(D) (S.C.))	Bail. [*BB*]
Bailey's Equity (See App. 3(D) (S.C.))	Bail. Eq. [*BB*]
Bankruptcy Reporter	B.R.
Barbour's Chancery Reports (See App. 3(D) (N.Y.))	Barb. Ch. [*BB*]
Barbour's Supreme Court Reports (See App. 3(D) (N.Y.))	Barb. [*BB*]
Bay (See App. 3(D) (S.C.))	Bay [*BB*]
Bibb (See App. 3(D) (Ky.))	Bibb [*BB*]
Binny (See App. 3(D) (Pa.))	Binn. [*BB*]
Black (See App. 3(A) (U.S.))	Black [*BB*]
Blackford (See App. 3(D) (Ind.))	Blackf. [*BB*]
Blume, [Michigan] Supreme Court Transactions (See App. 3(D) (Mich.))	Blume Sup. Ct. Trans. [*BB*]
Blume, Unreported Opinions (See App. 3(D) (Mich.))	Blume Unrep. Op. [*BB*]

REPORTER	ABBREVIATION
Board of Tax Appeals Reports	B.T.A.
Boyce (See App. 3(D) (Del.))	Boyce [*BB*]
Bradford (See App. 3(D) (Iowa))	Bradf. [*BB*]
Brayton (See App. 3(D) (Vt.))	Brayt. [*BB*]
Breese (See App. 3(D) (Ill.)	Breese [*BB*]
Brevard (See App. 3(D) (S.C.))	Brev. [*BB*]
Brief Times Reporter (Colo.)	Brief Times Rptr. [*BB*]
Burnett (See App. 3(D) (Wis.))	Bur. [*BB*]
Busbee's Equity (See App. 3(D) (N.C.))	Busb. Eq. [*BB*]
Busbee's Law (See App. 3(D) (N.C.))	Busb. [*BB*]
Bush (See App. 3(D) (Ky.))	Bush [*BB*]
Caines' Cases (See App. 3(D) (N.Y.))	Cai. Cas. [*BB*]
Caines' Reports (See App. 3(D) (N.Y.))	Cai. [*BB*]
California Appellate Reports	Cal.
California Appellate Reports Second Series	Cal. 2d
California Appellate Reports Third Series	Cal. 3d
California Appellate Reports Fourth Series	Cal. 4th
California Appellate Reports Supplement	Cal. App. Supp.
California Appellate Reports Supplement Second Series	Cal. App. Supp. 2d
California Appellate Reports Supplement Third Series	Cal. App. Supp. 3d
California Appellate Reports Supplement Fourth Series	Cal. App. Supp. 4th
[West's] California Reporter	Cal. Rptr.

<u>REPORTER</u>	<u>ABBREVIATION</u>
[West's] California Reporter Second Series	Cal. Rptr. 2d
[West's] California Reporter Third Series	Cal. Rptr. 3d
California Reports	Cal.
California Reports Second Series	Cal. 2d
California Reports Third Series	Cal. 3d
California Reports Fourth Series	Cal. 4th
Call (See App. 3(D) (Va.))	Call [*BB*]
Cameron & Norwood [Conference by] (See App. 3(D) (N.C.))	Cam. & Nor. [*BB*]
Carolina Law Repository (See App. 3(D) (N.C.))	Car. L. Rep. [*BB*]
Chandler (See App. 3(D) (Wis.))	Chand. [*BB*]
Cheves (See App. 3(D) (S.C.))	Chev. [*BB*]
Cheves' Equity (See App. 3(D) (S.C.))	Chev. Eq. [*BB*]
[D.] Chipman (See App. 3(D) (Vt.))	D. Chip. [*BB*]
[N.] Chipman (See App. 3(D) (Vt.))	N. Chip. [*BB*]
Clarke's Chancery Reports (See App. 3(D) (N.Y.))	Cl. Ch. [*BB*]
Coldwell (See App. 3(D) (Tenn.))	Cold. [*BB*]
Coleman & Caines' Cases (See App. 3(D) (N.Y.))	Cole. & Cai. Cas. [*BB*]
Coleman's Cases (See App. 3(D) (N.Y.))	Cole. Cas. [*BB*]
Colorado Court of Appeals Reports	Colo. App.
Colorado Journal	Colo. J. [*BB*]
Colorado Lawyer	Colo. Law.
Colorado Reports	Colo.
Conference by Cameron & Norwood (See App. 3(D) (N.C.))	Cam. & Nor. [*BB*]
Connecticut Appellate Reports	Conn. App.

REPORTER	ABBREVIATION
Connecticut Circuit Court Reports	Conn. Cir. Ct. [*BB*]
	Conn. Cir. [*ALWD*]
Connecticut Law Reporter	Conn. L. Rptr. [*BB*]
Connecticut Reports	Conn.
Connecticut Superior Court Reports	Conn. Super. Ct.
	[*BB*]
Connecticut Supplement	Conn. Supp.
Cooke (See App. 3(D) (Tenn.))	Cooke [*BB*]
Court of Claims Reports	Ct. Cl.
Court of Customs and Patent	
Appeals	C.C.P.A.
Court of International Trade	
Reporter Decisions	I.T.R.D. (BNA)
Court of International Trade	Ct. Int'l Trade [*BB*]
Reports	Ct. Intl. Trade
	[*ALWD*]
Court Martial Reports	C.M.R.
Cowen's Reports (See App. 3(D)	
(N.Y.))	Cow. [*BB*]
Cranch (See App. 3(A) (U.S.))	Cranch [*BB*]
Cranch, Circuit Court (See App. 3(C)	
(D.C.))	Cranch [*BB*]
Cushing (See App. 3(D) (Mass.))	Cush. [*BB*]
Customs Bulletin and Decisions	Cust. B. & Dec. [*BB*]
Dakota Reports	Dakota [*BB*]
Dallam's Opinions (See App. 3(D)	
(Tex.))	Dallam [*BB*]
Dallas (See App. 3(A) (U.S.))	Dall. [*BB*]
Dallas (See App. 3(D) (Pa.))	Dall. [*BB*]
Dana (See App. 3(D) (Ky.))	Dana [*BB*]
Day (See App. 3(D) (Conn.))	Day [*BB*]

REPORTER	ABBREVIATION
Decisiones de Puerto Rico	P.R. Dec. [*BB*]
	D.P.R. [*ALWD*]
Decisiones del Tribunal de Circuito de Apelaciones [de] Puerto Rico	T.C.A.
Decisions of the United States Court of Military Appeals	C.M.A.
Delaware Cases	Del. Cas. [*BB*]
Delaware Chancery Reports	Del. Ch.
Delaware Reports (See App. 3(D) (Del.) for nominatives incorporated in series)	Del.
Desaussure's Equity (See App. 3(D) (S.C.))	Des. Eq. [*BB*]
Devereux & Battle's Equity (See App. 3(D) (N.C.))	Dev. & Bat. Eq. [*BB*]
Devereux & Battle's Law (See App. 3(D) (N.C.))	Dev. & Bat. [*BB*]
Devereux's Equity (See App. 3(D) (N.C.))	Dev. Eq. [*BB*]
Devereux's Law (See App. 3(D) (N.C.))	Dev. [*BB*]
Digest of the Laws of Texas (Dallam's Opinions) (See App. 3(D) (Tex.))	Dallam [*BB*]
[District of Columbia] Appeals Cases	App. D.C. [*BB*]
District of Columbia Reports (See App. 3(C) (D.C.) for nominatives incorporated in series)	D.C. [*BB*]
Douglass (See App. 3(D) (Mich.))	Doug. [*BB*]
Dudley (See App. 3(D) (S.C.))	Dud. [*BB*]

REPORTER	ABBREVIATION
Dudley's Equity (See App. 3(D) (S.C.))	Dud. Eq. [*BB*]
Duvall (See App. 3(D) (Ky.))	Duv. [*BB*]
Edmond's Select Cases (See App. 3(D) (N.Y.))	Edm. Sel. Cas. [*BB*]
Edward's Chancery Reports (See App. 3(D) (N.Y.))	Edw. Ch. [*BB*]
[West's] Federal Appendix	F. App'x. [*BB*] Fed. Appx. [*ALWD*]
Federal Cases	F. Cas.
[West's] Federal Reporter	F.
[West's] Federal Reporter Second Series	F.2d
[West's] Federal Reporter Third Series	F.3d
[West's] Federal Rules Decisions	F.R.D.
[West's] Federal Supplement	F. Supp.
[West's] Federal Supplement Second Series	F. Supp. 2d
Florida Law Weekly	Fla. L. Weekly [*BB*]
Florida Law Weekly Supplement	Fla. L. Weekly Supp. [*BB*]
Florida Reports	Fla.
Florida Supplement	Fla. Supp.
Florida Supplement Second	Fla. Supp. 2d
Gildersleeve Reports (See App. 3(D) (N.M.)) (Gild., B.-W. ed., and John are unofficial and not preferred.)	Gild., E.W.S. ed. [*BB*]
Gill (See App. 3(D) (Md.))	Gill [*BB*]
Gill & Johnson (See App. 3(D) (Md.))	G. & J. [*BB*]
Gilman (See App. 3(D) (Ill.)	Gilm. [*BB*]
Gilmer (See App. 3(D) (Va.))	Gilmer [*BB*]
Georgia Appeals Reports	Ga. App.

REPORTER	ABBREVIATION
Georgia Reports	Ga.
Grant (See App. 3(D) (Pa.))	Grant [*BB*]
Grattan (See App. 3(D) (Va.))	Gratt. [*BB*]
Gray (See App. 3(D) (Mass.))	Gray [*BB*]
Greene (See App. 3(D) (Iowa))	Greene [*BB*]
Guam Reports	Guam
Gunby's Reports (See App. 3(D) (La.))	Gunby [*BB*]
Hardin (See App. 3(D) (Ky.))	Hard. [*BB*]
Harper (See App. 3(D) (S.C.))	Harp. [*BB*]
Harper's Equity (See App. 3(D) (S.C.))	Harp. Eq. [*BB*]
Harrington (See App. 3(D) (Del.))	Harr. [*BB*]
Harris & Gill (See App. 3(D) (Md.))	H. & G. [*BB*]
Harris & Johnson (See App. 3(D) (Md.))	H. & J. [*BB*]
Harris & McHenry (See App. 3(D) (Md.))	H. & McH. [*BB*]
Hawaii Appellate Reports	Haw. App.
[West's] Hawaii Reports	Haw.
Hawks (See App. 3(D) (N.C.))	Hawks [*BB*]
Hayward & Hazelton, Circuit Court (Circuit Court Reports, vols. 6-7) (See App. 3(C) (D.C.))	Hay. & Haz. [*BB*]
Haywood (See App. 3(D) (Tenn.))	Hayw. [*BB*]
Head (See App. 3(D) (Tenn.))	Head [*BB*]
Heiskell (See App. 3(D) (Tenn.))	Heisk. [*BB*]
Henning & Munford (See App. 3(D) (Va.))	Hen. & M. [*BB*]
Hill (See App. 3(D) (S.C.))	Hill [*BB*]
Hill & Denio Supplement (Labor) (See App. 3(D) (N.Y.))	Hill & Den. [*BB*]
Hill's Equity (See App. 3(D) (S.C.))	Hill Eq. [*BB*]
Hill's Reports (See App. 3(D) (N.Y.))	Hill [*BB*]

REPORTER	ABBREVIATION
Hoffman's Chancery Reports (See App. 3(D) (N.Y.))	Hoff. Ch. *[BB]*
Hopkins Chancery Reports (See App. 3(D) (N.Y.))	Hopk. Ch. *[BB]*
Houston (See App. 3(D) (Del.))	Houst. *[BB]*
Howard (See App. 3(A) (U.S.))	How. *[BB]*
Howard's Practice Reports (See App. 3(D) (N.Y.))	How. Pr. How. Pr. (n.s.) *[BB]*
Hughes (See App. 3(D) (Ky.))	Hughes *[BB]*
Humphreys (See App. 3(D) (Tenn.))	Hum. *[BB]*
Idaho Reports	Idaho
Illinois Appellate Court Reports	Ill. App.
Illinois Appellate Court Reports Second Series	Ill. App. 2d
Illinois Appellate Court Reports Third Series	Ill. App. 3d
Illinois Circuit Court Reports	Ill. Cir. *[ALWD]*
Illinois Court of Claims Reports	Ill. Ct. Cl. *[BB]* Ill. Cl. *[ALWD]*
Illinois Reports (See App. 3(D) (Ill.) for nominatives incorporated in series)	Ill.
Illinois Reports Second Series	Ill. 2d
Indiana Appellate Court Reports	Ind. App.
Indiana Court of Appeals Reports	Ind. App.
Indiana Reports	Ind.
Iowa Reports	Iowa
Iredell's Equity (See App. 3(D) (N.C.))	Ired. Eq. *[BB]*
Iredell's Law (See App. 3(D) (N.C.))	Ired. *[BB]*
Johnson's Cases (See App. 3(D) (N.Y.))	Johns. Cas. *[BB]*

REPORTER	ABBREVIATION
Johnson's Chancery Reports (See App. 3(D) (N.Y.))	Johns. Ch. [*BB*]
Johnson's Reports (See App. 3(D) (N.Y.))	Johns. [*BB*]
Jones' Equity (See App. 3(D) (N.C.))	Jones Eq. [*BB*]
Jones' Law (See App. 3(D) (N.C.))	Jones [*BB*]
Jurispurdencia del Tribunal Supremo de Puerto Rico	J.T.S. [*ALWD*]
Kansas Court of Appeals Reports	Kan. App.
Kansas Court of Appeals Reports Second Series	Kan. App. 2d
Kansas Reports	Kan.
Kentucky Appellate Reporter	Ky. App. [*BB*]
Kentucky Attorneys Memo	Ky. Att'y Memo. [*BB*]
Kentucky Law Reporter	Ky. L. Rptr. [*BB*]
Kentucky Law Summary	Ky. L. Summ. [*BB*]
Kentucky Opinions	Ky. Op. [*BB*]
Kentucky Reports (See App. 3(D) (Ky.) for nominatives incorporated in series)	Ky.
Kirby (See App. 3(D) (Conn.))	Kirby [*BB*]
Lansing's Chancery Reports (See App. 3(D) (N.Y.))	Lans. Ch. [*BB*]
Lansing's Reports (See App. 3(D) (N.Y.))	Lans. [*BB*]
Law Week Colorado	L. Week Colo. [*BB*]
Leigh (See App. 3(D) (Va.))	Leigh [*BB*]
Littell (See App. 3(D) (Ky.))	Litt. [*BB*]
Littell's Selected Cases (See App. 3(D) (Ky.))	Litt. Sel. Cas. [*BB*]

REPORTER

ABBREVIATION

Lockwood's Reversed Cases (See App. 3(D) (N.Y.))	Lock. Rev. Cas. [BB]
Louisiana Annual Reports	La. Ann. [BB]
Louisiana Reports	La.
Louisiana Term Reports (See App. 3(D) (La.))	Mart. (o.s.) [BB] Mart. (n.s.) [BB]
MacArthur (See App. 3(C) (D.C.))	MacArth. [BB]
MacArthur & Mackey (See App. 3(c) (D.C.))	MacArth. & M. [BB]
Mackey (See App. 3(C) (D.C.))	Mackey [BB]
Maine Reports	Me.
[A.K.] Marshall (See App. 3(D) (Ky.))	A.K. Marsh. [BB]
[J.J.] Marshall (See App. 3(D) (Ky.))	J.J. Marsh. [BB]
Martin (See App. 3(D) (N.C.))	Mart. [BB]
Martin (Louisiana Term Reports) (See App. 3(D) (La.))	Mart. (o.s.) [BB] Mart. (n.s.) [BB]
Martin & Yerger (See App. 3(D) (Tenn.))	Mart. & Yer. [BB]
Marvel (See App. 3(D) (Del.))	Marv. [BB]
Maryland Appellate Reports	Md. App.
Maryland Reports	Md.
Massachusetts Appeals Court Reports	Mass. App. Ct. [BB] Mass. App. [ALWD]
Massachusetts Appellate Decisions	Mass. App. Dec.
[Massachusetts] Appellate Division Advance Sheets	[year] Mass. App. Div. Adv. Sheet [page] [BB]
Massachusetts Appellate Division Reports	Mass. App. Div.
Massachusetts Law Reporter	Mass. L. Rptr.

REPORTER	ABBREVIATION
Massachusetts Reports (See App. 3(D) (Ma.) for nominatives incorporated in series)	Mass.
Massachusetts [Reports] Supplement	Mass. Supp.
McCahon (See App. 3(D) (Kan.))	McCahon [*BB*]
McCord (See App. 3(D) (S.C.))	McCord [*BB*]
McCord's Chancery (See App. 3(D) (S.C.))	McCord Eq. [*BB*]
McGloin (See App. 3(D) (La..))	McGl. [*BB*]
McMullan (See App. 3(D) (S.C.))	McMul. [*BB*]
McMullan's Eq. (See App. 3(D) (S.C.))	McMul. Eq. [*BB*]
Meigs (See App. 3(D) (Tenn.))	Meigs [*BB*]
Metcalf (See App. 3(D) (Ky.))	Met. [*BB*]
Metcalf (See App. 3(D) (Mass.))	Met. [*BB*]
Michigan Appeals Reports	Mich. App.
Michigan Court of Claims Reports	Mich. Ct. Cl. [*BB*]
Michigan Reports	Mich.
[West's] Military Justice Reporter	M.J.
Mill's Constitutional Court	Mill. [*BB*]
Minnesota Reports	Minn.
Minor (See App. 3(D) (Ala.))	Minor [*BB*]
Mississippi Decisions	Miss. Dec. [*BB*]
Mississippi Reports (See App. 3(D) (Miss.) for nominatives incorporated in series)	Miss.
Missouri Appeal Reports	Mo. App.
Missouri Reports	Mo.
Monaghan (See App. 3(D) (Pa.))	Monag. [*BB*]
[Ben] Monroe (See App. 3(D) (Ky.))	B. Mon. [*BB*]
[T.B.] Monroe (See App. 3(D) (Ky.))	T.B. Mon. [*BB*]

REPORTER	ABBREVIATION
Montana Reports	Mont.
Montana State Reporter	State Rptr. [*BB*]
Morris (See App. 3(D) (Iowa))	Morris [*BB*]
Munford (See App. 3(D) (Va.))	Munf. [*BB*]
Murphy (See App. 3(D) (N.C.))	Mur. [*BB*]
Navajo Reporter	Navajo Rptr. [*BB*]
	Navajo [*ALWD*]
Nebraska Appellate Reports	Neb. App.
Nebraska Reports	Neb.
Nevada Reports	Nev.
New Hampshire Reports	N.H.
New Jersey Equity Reports	N.J. Eq.
New Jersey Law Reports	N.J.L.
New Jersey Miscellaneous Reports	N.J. Misc.
New Jersey Reports	N.J.
New Jersey Superior Court Reports	N.J. Super.
New Jersey Tax Court Reports	N.J. Tax
New Mexico Reports	N.M.
(See App. 3(D) (N.M.) for nominatives incorporated in series)	
New York Appellate Division Reports	A.D.
New York Appellate Division Reports Second Series	A.D. 2d
New York Appellate Division Reports Third Series	A.D. 3d
New York Chancery Reports Annotated (See App. 3(D) (N.Y.))	N.Y. Ch. Ann. [*BB*]
New York Reports	N.Y.
New York Reports Second Series	N.Y.2d
New York Reports Third Series	N.Y.3d
New York Miscellaneous Reports	Misc.

REPORTER	ABBREVIATION
New York Miscellaneous Reports	
Second Series	Misc. 2d
New York Miscellaneous Reports	
Third Series	Misc. 3d
[West's] New York Supplement	N.Y.S.
[West's] New York Supplement	
Second Series	N.Y.S. 2d
North Carolina Court of Appeals	N.C. App.
North Carolina Reports	N.C.
(See App. 3(D) (N.C.) for	
nominatives incorporated in	
series)	
North Dakota Reports	N.D.
[West's] North Eastern Reporter	N.E.
[West's] North Eastern Reporter	
Second Series	N.E.2d
Norther Mariana Commonwealth	N. Mar. I. Commw.
Reporter	[*BB*]
	N. Mar. Cmmw.
	[*ALWD*]
Northern Mariana Islands Reporter	N. Mar. I. [*BB*]
	N. Mar. Is. [*ALWD*]
Nott & McCord (See App. 3(D) (S.C.))	Nott. & McC. [*BB*]
Official Translations of the Supreme	P.R. Offic. Trans.
Court of Puerto Rico	[*BB*]
Rico	P.R. Off. Trans.
	[*ALWD*]
Ohio Appellate Reports	Ohio App.
Ohio Appellate Reports Second	
Series	Ohio App. 2d
Ohio Appellate Reports Third	
Series	Ohio App. 3d
Ohio Bar Reports	Ohio B. [*BB*]

REPORTER	ABBREVIATION
Ohio Circuit Court Decisions	Ohio C.C. Dec. [BB]
Ohio Circuit Court Reports	Ohio C.C.
	Ohio C.C. (n.s.) [BB]
Ohio Decisions	Ohio Dec. [BB]
Ohio Decisions, Reprint	Ohio Dec. Reprint [BB]
Ohio Law Abstract	Ohio Law Abs. [BB]
Ohio Law Reporter	Ohio L.R. [BB]
Ohio Miscellaneous Reports	Ohio Misc.
Ohio Miscellaneous Reports Second Series	Ohio Misc. 2d
Ohio Nisi Prius Reports	Ohio N.P.
	Ohio N.P. (n.s.) [BB]
Ohio Opinions	Ohio Op.
Ohio Opinions Second Series	Ohio Op. 2d
Ohio Opinions Third Series	Ohio Op. 3d
Ohio Reports	Ohio
Ohio State Reports	Ohio St.
Ohio State Reports Second Series	Ohio St. 2d
Ohio State Reports Third Series	Ohio St. 3d
Ohio Unreported Cases	Ohio Unrep. Cas. [BB]
Oklahoma Criminal Reports	Okla. Crim.
[Okla.] Indian Territory Reports	Indian Terr.
Oklahoma Reports	Okla.
Oklahoma Tribal Court Reports	Okla. Trib. [BB]
Oregon Reports	Or.
Oregon Reports, Court of Appeals	Or. App.
Oregon Tax [Court] Reports	Or. Tax

REPORTER	ABBREVIATION
Overton (See App. 3(D) (Tenn.))	Overt. [*BB*]
[West's] Pacific Reporter	P.
[West's] Pacific Reporter Second Series	P.2d
[West's] Pacific Reporter Third Series	P.3d
Paige's Chancery Reports (See App. 3(D) (N.Y.))	Paige Ch. [*BB*]
Peck (See App. 3(D) (Tenn.))	Peck [*BB*]
Peltier's Decisions, Parish of New Orleans (See App. 3(D) (La.))	Pelt. [*BB*]
Pennewill (See App. 3(D) (Del.))	Penne. [*BB*]
Pennsylvania Commonwealth Court	Pa. Commw. [*BB*] Pa. Cmmw. [*ALWD*]
Pennsylvania County Court Reports	Pa. C. [*BB*]
Pennsylvania District Reports	Pa. D. [*BB*]
Pennsylvania District and County Reports	Pa. D. & C.
Pennsylvania District and County Reports Second Series	Pa. D. & C.2d
Pennsylvania District and County Reports Third Series	Pa. D. & C.3d
Pennsylvania District and County Reports Fourth Series	Pa. D. & C.4th
Pennsylvania State Reports	Pa.
Pennsylvania Superior Court Reports	Pa. Super.
Pennypacker (See App. 3(D) (Pa.))	Pennyp. [*BB*]
Penrose & Watts (See App. 3(D) (Pa.))	Pen. & W. [*BB*]
Peters (See App. 3(A) (U.S.))	Pet. [*BB*]
Phillips Equity (See App. 3(D) (N.C.))	Phil. Eq. [*BB*]
Phillips Law (See App. 3(D) (N.C.))	Phil. [*BB*]
Pickering (See App. 3(D) (Mass.))	Pick. [*BB*]

REPORTER	ABBREVIATION
Pinney (See App. 3(D) (Wis.))	Pin. [*BB*]
Porter (See App. 3(D) (Ala.))	Port. [*BB*]
Posey (See App. 3(C) (Tex.))	Posey [*BB*]
[Puerto Rico] Avazadas del Colegio de Abogados de Puerto Rico	C.A. [*ALWD*]
[Puerto Rico] Decisiones de Puerto Rico	P.R. Dec. [*BB*]
	D.P.R. [*ALWD*]
[Puerto Rico] Decisiones del Tribunal de Circuito de Apelaciones [de] Puerto Rico	T.C.A.
[Puerto Rico] Jurispurdencia del Tribunal Supremo de Puerto Rico	J.T.S. [*ALWD*]
[Puerto Rico] Official Translations of the Supreme Court of Puerto Rico	P.R. Offic. Trans. [*BB*]
	P.R. Off. Trans. [*ALWD*]
Puerto Rico Reports	P.R. [*BB*]
	P.R.R. [*ALWD*]
[Puerto Rico] Sentencias de Tribunal Supremo de Puerto Rico	P.R. Sent. [*BB*]
Randolph (See App. 3(D) (Va.))	Rand. [*BB*]
Rawle (See App. 3(D) (Pa.))	Rawle [*BB*]
Rhode Island Reports	R.I.
Rice (See App. 3(D) (S.C.))	Rice [*BB*]
Rice's Equity (See App. 3(D) (S.C.))	Rice Eq. [*BB*]
Richardson (See App. 3(D) (S.C.))	Rich. [*BB*]
Richardson's Cases (See App. 3(D) (S.C.))	
Richardson's Equity (See App. 3(D) (S.C.))	Rich. Cas. [*BB*]
	Rich. Eq. [*BB*]
Riley (See App. 3(D) (S.C.))	Ril. [*BB*]
Riley's Equity (See App. 3(D) (S.C.))	Ril. Eq. [*BB*]

REPORTER	ABBREVIATION
Robards (See App. 3(D) (Tex.))	Robards *[BB]*
Robinson (See App. 3(D) (La.))	Rob. *[BB]*
Robinson (See App. 3(D) (Va.))	Rob. *[BB]*
Root (See App. 3(D) (Conn.))	Root *[BB]*
Sadler (See App. 3(D) (Pa.))	Sadler *[BB]*
Sandford's Chancery Reports (See App. 3(D) (N.Y.))	Sand. Ch. *[BB]*
Sartoga Chancery Sentinel (See App. 3(D) (N.Y.))	Sarat. Ch. Sent. *[BB]*
Scammon (See App. 3(D) (Ill.)	Scam. *[BB]*
Sentencias de Tribunal Supremo de Puerto Rico	P.R. Sent. *[BB]*
Sergeant & Rawle (See App. 3(D) (Pa.))	Serg. & Rawle *[BB]*
Smedes & Marshall (See App. 3(D) (Miss.))	S. & M. *[BB]*
Sneed (See App. 3(D) (Ky.))	Sneed *[BB]*
Sneed (See App. 3(D) (Tenn.))	Sneed *[BB]*
South Carolina Equity Reports (See App. 3(D) (S.C.) for nominatives incorporated in series)	S.C. Eq. *[BB]*
South Carolina Law Reports (See App. 3(D) (S.C.) for nominatives incorporated in series)	S.C.L. *[BB]*
South Carolina Reports	S.C.
South Dakota Reports	S.D.
[West's] South Eastern Reporter	S.E.
[West's] South Eastern Reporter Second Series	S.E.2d
[West's] South Western Reporter	S.W.

REPORTER	ABBREVIATION
[West's] South Western Reporter Second Series	S.W.2d
[West's] South Western Reporter Third Series	S.W.3d
[West's] Southern Reporter	So.
[West's] Southern Reporter Second Series	So. 2d
Speers (See App. 3(D) (S.C.))	Speers [BB]
Speers Equity (See App. 3(D) (S.C.))	Speers Eq. [BB]
State Reporter (Montana)	State Rptr. [BB]
Stewart (See App. 3(D) (Ala.))	Stew. [BB]
Stewart & Porter (See App. 3(D) (Ala.))	Stew. & P. [BB]
Strobhart (See App. 3(D) (S.C.))	Strob. [BB]
Strobhart's Equity (See App. 3(D) (S.C.))	Strob. Eq. [BB]
[West's] Supreme Court Reporter	S. Ct.
Swan (See App. 3(D) (Tenn.))	Swan [BB]
Taylor (See App. 3(D) (N.C.))	Tay. [BB]
Taylor's North Carolina Term Reports (See App. 3(D) (N.C.))	Taylor [BB]
Teissier, Orleans Court of Appeals (See App. 3(D) (La.))	Teiss. [BB]
Tennessee Appeals Reports	Tenn. App.
Tennessee Criminal Appeals Reports	Tenn. Crim.
Tennessee Reports (See App. 3(D) (Tenn.) for nominatives incorporated in series)	Tenn.
Texas Civil Appeals Reports	Tex. Civ. App. [BB] Tex. Civ. [ALWD]

REPORTER	ABBREVIATION
Texas Court of Appeals Reports	Tex. Ct. App. [*BB*]
	Tex. App. [*ALWD*]
Texas Criminal Reports	Tex. Crim.
Texas Reports	Tex.
Texas Supreme Court Journal	Tex. Sup. Ct. J. [*BB*]
Texas Unreported Cases (Posey) (See App. 3(C) (Tex.))	Posey [*BB*]
Tredway (See App. 3(D) (S.C.))	Tread. [*BB*]
Tucker & Clephane (See App. 3(C) (D.C))	Tuck. & Cl. [*BB*]
Tyler (See App. 3(D) (Vt.))	Tyl. [*BB*]
Tyng (See App. 3(D) (Mass.))	Tyng [*BB*]
[United States] Board of Tax Appeals Reports	B.T.A.
United States Claims Court Reporter	Cl. Ct.
United States Court of Appeals Reports [D.C. Cir.]	U.S. App. D.C. [*BB*]
[United States] Court of Claims Reports	Ct. Cl.
[United States] Court of Customs and Patent Appeals	C.C.P.A.
[United States] Court of International Trade Reporter Decisions	I.T.R.D. (BNA)
[United States] Court of International Trade Reports	Ct. Int'l Trade [*BB*]
	Ct. Intl. Trade [*ALWD*]
United States Court of Military Appeals, [Decisions of the]	C.M.A.
United States Law Week	U.S.L.W.

REPORTER	ABBREVIATION
United States Reports	U.S.
United States Supreme Court Reports, Lawyers' Edition	L. Ed.
United States Supreme Court Reports, Lawyers' Edition, Second Edition	L. Ed. 2d
United States Tax Court	T.C.
Utah Reports	Utah
Utah Reports Second Series	Utah 2d
Vermont Reports	Vt.
[West's] Veterans Appeals Reporter	Vet. App.
Virgin Island[s] Reports	V.I.
Virginia Cases, Criminal (See App. 3(D) (Va.))	Va. Cas. [BB]
Virginia Circuit Court Opinions	Va. Cir.
Virginia Court of Appeals Reports	Va. App.
Virginia Reports (See App. 3(D) (Va.) for nominatives incorporated in series)	Va.
Walker (See App. 3(D) (Pa.))	Walk. [BB]
Wallace (See App. 3(A) (U.S.))	Wall. [BB]
Washington (See App. 3(D) (Va.))	Wash. [BB]
Washington Appellate Reports	Wash. App.
Washington Reports	Wash.
Washington Reports Second Series	Wash. 2d
Washington Territory Reports	Wash. Terr. [BB]
Watts (See App. 3(D) (Pa.))	Watts [BB]
Watts & Sergeant (See App. 3(D) (Pa.))	Watts & Serg. [BB]
Wendell's Reports (See App. 3(D) (N.Y.))	Wend. [BB]
West Virginia Reports	W. Va.

<u>REPORTER</u>	<u>ABBREVIATION</u>
Wharton (See App. 3(D) (Pa.))	Whart. [*BB*]
Wheaton (See App. 3(A) (U.S.))	Wheat. [*BB*]
White & Wilson (Condensed Reports of Decisions in Civil Causes in the Court of Appeals) (See App. 3(D) (Tex.))	White & W. [*BB*]
Williams (See App. 3(D) (Mass.))	Will. [*BB*]
Wilcox's Condensed Reports (See App. 3(D) (Ohio)	Wilc. Cond. Rep. [*BB*]
Wilson (Condensed Reports of Decisions in Civil Causes in the Court of Appeals) (See App. 3(D) (Tex.))	Wilson [*BB*]
Winston (See App. 3(D) (N.C.))	Win. [*BB*]
Wisconsin Reports	Wis.
Wisconsin Reports Second Series	Wis. 2d
Wright (See App. 3(D) (Ohio))	Wright [*BB*]
Wyoming Reports	Wyo.
Yates Select Reports (See App. 3(D) (N.Y.))	Yates Sel. Cas. [*BB*]
Yeates (See App. 3(D) (Pa.))	Yeates [*BB*]
Yerger (See App. 3(D) (Tenn.))	Yer. [*BB*]

APPENDIX 3

NOMINATIVE REPORTERS

A. EARLY NOMINATIVE U.S. SUPREME COURT REPORTERS

ALWD = *ALWD Citation Manual*
BB = *Bluebook*

REPORTER	BLUEBOOK ABBREV.	VOLUMES		DATES
Dallas *	Dall.	4 vols.	1-4 U.S.	1789-1800
Cranch	Cranch	9 vols.	5-13 U.S.	1801-1815
Wheaton	Wheat.	12 vols.	14-25 U.S.	1816-1827
Peters	Pet.	16 vols.	26-41 U.S.	1828-1842
Howard	How.	24 vols.	42-65 U.S.	1843-1860
Black	Black	2 vols.	66-67 U.S.	1861-1862
Wallace	Wall.	23 vols.	68-90 U.S.	1863-1874

[*BB*] *McCulloch v. Maryland*, 17 U.S. (4 Wheat.) 316 (1819); *Harrison v. Sterry*, 9 U.S. (5 Cranch) 289 (1809).

* Despite being part of the *United States Reports* series, volume 1 of Dallas' reports contains only Pennsylvania cases. Volumes 2-4 of Dallas' reports contain both U.S. Supreme Court cases and Pennsylvania cases. The *Bluebook* indicates that those Pennsylvania cases should be cited to *United States Reports* "along with a parallel citation to the appropriate lower court reporter."

[*BB*] *Ross v. Whittenhouse*, 2 U.S. (2 Dall.) 160, 1 Yeates 443 (Pa. 1795); *United States v. Ravara*, 2 U.S. (2 Dall.) 297, 27 F. Cas. 713 (C.C.D. Pa. 1793) (No. 16,122).

B. EARLY NOMINATIVE LOWER FEDERAL COURT REPORTERS

Early nominative federal court reports should be cited only to the *Federal Cases* set if they have been reprinted therein. The Federal Case No. should be appended parenthetically in *Bluebook* citations, but it is not included in *ALWD* citations.

[*BB*] *United States v. Ashton*, 24 F. Cas. 873 (C.C.D. Mass. 1834) (No. 14,470).

[*ALWD*] *U.S. v. Ashton*, 24 F. Cas. 873 (C.C.D. Mass. 1834).

C. EARLY NOMINATIVE REPORTERS FOR THE DISTRICT OF COLUMBIA

DISTRICT OF COLUMBIA

REPORTER	BLUEBOOK ABBREV.	VOLUMES	DATES
Cranch	Cranch	5 vols. 1-5 D.C.	1801-1840
Hayward & Hazleton	Hay. & Haz.	2 vols. —	1840-1863
—	—	2 vols. 6-7 D.C.	1863-1872
MacArthur	MacArth.	3 vols. 8-10 D.C.	1873-1879
MacArthur & Mackey	MacArth. & M.	1 vol. 11 D.C.	1879-1880
Mackey	Mackey	9 vols. 12-20 D.C.	1880-1872
Tucker & Clephane	Tuck. & Cl.	1 vol. 21 D.C.	1892-1893

"D.C." is the abbreviation for *District of Columbia Reports.*

[*BB*] *Merchant v. Cook*, 21 D.C. (Tuck. & Cl.) 145 (1892); *Gunton v. Zantzinger*, 10 D.C. (3 MacArth.) 262 (1879).

D. EARLY NOMINATIVE STATE REPORTERS

• If no jurisdiction-named official report is indicated under "Volumes," then the nominative reporter has not been incorporated into a jurisdiction-named series (e.g., *Cary v. Gregg*, 3 Stew. 433 (Ala. 1831).).

• If only one volume is indicated for a nominative reporter, then no volume number is used (e.g., *Apthrop v. Backus*, Kirby 407 (Conn. 1788).).

• When a jurisdiction-named official report is indicated under "Volumes," the nominative reporter has been incorporated into a jurisdiction-named series; *The Bluebook* requires the early nominative volume number and reporter be included in the citation (e.g., *Harris v. Porter*, 2 Del. (2 Harr.) 27 (Super. Ct. 1835).); many local court citation rules also do so.

• The pagination in the jurisdiction-named series and the nominative reporter is usually the same; however, if it differs, *The Bluebook* requires parallel citations be used (e.g., *Perkins v. Parker*, 1 Mass. 89 (Will. 117) (1804).).

ALABAMA

REPORTER	BLUEBOOK ABBREV.	VOLUMES		DATES
Minor	Minor	1 vol.	—	1820-1826
Stewart	Stew.	3 vols.	—	1827-1831
Stewart & Porter	Stew. & P.	5 vols.	—	1831-1834

ALABAMA (CONTINUED)

REPORTER	BLUEBOOK ABBREV.	VOLUMES		DATES
Porter	Port.	9 vols.	—	1834-1839

Connects to 1 Ala. (Alabama Reports) (1840)
West's Southern Reporter (So.) coverage begins in 1886.

[BB] *Keath v. Patton*, 2 Stew. 38 (Ala. 1829); *Jones v. Acre*, Minor 5 (Ala. 1820).

CONNECTICUT

REPORTER	BLUEBOOK ABBREV.	VOLUMES		DATES
Kirby	Kirby	1 vol.	—	1785-1789
Root	Root	2 vols.	—	1789-1798
Day	Day	5 vols.	—	1802-1813

Connects to 1 Conn. (Connecticut Reports) (1814)
West's Atlantic Reporter (A.) coverage begins in 1885.

[BB] *Whipple v. McClure*, 2 Root 216 (Conn. 1795); *Nicole v. Mumford*, Kirby 270 (Conn. Super. Ct. 1786).

DELAWARE

REPORTER	BLUEBOOK ABBREV.	VOLUMES	DATES
Harrington	Harr.	5 vols. 1-5 Del.	1832-1855
Houston	Houst.	9 vols. 6-14 Del.	1855-1893
Marvel	Marv.	2 vols. 15-16 Del.	1893-1897
Pennewill	Penne.	7 vols. 17-23 Del.	1897-1909
Boyce	Boyce	7 vols. 24-30 Del.	1909-1920

Connects to 31 Del. (Delaware Reports) (1920)
West's Atlantic Reporter (A.) coverage begins in 1886.

DELAWARE (CONTINUED)

[BB] *Pyle v. Gallaher*, 22 Del. (6 Penne.) 407 (Super. Ct. 1908).

ILLINOIS

REPORTER	BLUEBOOK ABBREV.	VOLUMES	DATES
Breese	Breese	1 vol. 1 Ill.	1819-1851
Scammon	Scam.	4 vols. 2-5 Ill.	1832-1843
Gilman	Gilm.	5 vols. 6-10 Ill.	1844-1849

Connects to 11 Ill. (Illinois Reports) (1849)
West's North Eastern Reporter (N.E.) coverage begins in 1886.

[BB] *Mears v. Morrison*, 1 Ill. (Breese) 223 (1827); *Mason ex rel. Mason v. Caldwell*, 10 Ill. (5 Gilm.) 196 (1848).

INDIANA

REPORTER	BLUEBOOK ABBREV.	VOLUMES	DATES
Blackford	Blackf.	8 vols. —	1817-1847

Connects to 1 Ind. (Indiana Reports) (1848)
West's North Eastern Reporter (N.E.) begins in 1885.

IOWA

REPORTER	BLUEBOOK ABBREV.	VOLUMES	DATES
Bradford	Bradf.	3 vols. in 1 —	1838-1841
Morris	Morris	1 vol. —	1839-1846
Greene	Greene	4 vols. —	1847-1854

For volumes 1-8 of Ia. (Iowa Reports) (1855), *The Bluebook* indicates that Clarke's edition should be cited, if available.

West's North Western Reporter (N.W.) coverage begins in 1879.

[BB] *Phelps v. Pierson*, 1 Greene 121 (Iowa 1848); *Cane v. Watson*, Bradf. 42 (Iowa 1840); *Pixler v. Nichols*, 8 Iowa 106 (1859). [The *Pixler* case is cited to Clarke's edition of Iowa Reports.]

KANSAS

REPORTER	BLUEBOOK ABBREV.	VOLUMES	DATES
McCahon	McCahon	1 vol. —	1858-1868

Connects to 1 Kan. (Kansas Reports) (1862)
West's Pacific Reporter (P.) coverage begins in 1883.

[BB] *Armstrong v. Wyandotte Bridge Co.*, McCahon 166 (Kan. 1860).

KENTUCKY

REPORTER	BLUEBOOK ABBREV.	VOLUMES		DATES
Hughes	Hughes	1 vol.	1 Ky.	1785-1801
Sneed	Sneed	1 vol.	2 Ky.	1801-1805

KENTUCKY (CONTINUED)

REPORTER	BLUEBOOK ABBREV.	VOLUMES		DATES
Hardin	Hard.	1 vol.	3 Ky.	1805-1808
Bibb	Bibb	4 vols.	4-7 Ky.	1808-1817
Marshall, A.K.	A.K. Marsh.	3 vols.	8-10 Ky.	1817-1821
Littell	Litt.	5 vols.	11-15 Ky.	1822-1824
Littell's Selected Cases	Litt. Sel. Cas.	1 vol.	16 Ky.	1795-1821
Monroe, T.B.	T.B. Mon.	7 vols.	17-23 Ky.	1824-1828
Marshall, J.J.	J.J. Marsh.	7 vols.	24-30 Ky.	1829-1832
Dana	Dana	9 vols.	31-39 Ky.	1833-1840
Monroe, Ben	B. Mon.	18 vols.	40-57 Ky.	1840-1857
Metcalf	Met.	4 vols.	58-61 Ky.	1858-1863
Duvall	Duv.	2 vols.	62-63 Ky.	1863-1866
Bush	Bush	14 vols.	64-77 Ky.	1866-1879

Connects to 78 Ky. (Kentucky Reports) (1879)
West's South Western Reporter (S.W.) coverage begins in 1886.

[BB] *Auditor v. Ballard*, 72 Ky. (9 Bush) 572 (1873); *Pope v. Campbell*, 3 Ky. (Hard.) 31 (1805).

LOUISIANA

REPORTER	BLUEBOOK ABBREV.	VOLUMES		DATES
Martin	Mart. (o.s.)	12 vols.	—	1809-1823
	Mart. (n.s.)	8 vols.	—	1823-1830
Louisiana Reports	La.	19 vols.	—	1830-1841

LOUISIANA (CONTINUED)

REPORTER	BLUEBOOK ABBREV.	VOLUMES		DATES
Robinson	Rob.	12 vols.	—	1841-1846
Louisiana Annual Reports	La. Ann.	52 vols.	—	1846-1900

Connects to 109 La. (Louisiana Reports) (1901)
West's Southern Reporter (So.) coverage begins in 1887.

[BB] *Galloway v. Legan*, 4 Mart. (n.s.) 167 (La. 1826); *Edwards v. Turner*, 6 Rob. 382 (La. 1844).

REPORTER	BLUEBOOK ABBREV.	VOLUMES		DATES
McGloin's Ct. of Appeals Reports	McGl.	2 vols.	—	1881-1884
Gunby's Reports	Gunby	1 vol.	—	1885
Teisser	Teiss.	14 vols.	—	1903-1917
Pelitier	Pelt.	7 vols.	—	1917-1924

Connects to 1 La. App. (Louisiana Court of Appeals Reports) (1924)
West's Southern Reporter (So.) coverage begins in 1928.

[BB] *Herbert v. Smylie*, Gunby 73 (La. Ct. App. 1885); *Marcuse v. Kramer*, 5 Teiss. 247 (La. Ct. App. 1908).

MARYLAND

REPORTER	BLUEBOOK ABBREV.	VOLUMES		DATES
Harris and McHenry	H. & McH.	4 vols.	—	1770-1799
Harris and Johnson	H. & J.	7 vols.	—	1800-1826
Harris and Gill	H. & G.	2 vols.	—	1826-1829
Gill and Johnson	G. & J.	12 vols.	—	1829-1842
Gill	Gill	9 vols.	—	1843-1851

Connects to 1 Md. (Maryland Reports) (1851)
West's Atlantic Reporter (A.) coverage begins in 1885.

[BB] *Bevans v. Sullivan*, 4 Gill 383 (Md. 1846).

MASSACHUSETTS

REPORTER	BLUEBOOK ABBREV.	VOLUMES		DATES
Williams	Will.	1 vol.	1 Mass.	1804-1805
Tyng	Tyng	16 vols.	2-17 Mass.	1806-1822
Pickering	Pick.	24 vols.	18-41 Mass.	1822-1839
Metcalf	Met.	13 vols.	42-54 Mass.	1840-1847
Cushing	Cush.	12 vols.	55-66 Mass.	1848-1853
Gray	Gray	16 vols.	67-82 Mass.	1854-1860
Allen	Allen	14 vols.	83-96 Mass.	1861-1867

Connects to 97 Mass. (Massachusetts Reports) (1867)
West's North Eastern Reporter (N.E.) coverage begins in 1885.

[BB] *Rohan v. Sawin*, 59 Mass. (5 Cush.) 281 (1850); *Clark v. King*, 2 Mass. 471, 1 Tyng 524 (1807). [Pagination differs]

MICHIGAN

REPORTER	BLUEBOOK ABBREV.	VOLUMES		DATES
Blume Sup. Ct. Transactions	Blume Sup. Ct. Trans.	6 vols.	—	1805-1836
Blume Unreported Opinions	Blume Unrep. Op.	1 vol.	—	1836-1843
Douglass	Doug.	2 vols.	—	1843-1847

Connects to 1 Mich. (Michgan Reports) (1847)
West's North Western Reporter (N.W.) coverage begins in 1879.

[BB] *People v. Moore*, 2 Doug. 1 (Mich. 1845); *Roby v. Reaume*, 3 Blume Sup. Ct. Trans. 376 (Mich. 1819).

MISSISSIPPI

REPORTER	BLUEBOOK ABBREV.	VOLUMES		DATES
Walker	Walker	1 vol.	1 Miss.	1818-1832
Howard	Howard	7 vols.	2-8 Miss.	1834-1843
Smedes and Marshall	S. & M.	14 vols.	9-22 Miss.	1843-1850

Connects to 23 Miss. (Mississippi Reports) (1851)
West's Southern Reporter (So.) coverage begins in 1886.

[BB] *Hill v. Robeson*, 10 Miss. (2 S. & M) 340 (1844).

NEW MEXICO

REPORTER	BLUEBOOK ABBREV.	VOLUMES		DATES
Gildersleeve (preferred edition)	Gild. E.W.S. ed.	4 vols.	1-4 N.M.	1852-1888

Connects to 5 N.M. (New Mexico Reports) (1888)
West's Pacific Reporter (P.) coverage begins in 1883.

[BB] *Bustamento v. Analla*, 1 N.M. (Gild. E.W.S. ed.) 255 (1857).

NEW YORK

REPORTER	BLUEBOOK ABBREV.	VOLUMES		DATES
Coleman	Cole.			
	Cases	1 vol.	—	1791-1800
Johnson	Johns.			
	Cas.	3 vols.	—	1799-1803
Coleman &	Coel. &			
	Cai.	1 vol.	—	1794-1805
Caines Cases	Cai. Cas.	2 vols.	—	1796-1805
Caines Reports	Cai.	3 vols.	—	1796-1805
Johnson	Johns.	20 vols.	—	1806-1823
Cowen	Cow.	9 vols.	—	1823-1829
Wendell	Wend.	26 vols.	—	1828-1841
Anthon's Nisi Prius Cas.	Ant. N.P. Cas.	1 vol.	—	1808-1851
Yates Select Cases	Yates Sel. Cas.	1 vol.	—	1809

NEW YORK (CONTINUED)

REPORTER	BLUEBOOK ABBREV.	VOLUMES		DATES
Edmond's Select Cases	Edm. Sel. Cas.	2 vols.	—	1834-1853
Hill	Hill	7 vols.	—	1841-1844
Hill & Denio Supp.	Hill & Den.	1 vol.	—	1842-1844
Denio	Denio	5 vols.	—	1845-1848
Lockwood's Reserved Cases	Lock. Rev. Cas.	1 vol.	—	1799-1847

Connects to 1 N.Y. (New York Reports) (1847)
West's North Eastern Reporter (N.E.) coverage begins in 1885.

[BB] *Livingston v. Van Ingen*, 9 Johns. 507 (N.Y. 1812); *Blodgett v. Washams*, Hill & Den. 65 (N.Y. 1843).

REPORTER	BLUEBOOK ABBREV.	VOLUMES		DATES
N.Y. Chan. Rep. Ann.	N.Y. Ch. Ann.	7 vols.	—	1814-1847
Johnson's Chancery	Johns. Ch..	7 vols.	—	1814-1823
Lansing Chancery	Lans. Ch.	1 vols	—	1824-1826
Hopkins Chancery	Hopk. Ch.	1 vol.	—	1823-1826
Hoffman's Chancery	Hoff. Ch.	1 vol.	—	1839-1840
Clarke's Chancery	Cl. Ch.	1 vol.	—	1839-1841

NEW YORK (CONTINUED)

REPORTER	BLUEBOOK ABBREV.	VOLUMES	DATES
Paige's Chancery	Paige Ch.	11 vols. —	1828-1841
Saratoga Chancery Sentinel	Sarat. Ch. Sentinel	6 vols. —	1841-1847
Sandford's Chancery	Sand. Ch.	4 vols. —	1843-1847
Babour's Chancery	Barb. Ch.	3 vols. —	1845-1848
Edward's Chancery	Edw. Ch.	4 vols. —	1831-1850

Connects to 1 N.Y. (New York Reports) (1847)

West's North Eastern Reporter (N.E.) coverage begins in 1885.

[*BB*] *People v. Mercein*, 8 Paige Ch. 47 (N.Y. 1839).

REPORTER	BLUEBOOK ABBREV.	VOLUMES	DATES
Barbour's Supreme Ct. Reports	Barb.	67 vols. —	1847-1877
Lansing's Reports	Lans.	7 vols. —	1869-1873

Connects to 1 A.D. (New York Appellate Division Reports) (1896)

West's New York Supplement (N.Y.S.) coverage begins in 1888.

[*BB*] *Hall v. Southmayd*, 15 Barb. 32 (N.Y. App. Div. 1853).

NEW YORK (CONTINUED)

REPORTER	BLUEBOOK ABBREV.	VOLUMES		DATES
Howard's Practice Reports	How. Pr., How. Pr. (n.s.)	70 vols.	—	1844-1886
Abbott's Practice Reports	Abb. Pr., Abb. Pr. (n.s.)	35 vols.	—	1854-1875
Abbott's New Cases	Abb. N. Cas.	32 vols.	—	1876-1894

Connects to 1 Misc. (New York Miscellaneous Reports) (1892)
West's New York Supplement (N.Y.S.) coverage begins in 1888.

[BB] *Loonam v. Brockway*, 28 How. Pr. 472 (N.Y. Sup. Ct. 1864).

NORTH CAROLINA

REPORTER	BLUEBOOK ABBREV.	VOLUMES		DATES
Martin	Mart.	1 vol.	1 N.C.	1778-1797
Taylor Conf. by	Tay.	1 vol.	1 N.C.	1798-1802
Cameron & Norwood	Cam. & Nor.	1 vol.	1 N.C.	1800-1804
Haywood	Hayw.	2 vols.	2-3 N.C.	1789-1806
Carolina Law Repository	Car. L. Rep.	2 vols.	4 N.C.	1811-1816

NORTH CAROLINA (CONTINUED)

Reporter	Bluebook Abbrev.	Volumes		Dates
Taylor's N.C. Term Reports	Taylor	1 vol.	4 N.C.	1816-1818
Murphey	Mur.	3 vols.	5-7 N.C.	1804-1813 1818-1819
Hawks	Hawks	4 vols.	8-11 N.C.	1820-1826
Devereux's Law	Dev.	4 vols.	12-15 N.C.	1826-1834
Devereux's Equity	Dev. Eq.	2 vols.	16-17 N.C.	1826-1834
Devereux & Battle's Law	Dev. & Bat.	4 vols.	18-20 N.C.	1834-1839
Devereux & Battle's Equity	Dev. & Bat. Eq.	2 vols.	21-22 N.C.	1834-1839
Iredell's Law	Ired.	13 vols.	23-35 N.C.	1840-1852
Iredell's Equity	Ired. Eq.	8 vols.	36-43 N.C.	1840-1852
Busbee's Law	Busb.	1 vol.	44 N.C.	1852-1853
Busbee's Equity	Busb. Eq.	1 vol.	45 N.C.	1852-1853
Jones' Law	Jones	8 vols.	46-53 N.C.	1853-1862
Jones' Equity	Jones Eq.	6 vols.	54-59 N.C.	1853-1863
Winston	Win.	2 vols.	60 N.C.	1863-1864
Phillips' Law	Phil.	1 vol.	61 N.C.	1866-1868

NORTH CAROLINA (CONTINUED)

REPORTER	BLUEBOOK ABBREV.	VOLUMES		DATES
Phillips' Equity	Phil. Eq.	1 vol.	62 N.C.	1866-1868

Connects to 63 N.C. (North Carolina Reports) (1868)
West's South Eastern Reporter (S.E.) coverage begins in 1887.

[BB] *State v. Mann*, 13 N.C. (2 Dev.) 263 (1829); *Turley v. Nowell*, 62 N.C. (Phil. Eq.) 301 (1868).

OHIO

REPORTER	BLUEBOOK ABBREV.	VOLUMES		DATES
Wright	Wright	1 vol.	—	1831-1834
Wilcox's Condensed Reports	Wilc. Cond. Rep.	5 vols.	—	1821-1836

Connects to Ohio Reports (Ohio) (1821-1851) and Ohio State Reports (Ohio St.) (1852)
West's North Eastern Reporter (N.E.) coverage begins in 1885.

[BB] *Stanberry's Lessee v. Nelson*, Wright 766 (Ohio 1834).

PENNSYLVANIA

REPORTER	BLUEBOOK ABBREV.	VOLUMES		DATES
Alden	Ald.	3 vols.	—	1754-1814
Dallas	Dall.	4 vols.	—	1754-1806
Addison	Add.	1 vol.	—	1791-1799

PENNSYLVANIA (CONTINUED)

REPORTER	BLUEBOOK ABBREV.	VOLUMES		DATES
Yeates	Yeates	4 vols.	—	1791-1808
Binney	Binn.	6 vols.	—	1799-1814
Sergeant & Rawle	Serg. & Rawle	17 vols.	—	1814-1828
Penrose & Watts	Pen & W.	3 vols.	—	1829-1832
Rawle	Rawle	5 vols.	—	1828-1835
Watts	Watts	10 vols.	—	1832-1840
Wharton	Whart.	6 vols.	—	1835-1841
Watts & Sergeant	Watts & Serg.	9 vols.	—	1841-1845
Grant	Grant	3 vols.	—	1814-1863
Pennypacker	Pennyp.	4 vols.	—	1881-1884
Walker	Walk.	4 vols.	—	1855-1885
Sadler	Sadler	10 vols.	—	1885-1889
Monaghan	Monag.	2 vols.	—	1888-1890

Pennsylvania State Reports (Pa.) begins in 1845.
West's Atlantic Reporter (A.) coverage begins in 1885.

[BB] *Prevost v. Nicholls*, 4 Yeates 479 (Pa. 1808); Hare v. Bedell, 98 Pa. 485, 1 Pennyp. 392 (1881). [Pagination differs]

SOUTH CAROLINA

REPORTER	BLUEBOOK ABBREV.	VOLUMES		DATES
Bay	Bay	2 vols.	1-2 S.C.L.	1783-1804
Brevard	Brev.	3 vols.	3-5 S.C.L.	1793-1816
Treadway	Tread.	2 vols.	6-7 S.C.L.	1812-1816

SOUTH CAROLINA (CONTINUED)

REPORTER	BLUEBOOK ABBREV.	VOLUMES		DATES
Mill Const. Court Reps.	Mill	2 vols.	8-9 S.C.L.	1817-1818
Nott & McCord	Nott & McC.	2 vols.	10-11 S.C.L.	1819-1820
McCord	McCord	4 vols.	12-15 S.C.L.	1821-1828
Harper	Harp.	1 vol.	16 S.C.L.	1823-1824
Bailey	Bail.	2 vols.	17-18 S.C.L.	1828-1832
Hill	Hill	3 vols.	19-21 S.C.L.	1833-1837
Riley	Ril.	1 vol.	22 S.C.L.	1836-1837
Dudley	Dud.	1 vol.	23 S.C.L.	1837-1838
Rice	Rice	1 vol.	24 S.C.L.	1838-1839
Cheves	Chev.	1 vol.	25 S.C.L.	1839-1840
McMullan	McMul.	2 vols.	26-27 S.C.L.	1840-1842
Speers	Speers	2 vols.	28-29 S.C.L.	1842-1844
Richardson	Rich.	2 vols.	30-31 S.C.L.	1844-1846
Strobhart	Strob.	5 vols.	32-36 S.C.L.	1846-1850
Richardson	Rich.	13 vols.	37-49 S.C.L.	1850-1868

Connects to 1 S.C. (South Carolina Reports) (1868)
West's South Eastern Reporter (S.E.) begins in 1887.

[BB] *State v. Brazil*, 24 S.C.L. (Rice) 257 (1839); *Ex parte Leland*, 10 S.C.L. (1 Nott & McC.) 460 (1819).

REPORTER	BLUEBOOK ABBREV.	VOLUMES		DATES
Desaussure's Equity	Des. Eq.	4 vols.	1-4 S.C. Eq.	1784-1817
Harper's Equity	Harp. Eq.	1 vol.	5 S.C. Eq.	1824

SOUTH CAROLINA (CONTINUED)

REPORTER	BLUEBOOK ABBREV.	VOLUMES		DATES
McCord's Chancery	McCord Eq.	2 vols.	6-7 S.C. Eq.	1825-1827
Bailey's Equity	Bail. Eq.	1 vol.	8 S.C. Eq.	1830-1831
Richardson's Cases	Rich. Cas.	1 vol.	9 S.C. Eq.	1831-1832
Hill's Chancery	Hill. Eq.	2 vols.	10-11 S.C. Eq.	1833-1837
Riley's Chancery	Ril. Eq.	1 vol..	12 S.C. Eq.	1836-1837
Dudley's Equity	Dud. Eq.	1 vol.	13 S.C. Eq.	1837-1838
Rice's Equity	Rice Eq.	1 vol.	14 S.C. Eq.	1838-1839
Cheves' Equity	Chev. Eq.	1 vol.	15 S.C. Eq.	1839-1840
McMullan's Equity	McMul. Eq.	1 vol.	16 S.C. Eq.	1840-1842
Speers' Equity	Speers Eq.	1 vol.	17 S.C. Eq.	1842-1844
Richardson's Equity	Rich. Eq.	2 vols.	18-19 S.C. Eq.	1844-1846
Strobhart's Equity	Strob. Eq.	4 vols.	20-23 S.C. Eq.	1846-1850
Richardson's Equity	Rich. Eq.	12 vols.	24-35 S.C. Eq.	1850-1868

Connects to 1 S.C. (South Carolina Reports) (1868)
West's South Eastern Reporter (S.E.) coverage begins in 1887.

[BB] *Sims v. Sims*, 11 S.C. Eq. (2 Hill) 61 (1834); *Harmon v. Dreher*, 17 S.C. Eq. (Speers Eq.) 87 (1843).

TENNESSEE

REPORTER	BLUEBOOK ABBREV.	VOLUMES		DATES
Overton	Overt.	2 vols.	1-2 Tenn.	1791-1816
Cooke	Cooke	1 vol.	3 Tenn.	1811-1814
Haywood	Hayw.	3 vols.	4-6 Tenn.	1816-1818
Peck	Peck	1 vol.	7 Tenn.	1821-1824
Martin & Yerger	Mart. & Yer.	1 vol.	8 Tenn.	1825-1828
Yerger	Yer.	10 vols.	9-18 Tenn.	1818-1837
Meigs	Meigs	1 vol.	19 Tenn.	1838-1839
Humphreys	Hum.	11 vols.	20-30 Tenn.	1839-1851
Swan	Swan	2 vols.	31-32 Tenn.	1851-1853
Sneed	Sneed	5 vols.	33-37 Tenn.	1853-1858
Head	Head	3 vols.	38-40 Tenn.	1858-1860
Coldwell	Cold.	7 vols.	41-47 Tenn.	1860-1870
Heiskell	Heisk.	12 vols.	48-59 Tenn.	1870-1874

Connects to 60 Tenn. (Tennessee Reports) (1872)
West's South Western Reporter (S.W.) coverage begins in 1886.

[BB] *Barton's Lessee v. Shall*, 7 Tenn. (Peck) 215 (1823); Craddock v. Cabiness, 31 Tenn. (1 Swan) 474 (1852).

TEXAS

REPORTER	BLUEBOOK ABBREV.	VOLUMES		DATES
Dallam (Digest of the Laws of Texas)	Dallam	1 vol.	—	1840-1844
Texas Law Review *	65 Tex. L. Rev. [page]	Not App.	—	1845-1846

TEXAS (CONTINUED)

Connects to 1 Tex. (Texas Reports) (1846)
West's South Western Reporter (S.W.) coverage begins in 1886.

* *The Bluebook* provides the following format for citing the previously unpublished cases from the 1845 Term:
[Case Name] [Tex. & year], 65 Tex. L. Rev. [page] (Reprint information [Paulsen rep.] & date [1986]).

[BB] *Republic v. DeWees* (Tex. 1845), 65 Tex. L. Rev. 372 (Paulsen rep. 1986).

Synopses of the Decisions of the Supreme Court of Texas Arising from Restraints by Conscript and Other Military Authorities is cited by *The Bluebook* as "Robards" (with no volume number).

REPORTER	BLUEBOOK ABBREV.	VOLUMES	DATES
White & Wilson *	White & W.	1 vol. —	1876-1883
Wilson *	Wilson	3 vols. —	1883-1892

* Condensed Reports of Decisions in Civil Causes in the Court of Appeals (4 volumes)

Connects to 1 Tex. Civ. App. (Texas Civil Appeals Reports) (1892)
West's South Western Reporter (S.W.) coverage begins in 1892.

[BB] *Lauve v. Balfour*, 1 White & W. § 727 (Tex. Ct. App. 1879).

For additional information on citation of early Texas courts and cases, see *Texas Rules of Form*.

VERMONT

REPORTER	BLUEBOOK ABBREV.	VOLUMES		DATES
N. Chipman	N. Chip.	1 vol.	—	1789-1791
Tyler	Tyl.	2 vols.	—	1800-1803
Brayton	Brayt.	1 vol.	—	1815-1819
D. Chipman	D. Chip.	2 vols.	—	1789-1824
Aikens	Aik.	2 vols.	—	1825-1828

Connects to 1 Vt. (Vermont Reports) (1826).
West's Atlantic Reporter (A.) coverage begins in 1885.

[BB] *Higley v. Smith*, 1 D. Chip. 409 (Vt. 1824); *Hathaway v. Allen*, Brayt. 152 (Vt. 1815).

VIRGINIA

REPORTER	BLUEBOOK ABBREV.	VOLUMES		DATES
Washington	Wash.	2 vols.	1-2 Va.	1790-1796
Va. Criminal Cases	Va. Cas.	2 vols.	3-4 Va.	1789-1826
Call	Call	6 vols.	5-10 Va.	1779-1825
Henning & Munford	Hen. & M.	4 vols.	11-14 Va.	1806-1810
Munford	Munf.	4 vols.	15-20 Va.	1810-1820
Gilmer	Gilmer	1 vol.	21 Va.	1820-1821
Randolph	Rand.	6 vols.	22-27 Va.	1821-1828
Leigh	Leigh	12 vols.	28-39 Va.	1829-1842
Robinson	Rob.	2 vols.	40-41 Va.	1842-1844
Grattan	Gratt.	33 vols.	42-74 Va.	1844-1880

Connects to 75 Va. (Virginia Reports) (1880)
West's South Eastern Reporter (S.E.) coverage begins in 1887.

VIRGINIA (CONTINUED)

[BB] *Baker v. Preston*, 21 Va. (Gilmer) 235 (1821); *Hunter v. Martin*, 18 Va. (4 Munf.) 1 (1813).

WISCONSIN

REPORTER	BLUEBOOK ABBREV.	VOLUMES		DATES
Burnett	Bur.	2 vols. *	—	1841-1843
Chandler	Chand.	4 vols.	—	1849-1852
Pinney	Pin.	3 vols.	—	1839-1852

Connects to 1 Wis. (Wisconsin Reports) (1853)
West's North Western Reporter (N.W.) coverage begins in 1889.

* Burnett's first volume is bound with the session laws for December 1841.

[BB] *Fisher v. Otis*, 3 Chand. 83 (Wis. 1850).

APPENDIX 4

STATUS OF OFFICIAL STATE COURT REPORTERS, PUBLIC DOMAIN CITATIONS, AND AVAILABILITY OF PARALLEL WEST CITATIONS

ALWD = *ALWD Citation Manual*
BB = *Bluebook*

[Highest Court Listed First] STATE COURT	WEST RPTR.	FIRST WEST CITE AVAILABLE FOR	LAST VOL. OF OFFICIAL REPORTER
Ala. Sup. Ct. (Ala. 1840 → 1976) Nominatives See App. 3(D)	So. So. 2d	80 Ala. 433 (1887)	295 Ala. (1976)
Ala. Civ. App. & Ala. Crim. App. (previously Ala. Ct. App.) (1910 → 1976)	So. So. 2d	1 Ala. App. (1910)	57 Ala. App. (1976)
Alaska Sup. Ct. (1960 →)	P.2d P.3d	Not App.	Not App.
Alaska Ct. App. (1980 →)	P.2d P.3d	Not App.	Not App.

[Highest Court Listed First] STATE COURT	WEST RPTR.	FIRST WEST CITE AVAILABLE FOR	LAST VOL. OF OFFICIAL REPORTER
Ariz. Sup. Ct. ‡ (Ariz. 1866 ➔)	P. P.2d P.3d	1 Ariz. 25 * (1866)	To Date

[* Early Arizona cases were published retrospectively in the Pacific Reporter.]

[‡ Beginning Jan. 1, 1998, opinions use paragraph numbering.]

Ariz. Ct. of App. ‡ (1965 ➔)	P.2d P.2d P.3d	1 Ariz. App. (1965 ➔ 1976) Ariz. (1976 ➔)	Not App. To Date

[‡ Beginning Jan. 1, 1998, opinions use paragraph numbering.]

Ark. Sup Ct. (Ark. 1837 ➔)	S.W. S.W.2d S.W.3d	47 Ark. (1885) (1886 ➔)	To Date

Ark. Ct. App. (1979 ➔)	S.W.2d S.W.3d	266 Ark. (1979 ➔ 1981) 1 Ark. App. (1981 ➔) Bound with Ark.	To Date

[Highest Court Listed First] STATE COURT	WEST RPTR.	FIRST WEST CITE AVAILABLE FOR	LAST VOL. OF OFFICIAL REPORTER
Cal. Sup. Ct. (Cal. Cal. 2d Cal. 3d Cal. 4th 1850 →)	P. P.2d P.3d Cal. Rptr. Cal. Rptr. 2d Cal. Rptr. 3d	64 Cal. (1883 →) 53 Cal. 2d (1960 →)	To Date To Date

---

| Cal. Ct. App. (previously Cal. Dist. Ct. App.) (Cal. App. Cal. App. 2d Cal. App. 3d Cal. App. 4th 1905 →) | P. P.2d Cal. Rptr. Cal. Rptr. 2d Cal. Rptr. 3d | 1 Cal. App. (1905 → 1959) * 175 Cal. App. 2d (1960 →) * To Date

[* Reported in the Pacific Reporter until 1960; then in West's California Reporter.] |

| Cal. Superior Ct., Appellate Departments (Cal. App. Supp. Cal. App. Supp. 2d Cal. App. Supp. 3d † [† Bound with Cal. App. 3d] Cal. App. Supp. 4th + [+ Bound with Cal. App. 4th] | P. P.2d Cal. Rptr. Cal. Rptr. 2d Cal. Rptr. 3d | 1 Cal. App. Supp. (1929 → 1959) * 175 Cal. App. 2d Supp. (1960 →) * To Date

[* Reported in the Pacific Reporter until 1960; then in West's California Reporter.] |

[Highest Court Listed First] STATE COURT	WEST RPTR.	FIRST WEST CITE AVAILABLE FOR	LAST VOL. OF OFFICIAL REPORTER
Colo. Sup. Ct. ‡ (Colo. 1864 ➜ 1980)	P. P.2d P.3d	7 Colo. (1883)	200 Colo. (1980)

[‡ In May 1994, the Colorado Supreme Court authorized optional citation using paragraph numbering, but to date paragraph numbers have not been included in the Pacific Reporter.]

Colo. Ct. App. ‡ (1891 ➜ 1980)	P. P.2d P.3d	1 Colo. App. (1891 ➜ 1905) (1912 ➜ 1915) (1970 ➜ 1980)	44 Colo. App. (1980)

[‡ In May 1994, the Colorado Supreme Court authorized optional citation using paragraph numbering, but to date paragraph numbers have not been included in the Pacific Reporter.]

Conn. Sup. Ct. (Conn. 1814 ➜) (Sup. Ct. of Errors before 1966) Nominatives See App. 3(D)	A. A.2d	53 Conn. (1885 ➜)	To Date

Conn. App. Ct. (1983 ➜)	A.2d	1 Conn. App. (1983 ➜)	To Date

[Highest Court Listed First] STATE COURT	WEST RPTR.	FIRST WEST CITE AVAILABLE FOR	LAST VOL. OF OFFICIAL REPORTER
Conn. Ct. of Common Pleas * (1935 → 1978)	A.2d	19 Conn. Supp. (1954 → 1978)	July 1, 1978

[* On July 1, 1978, the Connecticut Court of Common Pleas [and Juvenile Court] merged into the Connecticut Superior Court (see below).]

Conn. Cir. Ct. + (1961 → 1974)	A.2d	[*BB*] 1 Conn. Cir. Ct. [*ALWD*] 1 Conn. Cir.	6 Conn. Cir. Ct. (1974)

[+ On December 31, 1974, the Connecticut Circuit Court was merged into the Connecticut Court of Common Pleas (see above).]

Conn. Superior * Ct. (1935 →)	A.2d	19 Conn. Supp. (1954 →)	To Date

[* On July 1, 1978, the Connecticut Superior Court became the sole trial court of general jurisdiction in Connecticut.]

Del. Sup. Ct. (previously Ct. of Errors & Appeals) (Del. 1832 → 1966) Nominatives See App. 3(D)	A. A.2d	12 Del. (7 Houst.) (1886)	59 Del. (1966)

[Highest Court Listed First] STATE COURT	WEST RPTR.	FIRST WEST CITE AVAILABLE FOR	LAST VOL. OF OFFICIAL REPORTER
Del. Ct. of Chancery (Del. Ch. 1814 → 1968) See also Del. Cases (1792-1830)	A. A.2d	6 Del. Ch. (1886)	43 Del. Ch. (1968)
Del. Superior Ct.+ (previously Del. Super. Ct & Del. Orphans' Ct.) (1831 →)	A.2d (1951→)	No official state series	No App.

[+ The Delaware Superior Court is the highest level trial court and the court of general jurisdiction in Delaware; It also serves as an intermediate appellate court, hearing appeals on the record from the Court of Common Pleas, Family court, and most state administrative agencies.]

Del. Fam. Ct. (1977 →)	A.2d (1977 →)	No official state series	Not App.
Fla. Sup. Ct. (Fla. 1846 → 1948)	So. So. 2d (1886 →)	22 Fla. (1886)	160 Fla. (1948)
Fla. Dist. Ct. of App. (1957 →)	So. 2d (1957 →)	No official state series	Not App.

[Highest Court Listed First] STATE COURT	WEST RPTR.	FIRST WEST CITE AVAILABLE FOR	LAST VOL. OF OFFICIAL REPORTER
Fla. Cir. Ct., Fla. County Ct., Pubic Serv. Comm'n (P.S.C.), and other lower Fla. courts *		[* Cite to Fla. Supp. or Fla. Supp. 2d (1948 → 1992); Fla. L. Weekly Supp. (1978 →).]	
Ga. Sup. Ct. (Ga. 1846 →)	S.E. S.E.2d	77 Ga. (1886)	To Date
Ga. Ct. of App. (Ga. App. 1907 →)	S.E. S.E.2d	1 Ga. App. (1907)	To Date
Haw. Sup. Ct. (Haw. 1847 →1994) Continues with West's Hawaii Reports	P.2d P.3d	44 Haw. (1959)	75 Haw. (1994) Continues 76 Haw. →
Haw. Intermediate Ct. of App. (Haw. App. 1980 → 1994) Continues with West's Hawaii Reports	P.2d P.3d	1 Haw. App. (1980)	10 Haw. App. (1994) Continues 76 Haw. →
Idaho Sup. Ct. (Idaho 1866 →)	P. P.2d P.3d	2 Idaho (1881)	To Date
Idaho Ct. of App. (Idaho 1982 →)	P.2d P.3d	102 Idaho (1982)	To Date

[Highest Court Listed First] STATE COURT	WEST RPTR.	FIRST WEST CITE AVAILABLE FOR	LAST VOL. OF OFFICIAL REPORTER
Ill. Sup. Ct. (Ill., Ill. 2d 1819 ➔) Nominatives See App. 3(D)	N.E. N.E.2d	112 Ill. (1884)	To Date
Ill. App. Ct. (Ill. App. Ill. App. 2d, Ill App. 3d 1877 ➔)	N.E.2d	284 Ill. App. (1936)	To Date
Ill. Ct. of Claims (1889 ➔)*	[* Cite to [*BB*] Ill Ct. Cl. [*ALWD*] Ill. Cl.; one bound volume of opinions is generally issued per year.]		
Ill. Cir. Ct. (Ill. Cir. 1866 ➔ 1908)+	[+ Cite to Ill. Cir. Ct. Opinions; as a trial court of general jurisdiction, circuit court opinions are not generally published, but they occasionally appear in topical loose-leaf services.]		
Ind. Sup. Ct. (Ind. 1848 ➔ 1981) Nominatives See App. 3(D)	N.E. N.E.2d	102 Ind. (1884)	275 Ind. (1981)

[Highest Court Listed First] STATE COURT	WEST RPTR.	FIRST WEST CITE AVAILABLE FOR	LAST VOL. OF OFFICIAL REPORTER
Ind. Ct. of App. (before 1972, Ind. App. Ct.) (Ind. App. 1891 ➜ 1979)	N.E. N.E.2d	1 Ind. App. (1891)	182 Ind. App. (1979)
Iowa Sup. Ct. (Iowa 1855 ➜ 1968) Nominatives See App. 3(D)	N.W. N.W.2d	51 Iowa (1879)	261 Iowa (1968)
Iowa Ct. of App. (1977 ➜)	N.W.2d	No official state series	Not App.
Kan. Sup. Ct. (Kan. 1862 ➜) Nominatives See App. 3(D)	P. P.2d P.3d	30 Kan. (1883)	To Date
Kan. Ct. of App. (Kan. App. 1895 ➜ 1901) (Kan. App. 2d 1997 ➜)	40-63 P. P.2d P.3d	1 Kan. App. (1895) 1 Kan. App. 2d (1977)	10 Kan. App. * To Date

[* In volumes 8-10 of the first series of Kansas Appeals Reports, cases were reported in full, with opinion, in the Pacific Reporter, but were not reported in full in Kansas Appeals Reports.]

[Highest Court Listed First] STATE COURT	WEST RPTR.	FIRST WEST CITE AVAILABLE FOR	LAST VOL. OF OFFICIAL REPORTER
Ky. Sup. Ct. (before 1976, Ky. Ct. of App.) (Ky. 1785 → 1951) Nominatives See App. 3(D)	S.W. S.W.2d S.W.3d	84 Ky. (1886)	314 Ky. (1951)
Ky. Ct. of App. +	S.W.2d S.W.3d	No official state series	Not App.

[+ Intermediate appellate court after 1975; before1976, highest state court (see above)]

| La. Sup. Ct. + ‡ (La. Ann. 1846 → 1900; La. 1901 → 1972) Nominatives See App. 3(D) | So. So. 2d | 39 La. Ann. 104 La. (1887) | 263 La. (1972) |

[+ Before 1813, known as the Superior Court of Louisiana and the Superior Court of the Territory of Orleans.]

[‡ After Dec. 31, 1993, opinions and actions issued by Louisiana Supreme Court and Courts of Appeal are cited using a uniform public domain citation form, consisting of the case name, docket number excluding letters, court abbreviation, and month/day/year of issue. This information is followed by a parallel citation to West's Southern Reporter. If a pinpoint citation is needed, the page number designated by the court should follow the docket number, set off with a comma and the abbreviation "p." See App. 5 for examples.]

[Highest Court Listed First] STATE COURT	WEST RPTR.	FIRST WEST CITE AVAILABLE FOR	LAST VOL. OF OFFICIAL REPORTER
La. Ct. of App. ‡ (La. App. 1924 → 1932) Nominatives See App. 3(D)	So. So. 2d	9 La. App. (1928)	19 La. App. (1932)

[‡ See La. Sup. Ct. for public domain citation form. See App. 5 for examples.]

Maine Sup. Judicial Ct. ‡ (Me. 1820 → 1965)	A. A.2d	77 Me. (1884)	161 Me. (1965)

[‡ For opinions issued on or after Jan. 1, 1997, a public domain citation is used. It is based on the calendar year and the sequential number assigned to the opinion. The official publication of each opinion issued includes paragraph numbers assigned by the courts. See App. 5 for examples.]

Md. Ct. of App. (Md. 1851 →) Nominatives See App. 3(D)	A. A.2d	63 Md. (1884)	To Date
Md. Ct. of Special App. (1967 →)	A.2d	1 Md. App. (1967)	To Date

[Highest Court Listed First] STATE COURT	WEST RPTR.	FIRST WEST CITE AVAILABLE FOR	LAST VOL. OF OFFICIAL REPORTER
Mass. Sup. Judicial Ct. (Mass. 1804 →) Nominatives See App. 3(D)	N.E. N.E.2d	139 Mass. (1885)	To Date
Mass. App. Ct. (1972 →)	N.E.2d	[*BB*] 1 Mass. App. Ct. (1972) [*ALWD*] 1 Mass. App.	To Date
Mass. Dist Ct. * (Appellate Div.) (Mass. App. Div. Reports begin in 1936)	[* Cite to Massachusetts Appellate Division Reports (Mass. App. Div.), Massachusetts Reports Supplement (Mass. Supp.), Massachusetts Appellate Decisions (Mass. App. Dec.).]		
Mass. Superior Ct. (Mass. L. Rep. begins in 1993 →) +	[+ Cite to the Massachusetts Law Reporter (Mass. L. Rptr.).]		
Mich. Sup. Ct. (Mich. 1847 →) Nominatives See App. 3(D)	N.W. N.W.2d	41 Mich. (1879)	To Date
Mich. Ct. of App. (Mich. App. 1965 →)	N.W.2d	1 Mich. App. (1965)	To Date

[Highest Court Listed First] STATE COURT	WEST RPTR.	FIRST WEST CITE AVAILABLE FOR	LAST VOL. OF OFFICIAL REPORTER
Mich. Ct. of Claims *	[* Cite to Michigan Court of Claims Reporter [*BB*] (Mich. Ct. Cl.) (1939 → 1942)]		
Minn. Sup. Ct. (Minn. 1851 → 1977)	N.W. N.W.2d	26 Minn. (1879)	312 Minn. (1977)
Minn. Ct. of App. (1983 →)	N.W.2d	No official state series	Not App.
Miss. Sup. Ct. ‡ (Miss. 1818 → 1966) Nominatives See App. 3(D)	So. So. 2d	64 Miss. (1886)	254 Miss. (1966)

[‡ Mississippi cases (decided after July 1, 1997) may be cited by the case numbers as assigned by the Clerk's Office. Quotations from cases and authorities appearing in the text of briefs may be cited to the paragraph number of the decision after the case number has been assigned by the Clerk's Office. For cases decided prior to July 1, 1997, paragraphs may be cited by paragraph after the Clerk's Office has assigned a case number to a case in the new format. See App. 5 for examples.]

Miss. Ct. of App. (1995 →)	So. 2d	No official state series	Not App.

[Highest Court Listed First] STATE COURT	WEST RPTR.	FIRST WEST CITE AVAILABLE FOR	LAST VOL. OF OFFICIAL REPORTER
Mo. Sup. Ct. (Mo. 1821 → 1956)	S.W. S.W.2d S.W.3d	89 Mo. (1886)	365 Mo. (1956)
Mo. Ct. of App. (Mo. App. 1876 → 1952)	S.W. S.W.2d S.W.3d	93 Mo. App. (1902)	241 Mo. (1952)
Mont. Sup. Ct. ‡ (Mont. 1868 →)	P. P.2d P.3d	4 Mont. (1881)	To Date

[‡ Beginning on Jan. 1, 1998, the Court assigns a public domain citation that includes the case name, year of decision, the two-letter postal code (MT), and a sequential number. Beginning with the first paragraph of text, each paragraph is numbered consecutively beginning with a mark. In the case of opinions not to be cited as precedent ("unpublished"), the consecutive court assigned number is followed by an "N," opinions that have been withdrawn or vacated are designated with a "W," and opinions that have been amended will be identified with an "A." These citation formats are in addition to and supplement the current citation formats. See App. 5 for examples.]

Neb. Sup. Ct. (Neb. 1860 →)	N.W. N.W.2d	8 Neb. (1878)	To Date

[Highest Court Listed First] STATE COURT	WEST RPTR.	FIRST WEST CITE AVAILABLE FOR	LAST VOL. OF OFFICIAL REPORTER
Neb. Ct. of App. (Neb. App. 1992 ➔)	N.W.2d	1 Neb. App. (1992)	To Date
Nev. Sup. Ct. (Nev. 1865 ➔)	P. P.2d	17 Nev. (1883)	To Date
N.H. Sup. Ct. (N.H. 1816 ➔)	A. A.2d	63 N.H. (1883)	To Date
N.J. Sup. Ct. (before 1948, N.J. Ct. of Errors & Appeals) (1790 ➔)	A. A.2d	47 N.J.L. 290 40 N.J. Eq. 83 10 N.J. Misc. (1885)	To Date (N.J.) (1948 ➔)
N.J. Super. Ct. (App Div., Ch. Div., Law Div.) (previously Chancery Ct., Supreme Ct., ‡ and Prerogative Ct.) (1790 ➔)	A. A.2d	1 N.J. Super. 47 N.J.L 40 N.J. Eq. 10 N.J. Misc. (1885)	To Date (N.J. Super.) (1948)
[‡ After 1947, the highest N.J. court is called the N.J. Supreme Court (see above).]			
N.J. County Ct. & other lower cts. *	[* Cite A.2d, if therein, or another reporter.]		
N.J. Tax Ct. +	[+ Cite N.J. Tax Court Reports (N.J. Tax) (1979 ➔).]		

[Highest Court Listed First] STATE COURT	WEST RPTR.	FIRST WEST CITE AVAILABLE FOR	LAST VOL. OF OFFICIAL REPORTER
N.M. Sup Ct. ‡ (N.M. 1852 ➔) Nominatives See App. 3(D)	P. P.2d P.3d	3 N.M. (1884)	To Date

[‡ For opinions on or after Jan. 1, 1996, New Mexico Supreme Court opinions are issued with a public domain citation consisting of the case name, the year, hyphenated with "NMSC," followed by the hyphenated case number. Paragraph numbers are provided for pinpoint citations. See App. 5 for examples.]

N.M. Ct. of App. (N.M. 1967 ➔) ‡	P.2d P.3d	78 N.M. (1967)	To Date

[‡ For opinions on or after Jan. 1, 1996, New Mexico Supreme Court opinions are issued with a public domain citation consisting of the case name, the year, hyphenated with "NMCA," followed by the hyphenated case number. Paragraph numbers are provided for pinpoint citations. See App. 5 for examples.]

[Highest Court Listed First] STATE COURT	WEST RPTR.	FIRST WEST CITE AVAILABLE FOR	LAST VOL. OF OFFICIAL REPORTER
N.Y. Ct. of App. (N.Y., N.Y.2d, N.Y.3d 1847→) Nominatives See App. 3(D) (Before 1847, highest courts of law were Ct. for the Correction of Errors and Sup. Ct. of Judicature; highest equity court was N.Y. Ct. of Chancery.)	N.E. N.E.2d N.Y.S.2d *	99 N.Y. * (1885)	To Date

[* Cases in the first series of New York Reports (N.Y.) should not be cited to the first series of West's N.Y. Supplement (N.Y.S.) because N.Y.S. reprints the first series of N.Y. without any difference in pagination; coverage in N.Y.S. of N.Y.2d starts in 1956.]

| N.Y. Sup. Ct. Appellate Division (A.D., A.D.2d, A.D.3d 1894 →) (previously N.Y. Sup. Ct., General Term) Nominatives See App. 3(D) | N.Y.S. N.Y.S.2d | 1 A.D. (1896) | To Date |

[Highest Court Listed First] STATE COURT	WEST RPTR.	FIRST WEST CITE AVAILABLE FOR	LAST VOL. OF OFFICIAL REPORTER
Other N.Y. Lower Courts * (Misc., Misc. 2d, Misc. 3d 1892 →) Nominatives See App. 3(D)	N.Y.S. N.Y.S.2d	1 Misc. (1892 →)	To Date

[* includes N.Y. App. Term, N.Y. Sup. Ct., N.Y. Ct. Cl., N.Y. Civ. Ct., N.Y. Crim. Ct., N.Y. Fam. Ct., and others.]

N.C. Sup. Ct. (N.C. 1778 →) Nominatives See App. 3(D)	S.E. S.E.2d	96 N.C. (1887)	To Date
N.C. Ct. of App. (N.C. App. 1968 →)	S.E.2d	1 N.C. App. (1968 →)	To Date
N.D. Sup. Ct. ‡ (N.D. 1890 → 1953) (Dakota 1867 → 1889) +	N.W. N.W.2d	1 N.D. (1890)	74 N.D. (1953)

[+ The 1861 federal Act creating the Dakota territory established the Supreme Court of Dakota; Dakota Reports (Dakota) covers the pre-statehood period 1867 → 1889; cases in Dakota Reports also appear in early North Western Reporter volumes.]

[‡ After Dec. 31, 1996, the public domain citation consists of the calendar year in which the decision was filed, followed by "ND," followed by a sequential number assigned by the Clerk. For pinpoint citations, a paragraph citation should be placed following the sequential number assigned to the case. See App. 5 for examples.]

[Highest Court Listed First] STATE COURT	WEST RPTR.	FIRST WEST CITE AVAILABLE FOR	LAST VOL. OF OFFICIAL REPORTER
N.D. Ct. of App. ‡ (1987 →)	N.W.2d	No official state series	Not App.

[‡ After Dec. 31, 1996, the public domain citation consists of the calendar year in which the decision was filed, followed by "ND App," followed by a sequential number assigned by the Clerk. For pinpoint citations, a paragraph citation should be placed following the sequential number assigned to the case. See App. 5 for examples.]

| Ohio Sup. Ct. ‡ (Ohio 1821 → 1851 Ohio St., Ohio St. 2d, Ohio St. 3d 1852 →) Nominatives See App. 3(D) | N.E. N.E.2d | 43 Ohio St. (1885 →) | To Date |

[‡ For cases decided after Apr. 30, 2002, a public domain citation is constructed as follows: Year-Ohio-Decision Number. Pinpoint cites are made to paragraph numbers assigned by the court reporter. See App. 5 for examples.]

| Ohio Ct. of App. ‡ (Ohio App., Ohio App. 2d, Ohio App. 3d 1913 →) * | N.E. N.E.2d | 20 Ohio App. (1926) | To Date |

[* See also Ohio Ct. of Appeals Reports [BB] Ohio Ct. App. 1906 →1923)]

[‡ For cases decided after Apr. 30, 2002, a public domain citation is constructed in the same manner as described for the Ohio Sup. Ct., above. See App. 5 for examples.]

[Highest Court Listed First] STATE COURT	WEST RPTR.	FIRST WEST CITE AVAILABLE FOR	LAST VOL. OF OFFICIAL REPORTER
Other Ohio Lower Courts + (Ohio Misc., Ohio Misc. 2d, Ohio Op., Ohio Op. 2d, Ohio Op. 3d 1934 →)	N.E.2d	1 Ohio Misc. 1 (1964)	To Date

[+ includes Ohio Common Pleas Courts, Ohio Court of Claims, Ohio Municipal Courts, etc.]

Okla. Sup. Ct. ‡ (Okla. 1890 → 1953)	P. P.2d P.3d	1 Okla. (1890)	208 Okla. (1953)

[‡ After May 01, 1997, the public domain citation consists of the year of decision, the court designation for the Supreme Court is "OK," and opinion number. Pinpoint citations are to paragraph numbers. The public domain citation form is followed by a parallel citation to Pacific Reporter. See App. 5 for examples.]

Okla. Ct. of Crim. App. (Okla. Crim. 1908 → 1953)	P. P.2d P.3d	1 Okla. Crim. (1908)	97 Okla. Crim. (1953)

[Highest Court Listed First] STATE COURT	WEST RPTR.	FIRST WEST CITE AVAILABLE FOR	LAST VOL. OF OFFICIAL REPORTER
Okla. Ct. of Civ. App. (1969 ➔) ‡	P.2d P.3d	No official state series	Not App.

[‡ After May 01, 1997, the public domain citation consists of the year of decision, the court designation for the Supreme Court is "OK CIV APP," and opinion number. Pinpoint citations are to paragraph numbers. The public domain citation form is followed by a parallel citation to the Pacific Reporter. See App. 5 for examples.]

Okla. Ct. of App. of the Indian Territory (1896 ➔ 1907)	S.W.	1 Indian Terr. (1896)	7 Indian Terr. (1907)
Or. Sup. Ct. (Or. 1853 ➔)	P. P.2d P.3d	11 Or. (1883)	To Date
Or. Ct. of App. (Or. App. 1969 ➔)	P.2d P.3d	1 Or. App. (1969)	To Date
Or. Tax Ct. (Or. Tax. 1962 ➔)	[Cite Oregon Tax Court Reports (Or. Tax).]		
Pa. Sup. Ct. (Pa. 1845 ➔) Nominatives See App. 3(D)	A. A.2d	108 Pa. (1884)	To Date

[Highest Court Listed First] STATE COURT	WEST RPTR.	FIRST WEST CITE AVAILABLE FOR	LAST VOL. OF OFFICIAL REPORTER
Pa. Super. Ct. ‡ (Pa. Super. 1895 ➜ 1997)	A. A.2d	102 Pa. Super. (1930)	456 Pa. Super. (1997)

[‡ After Jan. 1, 1999, opinions issued by the Pennsylvania Superior Court contain a public domain (universal) citation using the following format: (Year) PA Super (Court-issued number). The opinions also have numbered paragraphs to be used for pinpoint citations. Citations made to opinions not yet in the Atlantic Reporter must use the public domain citation. Once the official citation has been issued, however, citation should be made only to the official citation, and not the public domain citation. See App. 5 for examples.]

| Pa. Common-wealth Ct. (1970 ➜ 1995) | A.2d | [*BB*] 1 Pa. Commw. [*ALWD*] 1 Pa. Cmmw. (1970) | [*BB*] 168 Pa. Commw. [*ALWD*] 168 Cmmw. (1995) |
| Pa. Dist. & Co. Cts. (Pa. D. & C. Pa. D. & C. 2d Pa. D. & C. 3d Pa. D. & C. 4th 1921 ➜) | [Cite to Pa. District and County Reports (1921 ➜), Pa. District ([*BB*] Pa. D.) (1892 ➜ 1921). Pa. County Court Reports ([*BB*] Pa. C.) (1870 ➜ 1921).] | | |

[Highest Court Listed First] STATE COURT	WEST RPTR.	FIRST WEST CITE AVAILABLE FOR	LAST VOL. OF OFFICIAL REPORTER
R.I. Sup. Ct. (R.I. 1828 → 1980)	A. A.2d	15 R.I. (1885)	122 R.I. (1980)
S.C. Sup. Ct. (S.C. 1868 →) Nominatives See App. 3(D)	S.E. S.E.2d	25 S.C. (1886)	To Date
S.C. Ct. of App. (S.C. 1983 →)	S.E.2d	279 S.C. (1983)	To Date
S.D. Sup Ct. ‡ (S.D. 1890 → 1976) (Dakota 1867 → 1889)+	N.W. N.W.2d	1 S.D. (1890)	90 S.D. (1976)

[+ The 1861 federal Act creating the Dakota territory established the Supreme Court of Dakota; Dakota Reports (Dakota) covers the pre-statehood period 1867 → 1889); cases in Dakota Reports also appear in early North Western Reporter volumes.]

[‡ After Jan. 1, 1996, the public domain citation consists of the calendar year in which the decision was filed, followed by "SD," followed by a sequential number assigned by the Clerk. For pinpoint citations, a paragraph citation should be placed following the sequential number assigned to the case. When available, initial citations shall include the volume and initial page number of the North Western Reporter. See App. 5 for examples.]

[Highest Court Listed First] STATE COURT	WEST RPTR.	FIRST WEST CITE AVAILABLE FOR	LAST VOL. OF OFFICIAL REPORTER
Tenn. Sup. Ct. (Tenn. 1791 → 1972) Nominatives See App. 3(D)	S.W. S.W.2d S.W.3d	85 Tenn. (1886)	225 Tenn. (1972)
Tenn. Ct. of App. (Tenn. App. 1925 → 1971)	S.W.2d S.W.3d	16 Tenn. App. (1932)	61 Tenn. App. (1971)
Tenn. Ct. of Crim. App. (1967 → 1971)	S.W.2d S.W.3d	[BB] 1 Tenn. Crim. App. [ALWD] Tenn. Crim. (1967)	[BB] 4 Tenn. Crim. App. (1971) [ALWD] 4 Tenn. Crim.
Tex. Sup. Ct. (Tex. 1846 → 1962) Nominatives See App. 3(D)	S.W. S.W.2d S.W.3d	66 Tex. (1886)	163 Tex. (1962)
Tex. Ct. of Crim. App. (1892 → 1963) (previously Tx. Ct. of App.) (See Tex. Court of Appeals Reports (Tex. Ct. App. 1876 → 1892) Nominatives See App. 3(D)	S.W. S.W.2d S.W.3d	31 Tex. Crim. (1892)	172 Tex. Crim. (1963)

[Highest Court Listed First] STATE COURT	WEST RPTR.	FIRST WEST CITE AVAILABLE FOR	LAST VOL. OF OFFICIAL REPORTER
Tex. Ct. of App. (before 1981, Tx. Ct. of Civ. App.) [See Tex. Civil Appeals Reports ([*BB*] Tex. Civ. App. [*ALWD*] Tex. Civ.) 1892 → 1911.]	S.W. S.W.2d S.W.3d	[*BB*] 1 Tex. Civ. App. [*ALWD*] 1 Tex. Civ. (1892)	[*BB*] 63 Tex. Civ. App. [*ALWD*] 63 Tex. Civ. (1911)

[N.B. See Texas Rules of Form re: the significance of the denial of writs of error by the Texas Supreme Court; Shepard's Citations is the most readily accessible source for writ history for most researchers.]

Tex. Commission of Appeals * (Tex. 1879 → 1892 Tex. 1918 → 1945)	S.W. S.W.2d	1 White & W. + (1880)	144 Tex. (1945)

[+ See App. 2 & App. 3(D) (Texas)]

[N.B. See Texas Rules of Form re: adoption by the Texas Sup. Ct.]

[* See also Texas Unreported Cases (Posey) (1879 → 1884) and Condensed Reports of Decisions in Causes in the Court of Appeals (White & Wilson) (1879 → 1883)].

[Highest Court Listed First] STATE COURT	WEST RPTR.	FIRST WEST CITE AVAILABLE FOR	LAST VOL. OF OFFICIAL REPORTER
Utah Sup. Ct. ‡ (Utah 1855 ➜ 1974)	P. P.2d P.3d	3 Utah (1881)	22 Utah 2d (1974)

[‡ Published opinions of the Utah Supreme Court and the Utah Court of Appeals released on or after January 1, 1999, have a public domain citation consisting of the case name, the year the opinion was issued, an identification of the court that issued the opinion ("UT" and "UT App"), and the sequential number assigned by the court. A comma and then a paragraph symbol are used to denote pinpoint citations. Initial citations should also include either the Utah Advance Reports citation or the volume and initial page number of the Pacific Reporter in which it is published. The year the case was published and the parallel page number for pinpoint citation to the Pacific Reporter is not needed. See App. 5 for examples.]

Utah Ct. of App. ‡ (1987 ➜)	P.2d P.3d	No official state series	Not App.

[‡ See public domain citation information in the entry for the Utah Sup. Ct., above.]

[Highest Court Listed First] STATE COURT	WEST RPTR.	FIRST WEST CITE AVAILABLE FOR	LAST VOL. OF OFFICIAL REPORTER
Vt. Sup. Ct. ‡ (Vt. 1826 ➜) Nominatives See App. 3(D)	A. A.2d	58 Vt. (1886)	To Date

[‡ After Jan. 1, 2003, Vermont Supreme Court opinions have a public domain citation consisting of the year, the abbreviated identification of the jurisdiction ("VT"), and the sequentially numbered opinion. The paragraphs are numbered for purposes of pinpoint citations. See App. 5 for examples.]

Va. Sup. Ct. (Va. 1790 ➜) Nominatives See App. 3(D)	S.E. S.E.2d	82 Va. (1884)	To Date
Va. Ct. of App. (Va. App. 1985 ➜)	S.E.2d	1 Va. App. (1985)	To Date
Va. Cir. Ct. (1985 ➜)	[Cite to Virginia Circuit Court Opinions (Va. Cir.)]		
Wash. Sup. Ct. (Wash., Wash. 2d 1890 ➜) (Wash. Territory Reports [*BB*] Wash. Terr. 1854 ➜ 1888)	P. P.2d P.3d	2 Wash. Terr. (1880) 1 Wash. (1890)	To Date

[Highest Court Listed First] STATE COURT	WEST RPTR.	FIRST WEST CITE AVAILABLE FOR	LAST VOL. OF OFFICIAL REPORTER
Wash. Ct. of App. (Wash. App. 1969 →)	P.2d P.3d	1 Wash. App. (1969)	To Date
W. Va. Sup. Ct. of App. (W. Va. 1864 →)	S.E. S.E.2d	29 W. Va. (1887)	To Date
W. Va. Ct. of Claims (1942 →)	[Cite to West Virginia Court of Claims Reports [*ALWD*] (W. Va. Cl.).]		
Wis. Sup. Ct. ‡ (Wis., Wis. 2d 1853 →) Nominatives See App. 3(D)	N.W. N.W.2d	46 Wis. (1879)	To Date

[‡ After Jan. 1, 2000, Wisconsin Supreme Court and Court of Appeals opinions have a public domain citation consisting of the year, the abbreviated identification of the court ("WT" or "WI App"), and the sequentially numbered opinion. The paragraphs are numbered for purposes of pinpoint citations. See App. 5 for examples.]

| Wis. Ct. of App. ‡ (Wis. 2d 1978 →) | N.W.2d | 85 Wis. 2d (1978) | To Date |

[‡ See entry for Wisconsin Supreme Court, above, for the public domain citation format. See App. 5 for examples.]

[Highest Court Listed First] STATE COURT	WEST RPTR.	FIRST WEST CITE AVAILABLE FOR	LAST VOL. OF OFFICIAL REPORTER
Wyo. Sup. Ct. ‡ (Wyo. 1883 → 1959)	P. P.2d P.3d	3 Wyo. (1883)	80 Wyo. (1959)

[‡ Beginning on Jan. 1, 2003, the Wyoming Supreme Court assigns a public domain citation that includes the case name, year of decision, the two-letter postal code (WY), and a sequential number. Beginning with the first paragraph of text, each paragraph is numbered consecutively beginning with a mark. In the case of opinions not to be cited as precedent ("unpublished"), the consecutive court assigned number is followed by an "N," opinions that have been withdrawn or vacated are designated with a "W," and opinions that have been amended will be identified with an "A." These citation formats are in addition to and supplement the current citation formats. See App. 5 for examples.]

APPENDIX 5

PARENTHETICAL COURT ABBREVIATIONS, COURT WEBSITES, AND PREFERRED REPORTERS

ALWD = *ALWD Citation Manual*
BB = *Bluebook*

Unless otherwise indicated below, the *ALWD* and *BB* form is the same.

See Appendix 3(D) for citation of early federal and state court cases, including nominative reporters.

For further information on the discontinuation of official state court reporters, see Appendix 4.

The highest court in a jurisdiction is listed first.

A. FEDERAL COURTS

U.S. Courts Website: http://www.uscourts.gov/
(U.S. Courts: The Federal Judiciary)

(Includes useful "Court Links" with a searchable map of the United States which can be used to find courts, probation offices, and pretrial services offices; it is also searchable by zip code, city/state, circuit, county/state, or telephone area code; searches lead to court locations, local map, contact information, and individual court websites.)
http://www.uscourts.gov/courtlinks/

UNITED STATES SUPREME COURT

<u>Court Website</u>: http://www.supremecourtus.gov/
(Supreme Court of the United States)

(Information about the Court and the Justices; the Court's docket; oral arguments, including transcripts; links for briefs on the merits; bar admissions; Court rules; case handling guidelines; opinions; slip opinions; orders; and the text of speeches delivered by the Justices.)

<u>Special Citation Interest</u>: "Dates of Supreme Court Decisions and Arguments; United States Reports (Volumes 2-107 (1791-1882)"
http://www.supremecourtus.gov/opinions/
datesofdecisions.pdf

(To find specific dates of early U.S. Supreme Court decisions because the dates do not appear below the case name in *United States Reports*; beginning in 1854, dates are given in the *Lawyers' Edition* , but there are some errors or omissions.)

U.S. Supreme Court (U.S.) [*BB*] Cite to U.S., S. Ct., L. Ed., or U.S.L.W. in that order of preference.

See Chapter 2(C)(2)(*a*), above, for a discussion of which reporter should be cited.

Lockyer v. Andrade, 538 U.S. 63 (2003)*; Lockyer v. Andrade*, 538 U.S. 63, 123 S. Ct. 1166, 155 L. Ed. 2d 144 (2003); *Lockyer v. Andrade*, 123 S. Ct. 1166 (2003); *Lockyer v. Andrade*, 155 L. Ed. 2d 144 (2003); *Lockyer v. Andrade*, 71 U.S.L.W. 4125 (U.S. 2003).

The individual U.S. Supreme Court Justices are allotted as Circuit Justices among the circuits. As such, some applications are made to individual members of the Supreme Court as Circuit Justices. However, individual Justices, as

Circuit Justices, do not possess the supervisory powers of a court of appeals concerning the activities of the district courts within its circuit. As Circuit Justices, they primarily grant stays, arrange bails, and provide for other ancillary relief. Individual Justices of the Supreme Court have no power to dispose of cases on their merits. Nor do Circuit Justices have authority to revise, modify, or reverse an order of a United States Court of Appeals on the merits of a controversy.

Opinions by Supreme Court Justices sitting alone in their individual capacities as Circuit Justices are cited as follows: [BB] *Autry v. Estelle*, 464 U.S. 1301 ((White, Circuit Justice, (1983); *D'Aquino v. United States*, 180 F.2d 271 (Douglas, Circuit Justice, 1950); *Hovey v. Stevens*, 12 F. Cas. 609 (Woodbury, Circuit Justice, C.C.D. Mass. 1846) (No. 6745).

UNITED STATES COURTS OF APPEALS

U.S. Courts of Appeals Websites: See access information for the federal courts at the beginning of this subdivision.

The United States Courts of Appeals are the principal intermediate appellate courts in the United States. They were previously called United States Circuit Courts of Appeals. The designation of United States Courts of Appeals is discussed in Chapter 2(D)(2). See also the next entry for the United States Court of Appeals for the Federal Circuit below.

Breard v. Pruett, 134 F.3d 615 (4th Cir. 1998); *Skaggs v. Carle*, 110 F.3d 831 (D.C. Cir. 1997); [BB] *Wilcher v. Anderson*, 188 F. App'x 279 (5th Cir. 2006); [ALWD] *Wilcher v. Anderson*, 188 Fed. Appx. 279 (5th Cir. 2006).

UNITED STATES COURT OF APPEALS
FOR THE FEDERAL CIRCUIT
(AND ITS PREDECESSORS)

Court Website: http://www.cafc.uscourts.gov/
(United States Court of Appeals for the Federal Circuit)

The current United States Court of Appeals for the Federal Circuit was created in 1982. It primarily hears appeals from U.S. district and territorial courts in patent and trademark cases, but it also hears appeals in cases in which the United States or its agencies is a defendant, as in alleged breaches of contract or in tax disputes. Its decisions are reported in the Federal Reporter.

In re Alappat, 33 F.3d 1526 (Fed. Cir. 1994).

The Court of Appeals for the Federal Circuit was the result of a merger of (1) the United States Court of Customs and Patent Appeals (C.C.P.A.) (1929 → 1982) (34 F.2d → 691 F.2d) (official: 17 C.C.P.A. → 69 C.C.P.A) and (2) the *appellate* jurisdiction of the Court of Claims (Ct. Cl.) (See the next subsection for further information on the Court of Claims.) Before the merger, the preferred [*BB*] citation for these two courts is to Federal Reporter.

In re Druey, 319 F.2d 237 (C.C.P.A. 1963); [*BB*] *Gearinger v. United States*, 412 F.2d 862 (Ct. Cl. 1969); [*ALWD*] *Gearinger v. U.S.*, 412 F.2d 862 (Ct. Cl. 1969).

Prior to 1929, the United States Court of Claims and Patent Appeals was the U.S. Court of Customs Appeals [*BB*] (Ct. Cust. App.) [*ALWD*] (Cust. App.) (1910 → 1929) (official: 1 Ct. Cust. → 16 Ct. Cust.).

[*BB*] *Nicholas & Co. v. United States*, 7 Ct. Cust. 97 (1916); [*ALWD*] *Nicholas & Co. v. U.S.*, 7 Ct. Cust. 97 (1916).

UNITED STATES COURT OF FEDERAL CLAIMS
(AND ITS PREDECESSORS)

<u>Court Website</u>: http://www.uscfc.uscourts.gov/
(United States Court of Federal Claims)

The United States Court of Federal Claims has jurisdiction over money claims against the United States or any of its branches, departments, or agencies based on the U.S. Constitution, federal laws, executive regulations, or an express or implied contract with the government. Among the cases handled by this trial court are those arising from supply and construction contracts, those involving compensation for property taken, those arising from claims for back pay or tax refunds, and those involving alleged government infringement or misinterpretation of private patents, trademarks, copyrights, or licenses. It also handles cases in which the United States is a defendant.

The naming of this court has a confusing history. The current United States Court of Federal Claims (Fed. Cl.) received its present name in 1992; between 1992 and its creation in 1982, it was called the United States Claims Court (Cl. Ct.). Cases should be cited to the following West reporters:

West's United States Claims Court Reporter (1983 ➔ 1992) (1 Cl. Ct. ➔ 26 Cl. Ct.)
West's Federal Claims Reporter (1992 ➔) (27 Fed. Cl. ➔)
[The United States Claims Court Reporter was renamed as the Federal Claims Reporter, commencing with volume 27).]

[*BB*] *Bowles v. United States*, 31 Fed. Cl. 37 (1994); *Winstar Corp. v. United States*, 25 Cl. Ct. 541 (1992).

[*ALWD*] *Bowles v. U.S.*, 31 Fed. Cl. 37 (1994); *Winstar Corp. v. U.S.*, 25 Cl. Ct. 541 (1992).

The United States Claims Court (created in 1982, see above) was the successor to the *original* jurisdiction of the Court of Claims (Ct. Cl.) (1855 ➔ 1982). (The *appellate* jurisdiction of the Court of Claims was part of the merger creating the present Court of Appeals for the Federal Circuit, as discussed in the preceding subsection.) Over time, decisions of Court of Claims have appeared in various reporters. These decisions may be cited [BB] to one of these reporters:

Federal Reporter (1930 ➔ 1932, 1960 ➔ 1982)
Federal Supplement (1932 ➔ 1960)
Court of Claims Reports (Ct. Cl.) (official) (1863 ➔ 1982).

[BB] *Freedman v. United States*, 320 F.2d 359 (Ct. Cl. 1963); *Ottinger v. United States*, 88 F. Supp. 881 (Ct. Cl. 1950); *Paridy v. United States*, 64 Ct. Cl. 375 (1928).

[ALWD] *Freedman v. U.S.*, 320 F.2d 359 (Ct. Cl. 1963); *Ottinger v. U.S.*, 88 F. Supp. 881 (Ct. Cl. 1950); *Paridy v. U.S.*, 64 Ct. Cl. 375 (1928).

COURT OF INTERNATIONAL TRADE (FORMERLY THE UNITED STATES CUSTOMS COURT)

<u>Court Website</u>: http://www.cit.uscourts.gov/
(United States Court of International Trade)

Pursuant to the Customs Act of 1980, the Court of International Trade ([BB] Ct. Int'l Trade [ALWD] Intl. Trade) replaced the United States Customs Court (Cust. Ct.). The Court of International Trade has jurisdiction over protests filed with U.S. Customs and Border Protection, decisions regarding Trade Adjustment Assistance by the U.S. Department of Labor or U.S. Department of Agriculture, customs broker licensing, and disputes relating to determinations made by the U.S. International Trade Commission and the Department of Commerce's International Trade Administration regarding antidumping and countervailing duties (except special NAFTA disputes). The preferred [*BB* and *ALWD*] citation is to the official report (Court of International Trade Reports) ([*BB*] Ct. Int'l Trade [*ALWD*] Ct. Intl. Trade). If that reporter is unavailable, *The Bluebook* indicates that the Federal Supplement (F. Supp., F. Supp. 2d 1980 ➔), the Customs Bulletin and Decisions (Cust. B. & Dec. 1967 ➔), or the International Trade Reporter Decisions (I.T.R.D. (BNA) 1980 ➔) should be cited (in that order of preference).

[*BB*] *Daewoo Elecs. Co. v. United States*, 10 Ct. Int'l Trade 754 (1986); *Tembec, Inc. v. United States*, 441 F. Supp. 2d 1302 (Ct. Int'l Trade 2006); *Crawfish Processors Alliance v. United States*, 28 I.R.T.D. (BNA) 1383 (Ct. Int'l Trade 2005).

[*ALWD*] *Daewoo Elecs. Co. v. U.S.*, 10 Ct. Intl. Trade 754 (1986); *Tembec, Inc. v. U.S.*, 441 F. Supp. 2d 1302 (Intl. Trade 2006); *Crawfish Processors Alliance v. U.S.*, 28 I.R.T.D. (BNA) 1383 (Intl. Trade Dec. 29, 2005).

For the earlier United States Customs Court (Cust. Ct.), the preferred [*BB*] citation is to the official report (Customs Court Reports [*BB*] Cust. Ct. 1938 ➔ 1980). If that report is unavailable, *The Bluebook* indicates that the Federal Supplement (F. Supp., F. Supp. 2d 1980 ➔) or the Customs Bulletin and Decisions (Cust. B. & Dec. 1967 ➔) should be cited (in that order of preference).

[*BB*] *Klingerit, Inc. v. United States*, 14 Cust. Ct. 435 (1945); *J.E. Bernard & Co. v. United States*, 324 F. Supp. 496 (Cust. Ct. 1971).

[*ALWD*] *Klingerit, Inc. v. U.S.*, 14 Cust. Ct. 435 (1945); *J.E. Bernard & Co. v. U.S.*, 324 F. Supp. 496 (Cust. Ct. 1971).

EMERGENCY COURT OF APPEALS

The Emergency Court of Appeals ([*BB*] Emer. Ct. App. [*ALWD*] Emerg. Ct. App.) was established in 1942 to hear appeals in cases involving wartime price control measures. It heard its last case in 1961 and was abolished in that year.

[*BB*] *Bowman v. Bowles*, 140 F.2d 974 (Emer. Ct. App. 1944).

[*ALWD*] *Bowman v. Bowles*, 140 F.2d 974 (Emerg. Ct. App. 1944).

TEMPORARY EMERGENCY COURT OF APPEALS

The Temporary Emergency Court of Appeals ([*BB*] Temp. Emer. Ct. App. [*ALWD*] Temp. Emerg. Ct. App.) was established in 1971 to hear appeals from the U.S. District Courts arising under the wage and price control program established by the Economic Stabilization Act of 1970. That Act expired in 1974, but Congress extended the operation of the court in the Emergency Petroleum Allocation Act of 1973. The court exercised the judicial review provisions of the energy price stabilization program established by that Act. Its jurisdiction was further expanded in the Energy Policy and Conservation Act of 1975 and the Emergency Natural Gas Act of 1977.

In 1992, Congress abolished this court and transferred both its jurisdiction and its pending cases to the U.S. Court of Appeals for the Federal Circuit (discussed above).

[*BB*] *Gulf Oil Corp. v. Simon*, 502 F.2d 1154 (Temp. Emer. Ct. App. 1974).

[ALWD] *Gulf Oil Corp. v. Simon*, 502 F.2d 1154 (Temp. Emerg. Ct. App. 1974).

UNITED STATES COMMERCE COURT

The United States Commerce Court ([*BB*] Comm. Ct.) [*ALWD*] Com. Ct. 1910 ➔ 1913) had appellate jurisdiction over orders from the Interstate Commerce Commission. Its decisions were reported in the Federal Reporter.

[*BB*] *Crane Iron Works v. United States*, 209 F. 238 (Comm. Ct. 1912).
[*ALWD*] *Crane Iron Works v. U.S.*, 209 F. 238 (Com. Ct. 1912).

UNITED STATES DISTRICT COURTS

U.S. District Court Websites: See access information for the federal courts at the beginning of this subdivision.

The United States District Courts are the principal trial courts in the federal system. Opinions from these courts are primarily reported in the Federal Reporter (1880 ➔ 1932) and the Federal Supplement (1932 ➔). Opinions involving procedural issues are reported in Federal Rules Decisions (1938 ➔). Some early district court cases appear in the Federal Cases set.

For United States District Court citations, the district but not division is cited in the parenthetical containing the date. The following citations illustrate the various combinations of spacing for the district and the state as well as the form for the above reporters. For cases not appearing in the above reporters, *The Bluebook* indicates that the Federal Rules Service series (Fed. R. Serv., Fed. R. Serv. 2d, Fed. R. Serv. 3d) should be cited.

Ocasek v. Hegglund, 116 F.R.D. 154, 155 (D. Wyo. 1987); *Carson v. Squirrel Inn Corp.*, 298 F. Supp. 1040 (D.S.C. 1969); *Dietrich v. Bauer*, 126 F. Supp. 2d 759 (S.D.N.Y. 2001); *Sapp v. Brooks-Scanlon Corp.*, 285 F. 578 (S.D. Fla. 1922); [*BB*] *Hale v. Stimpson*, 11 F. Cas. 187 (D. Mass. 1865) (No. 5915);

[*ALWD*] *Hale v. Stimpson*, 11 F. Cas. 187 (D. Mass. 1865); [*BB*] *Smith v. CSX Transp., Inc.*, 29 Fed. R. Serv. 3d (West) 1439 (E.D.N.C. 1994); [*BB*] *Smith v. CSX Transp., Inc.*, 29 Fed. R. Serv. 3d (West) 1439 (E.D.N.C. May 18, 1994).

See also the entry for Bankruptcy Courts below.

UNITED STATES BANKRUPTCY COURTS

Court Websites: See access information for the federal courts at the beginning of this subdivision.

Each of the ninety-four United States judicial districts handles bankruptcy matters. In almost all districts, bankruptcy cases are filed in the United States Bankruptcy Court (Bankr.) (as a result of major changes in the bankruptcy laws enacted in 1978).

Beginning in 1980, cases from the United States Bankruptcy Courts (and those cases from the United States District Courts that deal with bankruptcy matters no longer reported in the Federal Supplement) are reported in West's Bankruptcy Reporter (B.R.) and various bankruptcy services. Districts are designated in the same way as they are for United States District Courts (see above).

In re Rittenhouse Carpet, Inc., 56 B.R. 131 (Bankr. E.D. Pa. 1985).

See also Bankruptcy Appellate Panels in the next subsection.

BANKRUPTCY APPELLATE PANELS

<u>Appellate Panel Websites</u>: See access information for the federal courts at the beginning of this subdivision. (Bankruptcy Appellate Panels can be found through the "Court of Appeals").

Bankruptcy Appellate Panels (*[BB]* B.A.P. *[ALWD]* Bankr. App.) hear appeals from the Bankruptcy Courts. They were instituted as an alternative forum to the district courts for hearing bankruptcy appeals. Panel decisions are reported in the Bankruptcy Reporter (B.R.) (1979 ➜). The applicable circuit is also indicated in the parenthetical.

[BB] Younie v. Gonya (In re Younie), 211 B.R. 367 (B.A.P. 9th Cir. 1997).

[ALWD] Younie v. Gonya, 211 B.R. 367 (Bankr. App. 9th Cir. 1997). Adding the nonadversary name parenthetically is optional: *[ALWD] Younie v. Gonya (In re Younie)*, 211 B.R. 367 (Bankr. App. 9th Cir. 1997).

JUDICIAL PANEL ON MULTIDISTRICT LITIGATION

<u>Judicial Panel on Multidistrict Litigation Website</u>:
http://www.jpml.uscourts.gov/
(United States Judicial Panel on Multidistrict Litigation)

Opinions by the Judicial Panel on Multidistrict Litigation (*[BB]* J.P.M.L. *[ALWD]* M.D.L.) are published in the Federal Supplement (1968 ➜).

[BB] In re Commodity Credit Litig., 364 F. Supp. 462 (J.P.M.L. 1973).

[ALWD] In re Commodity Credit Corp. Litig., 364 F. Supp. 462 (M.D.L. 1973).

UNITED STATES TAX COURT

<u>Court Website</u>: http://www.ustaxcourt.gov/
(United States Tax Court)

The United States Tax Court (T.C.) was created in 1942. It is authorized "to hear tax disputes concerning notices of deficiency, notices of transferee liability, certain types of declaratory judgment, readjustment and adjustment of partnership items, review of the failure to abate interest, administrative costs, worker classification, relief from joint and several liability on a joint return, and review of certain collection actions."

The preferred citation is to the official report, United States Tax Court Reports (T.C.) (1942 →) (titled Tax Court of the United States Reports from 1942 → 1968, which reflected the name of the court during that period). Otherwise, one of the several tax services should be cited, depending on availability.

[*BB* Citation Sentences or Clauses]   *Estate of Smith v. Comm'r*, 57 T.C. 650 (1972).

[*ALWD* Citation Sentences or Clauses] *Estate of Smith v. Commr.*, 57 T.C. 650 (1972).

Prior to 1942, the functions of the Tax Court were performed by the Board of Tax Appeals ([*BB*] B.T.A.). The official report for the Board of Tax Appeals was the Reports of the United States Board of Tax Appeals (1924 → 1942). The Board's memorandum decisions are also reported in various tax services. Older tax decisions, such as these, often use the "administrative style of the case," which is the plaintiff's full name in lieu of adversarial parties. In accord with practice, the *ALWD Manual* specifically recommends converting administrative styling of the case to an adversarial one (as shown below).

[*BB* Citation Sentences or Clauses] *Dahlinger v. Comm'r*, 20 B.T.A. 176 (1930).

[*ALWD* Citation Sentences or Clauses] *Dahlinger v. Commr.*, 20 B.T.A. 176 (1930).

UNITED STATES COURT OF APPEALS FOR THE ARMED FORCES

<u>Court Website</u>: http://www.armfor.uscourts.gov/
(United States Court of Appeals for the Armed Forces)

The United States Court of Appeals for the Armed Forces ([*BB*] C.A.A.F.) [*ALWD*] App. Armed Forces) exercises worldwide appellate jurisdiction over members of the armed forces on active duty and other persons subject to the Uniform Code of Military Justice (UCMJ). The Court was previously called the United States Court of Military Appeals ([*BB*] C.M.A.) (1951 → 1968). The preferred citation is to Decisions of the United States Court of Military Appeals (C.M.A. 1951 → 1975) or West's Military Justice Reporter (M.J. 1978 →). Another source is Court Martial Reports ([*BB*] C.M.R. 1951 → 1975).

[*BB*] *United States v. Marcum*, 60 M.J. 198 (C.A.A.F. 2004); *United States v. Frischholz*, 16 C.M.A. 150 306 (1966); *United States v. Wilson*, 26 C.M.R. 3 (C.M.A. 1958).

[*ALWD*] *U.S. v. Marcum*, 60 M.J. 198 (App. Armed Forces 2004).

MILITARY SERVICE COURTS OF CRIMINAL APPEALS

<u>Court Websites</u>:

https://www.jagcnet.army.mil/acca
(United States Army Court of Criminal Appeals)
http://afcca.law.af.mil/
(United States Air Force Court of Criminal Appeals)
http://www.uscg.mil/legal/cca/
(CG Court of Criminal Appeals)
http://www.jag.navy.mil/FieldOffices/NMCCA.htm
(NMCA (Code 7))

If the sentence in a courts-martial proceeding includes death, a bad-conduct or dishonorable discharge, dismissal of an officer, or confinement for one year or more, the case is reviewed by an intermediate appellate court: the Army Court of Criminal Appeals ([*BB*] A. Ct. Crim. App.), the Navy-Marine Corps Court of Criminal Appeals ([*BB*] N-M. Ct. Crim. App.), the Air Force Court of Criminal Appeals [*BB*] A.F. Ct. Crim. App.), and the Coast Guard Court of Criminal Appeals ([*BB*] C.G. Ct. Crim. App.). These courts were previously called Boards of Review ([*BB*] A.B.R., A.F.B.R., etc.). *The Bluebook* indicates that decisions after 1950 should be cited to either West's Military Justices Reporter (M.J.) or Court Martial Reports (C.M.R.), if therein.

[*BB*] *United States v. Schap*, 44 M.J. 512 (A. Ct. Crim. App. 1996); *United States v. Maxwell*, 42 M.J. 568 (A.F. Crim. App. 1995); *United States v. Quintanilla*, 60 M.J. 852 (N-M.Ct. Crim. App. 2005); *United States v. Padgett*, 45 M.J. 520 (C.G. Ct. Crim. App. 1996).

For more detailed citation information and guidance, consult the latest edition of the *Military Citation Guide* compiled by the editors of the *Military Law Review* and

The Army Lawyer [See the Tenth Edition (Aug. 2005) in Army Law. 7 (Sept. 2005)].

UNITED STATES COURT OF APPEALS FOR VETERANS CLAIMS

Court Website: http://www.vetapp.uscourts.gov/
(United States Court of Appeals for Veterans Claims)

The purposes of the United States Court of Appeals for Veterans Claims (Vet. App.) is to provide veterans with "an impartial judicial forum for review of administrative decisions by the Board of Veterans' Appeals that are adverse to the veteran-appellant's claim of entitlement to benefits for service-connected disabilities, survivor benefits and other benefits such as education payments and waiver of indebtedness."

This court was created in 1988. At the outset it was called the United States Court of Veterans Appeals, but its name changed to the present one in 1999. Opinions are cited to West's Veterans Appeals Reporter (Vet. App.).

Bobbitt v. Principi, 17 Vet. App. 547 (2004).

SPECIAL COURT FOR REGIONAL RAIL REORGANIZATION ACT

The Regional Rail Reorganization Act of 1973 created a Special Court with jurisdiction over disputes and matters relating to the final system plan implemented under the Act. This special court ([*BB*] Reg'l Rail Reorg. Ct. [*ALWD*] Regl. Rail Reorg.) was abolished in 1997, and all jurisdiction and other functions of the court were assumed by the United States District Court for the District of Columbia. Decisions of the special court (1973 → 1997) were published in the Federal Supplement.

[BB] *In re Penn Cent. Transp. Co.*, 384 F. Supp. 895 (Reg'l Rail Reorg. Ct. 1974).

[ALWD] *In re Penn Cent. Transp. Co.*, 384 F. Supp. 895 (Regl. Rail Reorg. 1974).

B. STATE COURTS AND THE DISTRICT OF COLUMBIA

ALABAMA

Court Website: http://www.judicial.state.al.us/
(Alabama Judicial System Online)

ALABAMA SUPREME COURT (Ala.)

Osoinach v. Watkins, 180 So. 577 (Ala. 1938); *Hollis v. City of Brighton*, 885 So. 2d 135 (Ala. 2004); *Osoinach v. Watkins*, 235 Ala. 564, 180 So. 577 (1938); *White v. State*, 294 Ala. 265, 314 So. 2d 857 (1975).

ALABAMA COURT OF CIVIL APPEALS (Ala. Civ. App.)

Chapman v. Boise Cascade Corp., 726 So. 2d 729 (Ala. Civ. App. 1999); *Sutton v. Sutton*, 314 So. 2d 707 (Ala. Civ. App. 1975); *Sutton v. Sutton*, 55 Ala. App. 254, 314 So. 2d 707 (1975).

ALABAMA COURT OF CRIMINAL APPEALS (Ala. Crim. App.)

Rumpel v. State, 847 So. 2d 399 (Ala. Crim. App. 2002); *Barton v. State*, 326 So. 2d 695 (Ala. Crim. App. 1975) *Barton v. State*, 57 Ala. App. 167, 326 So. 2d 695 (Crim. App. 1975).

ALABAMA COURT OF APPEALS ([BB] Ala. Ct. App. [ALWD] Ala. App.) (before 1969)

[BB] *Alexander v. State*, 102 So. 597 (Ala. Ct. App. 1925); [ALWD] *Alexander v. State*, 102 So. 597 (Ala. App. 1925); *Alexander v. State*, 20 Ala. App. 432, 102 So. 597 (1925).

ALASKA

<u>Court Websites</u>: http://www.state.ak.us/courts/
(Alaska Court System)
http://www.appellate.courts.state.ak.us/
(Alaska Appellate Courts Case Management System)

ALASKA SUPREME COURT (Alaska)

Sanders v. Barth, 12 P.3d 766 (Alaska 2000).

ALASKA COURT OF APPEALS ([*BB*] Alaska Ct. App. [*ALWD*]
Alaska App.)

[*BB*] *Nease v. State*, 105 P.3d 1145 (Alaska Ct. App. 2005);
[*ALWD*] *Nease v. State*, 105 P.3d 1145 (Alaska App. 2005).

ARIZONA

<u>Court Website</u>: http://www.supreme.state.az.us/
(Arizona Judicial Branch)

ARIZONA SUPREME COURT (Ariz.)

State v. Ring, 25 P.3d 1139 (Ariz. 2001); *State v. Ring*, 200
Ariz. 267, 25 P.3d 1139 (2001).

ARIZONA COURT OF APPEALS ([*BB*] Ariz. Ct. App.) [*ALWD*]
Ariz. App. ___ Div.)

[*BB*] *State v. Freitag*, 130 P.3d 544 (Ariz. Ct. App. 2006);
[*ALWD*] *State v. Freitag*, 130 P.3d 544 (Ariz. App. 1st Div.
2006); [*BB*] *State v. Freitag*, 212 Ariz. 269, 130 P.3d 544 (Ct.
App. 2006); [*ALWD*] *State v. Freitag*, 212 Ariz. 269, 130 P.3d
544 (App. 1st Div. 2006); [*BB*] *Purcell v. Zimbelman*, 18 Ariz.
App. 75, 500 P.2d 335 (1972); [*ALWD*] *Purcell v. Zimbelman*,
18 Ariz. App. 75, 500 P.2d 335 (2d Div. 1972); *Fish v. Redeker*,
2 Ariz. App. 602, 411 P.2d 40 (1966) [no appellate court
divisions at the time of this decision].

ARKANSAS

<u>Court Website</u>: http://courts.state.ar.us/
(Arkansas Judiciary)

<u>ARKANSAS SUPREME COURT</u> (Ark.)

Linder v. Linder, 72 S.W.3d 841 (Ark. 2002); *Linder v. Linder*, 348 Ark. 322, 72 S.W.3d 841 (2002).

<u>ARKANSAS COURT OF APPEALS</u> ([*BB*] Ark. Ct. App. [*ALWD*] Ark. App. Div. ___)

[*BB*] *Eagle Bank & Trust Co. v. Dixon*, 15 S.W.3d 695 (Ark. Ct. App. 2000); [*ALWD*] *Eagle Bank & Trust Co. v. Dixon*, 15 S.W.3d 695 (Ark. App. Div. III 2000); [*BB*] *Eagle Bank & Trust Co. v. Dixon*, 70 Ark. App. 146, 15 S.W.3d 695 (2000); [*BB*] *Eagle Bank & Trust Co. v. Dixon*, 70 Ark. App. 146, 15 S.W.3d 695 (Div. III 2000); [*BB*] *Caldwell v. State*, 594 S.W.2d 24 (Ark. Ct. App.1980) [*ALWD*] *Caldwell v. State*, 594 S.W.2d 24 (Ark. App.1980) [no appellate court divisions at the time of this decision]; [*BB*] *Caldwell v. State*, 267 Ark. 1053, 594 S.W.2d 24 (Ct. App.1980) [Court of Appeals cases reported in Arkansas Reports 1979 → 1981]; [*ALWD*] *Caldwell v. State*, 267 Ark. 1053, 594 S.W.2d 24 (App.1980).

CALIFORNIA

<u>Court Website</u>: http://www.courtinfo.ca.gov/
(California Courts: The Judicial Branch of California)

<u>CALIFORNIA SUPREME COURT</u> (Cal.)

In re George T., 93 P.3d 1007 (Cal. 2004); [*BB*] *In re George T.*, 33 Cal. 4th 620, 93 P.3d 1007, 16 Cal. Rptr. 3d 61 (2004); [*ALWD*] *In re George T.*, 33 Cal. 4th 620, 16 Cal. Rptr. 3d 61, 93 P.3d 1007 (2004); *People v. Alcalde*, 148 P. 2d 627 (1944); *People v. Alcalde*, 24 Cal. 2d 177, 148 P. 2d 627 (1944) [West's Cal. Rptr. begins in 1960 and thus cannot be cited].

CALIFORNIA COURT OF APPEAL (*[BB]* Cal. Ct. App. *[ALWD]* Cal. App. ___ Dist.)

[BB] In re David S., 133 Cal. App. 4th 1160, 35 Cal. Rptr. 3d 309 (2005); *[ALWD] In re David S.*, 133 Cal. App. 4th 1160, 35 Cal. Rptr. 3d 309 (1st Dist. 2005); *[BB] People v. Montecino*, 66 Cal. App. 2d 85, 152 P.2d 5 (1944) [West's Cal. Rptr. begins in 1960 and thus cannot be cited]; *[ALWD] People v. Montecino*, 66 Cal. App. 2d 85, 152 P.2d 5 (2d Dist. 1944).

CALIFORNIA SUPERIOR COURT, APPELLATE DEPARTMENT (*[BB]* Cal. App. Dep't Super. Ct. *[ALWD]* Cal. Super. App. Dept.])

[BB] People v. Tisbert, 14 Cal. Rptr. 2d 128 (App. Dep't Super. Ct. 1992); *[ALWD] People v. Tisbert*, 14 Cal. Rptr. 2d 128 (Super. App. Dept. 1992); *People v. Tisbert*, 11 Cal. App. Supp. 4th 1, 14 Cal. Rptr. 2d 128 (1992); *People v. Hecht*, 119 Cal. App. Supp. 778, 3 P.2d 399 (1931).

COLORADO

Court Website: http://www.courts.state.co.us/ (Colorado Judicial Branch)

COLORADO SUPREME COURT (Colo.)

People ex rel. Salazar v. Davidson, 79 P.3d 1221 (Colo. 2003); *Beebe v. Pierce*, 521 P.2d 1263 (Colo. 1974); *Beebe v. Pierce*, 185 Colo. 34, 521 P.2d 1263 (1974).

COLORADO COURT OF APPEALS (*[BB]* Colo. Ct. App. *[ALWD]* Colo. App.)

[BB] People v. Sharp, 155 P.3d 577 (Colo. Ct. App. 2006); *[ALWD] People v. Sharp*, 155 P.3d 577 (Colo. App. 2006); *[BB] People v. Trujillo*, 586 P.2d 235 (Colo. Ct. App. 1978); *[ALWD] People v. Trujillo*, 586 P.2d 235 (Colo. App. 1978); *People v. Trujillo*, 41 Colo. App. 223, 586 P.2d 235 (1978).

CONNECTICUT

Court Website: http://www.jud.state.ct.us/
(State of Connecticut Judicial Branch)

CONNECTICUT SUPREME COURT (previously Connecticut Supreme Court of Errors) (Conn.)

Roth v. Weston, 789 A.2d 431 (Conn. 2002); *Roth v. Weston*, 259 Conn. 202, 789 A.2d 431 (2002).

CONNECTICUT APPELLATE COURT ([*BB*] Conn. App. Ct. [*ALWD*] Conn. App.)

[*BB*] *Rosengarten v. Downes*, 802 A.2d 170 (Conn. App. Ct. 2002); [*ALWD*] *Rosengarten v. Downes*, 802 A.2d 170 (Conn. App. 2002); *Rosengarten v. Downes*, 71 Conn. App. 372 802 A.2d 170 (2002).

CONNECTICUT SUPERIOR COURT ([*BB*] Conn. Super. Ct. [*ALWD*] Conn. Super.)

[*BB*] *Jarboe v Edwards*, 223 A.2d 402 (Conn. Super. Ct. 1966); [*ALWD*] *Jarboe v Edwar ds*, 223 A.2d 402 (Conn. Super. 1966); [*BB*] *Jarboe v Edwards*, 26 Conn. Supp. 350, 223 A.2d 402 (Super. Ct. 1966); [*ALWD*] *Jarboe v Edwards*, 26 Conn. Supp. 350, 223 A.2d 402 (Super. 1966); *Abbhi v. AMI*, 19 Conn. L. Rptr. 493 (Super. Ct.1997).

CONNECTICUT CIRCUIT COURT ([*BB*] Conn. Cir. Ct. [*ALWD*] Conn. Cir.)

[*BB*] *State v. Bell*, 186 A.2d 805 (Conn. Cir. Ct. 1962); [*ALWD*] *State v. Bell*, 186 A.2d 805 (Conn. Cir. 1962); [*BB*] *State v. Bell*, 1 Conn. Cir. Ct. 421, 186 A.2d 805 (1962); [*ALWD*] *State v. Bell*, 1 Conn. Cir. 421, 186 A.2d 805 (1962).

CONNECTICUT COURT OF COMMON PLEAS ([*BB*] Conn. C.P. [*ALW*D] Com. Pleas)

[*BB*] *Nesko Corp. v. Fontaine*, 110 A.2d 631 (Conn. C.P. 1954); [*ALWD*] *Nesko Corp. v. Fontaine*, 110 A.2d 631 (Conn. Com. Pleas 1954); [*BB*] *Nesko Corp. v. Fontaine*, 19 Conn. Supp. 160, 110 A.2d 631 (C.P. 1954); [*ALWD*] *Nesko Corp. v. Fontaine*, 19 Conn. Supp. 160, 110 A.2d 631 (Com. Pleas 1954).

DELAWARE

Court Website: http://courts.delaware.gov/
(Delaware State Courts)

DELAWARE SUPREME COURT (previously Delaware High Court of Errors and Appeals) (Del.)

Ortiz v. State, 869 A.2d 285 (Del. 2005); *Rickards v. State*, 77 A.2d 199 (Del. 1950); *Rickards v. State*, 45 Del. 573, 77 A.2d 199 (1950).

DELAWARE COURT OF CHANCERY (Del. Ch.)

Jedwab v. MGM Grand Hotels, Inc., 509 A.2d 584 (Del. Ch. 1986); *Beard v. Elster*, 160 A.2d 731 (Del. Ch. 1960); *Beard v. Elster*, 39 Del. Ch. 153, 160 A.2d 731 (1960).

DELAWARE SUPERIOR COURT ([*BB*] Del. Super. Ct. [*ALWD*] Del. Super.)

[*BB*] *Grobow v. Perot*, 539 A.2d 180 (Del. Super. Ct. 1988); [*ALWD*] *Grobow v. Perot*, 539 A.2d 180 (Del. Super. 1988).

DELAWARE FAMILY COURT ([*BB*] Del. Fam. Ct. [*ALWD*] Del. Fam.)

[*BB*] *Murphy v. Murphy*, 467 A.2d 129 (Del. Fam. Ct. 1983); [*ALWD*] *Murphy v. Murphy*, 467 A.2d 129 (Del. Fam. 1983).

D<small>ELAWARE</small> O<small>RPHANS</small>' C<small>OURT</small> ([*BB*] Del. Orphans' Ct.)

[*BB*] *In re Panousseris' Will*, 151 A.2d 518 (Del. Orphans' Ct. 1959); [*BB*] *In re Panousseris' Will*, 52 Del. 21, 151 A.2d 518 (Orphans' Ct. 1959).

DISTRICT OF COLUMBIA

Court Website: http://www.dccourts.gov/dccourts/index.jsp (Welcome to the District of Columbia Courts)

D<small>ISTRICT OF</small> C<small>OLUMBIA</small> C<small>OURT OF</small> A<small>PPEALS</small> (D.C.) (previously Municipal Court of Appeals ([*BB*] D.C. [*ALWD*] D.C. Mun. App.)

Rockler v. Sevareid, 691 A.2d 97 (D.C. 1997); [*BB*] *Hyde v. Brandler*, 118 A.2d 398 (D.C. 1955); [*ALWD*] *Hyde v. Brandler*, 118 A.2d 398 (D.C. Mun. App. 1955).

FLORIDA

Court Website: http://www.flcourts.org/ (Florida State Courts)

F<small>LORIDA</small> S<small>UPREME</small> C<small>OURT</small> (Fla.)

Posner v. Posner, 233 So. 2d 381 (Fla. 1970); *Wildman v. State*, 25 So. 2d 808 (Fla. 1946); *Wildman v. State*, 157 Fla. 334, 25 So. 2d 808 (1946).

F<small>LORIDA</small> D<small>ISTRICT</small> C<small>OURT OF</small> A<small>PPEAL</small> ([*BB*] Fla. Dist. Ct. App. [*ALWD*] Fla. ___ Dist. App.)

[*BB*] *State v. Pinault*, 933 So. 2d 1287 (Fla. Dist. Ct. App. 2006); *State v. Pinault*, 933 So. 2d 1287 (Fla. 4th Dist. App. 2006).

FLORIDA CIRCUIT COURT (*[BB]* Fla. Cir. Ct. *[ALWD]* Fla. ___ Cir.)

[BB] Ash v. Dade County, 18 Fla. Supp. 2d 185 (Cir. Ct. 1986); *[ALWD] Ash v. Dade Co.*, 18 Fla. Supp. 2d 185 (11th Cir. 1986).

FLORIDA COUNTY COURT (*[BB]* Fla. [Name of County] County Ct. *[ALWD]* Fla. [Name of County] Co. Ct.)

[BB] In re Kent's Estate, 23 Fla. Supp. 133 (Palm Beach County Ct. 1964); *[ALWD] In re Kent's Estate*, 23 Fla. Supp. 133 (Palm Beach Co. Ct. 1964).

GEORGIA

Court Website: http://www.georgiacourts.org/
(Judicial Branch of Georgia)

GEORGIA SUPREME COURT (Ga.)

Kruse v. Todd, 389 S.E.2d 488 (Ga. 1990); *Kruse v. Todd*, 260 Ga. 63, 389 S.E.2d 488 (1990).

GEORGIA COURT OF APPEALS (*[BB]* Ga. Ct. App. *[ALWD]* Ga. App.)

[BB] Price v. State, 469 S.E.2d 333 (Ga. Ct. App. 1996); *[ALWD] Price v. State*, 469 S.E.2d 333 (Ga. App. 1996); *Price v. State*, 220 Ga. App. 176, 469 S.E.2d 333 (1996).

HAWAII

Court Website: http://www.courts.state.hi.us/index.jsp
(Hawaii State Judiciary)

HAWAII SUPREME COURT (Haw.)

Bynum v. Magno, 101 P.3d 1149 (Haw. 2004); *Bynum v. Magno*, 106 Haw. 81, 101 P.3d 1149 (2004); *Breiner v. Takao*,

835 P.2d 637 (Haw. 1992); *Breiner v. Takao*, 73 Haw. 499, 835 P.2d 637 (1992).

HAWAII INTERMEDIATE COURT OF APPEALS ([*BB*] Haw. Ct. App. [*ALWD*] Haw. App.)

[*BB*] *JAZ, Inc. v. Foley*, 85 P.3d 1099 (Haw. Ct. App. 2004); [*ALWD*] *JAZ, Inc. v. Foley*, 85 P.3d 1099 (Haw. App. 2004); [*BB*] *JAZ, Inc. v. Foley*, 104 Haw. 148, 85 P.3d 1099 (Ct. App. 2004); [*ALWD*] *JAZ, Inc. v. Foley*, 104 Haw. 148, 85 P.3d 1099 (App. 2004); [*BB*] *BATS, Inc. v. Shikuma*, 617 P.2d 575 (Haw. Ct. App. 1980); [*ALWD*] *BATS, Inc. v. Shikuma*, 617 P.2d 575 (Haw. App. 1980); *BATS, Inc. v. Shikuma*, 1 Haw. App. 231, 617 P.2d 575 (1980).

IDAHO

Court Website: http://www.isc.idaho.gov/
(Idaho State Judiciary)

IDAHO SUPREME COURT (Idaho)

Lapham v. Stewart, 51 P.3d 396 (Idaho 2002); *Lapham v. Stewart*, 137 Idaho 582, 51 P.3d 396 (2002).

IDAHO COURT OF APPEALS ([*BB*] Idaho Ct. App. [*ALWD*] Idaho App.)

Pinnacle Performance, Inc. v. Hessing, 17 P.3d 308 (Idaho Ct. App. 2001); [*BB*] *Pinnacle Performance, Inc. v. Hessing*, 135 Idaho 364, 17 P.3d 308 (Ct. App. 2001); [*ALWD*] *Pinnacle Performance, Inc. v. Hessing*, 135 Idaho 364, 17 P.3d 308 (App. 2001).

ILLINOIS

Court Website: http://www.state.il.us/court/
(Welcome to Illinois Courts)

ILLINOIS SUPREME COURT (Ill.)

People v. Thompson, 853 N.E.2d 378 (Ill. 2006); *People v. Thompson*, 222 Ill. 2d 1, 853 N.E.2d 378 (2006).

ILLINOIS APPELLATE COURT (*[BB]* Ill. App. Ct. *[ALWD]* Ill. App. __ Dist.)

[BB] Cohen v. McDonald's Corp., 808 N.E.2d 1 (Ill. App. Ct. 2004); *[ALWD] Cohen v. McDonald's Corp.*, 808 N.E.2d 1 (Ill. App. 2004); *Cohen v. McDonald's Corp.*, 347 Ill. App. 3d 627, 808 N.E.2d 1 (Ill. App. Ct . 2004).

ILLINOIS COURT OF CLAIMS (*[BB]* Ill. Ct. Cl. [ALWD] Ill. Cl.)

[BB] Phillips v. State, 44 Ill. Ct. Cl. 89 (1992); *[ALWD] Phillips v. State*, 44 Ill. Cl. 89 (1992).

INDIANA

Court Website: http://www.in.gov/judiciary/
(Indiana Courts)

INDIANA SUPREME COURT (Ind.)

Peterson v. Borst, 786 N.E.2d 668 (Ind. 2003); *Howard v. State*, 342 N.E.2d 604 (Ind. 1976); *Howard v. State*, 264 Ind. 275, 342 N.E.2d 604 (1976).

INDIANA COURT OF APPEALS (*[BB]* Ind. Ct. App *[ALWD]* Ind. App. __ Dist.) (before 1972, Indiana Appellate Court (*[BB]* Ind. App. *[ALWD]* Ind. App. __ Dist.)

[BB] Quinn v. Quinn, 498 N.E.2d 1312 (Ind. Ct. App. 1986); *[ALWD] Quinn v. Quinn*, 498 N.E.2d 1312 (Ind. App. 1st Dist. 1986); *[BB] Cox v. State*, 392 N.E.2d 496 (Ind. Ct. App. 1976); *[ALWD] Cox v. State*, 392 N.E.2d 496 (Ind. App. 1st Dist. 1976); *[BB] Cox v. State*, 181 Ind. App. 476, 392 N.E.2d 496 (1976); *[ALWD] Cox v. State*, 181 Ind. App. 476, 392 N.E.2d 496 (1st Dist. 1976); *Kiste v. Red Cab, Inc.*, 106 N.E.2d 395

(Ind. App. 1952) (in banc); *Kiste v. Red Cab, Inc.*, 122 Ind. App. 587, 106 N.E.2d 395 (1952) (in banc).

IOWA

Court Website: http://www.judicial.state.ia.us/
(Iowa Judicial Branch)

IOWA SUPREME COURT (Ia.)

State v. Seering, 701 N.W.2d 655 (Iowa 2005); *Lehr v. Switzer*, 239 N.W. 564 (Iowa 1931); *Lehr v. Switzer*, 213 Iowa 658, 239 N.W. 564 (1931).

IOWA COURT OF APPEALS ([*BB*] Iowa Ct. App. [*ALWD*] Iowa App.)

[*BB*] *Montgomery v. Wells*, 708 N.W.2d 704 (Iowa Ct. App. 2005); [*BB*] *Montgomery v. Wells*, 708 N.W.2d 704 (Iowa App. 2005).

KANSAS

Court Website: http://www.kscourts.org/
(Kansas Judicial Branch)

KANSAS SUPREME COURT (Kan.)

State v. Alston, 887 P.2d 681 (Kan. 1994); *State v. Alston*, 256 Kan. 571, 887 P.2d 681 (1994).

KANSAS COURT OF APPEALS ([*BB*] Kan. Ct. App. [*ALWD*] Kan. App.)

[*BB*] *State v. Robinson*, 109 P.3d 185 (Kan. Ct. App. 2005); [*ALWD*] *State v. Robinson*, 109 P.3d 185 (Kan. App. 2005); *State v. Robinson*, 33 Kan. App. 2d 773, 109 P.3d 185 (2005).

KENTUCKY

Court Website: http://courts.ky.gov/
(Kentucky: Court of Justice)

KENTUCKY SUPREME COURT (before 1976, Kentucky Court of
Appeals) (Ky.)

Baze v. Rees, 217 S.W.3d 207 (Ky. 2006); *Miller v. Quertermous*, 202 S.W.2d 389 (Ky. 1947); *Miller v. Quertermous*, 304
Ky. 733, 202 S.W.2d 389 (1947).

KENTUCKY COURT OF APPEALS (only for cases after 1975)
([*BB*] Ky. Ct. App. [*ALWD*] Ky. App.)

[*BB*] *Meade v. Richardson Fuel, Inc.*, 166 S.W.3d 55 (Ky. Ct.
App. 2005); [*ALWD*] *Meade v. Richardson Fuel, Inc.*, 166
S.W.3d 55 (Ky. App. 2005).

LOUISIANA

Court Websites: http://www.lasc.org/
(Louisiana Supreme Court)
http://www.la-fcca.org/
(Louisiana Court of Appeal First Circuit)
http://www.lacoa2.org/
(Second Circuit Court of Appeal)
http://www.la3circuit.org/
(Third Circuit Court of Appeal)
http://www.4thcir-app.state.la.us/
(State of Louisiana 4th Cir. Court of Appeal)
http://www.fifthcircuit.org/
(Louisiana Fifth Circuit Court of Appeal)

LOUISIANA SUPREME COURT (La.)

[*BB* & *ALWD* Public Domain] *Theisges v. Boudreaux*, 99-
1458 (La. 7/2/99); 747 So. 2d 4; [*ALWD* Optional] *Theisges v.
Boudreaux*, 747 So. 2d 4 (La. 1999); *State v. Bates*, 397 So. 2d

1331 (La. 1980); *Ducuy v. Falgoust*, 83 So. 2d 118 (La. 1955); *Ducuy v. Falgoust*, 228 La. 533, 83 So. 2d 118 (1955).

LOUISIANA COURT OF APPEAL ([*BB*] La. Ct. App. [*ALWD*] La. App. ___ Cir.)

[*BB* & *ALWD* Public Domain] *Bridges v. Wilcoxon*, 34-660 (La. App. 2 Cir. 5/09/01); 786 So. 2d 264; [*ALWD* Optional] *Bridges v. Wilcoxon*, 786 So. 2d 264 (La. App. 2d Cir. 2001); [*BB*] *Flowers v. Morris*, 43 So. 2d 917 (La. Ct. App. 1950); [*ALWD*] *Flowers v. Morris*, 43 So. 2d 917 (La. App. 2d Cir. 1950); [*BB*] *Greco v. Frigero*, 3 La. App. 649 (1926) [Southern Reporter coverage begins in 1928].

MAINE

Court Website: http://www.courts.state.me.us/ (State of Maine Judicial Branch)

MAINE SUPREME JUDICIAL COURT (Me.)

Hayden v. Orfe, 2006 ME 56, 896 A.2d 968; *Hayden v. Orfe*, 896 A.2d 968 (Me. 2006); *Campbell v. Town of Machias*, 661 A.2d 1133 (Me. 1995); *Bragdon v. Shapiro*, 77 A.2d 598 (Me. 1951); *Bragdon v. Shapiro*, 146 Me. 83, 77 A.2d 598 (1951).

MARYLAND

Court Website: http://www.courts.state.md.us/ (Maryland Judiciary)

MARYLAND COURT OF APPEALS (Md.)

Johnson v. G.D. Searle & Co., 552 A.2d 29 (Md. 1989). *Johnson v. G.D. Searle & Co.*, 314 Md. 521, 552 A.2d 29 (1989).

MARYLAND COURT OF SPECIAL APPEALS (*[BB]* Md. Ct. Spec. App. *[ALWD]* Md. Spec. App.)

[BB] *Smith v. State*, 932 A.2d 773 (Md. Ct. Spec. App. 2007); *[ALWD]* *Smith v. State*, 932 A.2d 773 (Md. Spec. App. 2007); *Smith v. State*, 176 Md. App. 64, 932 A.2d 773 (2007).

MASSACHUSETTS

Court Website: http://www.mass.gov/courts/ (The Massachusetts Court System)

MASSACHUSETTS SUPREME JUDICIAL COURT (Mass.)

McCarthy v. Tobin, 706 N.E.2d 629 (Mass. 1999); *McCarthy v. Tobin*, 429 Mass. 84, 706 N.E.2d 629 (1999).

MASSACHUSETTS APPEALS COURT (*[BB]* Mass. App. Ct. *[ALWD]* Mass. App.)

[BB] *Bak v. Bak*, 511 N.E.2d 625 (Mass. App. Ct. 1987); *[ALWD]* *Bak v. Bak*, 511 N.E.2d 625 (Mass. App. 1987).

MASSACHUSETTS DISTRICT COURT, APPELLATE DIVISION (*[BB]* Mass. Dist. Ct. *[ALWD]* Mass Dist. App. Div.)

[BB] *Denaro v. 99 Rest., Inc.*, 2002 Mass. App. Div. 195 (Dist. Ct.); *[ALWD]* *Denaro v. 99 Rest., Inc.*, 2002 Mass. App. Div. 195 (Dist. App. Div.); *[BB]* *Whately v. Tetrault*, 29 Mass. App. Dec. 112 (Dist. Ct. 1964); *[ALWD]* *Whately v. Tetrault*, 29 Mass. App. Dec. 112 (Dist. App. Div. 1964).

MASSACHUSETTS SUPERIOR COURT (*[BB]* Mass. Super. Ct. *[ALWD]* Mass. Super.)

[BB] *Erickson v. Hart*, 10 Mass. L. Rptr. 613 (Super. Ct. 1999); *[BB]* *Erickson v. Hart*, 10 Mass. L. Rptr. 613 (Super. 1999).

MICHIGAN

<u>Court Website</u>: http://courts.michigan.gov/
(Michigan Courts)

Michigan Supreme Court (Mich.)

Rinke v. Rinke, 48 N.W.2d 201 (Mich. 1951); *Rinke v. Rinke*, 330 Mich. 615, 48 N.W.2d 201 (1951).

Michigan Court of Appeals ([*BB*] Mich. Ct. App. [*ALWD*] Mich. App.)

[*BB*] *People v. Boomer*, 655 N.W.2d 255 (Mich. Ct. App. 2002); [*ALWD*] *People v. Boomer*, 655 N.W.2d 255 (Mich. App. 2002); *People v. Boomer*, 250 Mich. App. 534, 655 N.W.2d 255 (2002).

MINNESOTA

<u>Court Website</u>: http://www.mncourts.gov/
(Minnesota Judicial Branch)

Minnesota Supreme Court (Minn.)

In re Ramirez, 719 N.W.2d 920 (Minn. 2006); *Danielson v. Fitzsimmons*, 44 N.W.2d 484 (Minn. 1950); *Danielson v. Fitzsimmons*, 232 Minn. 149, 44 N.W.2d 484 (1950).

Minnesota Court of Appeals ([*BB*] Minn. Ct. App. [*ALWD*] Minn. App.)

[*BB*] *Mon-Ray, Inc. v. Granite Re, Inc.*, 677 N.W.2d 434 (Minn. Ct. App. 2004); [*ALWD*] *Mon-Ray, Inc. v. Granite Re, Inc.*, 677 N.W.2d 434 (Minn. App. 2004).

MISSISSIPPI

<u>Court Website</u>: http://www.mssc.state.ms.us/
(Mississippi Supreme Court)

MISSISSIPPI SUPREME COURT (Miss.)

Biglane v. Under the Hill Corp., 2005-CA-01751-SCT (Miss. 2007); *Biglane v. Under the Hill Corp.*, 949 So. 2d 9 (Miss. 2007); *Cooper v. Crabb*, 587 So. 2d 236 (Miss. 1991); *Hewling v. Blake*, 70 So. 247 (Miss. 1915); *Hewling v. Blake*, 110 Miss. 225, 70 So. 247 (1915).

MISSISSIPPI COURT OF APPEALS (Miss. App.)

In re McSwain, 2005-CA-00943-COA (Miss. Ct. App. 2006); [*BB*] *In re McSwain*, 946 So. 2d 417 (Miss. Ct. App. 2006); [*ALWD*] *In re McSwain*, 946 So. 2d 417 (Miss. App. 2006).

MISSOURI

Court Website: http://www.courts.mo.gov/
(Your Missouri Courts: The Judicial Branch of State Government)

MISSOURI SUPREME COURT (Mo.)

State ex. rel. Simmons v. Roper, 112 S.W.3d 397 (Mo. 2003); *DeVault v. Truman*, 194 S.W.2d 29 (Mo. 1946); *DeVault v. Truman*, 354 Mo. 1193, 194 S.W.2d 29 (1946); *Ex parte Brown*, 72 Mo. 83 (1880).

MISSOURI COURT OF APPEALS ([*BB*] Mo. Ct. App. [*ALWD*] Mo. App. __ Dist.)

[*BB*] *Ford Motor Credit Co. v. Updegraff*, 218 S.W.3d 617 (Mo. Ct. App. 2007); [*ALWD*] *Ford Motor Credit Co. v. Updegraff*, 218 S.W.3d 617 (Mo. App. W.D. 2007); *Hickey v. Welch*, 91 Mo. App. 4 (1901).

MONTANA

Court Website: http://www.montanacourts.org/
(Montana Courts)

MONTANA SUPREME COURT **(Mont.)**

[BB & ALWD **Public Domain]** *In re Z.M.*, 2007 MT 122, 337 Mont. 278, 160 P.3d 490; *[ALWD* **Optional]** *In re Z.M.*, 160 P.3d 490 (Mont. 2007); *In re Z.M.*, 337 Mont. 278, 160 P.3d 490 (2007); *Bruce v. Bruce*, 877 P.2d 999 (Mont. 1994); *Bruce v. Bruce*, 265 Mont. 431, 877 P.2d 999 (1994).

NEBRASKA

Court Website: **http://www.supremecourt.ne.gov/ (Nebraska Judicial Branch)**

NEBRASKA SUPREME COURT **(Neb.)**

Hamilton v. Bares, 678 N.W.2d 74 (Neb. 2004); *Hamilton v. Bares*, 267 Neb. 816, 678 N.W.2d 74 (2004); *Renard v. Brown*, 7 Neb. 449 (1878).

NEBRASKA COURT OF APPEALS **([BB]** Neb. Ct. App. *[ALWD]* **Neb. App.)**

[BB] Pickrel v Pickrel, 717 N.W.2d 479 (Neb. Ct. App. 2006); *[ALWD] Pickrel v Pickrel*, 717 N.W.2d 479 (Neb. App. 2006); *Pickrel v Pickrel*, 14 Neb. App. 292, 717 N.W.2d 479 (2006).

NEVADA

Court Website: **http://www.nvsupremecourt.us/ (The Supreme Court of Nevada)**

NEVADA SUPREME COURT **(Nev.)**

Abbott v. State, 138 P.3d 462 (Nev. 2006); *Abbott v. State*, 122 Nev. 715, 138 P.3d 462 (2006); *State v. Pearce*, 15 Nev. 188 (1880).

NEW HAMPSHIRE

<u>Court Website</u>: http://www.courts.state.nh.us/
(Judicial Branch: State of New Hampshire)

New Hampshire Supreme Court (N.H.)

State v. City of Dover, 891 A.2d 524 (N.H. 2006); *State v. City of Dover*, 153 N.H. 151, 891 A.2d 524 (2006); *Young v. Stevens*, 48 N.H. 133 (1868).

NEW JERSEY

<u>Court Website</u>: http://www.judiciary.state.nj.us/
(New Jersey Courts Online)

New Jersey Supreme Court (previously New Jersey Court of Errors and Appeals) (N.J.)

State v. Moore, 902 A.2d 1212 (N.J. 2006); *State v. Moore*, 188 N.J. 182, 902 A.2d 1212 (2006); *Broad & Branford Place Corp. v. J.J. Hockenjos Co.*, 39 A.2d 80 (N.J. 1944); *Broad & Branford Place Corp. v. J.J. Hockenjos Co.*, 132 N.J.L. 229, 39 A.2d 80 (1944); *Camden Trust Co. v. Handle*, 26 A.2d 865 (N.J. 1942); *Camden Trust Co. v. Handle*, 132 N.J. Eq. 97, 26 A.2d 865 (N.J. 1942); *Bell v. Gough*, 23 N.J.L. 624 (1852).

New Jersey Superior Court (*[BB]* N.J. Super. Ct. App. Div. *[ALWD]* N.J. Super. App. Div.; New Jersey Court of Chancery (*[BB]* N.J. Super. Ct. Ch. Div. *[ALWD]* N.J. Super. Ch. Div.); New Jersey Superior Court Law Division (*[BB]* N.J. Super. Ct. L. Div. *[ALWD]* N.J. Super. L. Div.)

[BB] *In re* Unanue, 710 A.2d 1036 (N.J. Super. Ct. App. Div. 1998); *[ALWD]* *In re* Unanue, 710 A.2d 1036 (N.J. Super. App. Div. 1998); *In re* Unanue, 311 N.J. Super. 589, 710 A.2d 1036 (App. Div. 1998); *[BB]* *In re Estate of Cole*, 491 A.2d 770 (N.J. Super. Ct. Ch. Div. 1984); *[ALWD]* *In re Estate of Cole*, 491 A.2d 770 (N.J. Super. Ch. Div. 1984); *In re Estate of Cole*,

200 N.J. Super. 369, 491 A.2d 770 (Ch. Div. 1984); [*BB*] *In re Diet Drug Litig.*, 895 A.2d 493, 497 (N.J. Super. Ct. Law Div. 2005); [*ALWD*] *In re Diet Drug Litig.*, 895 A.2d 493, 497 (N.J. Super. Law Div. 2005); *In re Diet Drug Litig.*, 384 N.J. Super. 546, 895 A.2d 493, 497 (Law Div. 2005).

(Before 1947, the New Jersey Superior Court was previously New York Court of Chancery (N.J. Ch.); New Jersey Supreme Ct. (N.J. Sup. Ct).; New Jersey Prerogative Court ([*BB*] N.J. Prerog. Ct. [*ALWD*] N.J. Prerog.))

Kreyling v. Kreyling, 23 A.2d 800 (N.J. Ch. 1942); *Kreyling v. Kreyling*, 20 N.J. Misc. 52, 23 A.2d 800 (Ch. 1942); *Stanfield v. Schneidewind*, 115 A. 339 (N.J. Sup. Ct. 1921); *Stanfield v. Schneidewind*, 96 N.J.L. 428, 115 A. 339 (Sup. Ct. 1921); [*BB*] *Smith v. Runkle*, 97 A. 296 (N.J. Pregog. Ct. 1915); [*ALWD*] *Smith v. Runkle*, 97 A. 296 (N.J. Pregog. 1915).

NEW JERSEY TAX COURT ([*BB*] N.J. Tax. Ct. [*ALWD*] N.J. Tax)

Marrinan v. State, 17 N.J. Tax. 47 (1997).

NEW JERSEY COUNTY COURTS (N.J. [Name of County] County Ct.)

State v. Walton, 179 A.2d 78 (N.J. Middlesex County Ct. 1962); *State v. Walton*, 72 N.J. Super. 527, 179 A.2d 78 (Middlesex County Ct. 1962).

NEW MEXICO

Court Website: http://www.nmcourts.com/
(New Mexico Courts: The Judicial Branch of New Mexico)

NEW MEXICO SUPREME COURT (N.M.)

[*BB & ALWD* Public Domain] *State v. DeGraff*, 2006-NMSC-011, 139 N.M. 211, 31 P.3d 61; [*ALWD* Optional] *State v. DeGraff*, 131 P.3d 61 (N.M. 2006); *State v. Gonzales*, 989 P.2d

419 (N.M. 1999); *State v. Gonzales*, 128 N.M. 44, 989 P.2d 419 (1999).

NEW MEXICO COURT OF APPEALS ([*BB*] N.M. Ct. App. [*ALWD*] N.M. App.)

[*BB* & *ALWD* Public Domain] *Estate of Haar v. Ulwelling*, 2007-NMCA-032, 141 N.M. 252, 154 P.3d 67; [*ALWD* Optional] *Estate of Haar v. Ulwelling*, 154 P.3d 67 (N.M. Ct. App. 2007); [*BB*] *Pollock v. Ramirez*, 870 P.2d 149 (N.M. Ct. App. 1994); [*ALWD*] *Pollock v. Ramirez*, 870 P.2d 149 (N.M. App. 1994); *Pollock v. Ramirez*, 117 N.M. 187, 870 P.2d 149 (1994).

NEW YORK

Court Website: http://www.courts.state.ny.us/
(New York State Unified Court System)

NEW YORK COURT OF APPEALS (after 1846) (N.Y.) (before 1847, New York Court for the Correction of Errors ([*BB*] N.Y. [*ALWD*] N.Y. Errors); New York Supreme Court of Judicature ([*BB*] N.Y. Sup. Ct. [*ALWD*] N.Y.); New York Court of Chancery (N.Y. Ch.))

Hernandez v. Robles, 855 N.E.2d 1 (N.Y. 2006); [*BB*] *Hernandez v. Robles*, 7 N.Y.3d 338, 855 N.E.2d 1, 821 N.Y.S.2d 770 (2006); [*ALWD*] *Hernandez v. Robles*, 7 N.Y.3d 338, 821 N.Y.S.2d 770, 855 N.E.2d 1 (2006); *Williams v. Quill*, 12 N.E.2d 547 (N.Y. 1938); *Williams v. Quill*, 277 N.Y. 1, 12 N.E.2d 547 (N.Y. 1938); *Loop v. Litchfield*, 42 N.Y. 351 (1870).

NEW YORK SUPREME COURT, APPELLATE DIVISION ([*BB*] N.Y. App. Div. [*ALWD*] N.Y. App. Div. ___ Dept.) (previously Supreme Court, General Term (N.Y. Gen. Term))

[*BB*] *In re Kennedy T.*, 835 N.Y.S.2d 85 (App. Div. 2007); [*ALWD*] *In re Kennedy T.*, 835 N.Y.S.2d 85 (App. Div. 1st Dept. 2007); [*BB*] *In re Kennedy T.*, 39 A.D.3d 408, 835

N.Y.S.2d 85 (2007); [*ALWD*] *In re Kennedy T.*, 39 A.D.3d 408, 835 N.Y.S.2d 85 (1st Dept. 2007); [*BB*] *In re Estate of Ball*, 146 N.Y.S. 499 (App. Div. 1914); [*ALWD*] *In re Estate of Ball*, 146 N.Y.S. 499 (App. Div. 2d Dept. 1914); [*BB*] *In re Estate of Ball*, 161 A.D. 79, 146 N.Y.S. 499 (1914); [*ALWD*] *In re Estate of Ball*, 161 A.D. 79, 146 N.Y.S. 499 (2d Dept. 1914); *People ex rel. Choate v. Barrett*, 9 N.Y.S. 321 (Gen. Term 1890).

NEW YORK APPELLATE TERM (NY. App. Term)

Kline v. Schaum, 673 N.Y.S.2d 992 (App. Term 1997); *Kline v. Schaum*, 174 Misc. 2d 988, 673 N.Y.S.2d 992 (App. Term 1997).

NEW YORK SUPREME COURT (N.Y. Sup. Ct.)

People v. Bell, 778 N.Y.S.2d 837 (Sup. Ct. 2003); *People v. Bell*, 3 Misc. 3d 773, 778 N.Y.S.2d 837 (Sup. Ct. 2003).

NEW YORK COURT OF CLAIMS (N.Y. Ct. Cl.)

Town of Esopus v. State, 631 N.Y.S.2d 213 (Ct. Cl. 1995); *Town of Esopus v. State*, 166 Misc. 2d 36, 631 N.Y.S.2d 213 (Ct. Cl. 1995).

NEW YORK CIVIL COURT (N.Y. Civ. Ct.)

Licitra v. Gateway, Inc., 734 N.Y.S.2d 389 (Civ. Ct. 2001); *Licitra v. Gateway, Inc.*, 189 Misc. 2d 721, 734 N.Y.S.2d 389 (Civ. Ct. 2001).

NEW YORK CRIMINAL COURT (N.Y. Crim. Ct.)

People v. Bezjak, 812 N.Y.S.2d 829 (Crim. Ct. 2006); *People v. Bezjak*, 11 Misc. 3d 424, 812 N.Y.S.2d 829 (Crim. Ct. 2006).

NEW YORK FAMILY COURT (N.Y. Fam.)

In re M.A.R., 832 N.Y.S.2d 794 (Fam. Ct. 2007); *In re M.A.R.*, 15 Misc. 3d 784, 832 N.Y.S.2d 794 (Fam. Ct. 2007).

NORTH CAROLINA

<u>Court Website</u>: http://www.nccourts.org/
(The North Carolina Court System)

<u>North Carolina Supreme Court</u> (N.C.)

State v. Hurst, 624 S.E.2d 309 (N.C. 2006); *State v. Hurst*, 360 N.C. 181, 624 S.E.2d 309 (2006); *Harrell v. Watson*, 63 N.C. 454 (1869).

<u>North Carolina Court of Appeals</u> (*[BB]* N.C. Ct. App. *[ALWD]* N.C. App.)

[BB] Deer Corp. v. Carter, 629 S.E.2d 159 (N.C. Ct. App. 2006); *[ALWD] Deer Corp. v. Carter*, 629 S.E.2d 159 (N.C. App. 2006); *Deer Corp. v. Carter*, 177 N.C. App. 314, 629 S.E.2d 159 (2006).

NORTH DAKOTA

<u>Court Websites</u>:
 http://www.court.state.nd.us/court/courts.htm
(North Dakota Courts)
http://www.ndcourts.gov/
(North Dakota Supreme Court)

<u>North Dakota Supreme Court</u> (N.D.)

[BB & ALWD Public Domain] *State v. Blue*, 2006 ND 134, 717 N.W.2d 558; *[ALWD* Optional] *State v. Blue*, 717 N.W.2d 558 (N.D. 2006); *[ALWD* Alternative Format] *State v. Blue*, 2006 N.D. 134, 717 N.W.2d 558.

<u>North Dakota Court of Appeals</u> (*[BB]* N.D. Ct. App. *[ALWD]* N.D. App.)

[BB & ALWD Public Domain] *City of Bismarck v. Glass*, 1998 ND App 1, 581 N.W.2d 474; *[ALWD* Optional] *City of Bismarck v. Glass*, 581 N.W.2d 474 (N.D. App. 1998); *[ALWD*

Alternative Format] *City of Bismarck v. Glass*, 1998 N.D. App. 1, 581 N.W.2d 474; *State v. Hanson*, 256 N.W.2d 364 (N.D. 1977); *Engstrom v. Larson*, 44 N.W.2d 97 (1950); *Engstrom v. Larson*, 77 N.D. 541, 44 N.W.2d 97 (1950).

OHIO

Court Website: http://www.sconet.state.oh.us/
(The Supreme Court of Ohio)

OHIO SUPREME COURT (Ohio)

[*BB & ALWD* Public Domain] *Robinson v. Bates*, 112 Ohio St. 3d 17, 2006-Ohio-6362, 857 N.E.2d 1195; [*ALWD* Optional] *Robinson v. Bates*, 857 N.E.2d 1195 (Ohio 2006); *Worth v. Huntington Bancshares, Inc.*, 540 N.E.2d 249 (Ohio 1989); *Worth v. Huntington Bancshares, Inc.*, 43 Ohio St. 3d 192, 540 N.E.2d 249 (1989); *Lange v. Werk*, 2 Ohio St. 519 (1853); *City of Cincinnati v. Rice*, 15 Ohio 225 (1846).

OHIO COURT OF APPEALS ([*BB*] Ohio Ct. App. [*ALWD*] Ohio App. ___ Dist.)

[*BB & ALWD* Public Domain] *Zahn v. Nelson*, 170 Ohio App. 3d 111, 2007-Ohio-667, 866 N.E.2d 58; [*ALWD* Optional] *Zahn v. Nelson*, 866 N.E.2d 58 (Ohio App. 4th Dist. 2007); [*BB*] *State v. Proffitt*, 596 N.E.2d 527 (Ohio Ct. App. 1991); [*ALWD*] *State v. Proffitt*, 596 N.E.2d 527 (Ohio App. 12th Dist. 1991); [*BB*] *State v. Proffitt*, 72 Ohio App. 3d 807, 596 N.E.2d 527 (1991); [*ALWD*] *State v. Proffitt*, 72 Ohio App. 3d 807, 596 N.E.2d 527 (12th Dist. 1991).

OHIO PROBATE COURTS (Ohio Prob. Ct.)

In re Estate of Kusar, 211 N.E.2d 535 (Ohio Prob. Ct. 1965); *In re Estate of Kusar*, 5 Ohio Misc. 23, 211 N.E.2d 535 (Prob. Ct. 1965).

OHIO COURT OF COMMON PLEAS ([*BB*] Ohio C.P. [*ALWD*] Ohio Com. Pleas)

[*BB*] *State v. Ventura*, 720 N.E.2d 1024 (Ohio C.P.1999); [*ALWD*] *State v. Ventura*, 720 N.E.2d 1024 (Ohio Com. Pleas 1999); [*BB*] *State v. Ventura*, 101 Ohio Misc. 2d 15, 720 N.E.2d 1024 (C.P. 1999); [*ALWD*] *State v. Ventura*, 101 Ohio Misc. 2d 15, 720 N.E.2d 1024 (Com. Pleas 1999).

OHIO MUNICIPAL COURT (Ohio Mun. Ct.)

Bound v. Biscotti, 663 N.E.2d 1376 (Mun. Ct. 1995); *Bound v. Biscotti*, 76 Ohio Misc. 2d 6, 663 N.E.2d 1376 (Mun. Ct. 1995).

OKLAHOMA

Court Website: http://www.oscn.net/
(The Oklahoma State Courts Network)

OKLAHOMA SUPREME COURT (Okla.)

[*BB & ALWD* Public Domain] *Zeier v. Zimmer, Inc.*, 2006 OK 98, 152 P.3d 861; [*ALWD* Optional] *Zeier v. Zimmer, Inc.*, 152 P.3d 861 (Okla. 2006); *Dennis v. Spillers*, 185 P.2d 465 (Okla. 1947); *Dennis v. Spillers*, 199 Okla. 311, 185 P.2d 465 (1947).

OKLAHOMA COURT OF CRIMINAL APPEALS (formerly Oklahoma Criminal Court of Appeals (Oka. Crim App.)

[*BB & ALWD* Public Domain] *Lambert v. State*, 2003 OK CR 11, 71 P.3d 30; [ALWD Optional] *Lambert v. State*, 71 P.3d 30 (Okla. Crim. App. 2003); *Fields v. State*, 322 P.2d 431 (Okla. Crim. App. 1958); *Collins v. State*, 55 P.2d 790 (Okla. Crim. App. 1936); *Collins v. State*, 59 Okla. Crim. 18, 55 P.2d 790 (1936).

OKLAHOMA COURT OF CIVIL APPEALS **(Okla. Civ. App.)**

[BB & ALWD **Public Domain]** *Eimen v. Eimen,* **2006 OK CIV APP 23, 131 P.3d 148;** *[ALWD* **Optional]** *Eimen v. Eimen,* **131 P.3d 148 (Okla. Civ. App. 2005);** *Bridges v. Ferrell,* **685 P.2d 409 (Okla. Civ. App. 1984).**

OKLAHOMA COURT OF APPEALS OF THE INDIAN TERRITORY **(Indian Terr.)**

In re Taylor's Estate, **82 S.W. 727 (Indian Terr. 1904);** *In re Taylor's Estate,* **5 Indian Terr. 219, 82 S.W. 727 (1904).**

OREGON

Court Website: **http://www.ojd.state.or.us/**
(Oregon Courts: Oregon Judicial Department)

OREGON SUPREME COURT **(Or.)**

Granewich v. Harding, **985 P.2d 788 (Or. 1999);** *Granewich v. Harding,* **329 Or. 47, 985 P.2d 788 (1999);** *State ex rel. Church v. Dustin,* **5 Or. 375 (1875).**

OREGON COURT OF APPEALS **(*[BB]* Or. Ct. App. *[ALWD]* Or. App.)**

[BB] *Cantua v. Creager,* **7 P.3d 693 (Or. Ct. App. 2000);** *[ALWD]* *Cantua v. Creager,* **7 P.3d 693 (Or. App. 2000);** *Cantua v. Creager,* **169 Or. App. 81, 7 P.3d 693 (2000).**

OREGON TAX COURT **(*[BB]* Or. T.C. *[ALWD]* Or. Tax)**

[BB] *Bryant v. Dep't of Revenue,* **6 Or. Tax 559 (1975);** *[ALWD]* *Bryant v. Dept. of Revenue,* **6 Or. Tax 559 (1975).**

PENNSYLVANIA

Court Website: **http://www.courts.state.pa.us/**
(Pennsylvania's Unified Judicial System)

PENNSYLVANIA SUPREME COURT (Pa.)

Sutliff v. Sutliff, 528 A.2d 1318 (Pa. 1987) *Sutliff v. Sutliff*, 515 Pa. 393, 528 A.2d 1318 (1987); *In re Helfenstein's Estate*, 77 Pa. 328 (1875).

PENNSYLVANIA SUPERIOR COURT ([*BB*] Pa. Super. Ct. [*ALWD*] Pa Super.]

[Public domain format prior to appearing in the Atlantic Reporter] *Schwarzwaelder v. Fox*, 2006 PA Super 61; [*BB*] *Schwarzwaelder v. Fox*, 895 A.2d 614 (Pa. Super. Ct. 2006); [*ALWD*] *Schwarzwaelder v. Fox*, 895 A.2d 614 (Pa. Super. 2006); [*BB*] *Litmans v. Litmans*, 673 A.2d 382 (Pa. Super. Ct. 1996); [*ALWD*] *Litmans v. Litmans*, 673 A.2d 382 (Pa. Super. 1996); *Litmans v. Litmans*, 449 Pa. Super. 209, 673 A.2d 382 (1996); *Husik v. Lever*, 95 Pa. Super. 258 (1929).

PENNSYLVANIA COMMONWEALTH COURT ([*BB*] Pa. Commw. Ct. [*ALWD*] Pa. Cmmw.)

[*BB*] *In re Estate of Berry*, 921 A.2d 1261 (Pa. Commw. Ct. 2007); [*ALWD*] *In re Estate of Berry*, 921 A.2d 1261 (Pa. Cmmw. Ct. 2007); [*BB*] *Blizzard v. Floyd*, 613 A.2d 619 (Pa. Commw. Ct. 1992); [*ALWD*] *Blizzard v. Floyd*, 613 A.2d 619 (Pa. Cmmw. 1992); [*BB*] *Blizzard v. Floyd*, 149 Pa. Commw. 503, 613 A.2d 619 (1992); [*ALWD*] *Blizzard v. Floyd*, 149 Pa. Cmmw. 503, 613 A.2d 619 (1992).

PENNSYLVANIA COURT OF COMMON PLEAS ([*BB*] Ct. C.P. [County] [*ALWD*] Com. Pleas [County])

[*BB*] *Pap's A.M. v. City of Erie*, 23 Pa. D. & C.4th 337 (Ct. C.P. Erie County 1995); [*ALWD*] *Pap's A.M. v. City of Erie*, 23 Pa. D. & C.4th 337 (Com. Pl. Erie Co. 1995).

RHODE ISLAND

Court Website: http://www.courts.state.ri.us/
(Judiciary of Rhode Island)

RHODE ISLAND SUPREME COURT (R.I.)

Kevorkian v. Glass, 913 A.2d 1043 (R.I. 2007); *Bailey v. Baronian*, 394 A.2d 1338 (R.I. 1978); *Bailey v. Baronian*, 120 R.I. 389, 394 A.2d 1338 (1978); *State v. Cozzens*, 2 R.I. 561 (1850).

SOUTH CAROLINA

Court Website: http://www.judicial.state.sc.us/
(South Carolina Judicial Department)

SOUTH CAROLINA SUPREME COURT (S.C.)

Chassereau v. Global-Sun Pools, Inc., 611 S.E.2d 305 (S.C. 2007); *Chassereau v. Global-Sun Pools*, Inc., 363 S.C. 628, 611 S.E.2d 305 (2007); *Norton v. Bradham*, 21 S.C. 375 (1884).

SOUTH CAROLINA COURT OF APPEALS ([*BB*] S.C. Ct. App. [*ALWD*] S.C. App.)

[*BB*] *Shaw v. Coleman*, 645 S.E.2d 252 (S.C. Ct. App. 2007); [*ALWD*] *Shaw v. Coleman*, 645 S.E.2d 252 (S.C. App. 2007); [*BB*] *Shaw v. Coleman*, 373 S.C. 485, 645 S.E.2d 252 (Ct. App. 2007); [*ALWD*] *Shaw v. Coleman*, 373 S.C. 485, 645 S.E.2d 252 (App. 2007).

SOUTH DAKOTA

Court Website: http://www.sdjudicial.com/
(South Dakota Unified Judicial System)

SOUTH DAKOTA SUPREME COURT (S.D.)

[*BB & ALWD* Public Domain] *Meldrum v. Novotny*, 1999 SD 127, 599 N.W.2d 651; [ALWD Optional] *Meldrum v. Novotny*, 599 N.W.2d 651 (S.D. 1999); [*ALWD* Alternative Format] *Meldrum v. Novotny*, 1999 S.D. 127, 599 N.W.2d 651; *Garrett v. BankWest, Inc.*, 459 N.W.2d 833 (S.D. 1990); *State v. Ferguson*, 175 N.W.2d 57 (S.D. 1970); *State v. Ferguson*, 84 S.D. 605, 175 N.W.2d 57 (1970).

TENNESSEE

Court Website: http://www.tsc.state.tn.us/
(Tennessee Administrative Office of the Courts)

TENNESSEE SUPREME COURT (Tenn.)

Givens v. Mullikin, 75 S.W.3d 383 (Tenn. 2002); *Canale v. Steveson*, 458 S.W.2d 797 (Tenn. 1970); *Canale v. Steveson*, 224 Tenn. 578, 458 S.W.2d 797 (1970); *Brown v. McClanahan*, 68 Tenn. 347 (1878).

TENNESSEE COURT OF APPEALS ([*BB*] Tenn. Ct. App. [*ALWD*] Tenn. App.)

[*BB*] *Wilhite v. Brownsville Concrete Co.*, 798 S.W.2d 772 (Tenn. Ct. App. 1990); [*ALWD*] *Wilhite v. Brownsville Concrete Co.*, 798 S.W.2d 772 (Tenn. App. 1990); [*BB*] *Pugh v. Richmond*, 425 S.W.2d 789 (Tenn. Ct. App. 1968); [*ALWD*] *Pugh v. Richmond*, 425 S.W.2d 789 (Tenn. App. 1968); *Pugh v. Richmond*, 58 Tenn. App. 62, 425 S.W.2d 789 (1968).

TENNESSEE COURT OF CRIMINAL APPEALS (Tenn. Crim. App.)

State v. Binion, 900 S.W.2d 702 (Tenn. Crim. App. 1994); *Brewer v. State*, 470 S.W.2d 47 (Tenn. Crim. App. 1970); [*BB*] *Brewer v. State*, 4 Tenn. Crim. App. 265, 470 S.W.2d 47 (1970); [*ALWD*] *Brewer v. State*, 4 Tenn. Crim. 265, 470 S.W.2d 47 (1970).

TEXAS

<u>Court Website</u>: http://www.courts.state.tx.us/
(Texas Courts Online)

<u>TEXAS SUPREME COURT</u> (Tex.)

In re J.P.B., 180 S.W.3d 570 (Tex. 2005); *Leonard v. Hare*, 336 S.W.2d 619 (Tex. 1960); *Leonard v. Hare*, 161 Tex. 28, 336 S.W.2d 619(1960); *Seeligson v. Taylor Compress Co.*, 56 Tex. 219 (1882).

<u>TEXAS COURT OF CRIMINAL APPEALS</u> (Tex. Crim. App.)

Ex parte O'Brien, 190 S.W.3d 677 (Tex. Crim. App. 2006); *Craig v. State*, 347 S.W.2d 255 (Tex. Crim. App. 1961); *Craig v. State*, 171 Tex. Crim. 256, 347 S.W.2d 255 (Tex. Crim. App. 1961).

<u>TEXAS COURT OF APPEALS</u> ([BB] Tex. App. [ALWD] Tex. App. ___ Dist.)

[BB] *Kent v. Holmes*, 139 S.W.3d 120 (Tex. App. 2004); [ALWD] *Kent v. Holmes*, 139 S.W.3d 120 (Tex. App. 6th Dist. 2004).

<u>TEXAS COURT OF CIVIL APPEALS</u> (Tex. Civ. App.)

Stacy v. Delery, 122 S.W. 300 (Tex. Civ. App. 1909) *Stacy v. Delery*, 57 Tex. Civ. App. 242, 122 S.W. 300 (1909).

UTAH

<u>Court Website</u>: http://www.utcourts.gov/
(Utah State Courts)

UTAH SUPREME COURT (Utah)

[*BB & ALWD* Public Domain] *Taylor v. State*, 2007 UT 12, 156 P.3d 739; [*ALWD* Optional] *Taylor v. State*, 156 P.3d 739 (Utah 2007); *State v. Kallin*, 877 P.2d 138 (Utah 1994); *Murdock v. Blake*, 484 P.2d 164 (Utah 1971); *Murdock v. Blake*, 26 Utah 2d 22, 484 P.2d 164 (1971).

UTAH COURT OF APPEALS ([*BB*] Utah Ct. App. [*ALWD*] Utah App.)

[*BB & ALWD* Public Domain] *Peterson v. Delta Air Lines, Inc.*, 2002 UT App 56, 42 P.3d 1253; [*ALWD* Optional] *Peterson v. Delta Air Lines, Inc.*, 42 P.3d 1253 (Utah App. 2002); [*BB*] *State v. Magee*, 837 P.2d 993 (Utah Ct. App. 1992); [*ALWD*] *State v. Magee*, 837 P.2d 993 (Utah App. 1992).

VERMONT

Court Website: http://www.vermontjudiciary.org/ (Vermont Judiciary)

VERMONT SUPREME COURT (Vt.)

Summits 7, Inc. v. Kelly, 886 A.2d 365 (Vt. 2005); *Summits 7, Inc. v. Kelly*, 178 Vt. 396, 886 A.2d 365 (2005); *Lincoln v. Smith*, 27 Vt. 328 (1855).

VIRGINIA

Court Website: http://www.courts.state.va.us/ (Virginia's Judicial System)

VIRGINIA SUPREME COURT (Va.)

Harris v. T.I., Inc., 413 S.E.2d 605 (Va. 1992); *Harris v. T.I., Inc.*, 243 Va. 63, 413 S.E.2d 605 (Va. 1992); [*BB*] *Temple v. Commonwealth*, 75 Va. 892 (1881); [*ALWD*] *Temple v. Cmmw.*, 75 Va. 892 (1881).

VIRGINIA COURT OF APPEALS (*[BB]* Va. Ct. App. *[ALWD]* Va. App.)

[BB] Hairston v. Commonwealth, 646 S.E.2d 32 (Va. Ct. App. 2007); *[ALWD] Hairston v. Cmmw.*, 646 S.E.2d 32 (Va. App. 2007); *[BB] Hairston v. Commonwealth*, 50 Va. App. 64, 646 S.E.2d 32 (2007); *[ALWD] Hairston v. Cmmw.*, 646 S.E.2d 32 (Va. App. 2007).

VIRGINIA CIRCUIT COURT (*[BB]* Va. Cir. Ct. *[ALWD]* Va. Cir.)

Domen v. Sugarman, 54 Va. Cir. 176 (2000).

WASHINGTON

Court Website: http://www.courts.wa.gov/
(Washington Courts)

WASHINGTON SUPREME COURT (Wash.)
Kim v. Lee, 31 P.3d 665 (Wash. 2001); *Kim v. Lee*, 145 Wash. 2d 79, 31 P.3d 665 (2001).

WASHINGTON COURT OF APPEALS (*[BB]* Wash. Ct. App. *[ALWD]* Wash. App.)
[BB] In re Riddell Testamentary Trust, 157 P.3d 888 (Wash. Ct. App. 2007); *[ALWD] In re Riddell Testamentary Trust*, 157 P.3d 888 (Wash. App. 2007); *In re Riddell Testamentary Trust*, 138 Wash. App. 485, 157 P.3d 888 (2007).

WEST VIRGINIA

Court Website: http://www.state.wv.us/wvsca/
(West Virginia Court System)

WEST VIRGINIA SUPREME COURT OF APPEALS (W. Va.)

State v. Mechling, 633 S.E.2d 311 (W. Va. 2006); *State v. Mechling*, 219 W. Va. 366, 633 S.E.2d 311 (2006); *Matthews v. Dunbar*, 3 W. Va. 138 (1869).

WISCONSIN

<u>Court Website</u>: http://www.wicourts.gov/
(Wisconsin Court System)

<u>WISCONSIN SUPREME COURT</u> (Wis.)

[*BB & ALWD* Public Domain] *State v. Malone*, 2004 WI 108, 274 Wis. 2d 540, 683 N.W.2d 1; [*ALWD* Optional] *State v. Malone*, 683 N.W.2d 1 (Wis. 2004); *Northridge Co. v. W.R. Grace & Co.*, 471 N.W.2d 179 (Wis. 1991); *Northridge Co. v. W.R. Grace & Co.*, 162 Wis. 2d 918, 471 N.W.2d 179 (1991); *Barker v. Dayton*, 28 Wis. 367 (1871).

<u>WISCONSIN COURT OF APPEALS</u> ([*BB*] Wis. Ct. App. [*ALWD*] Wis. App. Dist. ___)

[*BB & ALWD* Public Domain] *State v. Vogelsberg*, 2006 WI App 228, 297 Wis. 2d 519, 724 N.W.2d 649; [*ALWD* Optional] *State v. Vogelsberg*, 724 N.W.2d 649 (Wis. App. Dist. IV 2006); [*BB*] *Arneson v. Arneson*, 355 N.W.2d 16 (Wis. Ct. App. 1984); [*ALWD*] *Arneson v. Arneson*, 355 N.W.2d 16 (App.1984); [*BB*] *Arneson v. Arneson*, 120 Wis. 2d 236, 355 N.W.2d 16 (Ct. App.1984); [*ALWD*] *Arneson v. Arneson*, 120 Wis. 2d 236, 355 N.W.2d 16 (App.1984). [No specific district is given for the *Arneson* case.]

WYOMING

<u>Court Website</u>: http://www.courts.state.wy.us/
(Wyoming Judicial Branch)

<u>WYOMING SUPREME COURT</u> (Wyo.)

[*BB & ALWD* Public Domain] *Martin v. State*, 2007 WY 76, 157 P.3d 923 (Wyo. 2007); [*ALWD* Optional] *Martin v. State*, 157 P.3d 923 (Wyo. 2007); *In re Stone*, 288 P.2d 767 (Wyo.1955); *In re Stone*, 74 Wyo. 389, 288 P.2d 767 (1955); *Phillips v. Territory*, 1 Wyo. 82 (1872).

C. UNITED STATES TERRITORIES

AMERICAN SAMOA

<u>HIGH COURT OF AMERICAN SAMOA</u> (*[BB]* Am. Samoa *[ALWD]* Am. Sam.)

[BB] *Alamoana Recipe, Inc. v. ASG*, 25 Am. Samoa 2d 97 (1993); *[ALWD]* *Alamoana Recipe, Inc. v. ASG*, 25 Am. Sam. 2d 97 (1993).

GUAM

<u>Court Website</u>: http://www.justice.gov.gu/ (Unified Courts of Guam)

<u>SUPREME COURT OF GUAM</u> (Guam)

Taisipic v. Marion, 1996 Guam 9. [Public domain citation format]

NAVAJO NATION

<u>Court Website</u>: http://www.navajocourts.org/ (The Judicial Branch of the Navajo Nation)

<u>SUPREME COURT OF THE NAVAJO NATION</u> (previously Court of Appeals) (Navajo)

[BB] *In re Guardianship of Chewiwi*, 1 Navajo Rptr. 120 (1970); *[ALWD]* *In re Guardianship of Chewiwi*, 1 Navajo 120 (1970).

<u>NAVAJO DISTRICT COURT</u> (*[BB]* Navajo D. Ct. *[ALWD]* Navajo Dist.)

[BB] *Goldtooth v. Goldtooth*, 3 Navajo Rptr. 223 (D. Ct. 1982); *[ALWD]* *Goldtooth v. Goldtooth*, 3 Navajo 223 (Dist. 1982).

NORTHERN MARIANA ISLANDS

<u>Court Website</u>: http://www.justice.gov.mp/
(Unified Courts of the Commonwealth of the Northern
Mariana Islands)

<u>COMMONWEALTH SUPREME COURT OF THE NORTHERN MARIANA
ISLANDS</u> (*[BB]* N. Mar. I. *[ALWD]* N. Mar. Is.)

[Public domain citation format] *[BB]* *Commonwealth v.
Manglona*, 1997 MP 28, 5 N.M.I. 128; [Public domain
citation format] *[ALWD]* *Cmmw. v. Manglona*, 1997 MP 28,
5 N.M.I. 128; *[BB]* *Ito v. Macro Energy, Inc.*, 2 N. Mar. I. 459
(1992); *[ALWD]* *Ito v. Macro Energy, Inc.*, 2 N. Mar. Is. 459
(1992).

<u>COMMONWEALTH SUPERIOR COURT OF THE NORTHERN MARI-
ANA ISLANDS</u> (*[BB]* N. Mar. I. Commw. Super. Ct. *[ALWD]* N.
Mar. Is. Super.) (previously Northern Mariana Island
Commonwealth Trial Court *[BB]* N. Mar. I. Commw. Trial
Ct.)

[BB] *Bank of Haw. v. Teregeyo*, 3 N. Mar. I. Commw. 876
(Super Ct. 1989); *[ALWD]* *Bank of Haw. v. Teregeyo*, 3 N.
Mar. Cmmw. 876, 881 (Super 1989).
[Locally Preferred Citation] *Bank of Hawaii v. Teregeyo*, 3
CR 876, 881 (N.M.I. Super. Ct.1989).

PUERTO RICO

<u>Court Website</u>: http://www.tribunalpr.org/
(Rama Judicial)

<u>PUERTO RICO SUPREME COURT</u> (P.R.)

[Public domain format English] *Suárez Jiménez v.
Comisión Estatal de Elecciones*, 2004 PRSC 179; [Public
domain format Spanish] *Suárez Jiménez v. Comisión
Estatal de Elecciones*, 2004 TSPR 179; *[BB]* *Pérez v.*

Sampedro, 86 P.R. Dec. 530 (1962); [*ALWD*] *Pérez v. Sampedro*, 86 D.P.R. 526, 530 (1962); [*BB*] *Marina Indus., Inc. v. Brown Boveri Corp.*, 14 P.R. Offic. Trans. 86 (1983); [*ALWD*] *Marina Indus., Inc. v. Brown Boveri Corp.*, 14 P.R. Off. Trans. 86 (1983).

PUERTO RICO CIRCUIT COURT OF APPEALS (P.R. Cir.)

De Jesus v. Bacardi Corp., 97 DTA 19.

VIRGIN ISLANDS

Court Websites:
http://www.visupremecourt.org/
(Supreme Court of the Virgin Islands)
http://www.visuperiorcourt.org/
(Superior Court of the Virgin Islands)

TERRITORIAL COURT OF THE VIRGIN ISLANDS (V.I.) (Name changed to the Superior Court of the Virgin Islands in 2004; Supreme Court of the Virgin Islands created at the same time)

Greenaway v. Johnson, 13 V.I. 481 (Terr. Ct. 1977).

APPENDIX 6

FEDERAL AND STATE STATUTORY COMPILATIONS, SESSION LAWS, AND LEGISLATIVE WEBSITES

○ = Official Statutory Compilation

A. FEDERAL

<u>Legislative Websites</u>:
http://www.house.gov/
(United States House of Representative)
http://www.senate.gov/
(United States Senate)

○ United States Code	x U.S.C. § x (year)
United States Code Annotated	x U.S.C.A. § x (West year)
United States Code Service	x U.S.C.S. § (LexisNexis year) [*BB*]
	x U.S.C.S. § (Lexis year) [*ALWD*]
Gould's United States Code Unannotated	x U.S.C.U. § (Gould year) [*BB*]
United States Statutes at Large	vol. no. Stat. page no. (year)

B. STATE

ALABAMA

<u>Legislative Website</u>: http://www.legislature.state.al.us/
(Official Site of the Alabama Legislature)

○ Code of Alabama	Ala. Code § x-x-x (year) [*BB*]
	Ala. Code § x-x-x (West year) [*ALWD*]
Michie's Alabama Code [Service]	Ala. Code § x-x-x (LexisNexis year) [*BB*]
	Ala. Code § x-x-x (Lexis year) [*ALWD*]

Acts of Alabama	year Ala. Act act no. [*ALWD*]
Alabama Laws	year Ala. Laws page no. [*BB*]
West's Alabama Legislative Service	year Ala. Legis. Serv. page no. (West) [*BB*]
Michie's Alabama Code Advance Legislative Service (LexisNexis)	year-pamph. no. Ala. Adv. Legis. Serv. page no. (LexisNexis) [*BB*]

ALASKA

<u>Legislative Website</u>: http://w3.legis.state.ak.us/
(The Alaska State Legislature)

○ Alaska Statutes (LexisNexis) (Lexis)	Alaska Stat. § x.x.x. (year) [*BB*]
	Alaska Stat. § x.x.x. (Lexis year) [*ALWD*]

Session Laws of Alaska	year Alaska Sess. Laws page no. [*BB*]
	year Alaska Sess. Laws ch. x [*ALWD*]

ARIZONA

<u>Legislative Website</u>: http://www.azleg.gov/
(Arizona State Legislature)

O Arizona Revised Statutes Annotated (West)	Ariz. Rev. Stat. Ann. § x-x (year) [*BB*]
	Ariz. Rev. Stat. Ann. § x-x (West year) [*ALWD*]
Arizona Revised Statutes (LexisNexis) (Lexis)	Ariz. Rev. Stat. § x-x (LexisNexis year) [*BB*]
	Ariz. Rev. Stat. § x-x (Lexis year) [*ALWD*]

Session Laws [of] Arizona	year Ariz. Sess. Laws page no. [*BB*]
Arizona Legislative Service (West)	year Ariz. Legis. Serv. page no. (West) [*ALWD*]

ARKANSAS

<u>Legislative Websites</u>:
http://www.arkansas.gov/senate/
(Arkansas Senate)
http://www.arkansas.gov/house/
(Arkansas House of Representative)

O Arkansas Code (of 1987) Annotated (LexisNexis)	Ark. Code Ann. § x-x-x (year) [*BB*]
	Ark. Code Ann. § x-x-x (Lexis year) [*ALWD*]
West's Arkansas Code Annotated	Ark. Code Ann. § x-x-x (West year)

Acts of Arkansas (West)	year Ark. Acts page no. [*BB*]
Arkansas Acts	year Ark. Acts law no. [*ALWD*]
Arkansas Advance Legislative Service (LexisNexis)	year-pamph. no. Ark. Adv. Legis. Serv. page no. (LexisNexis) [*BB*]
Arkansas Legislative Service (West)	year Ark. Legis. Serv. page no. (West) [*BB*]

CALIFORNIA

Legislative Website: http://www.legislature.ca.gov/ (California State Legislature)

O West's Annotated California Codes	Cal. [abbrev. subject] Code § x (West year) [*BB*]
	Cal. [abbrev. subject] Code Ann.§ x (West year) [*ALWD*]
O Deering's California Code(s, Annotated) (LexisNexis)	Cal. [abbrev. subject] Code § x (Deering year) [*BB*]
	Cal. [abbrev. subject] Code Ann. § x (Lexis year)

See subject abbreviations in the next subdivision.

Subject abbreviations for California Codes (if any):

Agricultural (1972 renamed "Food And Agricultural")	Agric.
Business and Professions	Bus. & Prof.
Civil	Civ.
Civil Procedure	Civ. Proc.
Commercial	Com.
Corporations	Corp.
Education	Educ.
Elections	Elec.
Evidence	Evid.
Family	Fam.
Financial	Fin.
Fish and Game	Fish & Game
Food and Agricultural	Food & Agric.
Government	Gov't [*BB*]
	Govt. [*ALWD*]
Harbors and Navigation	Harb. & Nav.
Health and Safety	Health & Safety
Insurance	Ins.
Labor	Lab.
Military and Veterans	Mil. & Vet.
Penal	Penal
Probate	Prob.
Public Contract	Pub. Cont.
Public Resources	Pub. Res.
Public Utilities	Pub. Util.
Revenue and Taxation	Rev. & Tax.
Streets and Highways	Sts. & High.
Unemployment Insurance	Unemp. Ins.
Vehicle	Veh.
Water	Water
Welfare and Institutions	Welf. & Inst.

Statutes of California	year Cal. Stat. page no. [*BB*]
	year Cal. Stat. law no. [*ALWD*]
California Legislative Service (West)	year Cal. Legis. Serv. page no. (West) [*BB*]
Deering's California Advance Legislative Service(LexisNexis)	year-pamph. no. Cal. Adv. Legis. Serv. page no. (Deering) [*BB*]

COLORADO

<u>Legislative Website</u>: http://www.leg.state.co.us/
(Colorado General Assembly)

○ Colorado Revised Statutes (LexisNexis)	Colo. Rev. Stat. § x-x-x (year) [*BB*]
	Colo. Rev. Stat. § x-x-x (Lexis year) [*ALWD*]
West's Colorado Revised Statutes Annotated	Colo. Rev. Stat. Ann. § x-x-x (West year)

Session Laws of Colorado (LexisNexis)	year Colo. Sess. Laws page no. [*BB*]
	year Colo. Sess. Laws law no. [*ALWD*]
Colorado Legislative Service (West)	year Colo. Legis. Serv. page no. (West) [*BB*]

CONNECTICUT

<u>Legislative Website</u>: http://www.cga.ct.gov/
(State of Connecticut General Assembly)

○ General Statutes of Connecticut	Conn. Gen. Stat. § x-x (year)
Connecticut General Statutes Annotated (West)	Conn. Gen. Stat. Ann. § x-x (West year)

Connecticut Public & Special Acts	year Conn. Acts page no. (Reg. [Spec.] Sess.) [*BB*]
Connecticut Public Acts	year Conn. Pub. Acts page no. [*BB*]
	year Conn. Pub. Acts act no. [*ALWD*]
Connecticut Special Acts	year Conn. Spec. Acts page no. [*BB*]
	year Conn. Spec. Acts act no. [*ALWD*]
Connecticut Legislative Service (West)	year Conn. Legis. Serv. page no. (West) [*BB*]

DELAWARE

<u>Legislative Website</u>: http://legis.delaware.gov/
(Delaware General Assembly)

○ Delaware Code Annotated (LexisNexis)	Del. Code Ann. tit. x, § x (year) [*BB*]
	Del. Code Ann. tit. x, § x (Lexis year) [*ALWD*]

| Laws of Delaware | volume no. Del. Laws page no. (year) [*BB*] volume no. Del. Laws chapter no. (year) [*ALWD*] |
| Delaware Code Annotated   Advance Legislative   Services (LexisNexis) | year-pamph. no. Del. Code. Ann. Adv. Legis. Serv. page no. (LexisNexis) [*BB*] |

DISTRICT OF COLUMBIA

<u>Legislative Website</u>:
http://www.dccouncil.washington.dc.us/
(Council of the District of Columbia)

| ○ District of Columbia   Official Code (West) | D.C. Code § x-x (year) [*BB*] D.C. Code § x-x (West year) [*ALWD*] |
| (Lexis) District of Columbia   Code Annotated | D.C. Code Ann. § x-x (LexisNexis year) [*BB*] D.C. Code Ann. § x-x (Lexis year) [*ALWD*] |

District of Columbia Statutes at Large	year D.C. Stat. law no.
District of Columbia Register	volume no. D.C. Reg. page no. (month day, year) [*BB*]
Lexis District of Columbia Code Advance Legislative Service	year-pamph. no. D.C. Code Adv. Leg. Serv. page no. (LexisNexis) [*BB*]
District of Columbia Session Law Service (West)	year D.C. Sess. Law Serv. page no. (West) [*BB*]

| United States Statutes at Large | volume no. Stat. page no. (year) *[BB]* |

FLORIDA

<u>Legislative Website</u>: http://www.leg.state.fl.us/
(Official Internet Site of the Florida Legislature)

O Florida Statutes	Fla. Stat. § x-x (year)
West's Florida Statutes Annotated	Fla. Stat. Ann. § x-x (West year)
LexisNexis Florida Statutes Annotated	Fla. Stat. Ann. § x-x (LexisNexis year) *[BB]*

Laws of Florida	year Fla. Laws page no. *[BB]*
	year Fla. Laws chapter no. *[ALWD]*
West's Florida Session Law Service	year Fla. Sess. Law Serv. page no. (West) *[BB]*

GEORGIA

<u>Legislative Website</u>: http://www.legis.state.ga.us/
(Georgia General Assembly)

| O Official Code of Georgia Annotated (LexisNexis) | Ga. Code Ann. § x-x-x (year) |
| West's Code of Georgia Annotated | Ga. Code Ann. § x-x-x (West year) |

Georgia Laws	year Ga. Laws page no.
Official Code of Georgia	year-pamph. no. Ga. Code
Annotated Advance	Ann. Adv. Legis. Serv.
Legislative Service	page no. (LexisNexis)
(LexisNexis)	*[BB]*

HAWAII

Legislative Website: http://www.capitol.hawaii.gov/
(Hawaii State Legislature)

○ Hawaii Revised Statutes	Haw. Rev. Stat. § x-x (year)
(Michie's) Hawaii Revised	Haw. Rev. Stat. Ann. § x-x
Statutes Annotated	(LexisNexis year) *[BB]*
(LexisNexis)	Haw. Rev. Stat. Ann. § x-x
	(Lexis year)

Session Laws of Hawaii	year Haw. Sess. Laws page no. *[BB]*
	year Haw. Sess. Laws act. no. *[ALWD]*
Michie's Hawaii Revised	year-pamph. No. Haw. Stat. Ann. Adv. Legis. Serv. page no. *[BB]*

IDAHO

Legislative website: http://www.legislature.idaho.gov/
(State of Idaho Legislature)

○ Idaho Code Annotated	Idaho Code Ann. § x-x
(LexisNexis)	(year) *[BB]*
Idaho Code Annotated	Idaho Code Ann. § x-x
	(Lexis year) *[ALWD]*

| Idaho Session Laws | year Idaho Sess. Laws page no. [*BB*]
year Idaho Sess. Laws ch. ch. no. [*ALWD*] |
| Idaho Code Annotated Advance Legislative Service (LexisNexis) | year-pamph, no. Idaho Code Ann. Adv. Legis. Serv. page no. (LexisNexis) [*BB*] |

ILLINOIS

Legislative Website: http://www.ilga.gov/
(Illinois General Assemby)

○ Illinois Compiled Statutes	x Ill. Comp. Stat. x/x-x (year)
West's Smith-Hurd Illinois Compiled Statutes Annotated	x Ill. Comp. Stat. Ann. x/ x-x (West year)
○ Illinois Compiled Statutes Annotated (LexisNexis)	x Ill. Comp. Stat. Ann. x/ x-x (LexisNexis year) [*BB*] x Ill. Comp. Stat. Ann. x/ x-x (Lexis year) [*ALWD*]

Laws of Illinois	year Ill. Laws page no.
Illinois Legislative Service (West)	year Ill. Legis. Serv. page no. (West) [*BB*]
Illinois Compiled Statutes Annotated Advance Legislative Service (LexisNexis)	year-pamph. no. Ill. Comp. Stat. Ann. Adv. Legis. Serv. page no. (LexisNexis) [*BB*]

INDIANA

<u>Legislative Website</u>: http://www.in.gov/legislative/
(Indiana General Assembly)

○ Indiana Code	Ind. Code § x-x-x-x (year)
West's Annotated Indiana Code	Ind. Code Ann. § x-x-x-x (West year)
Burns Indiana Statutes (LexisNexis)	Ind. Code Ann. § x-x-x-x (LexisNexis year) [*BB*]
	Ind. Code Ann. § x-x-x-x (Lexis year) [*ALWD*]
Indiana Acts	year Ind. Acts page no.
West's Indiana Legislative Service	year Ind. Legis. Serv. page no. (West)
Burns Indiana Statutes Annotated Advance Legislative Service (LexisNexis)	year-pamph. no. Ind. Stat. An. Adv. Legis. Serv. page no. (LexisNexis) [*BB*]

IOWA

<u>Legislative Website</u>: http://www.legis.state.ia.us/
(The Iowa Legislative General Assembly)

○ Code of Iowa	Iowa Code § x.x (year)
West's Iowa Code Annotated	Iowa Code Ann. § x.x (West year)

Acts (and Joint Resolutions) of the State of Iowa	year Iowa Acts page no.
Iowa Legislative Service (West)	year Iowa Legis. Serv. page no. (West) [*BB*]

KANSAS

<u>Legislative Website</u>:
http://www.kslegislature.org/legsrv-legisportal/
(Kansas Legislature)

O Kansas Statutes Annotated	Kan. Stat. Ann. § x-x (year)
Vernon's Kansas Statutes Annotated	Kan. [abbrev. subject Code] Ann. § x-x (West year) [*BB*]
	Kan. [abbrev. subject Code] § x-x (West year) [*ALWD*]

See subject abbreviations in the next subdivision.

<u>Subject abbreviations for Kansas Codes (if any)</u>:

Uniform Commercial Code	U.C.C.
Code of Civil Procedure	Civ. Proc. Code [*BB*]
	Civ. P. Code or Civ. Proc. Code [*ALWD*]
Criminal Code	Crim. Code
Code of Criminal Procedure	Crim. Proc. Code [*BB*]
	Crim. P. Code or Crim. Proc. Code [*ALWD*]
General Corporation Code	Corp. Code [*BB*]
	Gen. Corp. Code [*ALWD*]
Probate Code	Prob. Code

Session Laws of Kansas	year Kan. Sess. Laws page no.

KENTUCKY

<u>Legislative Website</u>: http://www.lrc.ky.gov/
(Kentucky Legislature)

○ Baldwin's Kentucky Revised Statutes Annotated (West)	Ky. Rev. Stat. Ann. § x-x (West year)
○ (Michie's) Kentucky Revised Statutes Annotated(LexisNexis)	Ky. Rev. Stat. Ann. § x-x (LexisNexis year) [*BB*]
	Ky. Rev. Stat. Ann. § x-x (Lexis year) [*ALWD*]

Acts of Kentucky	year Ky. Acts page no.
Kentucky Revised Statutes and Rules Service (West)	year Ky. Rev. Stat. & R. Serv. page no. (West) [*BB*]
Michie's Kentucky Revised Statutes Advance Legislative Service (LexisNexis)	year-pamph, no. Ky. Rev. Stat. Adv. Legis. Serv. page no. (LexisNexis) [*BB*]

LOUISIANA

<u>Legislative Website</u>: http://www.legis.state.la.us/
(Louisiana State Legislature)

○ West's Louisiana Revised Statutes Annotated	La. Rev. Stat. Ann. § x-x (year)
West's Louisiana Code Annotated	La. [abbrev. subject Code] Ann. art. x (year)
See subject abbreviations in the next subdivision.	

Subject abbreviations for Louisiana Codes (if any):

Children's Code	Child. Code [*BB*]
	Children's Code [*ALWD*]
Civil Code	Civ. Code
Code of Civil Procedure	Code Civ. Proc. [*BB*]
	Code Civ. P. or Code Civ. Proc. [*ALWD*]
Code of Criminal Procedure	Code Crim. Proc. [*BB*]
	Code Crim. P. or Code Crim. Proc. [*ALWD*]
Code of Evidence	Code Evid.

State of Louisiana: Acts of the Legislature	year La. Acts page no.
West's Louisiana Session Law Service	year La. Sess. Law Serv. page no. (West) [*BB*]
	year La. Sess. Law Serv. page no. [*ALWD*]

MAINE

Legislative Website: http://janus.state.me.us/legis/ (Maine State Legislature)

Maine Revised Statutes Annotated (West)	Me. Rev. Stat. Ann. tit. x, § x (year)

Laws of the State of Maine	year Me. Laws page no.
Acts, Resolves and Constitutional Resolutions of the State of Maine	year Me. Acts page no.
Maine Legislative Services (West)	year Me. Legis. Serv. page no. (West) [*BB*]

MARYLAND

<u>Legislative Website</u>: http://mlis.state.md.us/
(Maryland General Assembly)

○ (Michie's) Annotated Code of Maryland (LexisNexis)	Md. Code Ann., [abbrev. subject] § x-x (LexisNexis year) [*BB*]
	Md. [abbrev. subject] Code Ann. (year) [*ALWD*]
○ (West's) Annotated Code of Maryland	Md. Code Ann., [abbrev. subject] § x-x (West year) [*BB*]

See subject abbreviations in the next subdivision.

○ Annotated Code of Maryland (1957)	Md. Ann. Code art. x, § x (year)

<u>Subject abbreviations for Maryland Codes (if any)</u>:

Agriculture	Agric.
Business Occupations & Professions	Bus. Occ. & Prof. [*BB*]
	Bus. Occ. & Professions [*ALWD*]
Business Regulation	Bus. Reg.
Commercial Law	Com. Law [*BB*]
	Commercial L. [*ALWD*]
Constitutions	Const. [*BB*]
	Consts. [*ALWD*]
Corporations & Associations	Corps. & Ass'ns [*BB*]
	Corps. & Assns. [*ALWD*]
Correctional Services	Corr. Servs. [*BB*]
	Correctional Servs. [*ALWD*]
Courts & Judicial Proceedings	Cts. & Jud. Proc. [*BB*]
	Cts. & Jud. P. or Cts. Jud. Proc. [*ALWD*]

Criminal Law	Crim. Law [*BB*]
	Crim. L. [*ALWD*]
Criminal Procedure	Crim. Proc. [*BB*]
	Crim. P. or Crim. Proc.
	[*ALWD*]
Education	Educ.
Election Law	Elec. Law [*BB*]
	Election L. [*ALWD*]
Environment	Envir. [*BB*]
	Env. [*ALWD*]
Estates & Trusts	Est. & Trusts [*BB*]
	Ests. & Trusts [*ALWD*]
Family Law	Fam. Law [*BB*]
	Fam. L. [*ALWD*]
Financial Institutions	Fin. Inst. [*BB*]
	Fin. Instns. [*ALWD*]
Health-General	Health-Gen.
Health Occupations	Health Occ.
Insurance	Ins.
Labor & Employment	Lab. & Empl.
Natural Resources	Nat. Res. [*BB*]
	Nat. Resources [*ALWD*]
Public Safety	Pub. Safety
Public Utility Companies	Pub. Util. Cos.
Real Property	Real Prop.
State Finance &	State Fin. & Proc. [*BB*]
Procurement	St. Fin. & Procure. [*ALWD*]
State Government	State Gov't [*BB*]
	St. Govt. [*ALWD*]
State Personnel & Pensions	State Pers. & Pens. [*BB*]
	St. Personnel & Pens.
	[*ALWD*]
Tax-General	Tax-Gen.

Tax-Property	Tax-Prop.
Transportation	Transp.

Laws of Maryland	year Md. Laws page no.
Michie's Annotated Code of Maryland Advance Legislative Service (LexisNexis)	year-pamph. no. Md. Code Ann. Adv. Legis. Serv. page no. (LexisNexis) *[BB]*

MASSACHUSETTS

Legislative Website: http://www.mass.gov/legis/
(General Court of the Commonwealth of Massachusetts)

○ General Laws of [the Commonwealth of] Massachusetts (Mass. Bar Ass'n/West)	Mass. Gen. Laws ch. x, § x (year)
Massachusetts General Laws Annotated (West)	Mass. Gen. Laws ch. x, § x (West year)
Annotated Laws of Massachusetts (LexisNexis)	Mass. Ann. Laws ch. x, § x (LexisNexis year) *[BB]* Mass. Ann. Laws ch. x, § x (Lexis year) *[ALWD]*

Acts and Resolves of Massachusetts	year Mass. Acts page no.
Massachusetts Legislative Service (West)	year Mass. Legis. Serv. page no. (West) *[BB]*
Massachusetts Advance Legislative Service (LexisNexis)	year-pamph. no. Mass. Adv. Legis. Serv. page no. (LexisNexis) *[BB]*

MICHIGAN

<u>Legislative Website</u>: http://www.legislature.mi.gov/
(Michigan Legislature)

O Michigan Compiled Laws (1979)	Mich. Comp. Laws § x.x (year)
Michigan Compiled Laws Annotated (West)	Mich. Comp. Laws Ann. § x.x (West year)
Michigan Compiled Laws Service (LexisNexis)	Mich. Comp. Laws Serv. § x.x (LexisNexis year) [BB]
Michigan Statutes Annotated (Lexis)	Mich. Stat. Ann. § x.x (Lexis year) [ALWD]

Public & Local Acts of the Legislature of the State of Michigan	year Mich. Pub. Acts page no. [BB] year Mich. Acts page no. [ALWD]
Michigan Legislative Service (West)	year Mich. Legis. Serv. page no. (West) [BB]
Michigan Advance Legislative Service (LexisNexis)	year-pamph. no. Mich. Adv. Legis. Serv. page no. (LexisNexis) [BB]

MINNESOTA

<u>Legislative Website</u>: http://www.leg.state.mn.us/
(Minnesota State Legislature)

O Minnesota Statutes	Minn. Stat. § x.x (year)
Minnesota Statutes Annotated (West)	Minn. Stat. Ann. § x.x (West year)

Laws of Minnesota	year Minn. Laws page no.
Minnesota Session Law	year Minn. Sess. Law
Service (West)	Serv. page no. (West) [*BB*]
	year Minn. Sess. L. Serv. ch.
	x (West) [*ALWD*]

MISSISSIPPI

<u>Legislative Website</u>: www.ls.state.ms.us/
(The Mississippi Legislature)

○ Mississippi Code (1972)	Miss. Code Ann. § x-x-x
Annotated (LexisNexis)	(year) [*BB*]
	Miss. Code Ann. § x-x-x
	(Lexis year) [*ALWD*]
West's Annotated	Miss. Code Ann § x-x-x
Mississippi Code	(West year)

General Laws of Mississippi	year Miss. Laws page no.
	[*BB*]
	Year Gen. Laws Miss. page
	no. [*ALWD*]
Mississippi General Laws	year pamph. no. Miss.
Advance Sheets	Laws Adv. Sh. page no.
(LexisNexis)	(LexisNexis) [*BB*]
West's Mississippi	year Miss. Legis. Serv.
Legislative Service	page no. (West) [*BB*]

MISSOURI

<u>Legislative Website</u>: http://www.moga.mo.gov/
(Missouri General Assembly)

O Missouri Revised Statutes	Mo. Rev. Stat. § x.x (year)

Vernon's Annotated
   Missouri Statutes
   (West)
	Mo. Ann. Stat. § x.x
	(West year)

Laws of Missouri	year Mo. Laws page no.
Missouri Legislative Service (West)	year Mo. Legis. Serv. page no. (West) [*BB*]

MONTANA

Legislative Website: http://leg.mt.gov/css/
(Montana State Legislature)

O Montana Code Annotated	Mont. Code Ann. § x-x-x (year)

Laws of Montana	year Mont. Laws page no.

NEBRASKA

Legislative Website: http://nebraskalegislature.gov/
(Nebraska Unicameral Legislature)

O Revised Statutes of Nebraska	Neb. Rev. Stat. § x-x (year)

Revised Statutes of
   Nebraska Annotated
   (LexisNexis)
	Neb. Rev. Stat. Ann. § x-x
	(LexisNexis year) [*BB*]
	Neb. Rev. Stat. Ann. § x-x
	(Lexis year) [*ALWD*]

Laws of Nebraska	year Neb. Laws page no.

NEVADA

<u>Legislative Website</u>: http://www.leg.state.nv.us/
(Nevada Legislature)

O Nevada Revised Statutes	Nev. Rev. Stat. § x-x (year)
Nevada Revised Statutes Annotated (LexisNexis)	Nev. Rev. Stat. Ann. § x.x (LexisNexis year) [*BB*]
	Nev. Rev. Stat. Ann. § x.x (Lexis year) [*ALWD*]
West's Nevada Revised Statutes Annotated	Nev. Rev. Stat. Ann. § x.x (West year)

Statutes of Nevada	year Nev. Stat. page no.

NEW HAMPSHIRE

<u>Legislative Website</u>: http://www.gencourt.state.nh.us/
(New Hampshire General Court)

O New Hampshire Revised Statutes Annotated (West)	N.H. Rev. Stat. Ann. § x:x (year) [*BB*]
	N.H. Rev. Stat. Ann. § x:x (West year) [*ALWD*]
Lexis New Hampshire Revised Statutes Annotated	N.H. Rev. Stat. Ann. § x:x (LexisNexis year) [*BB*]
	N.H. Rev. Stat. Ann. § x:x (Lexis year) [*ALWD*]

Laws of the State of New Hampshire	year N.H. Laws page no.

Lexis New Hampshire Revised Statutes Annotated Advance Legislative Service	year-pamph, no. N.H. Rev. Stat. Ann. Adv. Legis. Serv. page no. (LexisNexis) *[BB]*

NEW JERSEY

<u>Legislative Website</u>: http://www.njleg.state.nj.us/
(New Jersey Legislature)

○ New Jersey Statutes Annotated (West)	N.J. Stat. Ann . § x:x (West year)
New Jersey Revised Statutes (1937)	N.J. Rev. Stat. § x:x (year)

Laws of New Jersey	year N.J. Laws page no.
New Jersey Session Law Service (West)	year N.J. Sess. Law Serv. page no. (West) *[BB]*

NEW MEXICO

<u>Legislative Website</u>: http://legis.state.nm.us/
(New Mexico Legislature)

○ New Mexico Statutes (1978)	N.M. Stat. § x-x-x (year)
West's New Mexico Statutes Annotated	N.M. Stat. Ann. § x-x-x (West year)
Michie's Annotated Statutes of New Mexico (LexisNexis)	N.M. Stat. Ann. § x-x-x (LexisNexis year) *[BB]* N.M. Stat. Ann. § x-x-x (Lexis year)

Laws of [the State of] New Mexico	year N.M. Laws page no.
New Mexico Legislative Service (West)	year N.M. Legis. Serv. page no. (West) [*BB*]

NEW YORK

<u>Legislative Websites</u>: http://assembly.state.ny.us/
(New York State Assembly)
http://www.senate.state.ny.us/
(New York State Senate)

O McKinney's Consolidated Laws of New York Annotated (West)	N.Y. [abbrev. subject] Law § x (McKinney year)
O (New York) Consolidated Laws Service (LexisNexis)	N.Y. [abbrev. subject] Law § x (Consol. year)
O Gould's New York Consolidated Laws Unannotated	N.Y. [abbrev. subject] Law § x (Gould year)

See subject abbreviations in the next subdivision.

<u>Subject abbreviations for New York Consolidated Laws (if any)</u>:

Abandoned Property	Aband. Prop.
Agricultural Conservation & Adjustment	Agric. Conserv. & Adj.
Agriculture and Markets	Agric. & Mkts.
Alcoholic Beverage Control	Alco. Bev. Cont.
Alternative County Government	Alt. County Gov't [*BB*]
Arts & Cultural Affairs	Arts & Cult. Aff.
Banking	Banking [*BB*]

Benevolent Orders	Ben. Ord.
Business Corporation	Bus. Corp.
Canal	Canal
Civil Practice Law & Rules (Citations need not include additional designation as a section or rule. [*BB*])	N.Y.C.P.L.R.
Civil Rights	Civ. Rights
Civil Service	Civ. Serv. [*BB*]
Commerce	Com.
Cooperative Corporations	Coop. Corp.
Correction	Correct.
County	County
Criminal Procedure	Crim. Proc.
Debtor and Creditor	Debt. & Cred.
Domestic Relations	Dom. Rel.
Economic Development	Econ. Dev.
Education	Educ.
Election	Elec.
Eminent Domain Procedure	Em. Dom. Proc.
Employers' Liability	Empl'rs Liab. [*BB*]
	Emplrs. Liab. [*ALWD*]
Energy	Energy
Environmental Conservation	Envtl. Conserv.
Estates, Powers, & Trusts	Est. Powers & Trusts
Executive	Exec.
General Associations	Gen. Ass'ns [*BB*]
	Gen. Assns. [*ALWD*]
General Business	Gen. Bus.
General City	Gen. City
General Construction	Gen. Constr.
General Municipal	Gen. Mun.
General Obligations	Gen. Oblig.

Highway	High.
Indian	Indian
Insurance	Ins.
Judiciary Court Acts	Jud. Ct. Acts
Labor	Lab.
Legislative	Legis.
Lien	Lien
Limited Liability Company	Ltd. Liab. Co.
Local Finance	Local Fin.
Mental Hygiene	Mental Hyg.
Military	Mil.
Multiple Dwelling	Mult. Dwell.
Multiple Residence	Mult. Resid.
Municipal Home Rule & Statute of Local Governments	Mun. Home Rule
Navigation	Nav.
Not-for-Profit Corporation	Not-for-Profit Corp.
Parks, Recreation & Historic Preservation	Parks Rec. & Hist. Preserv.
Partnership	P'ship [*BB*]
	Pship. [ALWD]
Penal	Penal
Personal Property	Pers. Prop.
Private Housing Finance	Priv. Hous. Fin.
Public Authorities	Pub. Auth.
Public Buildings	Pub. Bldgs.
Public Health	Pub. Health
Public Housing	Pub. Hous.
Public Lands	Pub. Lands
Public Officers	Pub. Off.
Public Service	Pub. Serv.
Racing, Pari-Mutuel Wagering & Breeding	Rac. Pari-Mut. Wag. & Breed.

Railroad	R.R.
Rapid Transit	Rapid Trans.
Real Property	Real Prop.
Real Property Actions and Proceedings	Real Prop. Acts
Real Property Tax	Real Prop. Tax
Religious Corporations	Relig. Corp.
Retirement & Social Security	Retire. & Soc. Sec.
Rural Electric Cooperative	Rural Elec. Coop.
Second Class Cities	Second Class Cities
Social Services	Soc. Serv.
Soil & Water Conservation Districts	Soil & Water Conserv. Dist.
State	State
State Administrative Procedure Act	A.P.A.
State Finance	State Fin.
State Printing & Public Documents	State Print. & Pub. Docs.
State Technology	State Tech.
Statutes	Stat.
Surrogate's Court Procedure Act	Surr. Ct. Proc. Act
Tax	Tax
Town	Town
Transportation	Transp.
Transportation Corporations	Transp. Corp.
Unconsolidated	Unconsol.
Uniform Commercial Code	U.C.C.
Vehicle & Traffic	Veh. & Traf.
Village	Village
Volunteer Ambulance Workers' Benefit	Vol. Ambul. Workers' Ben.

Volunteer Firefighters' Benefit	Vol. Fire. Ben.
Worker's Compensation	Workers' Comp.

McKinney's Consolidated Laws	N.Y. [abbrev. law] § x (McKinney year) [*BB*]
Consolidated Laws Service	N.Y. [abbrev. law] § x (Consol. year) [*BB*]
Gould's New York Consolidated Laws Unannotated	N.Y. [abbrev. law] § x (Gould year) [*BB*]

See subject abbreviations for uncompiled laws in the next subdivision.

<u>Subject abbreviations for New York Uncompiled Laws</u>:

New York City Civil Court Act	City Civ. Ct. Act [*BB*]
New York City Criminal Court Act	City Crim. Ct. Act [*BB*]
Code of Criminal Procedure	Code Crim. Proc. [*BB*]
Court of Claims Act	Ct. Cl. Act [*BB*]
Family Court Act	Fam. Ct. Act [*BB*]
Uniform City Court Act	Uniform City Ct. Act [*BB*]
Uniform City District Court	Uniform Dist. Ct. Act [*BB*]
Uniform Justice Court Act	Uniform Just. Ct. Act [*BB*]

Laws of New York	year N.Y. Laws page no.
McKinney's New York Session Law Service (West)	year N.Y. Sess. Laws page no. (McKinney)
New York Consolidated Laws Service Advance Legislative Service (LexisNexis)	year-pamph. no. N.Y. Consol. Laws Adv. Legis. Serv. page no. (LexisNexis) [*BB*]

NORTH CAROLINA

<u>Legislative Website</u>: http://www.ncga.state.nc.us/
(North Carolina General Assembly)

○ General Statutes of North Carolina (LexisNexis)	N.C. Gen. Stat. § x-x (year) [*BB*] N.C. Gen. Stat. § x-x (Lexis year) [*ALWD*]
West's North Carolina General Statutes Annotated	N.C. Gen. Stat. Ann. § x-x (West year)
Session Laws of North Carolina	year N.C. Sess. Laws page no.
North Carolina Advance Legislative Services (LexisNexis)	year-pamph. no. N.C. Adv. Legis. Serv. page no. (LexisNexis) [*BB*]

NORTH DAKOTA

<u>Legislative Website</u>: http://www.legis.nd.gov/
(North Dakota Legislative Branch)

○ North Dakota Century Code (LexisNexis)	N.D. Cent. Code § x-x-x (year)
Laws of North Dakota	year N.D. Laws page no.

OHIO

<u>Legislative Website</u>: http://www.legislature.state.oh.us/
(Ohio General Assembly)

○ Page's Ohio Revised   Ohio Rev. Code Ann. § x.x
    Code Annotated   (LexisNexis year) [*BB*]
    (LexisNexis)   Ohio Rev. Code Ann. § x.x
                            (Lexis year) [*ALWD*]

○ Baldwin's Ohio Revised   Ohio Rev. Code Ann. § x.x
    Code Annotated (West)   (West year)

State of Ohio: Legislative   year Ohio Laws page no.
    Acts Passed & Joint
    Resolutions Adopted

Page's Ohio Legislative   year Ohio Legis. Bull.
    Bulletin (LexisNexis)   page no. (LexisNexis) [*BB*]
    (Anderson)   year Ohio Legis. Bull
                             pinpoint cite (Lexis) [*ALWD*]

Baldwin's Ohio Legislative   year Ohio Legis. Serv.
    Service Annotated   Ann. page no. (West) [*BB*]
                             year Ohio Legis. Serv.
                             pinpoint cite (West)

OKLAHOMA

Legislative Website: http://www.lsb.state.ok.us/
(Oklahoma Legislature)

○ Oklahoma Statutes (West) Okla. Stat. tit. x, § x (year)

Oklahoma Statutes   Okla. Stat. Ann. tit. x, § x
    Annotated (West)   (West year)

Oklahoma Session Laws   year Okla. Sess. Laws
    (West)   page no. [*BB*]
                           year Okla. Laws page no.
                           [*ALWD*]

Oklahoma Session Law   year Okla. Sess. Law
    Service (West)   Serv. page no. (West) [*BB*]

OREGON

<u>Legislative Website</u>: http://www.leg.state.or.us/
(Oregon State Legislature)

○ Oregon Revised Statutes	Or. Rev. Stat. § x.x (year)
West's Oregon Revised Statutes Annotated	Or. Rev. Stat. Ann. § x.x (West year)

Oregon Laws & Resolutions	year Or. Laws page no.
	Year Or. Laws Spec. Sess. page no. [*BB*]
	Year Or. Laws Adv. Sh. No. X, page no. [*BB*]

PENNSYLVANIA

<u>Legislative Website</u>: http://www.legis.state.pa.us/
(Pennsylvania General Assembly)

○ Pennsylvania Consolidated Statutes	x Pa. Cons. Stat. § x (year) [*BB*]
	x Pa. Consol. Stat. Ann. § x (year) [*ALWD*]
Purdon's Pennsylvania Consolidated Statutes Annotated (West)	x Pa. Cons. Stat. Ann. § x (West year) [*BB*]
	x Pa. Consol. Stat. Ann. § x (West year) [ALWD]
Purdon's Pennsylvania Statutes Annotated (West)	x Pa. Stat. Ann. § x (West year) [*BB*]
	Pa. Stat. Ann. x § x (West year) [*ALWD*]

| Laws of Pennsylvania | year Pa. Laws page no. |
| Purdon's Pennsylvania Legislative Service (West) | year Pa. Legis. Serv. page no. (West) [*BB*] |

RHODE ISLAND

Legislative Website: http://www.rilin.state.ri.us/
(State of Rhode Island General Assembly)

| O General Laws of Rhode Island (LexisNexis) | R.I. Gen. Laws. § x-x-x (year) |

Public Laws of Rhode Island (& Providence Plantations)	year R.I. Pub. Laws page no. [*BB*] year R.I. Laws page no. [*ALWD*]
Acts & Resolves of Rhode Island & Providence Plantations	year R.I. Acts & Resolves page no. [*BB*] year R.I. Acts & Resolves pinpoint [*ALWD*]
Rhode Island General Laws Advance Legislative Service (LexisNexis)	year-pamph, no. R.I. Gen. Laws Adv. Legis. Serv. page no. (LexisNexis) [*BB*]

SOUTH CAROLINA

Legislative Website: http://www.scstatehouse.net/
(South Carolina Legislature)

| O Code of Laws of South Carolina 1976 Annotated (West) | S.C. Code Ann. § x-x-x (year) |

Acts & Joint Resolutions   year S.C. Acts page no.
    [of] South Carolina

SOUTH DAKOTA

<u>Legislative Website</u>: http://legis.state.sd.us/
(South Dakota Legislature)

○ South Dakota Codified Laws (West)	S.D. Codified Laws § x-x-x (year)

Session Laws of South Dakota	year S.D. Sess. Laws page no. [*BB*] year S.D. Laws page no. [*ALWD*]
South Dakota Advance Code Service (LexisNexis)	year-pamph. no. S.D. Adv. Code Serv. page no. (LexisNexis) [*BB*]

TENNESSEE

<u>Legislative Website</u>: http://www.legislature.state.tn.us/
(The Tennessee General Assembly)

○ Tennessee Code Annotated(LexisNexis)	Tenn. Code Ann. § x-x-x (year) [*BB*] Tenn. Code Ann. § x-x-x (Lexis year) [*ALWD*]
West's Tennessee Code Annotated	Tenn. Code Ann. § x-x-x (West year)

Public Acts of the State of Tennessee	year Tenn. Pub. Acts page no. [BB] year Tenn. Pub. Acts ch. x [*ALWD*]

Tennessee Code Annotated Advance Legislative Service (LexisNexis)	year-pamph. no. Tenn. Code Ann. Adv. Legis. Serv. page no. (LexisNexis) *[BB]*
West's Tennessee Legislative Service	year Tenn. Legis. Serv. page no. (West) *[BB]*

TEXAS

<u>Legislative Website</u>: http://www.capitol.state.tx.us/ (Texas Legislature Online)

O Vernon's Texas Statutes & Codes Annotated (West)	Tex. [abbrev. subject] Code Ann. § x (Vernon year) *[BB]* Tex. [abbrev. subject] Code Ann. § x (year) *[ALWD]*

See subject abbreviations in the next subdivision.

Vernon's Texas Revised Civil Statutes Annotated (West)	Tex. Rev. Civ. Stat. Ann. art. x, § x (Vernon year) *[BB]* Tex. Rev. Civ. Stat. Ann. art. x (West year) *[ALWD]*
Vernon's Texas Business Corporation Act Annotated (West)	Tex. Bus. Corp. Act Ann. art. X (Vernon year) *[BB]*
Vernon's Texas Code of Criminal Procedure Annotated (West)	Tex. Code Crim. Proc. Ann. art. x (Vernon year) *[BB]*
Vernon's Texas Insurance Code Annotated (West)	Tex. Ins. Code Ann. art. x (Vernon year) *[BB]*
Vernon's Texas Probate Code Annotated (West)	Tex. Prob. Code Ann. § x (Vernon year) *[BB]*

Subject abbreviations for Texas Codes (if any):

Agriculture	Agric.
Alcoholic Beverage	Alco. Bev. *[BB]*
	Alcoh. Bev. *[ALWD]*
Business & Commerce	Bus. & Com.
Business Organizations	Bus. Orgs.
Civil Practice & Remedies	Civ. Prac. & Rem.
Education	Educ.
Election	Elec. *[BB]*
	Election *[ALWD]*
Family	Fam.
Financial	Fin.
Government	Gov't *[BB]*
	Govt. [ALWD]
Health & Safety	Health & Safety
Human Resources	Hum. Res.
Insurance	Ins.
Labor	Lab.
Local Government	Loc. Gov't *[BB]*
	Local Govt. *[ALWD]*
Natural Resources	Nat. Res. *[BB]*
	Nat. Resources *[ALWD]*
Occupations	Occ.
Parks & Wildlife	Parks & Wild. *[BB]*
	Parks & Wildlife *[ALWD]*
Penal	Penal
Property	Prop.
Special Districts	Spec. Dists.
Tax	Tax
Transportation	Transp.
Utilities	Util. *[BB]*
	Utils. *[ALWD]*
Water	Water

General & Special Laws of the State of Texas	year Tex. Gen. Laws page no. [*BB*] year Tex. Gen. Laws ch. x [*ALWD*]
Vernon's Texas Session Law Service (West)	year Tex. Sess. Law Serv. page no. (West) [*BB*] year Tex. Sess. L. Serv. pinpoint cite [*ALWD*]
Laws of the Republic of Texas	18xx Repub. Tex. Laws page no. [*BB*]

UTAH

<u>Legislative Website</u>: http://www.le.state.ut.us/ (Utah State Legislature)

| O Utah Code Annotated (LexisNexis) | Utah Code Ann. § x-x-x (year) [*BB*]
Utah Code Ann. § x-x-x (Lexis year) [*ALWD*] |
| West's Utah Code Annotated | Utah Code Ann. § x-x-x (West year) |

| Laws of Utah | year Utah Laws page no. [*BB*]
year Utah Laws ch. x |

VERMONT

<u>Legislative Website</u>: http://www.leg.state.vt.us/ (The State of Vermont Legislature)

| O Vermont Statutes Annotated (LexisNexis) | Vt. Stat. Ann. tit. x, § x (year) |

| Acts & Resolves of Vermont | year Vt. Acts & Resolves page no. |
| Vermont Advance Legislative Service (LexisNexis) | year-pamph. no Vt. Adv. Legis. Serv. page no. (LexisNexis) [BB] |

VIRGINIA

Legislative Website: http://legis.state.va.us/
(Virginia General Assembly)

O Code of Virginia (1950) Annotated (LexisNexis)	Va. Code Ann. § x-x (year) [BB]
	Va. Code Ann. § x-x (Lexis year) [ALWD]
West's Annotated Code of Virginia	Va. Code Ann. § x-x (West year)

Acts of the General Assembly of the Commonwealth of Virginia	year Va. Acts page no. [BB] year Va. Acts ch. x [ALWD]
Michie's Virginia Advance Legislative Service (LexisNexis)	year-pamph. no. Va. Adv. Legis. Serv. page no. (LexisNexis) [BB]
West's Virginia Legislative Service	year Va. Legis. Serv. page no. (West)

WASHINGTON

Legislative Website: http://www.leg.wa.gov/legislature
(Washington State Legislature)

| O Revised Code of Washington | Wash. Rev. Code § x.x.x (year) |

Revised Code of Washington Annotated (West)	Wash. Rev. Code Ann. § x.x.x (West year)
Annotated Revised Code of Washington (LexisNexis)	Wash. Rev. Code Ann. § x.x.x (LexisNexis year) [*BB*] Wash. Rev. Code Ann. § x.x.x (Lexis year)

Session Laws of Washington	year Wash. Sess. Laws page no. [*BB*] year Wash. Laws page no. [*ALWD*]
West's Washington Legislative Service	year Wash. Legis. Serv. page no. (West) [*BB*] year Wash. Legis. Serv. pinpoint [*ALWD*]

WEST VIRGINIA

Legislative Website: http://www.legis.state.wv.us/
(West Virginia Legislature)

○ West Virginia Code	W. Va. Code § x-x-x (year)
Michie's West Virginia Code Annotated (LexisNexis)	W. Va. Code Ann. § x-x-x (LexisNexis year) [*BB*] W. Va. Code Ann. § x-x-x (Lexis year) [*ALWD*]
West's Annotated Code of West Virginia	W. Va. Code Ann. § x-x-x (West year)

Acts of the Legislature of West Virginia	year W. Va. Acts page no. [*BB*] year W. Va. Acts ch. x [*ALWD*]

Michie's West Virginia Code Advance Legislative Service (LexisNexis)	year-pamph. no. W. Va. Code Adv. Legis. Serv. page no. (LexisNexis) [*BB*]

WISCONSIN

<u>Legislative Website</u>: http://www.legis.state.wi.us/
(Wisconsin State Legislature)

○ Wisconsin Statutes (West's) Wisconsin Statutes Annotated	Wis. Stat. § x-x (year) Wis. Stat. Ann. § x.x (West year)
Wisconsin Session Laws (Laws of Wisconsin)	year Wis. Sess. Laws page no. [*BB*] year Wis. Laws ch. x [*ALWD*]
West's Wisconsin Legislative Service	year Wis. Legis. Serv. page no. (West) [*BB*] Year Wis. Legis. Serv. pinpoint (West) [*ALWD*]

WYOMING

<u>Legislative Website</u>: http://legisweb.state.wy.us/
(Wyoming State Legislature)

○ Wyoming Statutes Annotated (LexisNexis)	Wyo. Stat. Ann. § x-x-x (year)

Session Laws of Wyoming	year Wyo. Sess. Laws page no. [BB] Year Wyo. Laws ch. x [ALWD]

C. UNITED STATES TERRITORIES

AMERICAN SAMOA

○ American Samoa Code Annotated	Am. Samoa Code Ann. § x (year)

GUAM

Legislative Website: http://www.guamlegislature.com/
(Guam Legislature)

○ Guam Code Annotated	Guam Code Ann. tit. x, § x (Year)

Guam Session Laws	Guam Sess. Laws page no.

NAVAJO NATION

Legislative Website:
http://www.navajonationcouncil.org/
(Navajo Nation Council)

○ Navajo Nation Code	Navajo Nation Code tit. x, § x (year) [BB] Navajo Nation Code tit. x, § x (Equity year) [ALWD]

NORTHERN MARIANA ISLANDS

<u>Legislative Website</u>: http://www.cnmileg.gov.mp/
(Northern Mariana Islands Commonwealth Legislature)

○ Northern Mariana Islands Commonwealth Code	x N. Mar. I. Code § x (year) [*BB*] x N. Mar. Is. Code § x (year) [*ALWD*]
Northern Mariana Islands Session Laws	year N. Mar. I. Pub. L. x-x [*BB*]

PUERTO RICO

○ Laws of Puerto Rico Annotated (LexisNexis)	P.R. Laws Ann. tit. x, § x (year)
Laws of Puerto Rico	year P.R. Laws page no.

VIRGIN ISLANDS

<u>Legislative Website</u>: http://www.legvi.org/
(Virgin Islands Legislature)

○ Virgin Islands Code Annotated (LexisNexis)	V.I. Code Ann. tit. x, § x (year)
Session Laws of the Virgin Islands	year V.I. Sess. Laws page no. [*BB*] year V.I. Laws page no. [*ALWD*]

APPENDIX 7

PERIODICAL ABBREVIATIONS

This appendix provides two ways of determining how to abbreviate the name of a periodical. Subdivision A provides the abbreviations for the statistically most frequently cited legal periodicals. Subdivision B provides a list of abbreviations that can be used in conjunction with the abbreviations in Appendix 1 to construct abbreviations for other periodical titles.

Unless otherwise indicated, *The Bluebook* and the *ALWD* abbreviations are the same.

A. FREQUENTLY CITED PERIODICALS

PERIODICAL TITLE	ABBREVIATION
Alabama Law Review	Ala. L. Rev.
American Criminal Law Review	Am. Crim. L. Rev.
American Journal of	Am. J. Int'l L. [*BB*]
International Law	Am. J. Intl. L. [*ALWD*]
Boston University Law Review	B.U. L. Rev.
Brooklyn Law Review	Brook. L. Rev.
Buffalo Law Review	Buff. L. Rev.
Business Lawyer	Bus. Law.
California Law Review	Cal. L. Rev.
Chicago-Kent Law Review	Chi.-Kent L. Rev.
Columbia Law Review	Colum. L. Rev.
Cornell Law Review	Cornell L. Rev.
Duke Law Journal	Duke L.J.

PERIODICAL TITLE	ABBREVIATION
Florida L. Rev.	Fla. L. Rev.
George Washington Law Rev.	Geo. Wash. L. Rev.
Georgetown Law Journal	Geo. L.J.
Georgia Law Review	Ga. L. Rev.
Harvard Civil Rights-Civil Liberties Law Review	Harv. C.R.-C.L. L. Rev. [BB] Harv. Civ. Rights-Civ. Libs. L. Rev. [ALWD]
Harvard International Law Journal	Harv. Int'l L.J. [BB] Harv. Intl. L.J. [ALWD]
Harvard Law Review	Harv. L. Rev.
Hastings Law Journal	Hastings L. Rev.
Indiana Law Journal	Ind. L.J.
Iowa Law Review	Iowa L. Rev.
Journal of Criminal Law & Criminology	J. Crim. L. & Criminology
Journal of Law & Economics	J.L. & Econ. [BB] J.L. & Econs. [ALWD]
Journal of Legal Education	J. Legal Educ. [BB] J. Leg. Educ. [ALWD]
Journal of Legal Studies	J. Legal Stud. [BB] J. Leg. Stud. [ALWD]
Law & Human Behavior	Law & Hum. Behav. [BB] L. & Hum. Behav. [ALWD]
Law & Contemporary Problems	Law & Contemp. Probs. [BB] L. & Contemp. Probs. [ALWD]

PERIODICAL TITLE	ABBREVIATION
Law & Social Inquiry	Law & Soc. Inquiry [BB]
	L. & Soc. Inquiry [ALWD]
Law & Society Review	Law & Soc'y Rev. [BB]
	L. & Socy. Rev. [ALWD]
Maryland Law Review	Md. L. Rev.
Michigan Law Review	Mich. L. Rev.
Minnesota Law Review	Minn. L. Rev.
New York University Law Review	N.Y.U. L. Rev.
North Carolina Law Review	N.C. L. Rev.
Northwestern University Law Review	Nw. U. L. Rev.
Notre Dame Law Review	Notre Dame L. Rev.
Ohio State Law Journal	Ohio St. L.J.
San Diego Law Review	San Diego L. Rev. [BB]
	S.D. L. Rev. [ALWD]
Southern California Law Review	S. Cal. L. Rev.
Stanford Law Review	Stan. L. Rev.
Texas Law Review	Tex. L. Rev.
Tulane Law Review	Tul. L. Rev.
UCLA Law Review	UCLA L. Rev.
University of California at Davis Law Review	U.C. Davis L. Rev. [BB]
	U. Cal. Davis L. Rev. [ALWD]
University of Chicago Law Review	U. Chi. L. Rev.
University of Cincinnati Law Review	U. Cin. L. Rev.
University of Colorado Law Review	U. Colo. L. Rev.

PERIODICAL TITLE	ABBREVIATION
University of Florida Law Review (now Florida Law Review)	U. Fla. L. Rev.
University of Miami Law Review	U. Miami L. Rev.
University of Pennsylvania Law Review	U. Pa. L. Rev.
University of Pittsburgh Law Review	U. Pitt. L. Rev.
Vanderbilt Law Review	Vand. L. Rev.
Virginia Law Review	Va. L. Rev.
William and Mary Law Review	Wm. & Mary L. Rev.
Wisconsin Law Review	Wis. L. Rev.
Yale Law Journal	Yale L.J.

B. CONSTRUCTING PERIODICAL ABBREVIATIONS

The Bluebook and the *ALWD Manual* provide an extensive list of abbreviations for periodical titles. They also provide the following method for constructing abbreviations.

STEP 1. Identify the name of the periodical. Use the title of the periodical being cited even if it previously or subsequently has a different title.

STEP 2. For *ALWD* citations, look up each word of the title in the listing below and Appendix 1. For *Bluebook* citations, look up each word of the title in the listing below and geographic words in Appendix 1(B). (Inconsistencies in *The Bluebook* and *ALWD Manual* have been retained and are noted in the listing below.) If a word is not abbreviated in these listings, then the word should not be abbreviated.

Colons, slashes, and everything following them in the title of a periodical should be omitted. Otherwise, the punctuation of the periodical title should be retained, except for commas.

STEP 3. Construct the abbreviated title omitting the following five words : "a", "an," "in," "of," and "the." In this regard, *The Bluebook* specifically adds that (1) "on" should be retained an d (2) "if the title consists of one word after the [above] words ... have been omitted," the remaining word should not be abbreviated. The *ALWD Manual* also cautions that these words should not be omitted if a reader would be unable to recognize the title of the publication.

STEP 4. Adjust the spacing. Adjacent capital letters should be closed up, but single capitals should not be closed up with longer abbreviations. However, *The Bluebook* provides that adjacent capitals should not be closed up "when one or more of the capitals refers to the name of an institutional entity." Instead, they should be "set ... off from other adjacent single capitals with a space." The *ALWD Manual* also indicates that "the institutional or geographic abbreviation" should be set "off from other parts of the abbreviation [by] insert[ing] "one space before and after a group of consecutive capital letters [denoting the] geographic or institutional entity."

New Mexico Law Review = N.M. L. Rev.
Loyola University of Chicago Law Journal =
    Loy. U. Chi. L.J.
UCLA Women's Law Journal = UCLA Women's L.J.

Unless otherwise indicated below, the abbreviations for *Bluebook* and *ALWD* citations are the same.

WORD OR PHRASE	ABBREVIATION
ABA	A.B.A. *[BB]* ABA *[ALWD]*
Abroad	Abroad
Academic	Acad. *[BB]* Academic *[ALWD]*
Academy	Acad.
Account	Acct. *[BB]* Account *[ALWD]*
Accountancy	Acct. *[BB]*
	Accountancy *[ALWD]*
Accountant	Acct. *[BB]* Accountant *[ALWD]*
Accountants	Acct. *[BB]*
	Accountants *[ALWD]*
Accounting	Acct. *[BB]* Acctg. *[ALWD]*
Activities	Activities
Adelaide	Adel. *[BB]* Adelaide *[ALWD]*
Administration	Admin.
Administrative	Admin.
Administrator	Admin. *[BB]* Adminstr. *[ALWD]*
Advertising	Advert.
Advisor	Advisor
Advocacy	Advoc.
Advocate	Advoc.
Affairs	Aff.
Africa	Afr.
African	Afr. *[BB]* African *[ALWD]*
Affordable	Affordable *[BB]* Afford. *[ALWD]*
Aging	Aging
Agricultural	Agric.
Agriculture	Agric.
Air	Air
Air Force	A.F.
Akron	Akron
Alabama	Ala.
Alaska	Alaska
Albany	Alb.

WORD OR PHRASE	ABBREVIATION
Alia	Alia
Allied	Allied
America	Am.
American	Am.
American Intellectual Property Law Association	AIPLA [*BB*]
American Law Institute	A.L.I. [*BB*] ALI [*ALWD*]
American Society of Composers, Authors, & Publishers	ASCAP
American Legal Studies Association: ALSA Forum;	ALSA F. [*BB*] ALSA Forum [*ALWD*]
ALSA Newsletter	ALSA Newsl. [*BB*] ALSA Newsltr. [*ALWD*]
Americas	Am. [*BB*] Ams. [*ALWD*]
AmLaw Tech	AmLaw Tech
Ancestry	Anc. [*BB*] Ancestry [*ALWD*]
And	&
Anglo-American	Anglo-Am.
Animal	Animal
Annals	Annals
Annotated	A. [*BB*] Ann. [*ALWD*]
Annual	Ann. [*BB*] Annual [*ALWD*]
Antitrust	Antitrust
Appalachian	Appalachian
Appellate	App.
Arbitration	Arb.
Arbitrators	Arb. [*BB*] Arbs. [*ALWD*]
Army	Army
Arizona	Ariz.
Arkansas	Ark.

WORD OR PHRASE	ABBREVIATION
Art	Art
Arts	Arts
Asian	Asian
Asian-Pacific	Asian-Pac. [BB]
	Asian-P. [ALWD]
Association	Ass'n [BB] Assn. [ALWD]
Association of Legal Writing Directors	ALWD [ALWD]
Association of Student International Law Societies	ASILS [ALWD]
Atlanta	Atlanta
Atomic	Atom. [BB] Atomic [ALWD]
Attorney	Att'y. [BB] Atty. [ALWD]
Attorneys	Att'ys [BB] Attys. [ALWD]
Auckland	Auckland
Ave Maria	Ave Maria
Bag	Bag
Baltimore	Balt.
Bankers	Bankers
Banking	Banking
Bankruptcy	Bankr.
Bar	B.
Barrister	Barrister
Barletter	Barletter [BB] Barltr. [ALWD]
Barry	Barry
Basin	Basin
Baylor	Baylor
Bee	Bee
Behavior	Behav.
Behavioral	Behav.
Bench	Bench
Benchmark	Benchmark

WORD OR PHRASE	ABBREVIATION
Benefits	Benefits
Berkeley	Berkeley
Beverly Hills	Beverly Hills
Bibliography	Bibliography [*BB*]
	Bibliog. [*ALWD*]
Bill	Bill
BioLaw	BioLaw
Black	Black
Blackletter	Blackletter [*BB*]
	Blackltr. [*ALWD*]
Boston	Boston
Boston College	B.C.
Boston University	B.U.
Brandeis	Brandeis
Brigham Young University	BYU
Briefcase	Briefcase
Briefs	Briefs [*BB*] Brs. [*ALWD*]
British	Brit.
Brooklyn	Brook.
Buffalo	Buff.
Bulletin	Bull.
Business	Bus.
California	Cal.
Cambridge	Cambridge
Camden	Cam. [*BB*] Camden [*ALWD*]
Campbell	Campbell
Canada	Can.
Canadian	Can.
Capital	Cap.
Cardozo	Cardozo
Care	Care
Case	Case

WORD OR PHRASE	ABBREVIATION
Casebook	Casebook
Cases	Cas. [BB] Cases [ALWD]
Catholic	Cath.
CBA	CBA
Censorship	Censorship
Center	Center [BB] Ctr. [ALWD]
Central	Cent. [BB] C. [ALWD]
Change	Change
Chapman	Chap. [BB] Chapman [ALWD]
Chartered	C. [BB]
Chicago	Chi.
Chicano	Chicano
Chicano-Latino	Chicano-Latino
Child	Child
Children	Child. [BB] Children [ALWD]
Children's	Child. [BB] Children's [ALWD]
China	China
Chinese	Chinese
Chronicle	Chron.
Church	Church
Cincinnati	Cin.
Circuit	Cir.
City	City
Civil	Civ.
Civil Liberty	C.L. [BB] Civ. Lib. [ALWD]
Civil Liberties	C.L. [BB] Civ. Libs. [ALWD]
Civil Rights	C.R. [BB] Civ. Rights [ALWD]
Claims	Claims
Clearinghouse	Clearinghouse
Cleveland	Clev.
Clinical	Clinical [BB] Clin. [ALWD]
Club	Club
Coastal	Coastal

WORD OR PHRASE	ABBREVIATION
College	C.
Colorado	Colo.
Columbia	Colum.
Columbia-VLA	Colum.-VLA
Columbus	Columbus
Comment	Comment [*BB*] Cmt. [*ALWD*]
Commentary	Comment. [*BB*]
	Commentary [*ALWD*]
Commerce	Com.
Commercial	Com.
Committee	Comm. [*ALWD*]
CommLaw Conspectus	CommLaw Conspectus [*BB*]
	CommLaw [*ALWD*]
Commodities	Commodities
Common	Common [*BB*] Com. [*ALWD*]
Communication	Comm. [*BB*] Commun. [*ALWD*]
Communications	Comm. [*BB*] Commun. [*ALWD*]
Community	Community
Companies	Cos. [*ALWD*]
Comparative	Comp.
Compleat	Compleat
Compliance	Compl. [*ALWD*]
Computer	Computer
Computers	Computers [*ALWD*]
Computer/Law Journal	Computer/L.J.
Computer Law Review & Technology Journal	Comp. L. Rev. & Tech. J. [*BB*]
Computing	Computing
Conciliation	Conciliation
Conference	Conf.
Confinement	Confinement
Conflict	Conflict

WORD OR PHRASE	ABBREVIATION
Congressional	Cong.
Connecticut	Conn.
Conspectus	Conspectus [BB]
Constitution	Const.
Constitutional	Const.
Construction	Construction [BB]
	Constr. [ALWD]
Consumer	Consumer
Contemporary	Contemp.
Contract	Cont. [BB] Contract [ALWD]
Contracts	Cont. [BB]
Conveyancer	Conv. [BB]
	Conveyancer [ALWD]
Conveyancer and Property Lawyer (new series)	Conv. & Prop. Law. (n.s.) [BB]
Copyright	Copyright [BB] Copy. [ALWD]
Copyright Law Symposium (American Association of Composers, Authors, & Publishers)	Copyright L. Sym. (ASCAP) [BB] Copy. L. Sym. (ASCAP)
Cornell	Cornell
Corporate	Corp.
Corporation	Corp.
Cosmetic	Cosm. [BB] Cosmetic [ALWD]
Counsel	Couns. (But College Counsel: C. Coun. [ALWD])
Counsel's	Counsel's [BB] Couns. [ALWD]
Counselor	Couns. [BB] Counselor [ALWD]
Counselor's	Couns. [BB] Counselor [ALWD]
Counselors	Couns. [BB] Counselor [ALWD]

WORD OR PHRASE	ABBREVIATION
County	Co. [*ALWD*]
Courant	Courant
Course	Course
Court	Ct.
Courts	Cts.
Coverage	Coverage
Creighton	Creighton
Crime	Crime
Criminal	Crim.
Criminology	Criminology
Cumberland	Cumb.
Current	Current
Currents: International Trade Law Journal	Currents: Int'l Trade L. J. [*BB*] Currents [*ALWD*]
Dalhousie	Dalhousie
Davis	See University of California at Davis
Dayton	Dayton
DCL	DCL
Dealer	Dealer
Defense	Def.
Delinquency	Delinq. [*BB*] Delinquency [*ALWD*]
Denver	Denv. (But U. Denver Water L. Rev. [*ALWD*])
Department	Dep't [*BB*] Dept. [*ALWD*]
DePaul	DePaul
DePaul-LCA	DePaul-LCA
Delaware	Del.
Derecho	Der. [*BB*] D. [*ALWD*]
Detroit	Det.
Development	Dev.
Developments	Dev. [*BB*] Devs. [*ALWD*]

WORD OR PHRASE	ABBREVIATION
Dickinson	Dick.
Dicta	Dicta
Digest	Dig.
Digest: The National Italian-American Bar Association Law Journal	Digest
Diplomacy	Dipl. *[BB]* Diplomacy *[ALWD]*
Directions	Directions
Disability	Disability
Dispatch	Dispatch
Dispute	Disp. *[BB]* Dis. *[ALWD]*
District of Columbia	D.C.
Divorce	Divorce
Doctor	Dr.
Drake	Drake
Drug	Drug
Duke	Duke
Duquesne	Duq.
East	E.
Eastern	E.
Ecology	Ecology *[BB]* Ecol. *[ALWD]*
Economic	Econ.
Economics	Econ.
	Econs. (But J.L. & Econs. and Res. L. & Econs. *[ALWD]*)
Economist	Economist
Economy	Econ.
Education	Educ.
Educational	Educ.
Elder	Elder
Emerging	Emerging

<u>WORD OR PHRASE</u>	<u>ABBREVIATION</u>
Eminent Domain	Eminent Domain [*BB*]
	Em. Dom. [*ALWD*]
Emory	Emory
Employee	Emp. [*BB*] Employee [*ALWD*]
Employment	Emp. [*BB*] Empl. [*ALWD*]
Energy	Energy
England	Eng.
English	Eng. [*BB*] English [*ALWD*]
Entertainment	Ent.
Environment	Env't [*BB*] Env. [*ALWD*]
Environmental	Envtl.
Estate	Est.
Estates	Est. [*BB*] Ests. [*ALWD*]
Estuarine	Estuarine
Ethics	Ethics
Ethnic	Ethnic
Europe	Eur.
European	Eur.
Examiner	Examiner [*BB*] Examr. [*ALWD*]
Executive	Executive [*BB*] Exec. [*ALWD*]
Faculty	Fac. [*BB*] Faculty [*ALWD*]
Family	Fam.
Federal	Fed.
Federation	Fed'n [*BB*] Fedn. [*ALWD*]
Feminism	Feminism
Fernando	Fern. [*BB*] Fernando [*ALWD*]
FICC	FICC
Fields	Fields
Fighting	Fighting
Finance	Fin.
Financial	Fin.
Firm	Firm
FJC	FJC

WORD OR PHRASE	ABBREVIATION
Florida	Fla.
Fletcher	Fletcher
Florida International University Law Review	Fla. Int'l U. L. Rev. [*BB*] FIU L. Rev. [*ALWD*]
Food	Food
For	for
Force	Force
Fordham	Fordham
Foreign	Foreign [*BB*] For. [*ALWD*]
Foreign Broadcast Information Service	F.B.I.S. [*BB*]
Forensic	Forensic
Forest	Forest
Fortnightly	Fort. [*BB*] Fortnightly [*ALWD*]
Fortune	Fortune
Forum	F. [*BB*] (But Forum in The Forum [*BB*] Forum [*ALWD*]
Foundation	Found.
Foundations	Found. [*BB*] Founds. [*ALWD*]
Franchise	Franchise [*BB*] Fran. [*ALWD*]
Gas	Gas
Gate	Gate
Gender	Gender
General	Gen.
George	Geo.
Georgetown	Geo.
Georgia	Ga.
Gestae	Gestae
Gifts	Gifts
Glendale	Glendale
Globe	Globe
Global	Global

WORD OR PHRASE	ABBREVIATION
Golden	Golden
Gonzaga	Gonz.
Governance	Goverance
Government	Gov't [BB] Govt. [ALWD]
Graven	Graven
Great	Great
Green	Green
Guide	Guide
Guild	Guild
Hamline	Hamline
Hartford	Hartford
Harvard	Harv.
Hastings	Hastings
Hawaii	Haw.
Health	Health
Herald	Herald
High	High
Higher	Higher
Hispanic	Hisp. [BB] Hispanic [ALWD]
Historical	Hist.
History	Hist.
Hofstra	Hofstra
Hospital	Hosp.
Houston	Hous.
Howard	How.
Human	Hum.
Humanities	Human. [BB]
	Humanities [ALWD]
Humanity	Human. [BB]
	Humanity [ALWD]
Hybrid	Hybrid
ICC	ICC
ICC's	ICC's

WORD OR PHRASE	ABBREVIATION
ICSID	ICSID
Idaho	Idaho
IDEA	IDEA
Illinois	Ill.
ILSA	ILSA
Imagines	Imagines
Immigration	Immigr.
Independent	Indep.
Indian	Indian
Indiana	Ind.
Indianapolis	Indianapolis
	Indian. [*ALWD*]
Individual	Indiv. [*ALWD*]
Industrial	Indus.
Inequality	Ineq. [*BB*] Inequal. [*ALWD*]
Information	Info.
Injury	Inj. [*BB*] Injury [*ALWD*]
Inquiry	Inquiry
Institute	Inst.
Institute on Federal Taxation	Inst. on Fed. Tax'n [*BB*] Inst. Fed. Taxn. [*ALWD*]
Insurance	Ins.
Intellectual	Intell.
Inter	Inter
Inter-American	Inter-Am.
Interdisciplinary	Interdisc.
Interest	Int. (But in The Public Interest Law Review: Pub. Interest L. Rev. [*ALWD*])
International	Int'l [*BB*] Intl . [*ALWD*]
Intramural	Intramural [*BB*] Intra. [*ALWD*]
Investment	Inv.
Investments	Inv.

WORD OR PHRASE	ABBREVIATION
Investors	Inv. [BB] Investors [ALWD]
Iowa	Iowa
I/S	I/S
ISL	ISL
Issues	Issues
JAG	JAG
JAMA	JAMA
Jewish	Jewish
John	J. [BB] John [ALWD]
John's	John's
Journal	J.
Journal of the American Medical Association	JAMA
Judge	Judge
Judges	Judges
Judicature	Judicature
Judicial	Jud.
Juridical	Jurid. [BB] Juridical [ALWD]
Jurimetrics: The Journal of Law, Science, and Technology	Jurimetrics J. [BB] Jurimetrics [ALWD]
Juris Doctor	Juris Dr. [BB] J.D. [ALWD]
Jurisprudence	Juris.
Jurist	Jurist
Justice	Just.
Juvenile	Juv.
Kansas	Kan.
Kent	Kent
Kentucky	Ky.
Keys	Keys
Labor	Lab.

WORD OR PHRASE	ABBREVIATION
Lakes'	Lakes'
Land	Land
La Raza	La Raza
Latino	Latino
Law	L.
Law [first word of title]	Law [*BB*] L. [*ALWD*]
Lawyer	Law.
Lawyers	Law. [*BB*] Laws. [*ALWD*]
Lawyer's	Law. [*BB*] Laws. [*ALWD*]
Leader	Leader
League	League
Lee	Lee
Legal	Legal [*BB*] Leg. [*ALWD*]
Legislation	Legis.
Legislative	Legis.
Lewis	Lewis
Liability	Liab.
Liberation	Liberation
Liberties	L. [*BB*] Libs. [*ALWD*]
Liberty	L. [*BB*] Liberty [*ALWD*]
Librarian	Libr.
Libraries	Libr. [*BB*] Libs. [*ALWD*]
Library	Libr. [*BB*] Lib. [*ALWD*]
Life	L. [*BB*] Life [*ALWD*]
Lincoln	Lincoln
Literature	Literature [*BB*] Lit. [*ALWD*]
Litigation	Litig.
Litigator	Litigator [*BB*] Litig. [*ALWD*]
Little Rock	See University of Arkansas at Little Rock
Local	Loc.
Logistics	Logistics

<u>WORD OR PHRASE</u>	<u>ABBREVIATION</u>
Los Angeles	L.A. See also University of West Los Angeles
Louisiana	La.
Louisville	Louisville [BB] Louis. [ALWD]
Loyola	Loy.
Magazine	Mag.
Maine	Me.
Major	Major [BB] Maj. [ALWD]
Management	Mgmt. [BB] (But Tax Mgm't Int'l J. [BB]) Mgt. [ALWD]
Marine	Marine
Margins/University of Maryland Journal of Race, Religion, Gender and Class	Margins [ALWD]
Maritime	Mar.
Market	Mkt.
Marquette	Marq.
Marshall	Marshall
Mary	Mary
Maryland	Md.
Mary's	Mary's
Massachusetts	Mass.
Mason	Mason
Materials	Materials
Matrimonial	Matrim. [BB] Matrimonial [ALWD]
Matrix	Matrix
McGeorge	McGeorge
McGill	McGill
Media	Media
Mediation	Mediation
Medical	Med.

WORD OR PHRASE	ABBREVIATION
Medicine	Med.
Medicolegal	Medicolegal
Melbourne	Melb. [BB] Melbourne [ALWD]
Memorandum	Memo. [ALWD]
Memphis	Mem.
Mental	Mental
Mercer	Mercer
Mexico	Mex.
Miami	Miami
Michigan	Mich.
Military	Mil.
Milwaukee	Milwaukee [BB] Milw. [ALWD]
Mineral	Min.
Minnesota	Minn.
Mississippi	Miss.
Missouri	Mo.
Mitchell	Mitchell
Monash	Monash
Monitoring	Monitoring
Montana	Mont.
Monthly	Monthly [BB] Mthly. [ALWD]
Moot	Moot
Morning	Morning [BB] Morn. [ALWD]
Mountain	Mtn. [BB] Mt. [ALWD]
MSL	MSL
Municipal	Mun.
Museum	Museum
National	Nat'l [BB] Natl. [ALWD]
Nationality	Nat'lity [BB] Nationality [ALWD]
Natural	Nat.
NDAA	NDAA [ALWD]
Negligence	Negl.

WORD OR PHRASE	ABBREVIATION
Negotiation	Negot.
Nevada	Nev.
New	New (See also next entries)
New England	New Eng.
New Jersey	N.J.
New Mexico	N.M.
New Orleans	New Orleans [BB]
	N.O. [ALWD]
New York	N.Y.
New York City	N.Y. City [BB] N.Y.C. [ALWD]
News	News
Newsletter	Newsl. [BB] Newsltr. [ALWD]
NEXUS: A Journal of Opinion	NEXUS
North	N.
Northern	N.
North Carolina	N.C.
North Dakota	N.D.
Northwest	Nw. [BB] N.W. [ALWD]
Northwestern	Nw.
Nota Bene	Nota Bene
Notes	Notes
Notre Dame	Notre Dame
Nova	Nova
Nursing	Nursing
Ocean	Ocean
Office	Off.
Ohio	Ohio
Oil	Oil
Oklahoma	Okla.
On	on
Online	Online
Orange	Orange

WORD OR PHRASE	ABBREVIATION
Orlando	Orlando
Order	Ord. [BB] Or. [ALWD]
Oregon	Or.
Organization	Org.
Oregonian	Oregonian
Osgoode	Osgoode
Otago	Otago
Ottawa	Ottawa
Pace	Pace
Pacific	Pac. [BB] P. [ALWD]
Parker	Parker
Patent	Pat.
Penn	Penn
Pennsylvania	Pa.
Pension	Pension
Pepperdine	Pepp.
Performing	Perf.
Personal	Pers. [BB] Personal [ALWD]
Perspective	Persp.
Perspectives	Persp. [BB] Persps. [ALWD]
Petersburg	Petersburg [BB] Pete. [ALWD]
Pharmacy	Phram. [ALWD]
Philadelphia	Phila.
Philosophical	Phil.
Philosophically	Phil.
Philosophy	Philosophy [BB] Phil. [ALWD]
Physical	Physical
Pittsburgh	Pitt.
Plain	Plain
Plains	Plains
Planning	Plan.
Police	Police
Policy	Pol'y [BB] Policy [ALWD]

WORD OR PHRASE	ABBREVIATION
Political	Pol.
Politics	Pol.
Portland	Portland [*ALWD* in Portland Oregonian: Port. Oregonian]
Post	Post
Potomac	Potomac
Poverty	Poverty [*BB*] Pov. [*ALWD*]
PAR	PAR
Practical	Prac.
Practice	Prac.
Practitioner	Prac. [*BB*] Pract. [*ALWD*]
Practitioners	Prac. [*BB*] Practs. [*ALWD*]
Press	Press
Preventive	Preventive
Preview	Preview
Prison	Prison
Private	Priv.
Probate	Prob.
Probation	Probation
Problems	Probs.
Procedure	Proc. [*BB*] P. [*ALWD*]
Proceedings	Proc. [*BB*] Procs. [*ALWD*]
Process	Process
Products	Prod. [*BB*] Prods. [*ALWD*]
Profession	Prof.
Professional	Prof.
Profit-Sharing	Profit-Sharing
Property	Prop.
Prosecutor	Prosecutor
Prospectus	Prospectus
Psychiatry	Psychiatry [*BB*] Psych. [*ALWD*]
Psychological	Psychol.

WORD OR PHRASE	ABBREVIATION
Psychologically	Psychol. [BB]
	Psychologically [ALWD]
Psychologist	Psychol. [ALWD]
Psychology	Psychol.
Public	Pub.
Publishing	Pub. [BB] Publg. [ALWD]
Puertorriqueno	P.R. [BB] P. [ALWD]
Puget	Puget
Puerto Rico	P.R.
QLR	QLR [ALWD]
Quarterly	Q.
Quarterly/Christian Legal Society	Q./CLS [ALWD]
Quinnipiac	Quinnipiac
Race	Race
Real	Real
Record	Rec.
Referees	Ref. [BB] Referees [ALWD]
Reference	Ref. [ALWD]
Reform	Reform
Refugee	Refugee
Regent	Regent
Register	Reg. [BB] Register [ALWD]
Regulation	Reg.
Regulatory	Reg.
Relations	Rel.
Religion	Religion
Report	Rep. [BB] Rpt. or Rep. [ALWD]
Reporter	Rep. [BB]
	Rptr. or Rep. [ALWD]
Reports	R. or Rep. [BB]
	Rpts. or Reps. [ALWD]
Reproduction	Reprod.

WORD OR PHRASE	ABBREVIATION
Reproductive	Reprod.
Republic	Republic
Res	Res
Research	Res.
Reserve	Res.
Resolution	Resol. [*BB*] Res. [*ALWD*]
Resources	Resources (But J. Energy, Nat. Res.; Envtl. L. & Nat. Res. & Env.; and Pub. Land & Res. L. Rev. [*ALWD*])
Responsibility	Resp.
Restitution	Restitution
Review	Rev.
Revista	Rev.
Rhode Island	R.I.
Richmond	Rich.
Rights	Rts. [*BB*] Rights [*ALWD*]
Rim	Rim
Risk	Risk
RISK: Health, Safety, & Environment	RISK [*BB*] Risk [*ALWD*]
Rocky	Rocky
Roger	Roger
Rutgers	Rutgers
Sacramento	Sacramento
Saint	St.
San Antonio	San Antonio
San Diego	San Diego [*BB*] S.D. [*ALWD*]
San Fernando	San Fern. [*BB*] San Fernando [*ALWD*]
San Francisco	S.F.
Santa Clara	Santa Clara
Scholar	Scholar

WORD OR PHRASE	ABBREVIATION
School	Sch.
Science	Sci.
Sciences	Sci.
Scientific	Sci.
Scottish	Scot. [BB] Scottish [ALWD]
Scribes	Scribes
Scrivener	Scrivener
Scroll	Scroll
Search	Search
Seattle	Seattle
Section	Sec.
Security	Sec. [ALWD]
Securities	Sec. (But Rev. Secs. & Commodities Reg.; Secs. & Fed. Corp. L. Rpt.; Secs. L. Rev.; Secs. Reg. L.J. [ALWD])
Seizure	Seizure
Sentencing	Sent'g [BB] Senten. [ALWD]
Sentinel	Sentinel [BB] Sent. [ALWD]
Series	S. [BB] Ser. [ALWD]
Service	Serv.
Services	Servs. [ALWD]
Seton Hall	Seton Hall
Sexuality	Sexuality
Signs	Signs
Small	Small
SMU	S.M.U. [ALWD]
Social	Soc.
Socialist	Socialist
Society	Soc'y [BB] Socy. [ALWD]
Sociological	Soc. [BB] Sociological [ALWD]
Sociologically	Soc. [BB] Sociologically [ALWD]

WORD OR PHRASE	ABBREVIATION
Sociology	Soc. *[BB]* Sociology *[ALWD]*
Software	Software
Solicitor	Solic. *[BB]* Sol. *[ALWD]*
Solicitors	Solic. *[BB]* Sols. *[ALWD]*
Solicitor's	Solic. *[BB]*
Solicitors'	Solic. *[BB]*
Solo	Solo
Sound	Sound
South	S.
South Carolina	S.C.
South Dakota	S.D.
Southeastern	S.E. *[ALWD]*
Southern	S.
Southern Methodist University	SMU *[BB]*
Southwestern	Sw.
Space	Space (But Journal of Space Law: J. S. L. *[ALWD]*)
Sport	Sport
Sports	Sports
Stanford	Stan.
State	St.
States	S.
Statistical	Stat. *[BB]* Statistical *[ALWD]*
Statistics	Stat. *[BB]* Statistics *[ALWD]*
Stetson	Stetson
Strategies	Strategies
Street	St.
Student	Student
Studies	Stud.
Suffolk	Suffolk
Supreme	Sup. *[BB]* S. *[ALWD]*
Sun	Sun

WORD OR PHRASE	ABBREVIATION
Survey	Surv. [*BB*] Surv. [*ALWD*]
Sydney	Sydney
Symposium	Symp. (But Widener L. Symposium J. [*ALWD*])
Syracuse	Syracuse
System	Sys.
Tax	Tax
Taxation	Tax'n [*BB*] Taxn. [*ALWD*]
Taxes	Taxes
Teacher	Tchr. [*BB*] Teacher [*ALWD*]
Teachers	Tchrs. [*BB*] Teachers [*ALWD*]
Tech	Tech
Technique	Tec. [*BB*] Technique [*ALWD*]
Technology	Tech.
Telecommunications	Telecomm.
Telegram	Telegram [*BB*] Teleg. [*ALWD*]
Temple	Temp.
Tennessee	Tenn.
Texas	Tex.
Theory	Theory
Third	Third
Thomas	T. [*BB*] Thomas [*ALWD*]
Thomas Jefferson	T. Jefferson [*BB*] Thomas Jefferson [*ALWD*]
Thomas M. Cooley	T.M. Cooley [*BB*] Thomas M. Cooley [*ALWD*]
Thurgood	T. [*BB*] Thurgood [*ALWD*]
Times	Times
Toledo	Tol. [*BB*] Toledo [*ALWD*]
Tort	Tort
Touro	Touro
Toxics	Toxics

WORD OR PHRASE	ABBREVIATION
Trade	Trade
Trademark	Trademark
Transatlantic	Transatlantic
Transition	Transition
Transnational	Transnat'l [*BB*]
	Transnatl. [*ALWD*]
Transportation	Transp.
Trauma	Trauma
Trial	Trial [*BB*] Tr. [*ALWD*]
Tribune	Trib.
Trust	Tr. [*BB*] Trust [*ALWD*]
Trusts	Tr. [*BB*] Trusts [*ALWD*]
Tulane	Tul.
Tulsa	Tulsa
UCLA	UCLA
UMKC	UMKC
UN Monthly Chronicle	UN Monthly Chron. [*BB*]
Unbound	Unbound
Underwriters	U. [*BB*] Underwriters [*ALWD*]
Uniform Commercial Code	UCC [*BB*] U.C.C. [*ALWD*]
Union	Union
United	U.
United States Air Force	U.S. Air Force [*BB*]
	U.S.A.F. [*ALWD*]
	U.S. A.F. [*ALWD* in J. Leg. Stud./
	U.S. A.F. Academy]
Universal	Universal
University	U.
University of Arkansas at Little Rock	U. Ark. Little Rock [*BB*]
	UALR [*ALWD*]

WORD OR PHRASE	ABBREVIATION
University of California at Davis	U.C. Davis [BB] U. Cal. Davis [ALWD]
University of the District of Columbia David Clarke School of Law	UDC/DCSL [BB]
University of West Los Angeles	UWLA [BB] U.W.L.A. [ALWD]
Urban	Urb.
U.S.A.	USA (But Journal of the Copyright Society of th e U.S.A.: J. Copy. Socy. [ALWD])
USA	USA
Use	Use
Utah	Utah
Utilities	Util. [BB] Utils. [ALWD]
Utility	Util.
UWLA	UWLA
Valley	V. [BB] Valley [ALWD]
Valparaiso	Val.
Vanderbilt	Vand.
VBA	VBA
Vermont	Vt.
Villanova	Vill.
Virginia	Va.
VLA	VLA [BB]
Wake	Wake
Wall	Wall
Warsaw	Warsaw
Washburn	Washburn
Washington	Wash.
Water	Water

WORD OR PHRASE	ABBREVIATION
Wayne	Wayne
Week	Wk. [*BB*] Week [*ALWD*]
Weekly	Wkly.
Welfare	Welfare
Wesleyan	Wesleyan [*BB*] Wes. [*ALWD*]
West-Northwest	W.-Nw. [*BB*] W.-N.W. [*ALWD*]
West Virginia	W. Va.
Western	W.
Whittier	Whittier
Widener	Widener
Wildlife	Wildlife
Willamette	Willamette
William	Wm.
Williams	Williams
Wisconsin	Wis.
Women	Women
Women's	Women's
World	World
Writing	Writing
Wyoming	Wyo.
Yearbook	Y.B.
Young	Young
Zoning	Zoning

APPENDIX 8

ABBREVIATIONS FOR LOOSELEAF SERVICES AND REPORTERS

Looseleaf services primarily cover regulation-intensive subjects, such as energy, environmental, government contracts, labor, securities, and tax law. Looseleaf services frequently are referred as to sources of "one-stop shopping" or "one-stop research." Indeed, they have been aptly analogized to "vacuum cleaners pulling together everything on a subject." However, "[u]nlike vacuum cleaners, when you open . . . looseleaf service[s], everything is in order and easy to find. . . . [They] will save hours of research time as the editors have gathered the materials from many separate sources."

A. ABBREVIATIONS OF SELECTED LOOSELEAF PUBLISHERS

PUBLISHER	ABBREVIATION
American Bar Association	ABA
Aspen Publishers	Aspen Law & Bus. [*BB*]
	Aspen [*ALWD*]
Bureau of National Affairs	BNA
Clark Boardman Callaghan	CBC
Commerce Clearing House	CCH
Environmental Law Institute	Envtl. Law Inst. [*BB*]
	ELI [*ALWD*]

PUBLISHER	ABBREVIATION
LexisNexis	LexisNexis [*BB*] Lexis [*ALWD*]
Matthew Bender	MB [*BB*] Matthew Bender [*ALWD*]

National Association of
    College and University
    Attorneys
	Nat'l Ass'n Coll. & Univ.
	Att'ys [*BB*]
	NACUA [*ALWD*]

Pike & Fisher	P & F
Research Institute of America	RIA
University Publishing Group	Univ. Pub. Group [*BB*] U. Pub. Group [*ALWD*]
West Group	West

B. ABBREVIATING TITLES OF LOOSELEAF SERVICES AND REPORTERS

Bluebook Table T.15 ("Services") provides an extensive listing of abbreviations for frequently cited looseleaf services and reporters and corresponding bound services. The *ALWD Manual* treats looseleaf services titles like reporter titles and abbreviates words listed in Appendix 1 of this book. The following illustrates how cases, commentary, and other material are cited to looseleaf services.

Copyright Law Reporter

[*BB*] *Clark Equip. Co. v. Lift Parts Mfg. Co.*, 32 Copyright L. Rep. (CCH) ¶ 20,528 (N.D. Ill. 1986). [*ALWD*] *Clark Equip. Co. v. Lift Parts Mfg. Co.*, 32 Copy. L. Rep. (CCH) ¶ 20,528 (N.D. Ill. Apr. 8, 1986).

Criminal Law Reporter

Alexei Alexis, *Bush Signs Bill Renewing PATRIOT Act with New Provisions to Safeguard Data*, 78 Crim. L. Rep. (BNA) 669 (Mar. 15, 2006).

Environment Reporter (bound as Environment Reporter Cases)

[BB] *United States v. Tyson*, 25 Env't Rep. Cas. (BNA) 1897 (E.D. Pa. 1986). [ALWD] *U.S. v. Tyson*, 25 Envtl. Rep. Cases (BNA) 1897 (E.D. Pa. Aug. 21, 1986).

Family Law Reporter (bound as Family Law Reporter)

[BB] Ill. State Bar Ass'n Comm. on Prof'l Ethics, Op. 04-03, 31 Fam. L. Rep. (BNA) 1319 (May 17, 2005). [ALWD] Ill. St. B. Assn. Comm. on Prof. Ethics, Op. 04-03, 31 Fam. L. Rep. (BNA) 1319 (May 17, 2005).

Media Law Reporter (bound as Media Law Reporter)

[BB] *Stratton Oakmont, Inc. v. Prodigy Servs. Co.*, 23 Media L. Rep. 1794 (N.Y. Sup. Ct. 1995). [ALWD] *Stratton Oakmont, Inc. v. Prodigy Servs. Co.*, 23 Media L. Rep. 1794 (N.Y. Sup. Ct. May, 24, 1995).

Standard Federal Tax Reports (bound as U.S. Tax Cases)

[BB] *Miller v. United States*, 1993-1 U.S. Tax Cas. (CCH) ¶ 50,018 (W.D. Wash. 1992). [ALWD] *Miller v. U.S.*, 1993-1 U.S. Tax Cases (CCH) ¶ 50,018 (W.D. Wash. Dec. 1, 1992).

Trade Regulation Reporter (bound as Trade Cases)

[BB] *Kohler Co. v. Briggs & Stratton Corp.*, 1986-1 Trade Cas. (CCH) ¶ 67,047 (E.D. Wis. 1986). [ALWD] *Kohler Co. v. Briggs & Stratton Corp.*, 1986-1 Trade Cases (CCH) ¶ 67,047 (E.D. Wis. Mar. 13, 1986).

APPENDIX 9

TECHNICAL *BLUEBOOK* AND *ALWD* RULES GOVERNING THE ORDER OF CITATION OF AUTHORITIES

The following summarizes *The Bluebook* and *ALWD Rules* governing the order of citation of authorities *within a single signal*. Here, the rules are at their absolute zenith, and as discussed in Chapter 1(F)(3)(*g*), they are excellent candidates for being ignored unless one is absolutely forced into following them.

The Bluebook

(1) constitutions
(2) statutes (including rules of evidence and procedure)
(3) treaties
(4) cases
(5) legislative sources
(6) administrative and executive sources
(7) intergovernmental sources or decisions
(8) records, briefs, petitions, etc.
(9) secondary sources

ALWD

(1) constitutions
(2) statutes
(3) rules of evidence and procedure
(4) treaties and international agreements
(5) cases
(6) briefs, records, pleadings, etc.
(7) administrative and executive sources
(8) intergovernmental sources
(9) legislative materials
(10) secondary sources

Within each of the above categories, *The Bluebook* and *ALWD Manual* have further, very detailed "citation ordering" rules. Generally speaking, the following general rules apply:

● Within any category, federal authorities should appear before state authorities.

● When citing cases, state court decisions should be listed alphabetically by state, and the decisions should appear in reverse chronological order.

● Courts within the same state should be listed in order of the superiority of jurisdiction (*e.g.*, higher courts are listed before those of a lower appellate court).

The Bluebook treats all U.S. Courts of Appeals (including the D.C. Circuit and the Federal Circuit) as one court. Thus, cases from those courts would be cited in reverse chronological order. The same is true for the United States District courts.

[BB] *Haw. v. Standard Oil Co.*, 405 U.S. 251 (1972); *Guthrie v. Harkness*, 199 U.S. 148 (1905); *Wells Fargo Bank v. Boutris*, 419 F.3d 949 (9th Cir. 2005); *Shevin v. Exxon Corp.*, 526 F.2d 266 (5th Cir. 1976); *In re Multidistrict Motor Vehicle Air Pollution Control Litig.*, 481 F.2d 122 (9th Cir. 1973); *Illinois v. Bristol-Myers Co.*, 470 F.2d 1276 (D.C. Cir. 1972); *Hulme v. Madison County*, 188 F. Supp. 2d 1041 (S.D. Ill. 2001); *Illinois v. Associated Milk Producers, Inc.*, 351 F. Supp. 436 (N.D. Ill. 1972); *Derryberry v. Kerr-McGee Corp.*, 516 P.2d 813 (Okla. 1973).

Thus, in the above example, the two U.S. Supreme Court cases were cited first in reverse chronological order. Those cases were followed by the five U.S.

Court of Appeals cases in reverse chronological order (i.e., the 2005 cases, then the ones from 1976, 1973, and 1972, regardless of circuit). Next, the two U.S. District Court cases were cited next in reverse chronological order (i.e., 2001 and 1972). Then, the state court case was cited (after all of the federal court cases).

In contrast, the *ALWD Manual* requires that the U.S. Courts of Appeals be cited in order of circuit number (1st Cir., 2d Cir., etc.), followed by the the District of Columbia Circuit (D.C. Cir.),, and then the Federal Circuit (Fed. Cir.). When more than one case is cited from a particular circuit, then those cases would be cited in reverse chronological order.

In addition, the *ALWD Manual* requires United States District Courts cases be cited in alphabetically by state (e.g., Alabama cases first, then Arizona cases, etc.). Furthermore, for district courts from the same state, they must be cited alphabetically by district (e.g., Central District cases, then Northern District cases, and then Southern District cases). The order of the sources in the previous example would be altered to be as follows:

[*ALWD*] *Haw. v. Standard Oil Co.*, 405 U.S. 251 (1972); *Guthrie v. Harkness*, 199 U.S. 148 (1905); *Shevin v. Exxon Corp.*, 526 F.2d 266 (5th Cir. 1976); *Wells Fargo Bank v. Boutris*, 419 F.3d 949 (9th Cir. 2005); *In re Multidistrict Motor Vehicle Air Pollution Control Litig.*, 481 F.2d 122 (9th Cir. 1973); *Ill. v. Bristol-Myers Co.*, 470 F.2d 1276 (D.C. Cir. 1972); *Ill. v. Associated Milk Producers, Inc.*, 351 F. Supp. 436 (N.D. Ill. 1972); *Hulme v. Madison Co.*, 188 F. Supp. 2d 1041

(S.D. Ill. 2001); *Derryberry v. Kerr-McGee Corp.*, 516 P.2d 813 (Okla. 1973).

Thus, the U.S. Supreme Court cases remain first, in reverse chronological order. Next, the U.S. Court of Appeals cases are cited in order of circuit (i.e., the 5th Cir. case, the two 9th Cir. cases in chronological reverse order, and then the D.C. Cir. case). The two U.S. District court cases are cited next. Because they are from the same state (i.e., Illinois), they are cited in alphabetical order by district (i.e., Northern District first and then the Southern District case).

In sum, these "citation ordering" rules may make perfect sense in many circumstances. For example, if a legal writer is citing all state statutes dealing with a topic, it is logical and appropriate to cite them alphabetically by state. On the other hand, to the extent that the above "citation ordering" rules interfere with the persuasive process in documents like appellate briefs, many legal writers would say such rules are "perfect candidates for intentional violation."

APPENDIX 10

ABBREVIATIONS OF TITLES OF JUDGES AND OTHER OFFICIALS

Unless otherwise indicated, *The Bluebook* and *ALWD Manual* abbreviations are the same.

TITLE	ABBREVIATION
Magistrate Judge	Mag. J. *[BB]*
	Mag. *[ALWD]*
Master of the Rolls	M.R.
Mediator	Med.
President	Pres. *[ALWD]*
Referee	Ref. *[BB]*
Representative	Rep.
Senator	Sen.
Vice Chancellor	V.C. *[BB]*
	Vice Chan. *[ALWD]*

APPENDIX 11

ABBREVIATIONS OF LEGISLATIVE DOCUMENTS

Unless otherwise indicated, *The Bluebook* and *ALWD Manual* abbreviations are the same.

For possible additional *ALWD* abbreviations, see Appendix 1. *The Bluebook* permits abbreviation of words containing seven letters or more to be abbreviated unambiguously if they are not listed below. In addition, *The Bluebook* indicates that "all articles and prepositions [should be omitted] from any abbreviated title [of a document] if [it] can [still] be unambiguously identified without them."

TITLE	ABBREVIATION
Annals	Annals
Annual	Ann. [*BB*]
	Annual [*ALWD*]
Assembly	Assemb. [*BB*]
	Assembly [*ALWD*]
Assemblyman	Assemb. [*BB*]
Assemblywoman	Assemb. [*BB*]
Bill	B. (omitted in citations of unenacted bills)
Committee	Comm.
Concurrent	Con.
Conference	Conf.

TITLE	ABBREVIATION
Congress	Cong.
Congressional	Cong.
Debate	Deb. [BB]
	Debate [ALWD]
Delegate	Del. [BB]
	Delegate [ALWD]
Document	Doc.
Documents	Doc. [BB]
	Docs. [ALWD]
Executive	Exec.
Federal	Fed. [BB]
	Fed. or F. [ALWD]
File	File
General	Gen.
House	H.
House of Delegates	H.D. [BB]
	H. [ALWD]
House of Representatives	H.R. [BB]
	H.R. (Federal) [ALWD]
	H. (State) [ALWD]
Joint	J. [BB]
	Jt. [ALWD]
Legislation	Legis.
Legislative	Legis.
Legislature	Leg.
Miscellaneous	Misc.
Number	No.
Order	Order [BB]
	Or. [ALWD]
Record	Rec.
Register	Reg. [BB]
	Register [ALWD]

<u>TITLE</u>	<u>ABBREVIATION</u>
Regular	Reg.
Report	Rep. *[BB]*
	Rpt. (or Rep.) *[ALWD]*
Representative	Rep.
Resolution	Res.
Senate	S. *[BB]*
	Sen. *[ALWD]*
Senator	Sen.
Service	Serv.
Session	Sess.
Special	Spec.
Subcommittee	Subcomm.

APPENDIX 12

ABBREVIATIONS OF LITIGATION DOCUMENTS

These abbreviations are used for litigation (court) documents in absence of a contrary court rule or local custom.

For possible additional *ALWD* abbreviations, see Appendix 1. *The Bluebook* permits abbreviation of words containing seven letters or more to be abbreviated unambiguously if they are not listed below.

TITLE	ABBREVIATION
Admission	Admis.
Affidavit	Aff.
Affirm	Affirm
Amended	Am. *[BB]*
	Amend. *[ALWD]*
Answer	Answer *[BB]*
	Ans.
Answers	Answers *[BB]*
	Ans. *[ALWD]*
Appeal	Appeal *[BB]*
	App. *[ALWD]*
Appellant	Appellant
Appellee	Appellee
Appendix	App.
	(See also Joint App.)
Attorney	Att'y *[BB]*
	Atty. *[ALWD]*

TITLE	ABBREVIATION
Attorneys	Att'ys [*BB*]
	Attys. [*ALWD*]
Brief	Br.
Certiorari	Cert.
Compel	Compel
Complaint	Compl.
Counterclaim	Countercl. [*BB*]
	Counterclaim [*ALWD*]
Court	Ct.
Cross-claim	Cross-cl. [*BB*]
Declaration	Decl.
Defendant	Def.
Defendant's	Def.'s
Defendants	Defs.
Defendants'	Defs.'
Demurrer	Dem. [*BB*]
	Demr. [*ALWD*]
Deny	Den. [*BB*]
	Deny [*ALWD*]
Denying	Den. [*BB*]
	Denying [*ALWD*]
Deposition	Dep. [*BB*]
	Depo. [*ALWD*]
Discovery	Disc. [*BB*]
	Discovery [*ALWD*]
Dismiss	Dismiss
Document	Doc.
Documents	Docs.
Exhibit	Ex. [*BB*]
	Exhibit [*ALWD*]
Grant	Grant

<u>TITLE</u>	<u>ABBREVIATION</u>
Hearing	Hr'g [*BB*]
	Hrg. [*ALWD*]
Injunction	Inj.
Interrogatory	Interrog.
Interrogatories	Interrogs.
Joint Appendix	J.A. [*BB*]
	J.A. or Jt. App. [*ALWD*]
Judgment	J. [*BB*]
	Judm. [*ALWD*]
Memorandum	Mem. [*BB*]
	Memo. [*ALWD*]
Minutes	Mins. [*BB*]
	Minutes [*ALWD*]
Motion	Mot.
Opinion	Op.
Opposition	Opp'n [*BB*]
	Opposition [*ALWD*]
Order	Order [*BB*]
	Or. [*ALWD*]
Petition	Pet.
Petitioner	Pet'r [*BB*]
	Petr. [*ALWD*]
Plaintiff	Pl.
Plaintiff's	Pl.'s
Plaintiffs	Pls.
Plaintiffs'	Pls.'
Points and Authorities	P. & A. [*BB*]
	Points & Auths. [*ALWD*]
Preliminary	Prelim.
Produce	Produc. [*BB*]
	Produce [*ALWD*]

TITLE	ABBREVIATION
Production	Produc. [BB]
	Prod. [ALWD]
Quash	Quash
Reconsideration	Recons. [BB]
	Reconsideration [ALWD]
Record	R.
Rehearing	Reh'g [BB]
	Rehearing [ALWD]
Reply	Reply
Reporter	Rep. [BB]
	Rep. or Rptr. [ALWD]
Request	Req. [BB]
	Request [ALWD]
Respondent	Resp't [BB]
	Respt. [ALWD]
Response	Resp. [BB]
	Response [ALWD]
Stay	Stay
Subpoena	Subpoena [BB]
	Subp. [ALWD]
Summary	Summ. [BB]
	Summary [ALWD]
Summary Judgment	Summ. J. [BB]
	S.J. [ALWD]
Support	Supp. [BB]
	Support [ALWD]
Suppress	Suppress
Temporary Restraining Order	T.R.O.
Testimony	Test.
Transcript	Tr. [BB]
	Transcr. [ALWD]

TITLE	ABBREVIATION
Verified Statement	V.S. *[BB]* Verified Statement *[ALWD]*

*

INDEX

INDEX   475
References are to Pages

DEBATES
See Legislative History

DEPUBLISHED OPINIONS
Indication of, 217

DESCRIPTIONS OF A PARTY ALREADY NAMED
See Case Names

DICTIONARIES
Citation of, 189
Typeface, 189

DOING BUSINESS AS (d/b/a)
See Case Names

EDITIONS
See Texts and Treatises

EDITORIALS
See Newspapers

EDITORS
See Citation Parentheticals; Texts and Treatises

EMERGENCY COURT OF APPEALS
See Court Designations

EN BANC OPINIONS
See Citation Parentheticals

ENCYCLOPEDIAS
See Legal Encyclopedias

ENGLISH REPORTS, FULL REPRINT
See Reporters

ENGLISH STATUTES AT LARGE
See Statutes at Large

LETTERS TO THE EDITOR
See Newspapers

LEXIS
   See also Date of Decision; State Statutes
Adaption of traditional citation rules for cases in, 32-34
Administrative regulations, 172-173
Citing cases on, 32-34, 134-135
Docket number, not used in citations, 33, 135
Reporter tables, opinions in but reported on, 135
Pinpoint citations, 33-34
Screen numbers (pages), 33-34
Unreported opinions, 216

LITIGATION DOCUMENTS
See Court Documents

"LONG" CASE NAMES
See Case Names

LOOSELEAF SERV ICES
Abbreviations, App. 8
Cases in, 136-137
Citation of, 205
Special subject reporters, 136
Usefulness, 455

MEDIUM NEUTRAL CITATIONS
See Public Domain Citations

MEMORANDUM OPINIONS
See Citation Parentheticals

MILITARY SERVICE COURTS OF APPEALS
See Court Designations

MODEL ACTS
   See also Citation Parentheticals; Dates
Citation of, 176-177

PINCITES
See Pinpoint References

PINPOINT REFERENCES
A.L.R. annotations, 61
Citation, use in, generally, 21, 89
Congressional hearings, 168
Court documents, 211-212
Defined, 11
First page, specific reference to, 11
Legal periodicals, short forms, 199-200
LEXIS, screen numbers or pages, 34
Quotations, 30, 62
Passim, used in lieu of, 75
Practitioner documents, 211-212
Public domain citations, 35
Sections
    Statutes, 38
    Within, 203
Texts and treatises, 181
Treaties, 52, 169
WESTLAW, screen numbers or pages, 33

PROCEDURAL PHRASES
    See also Case Names
Accounting of, 97
Estate of, 97
Ex parte, 7
Ex rel., 8, 96-98
In re, 7, 97-98
Marriage of, 97
Relators, 8, 96-97
Succession of, 97
Will of, 97-98

**UNITED STATES COURT OF APPEALS FOR THE
ARMED FORCES**
See Court Designations

**UNITED STATES COURT OF APPEALS FOR THE
FEDERAL CIRCUIT**
See Court Designations

**UNITED STATES COURT OF APPEALS FOR VETERANS
CLAIMS**

UNITED STATES COURT OF FEDERAL CLAIMS
See Court Designations

UNITED STATES CUSTOMS COURT
See Court Designations

UNITED STATES DISTRICT COURTS
See Court Designations

UNITED STATES OF AMERICA
See Case Names

UNITED STATES SUPREME COURT
See Court Designations; Parallel Citations; Reporters

UNITED STATES TAX COURT
See Court Designations

UNIVERSAL CITATIONS
See Public Domain Citations

*